Legal Theory Today

Observing Law through Systems Theory

Legal Theory Today

Founding Editor

John Gardner, Professor of Jurisprudence, University College, Oxford

TITLES IN THIS SERIES

Law in its Own Right by Henrik Palmer Olsen and Stuart Toddington
Law as a Social Institution by Hamish Ross
Evaluation and Legal Theory by Julie Dickson
Law and Aesthetics by Adam Gearey
Risks and Legal Theory by Jenny Steele
A Sociology of Jurisprudence by Richard Nobles and David Schiff
Costs and Cautionary Tales: Economic Insights for the Law by Anthony Ogus
Legal Norms and Normativity: An Essay in Genealogy by Sylvie Delacroix
Consent in the Law by Deryck Beyleveld and Roger Brownsword
Law and Politics at the Perimeter: Re-Evaluating Key Debates in Feminist Theory by Vanessa Munro
Law's Meaning of Life: Philosophy, Religion, Darwin and the Legal Person by Ngaire Naffine
Answering for Crime: Responsibility and Liability in the Criminal Law by Antony Duff

Observing Law through Systems Theory

Richard Nobles and David Schiff

·HART·
PUBLISHING

OXFORD AND PORTLAND OREGON
2013

Published in the United Kingdom by Hart Publishing Ltd
16C Worcester Place, Oxford, OX1 2JW
Telephone: +44 (0)1865 517530
Fax: +44 (0)1865 510710
E-mail: mail@hartpub.co.uk
Website: http://www.hartpub.co.uk

Published in North America (US and Canada) by
Hart Publishing
c/o International Specialized Book Services
920 NE 58th Avenue, Suite 300
Portland, OR 97213-3786
USA
Tel: +1 503 287 3093 or toll-free: (1) 800 944 6190
Fax: +1 503 280 8832
E-mail: orders@isbs.com
Website: http://www.isbs.com

British Library Cataloguing in Publication Data
Data Available

ISBN: 978-1-84946-218-1

Typeset by Hope Services Ltd, Abingdon
Printed and bound in Great Britain by
Lightning Source UK Ltd

Preface

This book is complementary to our book *A Sociology of Jurisprudence*,[1] although it is not necessary for readers to have read that book in order to engage with what we present here. In *A Sociology of Jurisprudence* we offered a way of exploring general jurisprudence and legal theory as law's self-description,[2] adopting a particular version of general systems theory[3] to enable us to do so. This particular, modern version of general systems theory, often referred to as neo-systems theory or autopoiesis theory, provides an abstract theoretical underpinning from which to observe on the manner in which systems construct themselves, and construct what they are not (their environment). The theory is most closely associated with the writings of the German social theorist Niklas Luhmann.[4] Exploring jurisprudence as law's self-description enabled us to reconsider a number of jurisprudential theories about law's nature, its essential or implicit character, or what unifies law, and offer further commentary on those theories.

For the purpose of understanding jurisprudence as self-description, self-description has to be contrasted with external description.[5] Law's self-description is both generated by legal operations, and in turn stabilises those operations. In this sense self-description is not different from self-observation, or what others might portray as the internal understandings or implicit assumptions of those most closely associated with the practice of law.[6] However, the distinction between self-observation and self-description

[1] Nobles and Schiff, 2006.

[2] For a short statement of this approach and its application to natural law and legal positivist theories, and the differences between them, see Nobles and Schiff, 2009.

[3] See von Bertalanffy, 1976.

[4] His writings are not easily accessible to the uninitiated. For our purposes, the main general works that represent his fully developed theory are: *Social Systems* (1995), being built on his earlier work *The Differentiation of Society* (1982), and his last major work, the two volumes of *Die Gesellschaft der Gesellschaft* (1997), a translation of which is about to be published in English. For a valuable introduction to his general theory, see Moeller, 2006. Luhmann's major later work on law *Das Recht der Gesellschaft* (1993) is translated in English as *Law as a Social System* (2004). Difficulties abound in reading Luhmann's 70 books and over 400 scholarly articles as the theory that he develops shares some of the features of Marxism, in that alongside the works of Luhmann, one also has the work of various 'Luhmannians' who take a variety of approaches. These range from 'strict literalists' who insist that a correct interpretation of the theory requires fidelity to Luhmann's own works; 'liberals' who re-interpret and elaborate on his basic concepts; and 'pragmatists' who take some of his concepts and seek to apply them to their own subject areas (see Priban, 2010).

[5] As a clear example of this difference, see the account of the theoretical writings of the Critical Legal Studies movement in Nobles and Schiff, 2006, ch 6.

[6] We adopt the phrases self-description and self-observation, as understood from a particular sociological perspective (that of systems theory). This is close, as a sociological equivalent,

arises at the level of generality. Whereas self-observation has as its object particular operations within the legal system, self-description is the system's attempt to describe itself to itself as a unity.[7] But in describing itself in this way self-description is reflecting on self-observations, and guiding those self-observations, as well as guiding more mundane, local or particular legal operations. In *A Sociology of Jurisprudence* our concern was with how law generates its self-description, and the role played by that self-description in guiding laws' operations. In this book we are concerned less with law's self-description than a number of law's general, significant and often controversial self-observations, and in particular how those self-observations can be contrasted with the understanding and use of similar observations constructed within other subsystems, namely those observations reflecting on the same subject-matter but generated within other functionally differentiated subsystems in modern societies (such as the political system, the mass media, the economic system, etc).[8]

In writing this book we are seeking to demonstrate that observing systems using systems theory makes a difference: that it can increase our understanding of the legal system. In our last book, with its focus on law's self-description, that difference was at a high level of generality. But self-description does not operate in isolation from the rest of a system. It involves a relationship between the most particular[9] and most general kinds of system communications. The premise of systems theory is that a system's self-description is generated through that system's operations, observation on those operations, and observation on those observations. Thus, although a self-description is a system's description of itself as a totality, it

to the philosophical understanding that has recently been developed by Nigel Simmonds as an example of law's 'reflexivity' and the role of jurisprudence in this. 'Legal thought and practice exhibit reflexivity in so far as they explicitly or implicitly appeal to the idea of law. For the idea of law is not one that simply describes existing practices; rather, the idea of law plays a vital part *within* the practices that make up the existence of a legal order' (Simmonds, 2010, 1). The point at which this philosophical account diverges from the sociological account adopted here is well represented in Simmonds' statement about the inability to describe the social practices represented by the idea of law he is alluding to: 'The idea of law is the focal point that enables us to make coherent sense of the otherwise diverse features of practice, but it is not itself a matter of observable practice. It resembles a notional point in space that enables us to grasp the relationship between various parts of a complex drawing, although in itself it forms no part of the drawing' (at 18). Rather than a 'notional point in space', for systems theory the empirical evidence of this idea can be found in the actual communications used within the legal system, whether as self-description or self-observation.

[7] On Luhmann's analysis of the self-description of society as a whole, and in particular modern society, see N Luhmann, 1984.

[8] On functionally differentiated subsystems, see Luhmann, 1982, or in a short form, Luhmann, 1977.

[9] 'Nobody can deny the importance of law in society. Thus, a theory of society needs to occupy itself with society's law. This applies to the most intricate refinements of judicial semantics as well as to each decision made in law – even when they refer only to the diameter of apples or the ingredients of different kinds of beer which can be sold – because even the most detailed legal propositions happen to emerge in society and society alone' (Luhmann, 2004, Preface).

operates reflexively, by stabilising the self-observations which generate it, which in turn stabilise the system's operations. The most general, and the most particular, have a relationship to each other. Our book was called *A Sociology of Jurisprudence* because it offered a sociological explanation for the generation and role played by jurisprudence within the legal system, in linking law's operations to its most general kinds of communications. We attempted to demonstrate that jurisprudence, as philosophy, and as a sociological approach to law, does not identify different issues, and that a sociological approach to law, informed by systems theory, could improve our understanding of how the legal system generates the issues which philosophy has attempted to describe and evaluate.

In this book we have moved below the level of self-description to that of self-observation. And at this lower level of analysis the theme which unites the different Chapters in this book is our attempt to demonstrate that systems theory has the potential to increase our understanding of issues which other approaches (both sociological and philosophical) have already identified and imbued with significance. As with our earlier book, this endeavour is our response to assertions that systems theory is too abstract, general and complex to be used to undertake such a task. Unlike that book, we cannot claim that all of our Chapters here explore a single, central theme. But we do believe that the Chapters build upon one another, in the sense that issues dealt with within one Chapter provide a basis, or starting point, for those dealt with in others.[10]

One of the key self-observations that coalesce in so many of the communications of legal practitioners, and especially judges, is that they operate within and as part of the legal system. Communications by others than legal practitioners also offer what appear to be the 'same' observation, namely that lawyers and judges, and indeed law in general, operates within and as part of the legal system in general, or particular legal systems. But what is the nature of any legal system, or indeed of any social system? There are those who have doubted the characterisation of law as operating as a system, and those who have given that notion some specific content (and in both cases such characterisations have been offered differently by different people). Systems theory is well placed to observe on such attempts since it is most closely concerned with how the modern social world has evolved and has splintered into one in which subsystems, or functionally differentiated systems, operate. Even more, it has established ways of understanding how society operates as a system.

Right from the beginning of what is offered in this book, an attempt will be made to show how this sociological approach and its understanding of the modern social world, and its observations on systems and the legal

[10] And this is very different from an approach that might try to utilise 'bits and pieces' of systems theory, rather than the whole theory, to account for law's operation in society (for example, Galligan, 2007, 43).

system in particular, makes a significant difference. It highlights and sheds light on issues that have seemed to be so intractable: issues that throw up problems that we seem to fail to resolve with any degree of adequacy. In doing so it does not shy away from describing modern society in a manner which is adequate to both its modernity[11] and its complexity.[12] From the vantage point of systems theory society is a system made up of the sum total of its communications,[13] including the communications of each of its subsystems. Namely, society itself and each of its subsystems can be observed through their communications: those that construct society, and each subsystem, as themselves.[14] But, since systems theory makes the claim that systems construct themselves through their own operations, it follows that, for example in relation to law, what needs to be observed most closely is how the law communicates what it itself constructs as itself, as distinct from how other systems might communicate about law.

Chapter 2 addresses two interrelated issues. Within general discussions of systems theory, a central concern is the role played by individuals within a social system. To those used to analysing social events by reference to the thoughts, motivations and interests of human actors, placing individuals at the centre of any explanation, a theory that makes systems the subject of its propositions ('the legal system thinks this', or 'the political system does that')[15] has alarming elements of reification and socio-animism.[16] In this Chapter we seek to address the question of how individuals participate within systems and, by taking the example of judges, offer this explanation as an answer to one of the questions which has occupied much of legal philosophy: the nature of judicial discourse. Individuals who wish to achieve the operations which a legal system makes possible have to utilise the communications through which such operations occur, and in so doing, they are necessarily

[11] For a short account of Luhmann's systems theory as 'A Theory of Modernity', see Muller, 1994, especially section III (47–51). For a systems theory account of modernity, see Luhmann, 1998, ch 1, 'Modernity in Contemporary Society', and more generally, see Rasch, 2000.

[12] There are many attributes to systems theory's expression of complexity (as there are of the study of complex systems, complexity theory, network theory, and other terms that deal with the modelling of complex systems). To give one succinct example, see Luhmann's short account of the relationship between complexity and meaning: 1990, ch 3, 'Complexity and Meaning' 80–5; see also Luhmann, 1995a.

[13] Throughout this book the meaning of communications, communicative meaning, and epistemological implications of the communicative turn in social theory will be advanced. As background some readers might wish, at this stage, to reflect on the different meanings that can be attributed to the notion of communication, for example, in relation to science: consider Luhmann, 1996. Also one might wish to reflect on some improbabilities of communication: Luhmann, 1981, and some of communications' main characteristics: Luhmann, 1994.

[14] This can be described as 'a second-order cybernetics that observes observations' (Rasch and Knodt, 1994, 3). Such a disposition entails significant epistemological questions, which it is not our intention to engage with here. For short accounts of these epistemological questions of 'second-order cybernetics', see Luhmann, 2002, ch 9, 'I see something you don't see', esp 190–3; Rasch and Knodt, 1994.

[15] For example, see Teubner, 1989.

[16] Teubner, Nobles, Schiff, 2002, 918.

constrained in the meanings which can be generated. When participating within the legal system, especially at the level of judges, individuals have no means to carry out legal operations other than through the use of communications which generate explicit or implicit meanings, which include a commitment to the validity of the legal system. This discussion demonstrates why commitment is something internal to the legal system, a feature of its communications, rather than something internal to the individuals who participate in that system. It also considers why judges continue to speak, in their judgments, as if they were recognising a law that already existed, even though their law-making role is generally acknowledged, even by themselves, in other contexts. This discussion will introduce the reader to the difference between social and physic systems, as well as the manner in which redundancy (a concept which explains how information is extracted from communications) limits an individual's freedom to choose what meanings she/he can generate.

The Chapter on judicial discourse offers, we believe, a useful starting point for the understanding of how different commitments operate within different systems, and in particular the legal and political systems. The following Chapter introduces Luhmann's ideas on the nature of political legitimacy, and the role played by law within the political system, in establishing the legitimacy of political decisions. The particular issue which allows us to explore this is that of civil disobedience: the claim that it is, in certain situations, right to disobey law. In keeping with our approach to judicial speech, we explore the constraints which systems place upon individuals who seek to assert this right. Starting with the legal system, we consider the difficulties of acknowledging such a right within legal decisions. Next, we consider the problems of articulating such a right within the political system, and why civil disobedience can exist as protest, but not form part of the distribution of political power through government.

In Chapter 4 our focus shifts from issues which have been addressed by legal and political theory to one that has received more attention from anthropology and the sociology of law: the nature and study of legal pluralism. We take up the claim made by Gunther Teubner, a leading exponent of systems theory with particular reference to law, and its dismissal by Brian Tamanaha, a leading exponent of legal pluralism, that systems theory could make an important difference to our understanding of plural legal orders. Teubner has claimed explicitly, and in much recent writing continues to claim implicitly, that legal pluralism could be explored though the identification of the legal with a system that codes in terms of the distinction legal/illegal. In this Chapter, we consider the nature of codes (both in law and other systems) and the capacity of codes to provide criteria which can separate the legal from the rest of the social in a manner that does not reduce that distinction to the subjective opinion of a given individual, whether or not that assessment is shared with significant numbers of other individuals. This Chapter also explores the difference between a society that exhibits functional differentiation (one where it is meaningful to speak of separate religious, economic, legal and political norms) and one that does not, and the problem of seeking to find criteria for law that applies adequately to both.

When considering issues of pluralism one is principally concerned with normative space – which norms operate in which settings, locally, nationally, trans-nationally, regionally, internationally. But such consideration should not ignore a dimension that underpins these possibilities, namely time. That which has an existence needs to exist not only in space, but also in its allied temporality. This dimension of meaning is often studied in its application to society and its systems by utilising the various methods of historical analysis to help us understand how we came to where we currently are, and various other forms of analysis to anticipate from where we are to where we might be heading. Moving through time, past, present and future, and linking those moments involve the application of methods of analysis, explanation and understanding.[17] Systems theory offers one such method by its observations on how subsystems construct time within their own operations. In this Chapter our question is: how does law construct time and what can we learn from exploring those constructions as evidenced by its communications? We first introduce readers to the counter-intuitive idea that time can only exist socially within the meanings constructed by society's communications. As such, time can have different meanings as societies evolve and, when those societies evolve to produce functionally differentiated social subsystems (political, economic, religious, legal, mass media, etc), different meanings within those different social subsystems. With this starting point the Chapter looks at a number of ways in which time has particular meanings, or significance, for law. The need to bind time, to create expectations that meanings generated in the past will guide the generation of meanings in the future, are essential to all systems' operations. But the nature of that time binding differs between systems. We look at two examples. First, the presumption of innocence, which requires a defendant's guilt to be postponed until conviction regardless of the communications generated within the mass media, or the political system. Second, and this is a more complex example, we examine a claim that can be attributed to some natural law theorists (such as Lon Fuller) that law is inherently prospective in nature. We consider this claim in light of the routine retrospective character of law created through adjudication, and the difficulties of acknowledging this, and reforming law to prevent its occurrence. We also consider the reasons why attempts to create retrospective law remain an exceptional practice within the political system, and

[17] What Abbott calls 'temporality defined by relation' (Abbott, 2001, 239, see particularly ch 7).

further why political constructions of time might cause particular difficulties for legal operations.

Whilst Chapter 5 touches on some aspects of the relationship between law and politics, Chapter 6 attempts to re-examine the general relationship between these two subsystems using Luhmann's concept of structural coupling. We begin by considering the possibilities for co-ordinating law and politics, and the implications for both systems if political power is brought directly to bear on judges on anything other than an exceptional basis. Rule by way of law (legislation) represents a structural coupling through which politics increases its ability to distribute political power, but at the cost of relinquishing the ability to apply political power in illegal ways. Our discussion of 'the rule of law' provides a foundation for us to look at the development of constitutional law, and then human rights. The Chapter attempts to demonstrate how the self-limitation of politics represented by the rule of law, constitutional law, and human rights are generated by dynamics within a political system that has differentiated itself from the legal system. The motivation for political actors to make communications which affirm the rule of law is a consequence of the increased complexity which arises from the distribution of political power through legality. The evolutionary increase in the use of this technique provides the background for a change in the nature of constitutions, from 'fundamental laws' which exist only within the political system, to constitutional law, which can be the subject of adjudication within the legal system. The last section of this Chapter considers a systems theory explanation for the rise of human rights as part of this evolution, and whether human rights can operate as self-limiting for systems other than politics through processes of societal constitutionalism.

Chapter 6 deals with the structural coupling and co-evolution of the legal and political systems, which is a vast subject, while Chapter 7, too, deals with the equally vast subject of the co-evolution between the legal and other subsystems, not only the political system. Again, the aim is not to give adequate coverage of this wide-ranging topic, but rather to show how a systems theory understanding might make a difference to how we approach it. In this Chapter we briefly consider subjects associated with the idea of 'control through law', especially with the use of law (including both adjudication and legislation) to resolve issues and disputes. We explore a number of potential reasons for law's regulatory failure – either in terms of why it fails to have the impact that is aimed at (a failure of steering), or causes debilitating consequences for other systems, or for itself as a system in response to other's expectations of it. We ask tentatively whether the better understanding available from the perspective and application of systems theory (whether in terms of structural coupling, social constitutionalism or reflexive law) could engender practical solutions to the systemic difficulties and consequent problems demonstrated (not only in this Chapter but throughout the analysis in this book).

The analysis involved in Chapter 7 introduces many issues concerning the inter-systemic complexity of systems and the possibilities of structural coupling and co-evolution. The related final Chapter, Chapter 8, explores a similar analysis of inter-system coupling, but between law and the media in relation to convictions and appeals. It starts by addressing the meaning of appeals in law to itself through the evolution of doctrine, and goes on to offer some analysis of what the meaning of appeals in law has for the mass media. This Chapter also provides an example of the manner in which systems maintain closure, and why the participation of individuals in different systems, and their knowledge of each system's operations, does not overcome the system's closure, and allow each system to 'learn' what these individuals 'know'. The Chapter ends with a postscript both to Chapter 8 and the book as a whole about the place of individuals within systems.

This book explores themes that are represented in some of the most general and sustained observations about law characteristic of the communications of lawyers, law teachers, but also politicians, economists, journalists, and many others as they engage with law from the various vantage points offered to them within the systems that they are operating in. It demonstrates that a focus on systems offers a perceptive perspective from which to explore the modern social world and law's operation within it. But we recognise that our attempt to engage in this exploration is problematic as readers may, we hope, after reading our book well understand. Indeed, how can social scientific observations, engendered by research undertaken within the education system, construct insights and suggestions that can be adequately understood and used within the legal or political systems? *A Sociology of Jurisprudence* was a precursor to this book as it reflected on law's constructions of its unity, its jurisprudence. In this book we have moved from those constructions to an exploration of a number of law's general self-observations as they reflect its substantive differences from the external constructions by its social, economic and political environment. But in neither book have we systematically moved from applying some of the insights of systems theory and the understanding that this can engender, to a sustained account of the potential use of those applications and understandings. Although we have glimpsed the suggestions of others about how systems theory insight may be useful, we have yet to find a way to offer any sustained analysis of this ourselves.

Acknowledgements

We are grateful to the editors of the *International Journal of the Sociology of Law*, *The Modern Law Review*, *Law and Society Review*, and *Current Legal Issues* for permission to include material from the following articles/chapters.

'Why do judges talk the way they do?' (2009) 5 *International Journal of Law in Context* 25–49, an amended version of which is produced here as Chapter 2.

'Disobedience to Law, Debbie Purdy's case' (2010) 73 *Modern Law Review* 295–304, part of an amended version of which is incorporated in Chapter 3.

'Using systems theory to explore legal pluralism – what could be gained?' (2012) 46 *Law & Society Review* 265–96, part of an amended version of which is incorporated in Chapter 4.

'Legal pluralism: a systems theory approach to language, translation and communication' in Michael Freeman and Fiona Smith (eds), *Law and Language*, Current Legal Issues, Volume 15 (Oxford, Oxford University Press, 2013) ch 7, part of an amended version of which is incorporated in Chapter 4.

We wish to thank the many colleagues who have read or commented in seminars or workshops on drafts of sections of Chapters, but in particular Peter Alldridge, Roger Cotterrell, and Prakash Shah of Queen Mary University of London, Michael King of Reading University, and Andrew Halpin of the National University of Singapore.

We wish to thank Ann Adler for translating into English some of Luhmann's work as yet unpublished in English.

We also wish to thank those at Hart Publishing who have given us helpful and efficient advice, in particular Rachel Turner and Richard Hart.

Richard Nobles would like to thank Christine Doddington for her intellectual support.

Richard Nobles and David Schiff, London, 1 March 2012

Acknowledgements

Contents

1

Is the Legal System a System?

It is not sensible to launch into applications and implications of a theory that operates on the assumption that the legal system is both a system and one that describes and observes itself through its own operations, without giving some attention to what systems theorists mean by a system and, therefore, what makes the legal system a system for these purposes. This does not require us to restate all of the elements of autopoietic systems theory, but will inevitably involve some comparison between this version of systems theory and legal theories that have attempted to describe the legal system as a system, the most notable being that of HLA Hart. Nor is it necessary for us to explore all of the different meanings and approaches to systems, what it means to think and learn in systems[1] or in terms of systems.[2] Rather, for our purposes, such an introductory analysis of law's operation as a system addresses some of the most general questions in jurisprudence and, as we will demonstrate, displaces some of the answers provided by conventional legal theories.

What kind of system is the legal system?[3] Despite the ubiquitous use of the phrase 'legal system' there is no obvious consensus on what it means for law to operate as a system, how its systematic qualities are generated or maintained, or even that law operating as a system has a distinct character that could be distinguished from, or could distinguish itself from, any other part of society. This is so despite the fact that there have been many attempts to present law as a system.[4] Perhaps the most famous, that of Hart in *The*

[1] Consider the difference between 'systems engineering' (SE) and 'soft systems methodology' (SSM): Checkland, 2001.

[2] See Meadows, 2009; Midgley, 2000, ch 3, 'The Systems Idea'.

[3] This is a question that many others have addressed. For example, in the Preface to the French edition of their book, Van de Kerchove and Ost, 1994, ix: 'The starting point of this essay will be the obvious fact that law – at least modern, Western law – takes the form of a system. The central question throughout will be: in exactly what sense is law a system?'

[4] Joseph Raz makes this point succinctly: 'Laws are part of legal systems; a particular law is a law if it is part of American law or French law or some other legal system. Legal philosophers have persistently attempted to explain why we think of laws as forming legal systems, to evaluate the merits of this way of thinking about the law, and to make it more precise by explicating the features that account for the unity of legal systems. Various theories have been suggested but none have been accepted as completely satisfactory, and the continuing debate owes much to the intricacy of the problems involved' (2009, 78).

Concept of Law,[5] elaborated on law as a system of rules, separated from other social rules by the presence of a pedigree test for which rules count as legal rules, namely the 'rule of recognition'. Much of the writing in Anglo-American jurisprudence since this seminal work can be seen as a debate about the claim that law exists as a system, with some providing alternative accounts of law's systematic qualities (for example Dworkin – law as the systematic articulation of justificatory principles; Raz – law as the provision of source-based reasons for action within legal systems which are comprehensive in that they claim 'authority to regulate any type of behaviour', supreme, in that they claim 'authority to regulate the setting up and application of other institutionalized systems by its subject-community', and open, in giving 'binding force within the system to norms which do not belong to it'[6]), or denials or serious questioning of its systematic character (for example Sampford – law as mêlée;[7] Van de Kerchove and Ost – law operating between order and disorder;[8] much critical legal studies writing which, from a variety of theoretical perspectives, seeks to challenge claims that law is systematic and distinct, especially from politics).

Classical ideas of what a system is go back to the Greeks (Plato, Aristotle and Euclid), who explored ideas of wholeness, or union. The most general idea of system expressed is that of a distinct whole which has internal relationships between its various parts. The wholeness of a system requires it to be separated from its surroundings. There must be a boundary. The notion that the parts of the whole have a relationship with each other, and with the whole of which they form a part, is captured in the following statement by American philosopher John Dewey: 'It differs from such terms as aggregate, collection and inventory, in expressly conveying the way inherent bonds bind together . . . the parts of the whole [and] it differs from such terms as organism, totality and whole in expressly connoting that the parts are interdependent.'[9] The features of wholeness, a whole formed out of the

[5] 1961/1994. It is not only legal theorists who represent law in this way, sociological and political theory analysis of law also characterises the operation of law in similar terms. For what is now a classic statement to this effect, see Friedman, 1975, ch 1, 'The Legal System'.

[6] Raz, 2009, 115–21.

[7] Sampford, 1989.

[8] Van de Kerchove and Ost, 1994.

[9] Dewey 1901, quoted by Sampford, 1989, 14. There are, of course, many modern alternative definitions of system and systems, especially those that both inform systems science in itself and in relation to complexity science (see, for example, Castellani, 2009, 8: 'the celebrated insight of complexity science: all social systems, by definition, are complex'; Urry, 2005). There might be some agreement about the most general definition of a system (such as that offered by Webster's New World Dictionary: 'a set or arrangement of things so related or connected as to form a unity or organic whole') but this does not mean that modern theorists who explore systems, systems theory and systems science in depth, rely on the same definition or adopt similar methodologies in their study of systems. (Webster's definition is quoted by Klir, 2001, who also says (at 4): 'The term "system" is unquestioningly one of the mostly widely used terms not only in science, but in other areas of human endeavor as well. It is a highly overworked term, which enjoys different meanings under different circumstances and for different people. However, when separated from its specific connotations and uses,

relationship between the parts, points in turn to the concept of structure. The relationship between the parts forms the structure of the whole, and gives it its character as a particular system, distinct from other entities. Thus, with this formulation of what it means to be a system, structure also establishes the border or boundary of the system. By establishing what forms part of the system, the structure necessarily also establishes what does not form part of the system and hence establishes the system's boundary.

Using these ideas of system, Charles Sampford in *The Disorder of Law* undertakes a sustained attack on the possibilities of law existing as a system.[10] He presents legal positivism, as represented by the works of Hart, Kelsen, Raz and MacCormick, natural law, as represented by Dworkin, and sociological approaches to law, as represented by Parsons, as three unsuccessful attempts to understand law as a system. His presentation of these three approaches, and his reasons for concluding that they fail to explain how law could exist as a system, provides a useful starting point to our own explanation of how law operates as a separate and autonomous social system.

Legal positivism relies on a hierarchical structure, which sets out, in many different versions, to present law as the consequence of relationships of validity stretching between higher and lower norms. To Sampford all such versions fail to account for all of the possibilities of what can become law. Some norms become legal norms that are not selected as such by the highest norms in the system, and there are occasions when the highest norms are themselves altered. The structures identified by positivist legal theories cannot account for all that is commonly accepted to be law and, in particular, they cannot account satisfactorily for the capacity of law to evolve. Dworkin's attempt to describe law, using a hierarchy of principles and other background values, explains the capacity of law to exist, and evolve, by reference to relationships between levels of justification.[11] In particular, justifying the use of coercion involves a combination of consistency and appeal to community values. Community values themselves change, so some earlier justifications lose their persuasive force. Totally ad hoc justification would appear arbitrary, so some part of whatever has been justified in the past (especially the very recent past) must operate as a restraint on the ability to

the term "system" is almost never explicitly defined.') Nevertheless, despite the many significantly different uses of the term, there are those who suggest that there is a developing consensus on at least how to approach social systems (see Bausch, 2001) and how the paradigm of systems thinking provides an alternative to the prevailing analytic mode.

[10] Indeed his book (1989) attacks the possibility of any part of society qualifying as a system. Sampford identifies society as the aggregate of individual experience of interactions between individuals, locates this in each individual's mind, points to the asymmetry in any two individuals' experience of the same interaction, and claims that these disparate experiences could never create systems, but merely overlapping similarities. If we refer to Dewey's definition, the best that can be produced is aggregation, collection or inventory.

[11] For a later clarification of the approach which Sampford refers to, see Dworkin, 2006, ch 2, 'In Praise of Theory', esp 53–57.

offer wholly new and novel versions of what can be law. But once we abandon the pretence that any human judge could generate a single consistent set of justifications for what counts as law (producing replacement sets as social values alter) then this structure of reasoning does not account for the possibility of what can become law. Sampford feels that it has not established a relationship of the whole to its parts, and therefore it has also failed to establish law's boundaries, and its existence as a system. Parsons' version of systems theory sought to establish law as a separate system by reference to his account of functionalism.[12] Starting from the premise that society could not continue to exist unless certain functions (which include adaptive functions producing evolution) were carried out, Parsons sought to identify how these functions are achieved.[13] He identified particular functions with particular subsystems, one of which was the legal system.[14] Within this theory, law has an integrative and legitimating function, by means of the resolution of conflict. The actions of participants within each system are co-ordinated through their taking the form of roles, which are in turn co-ordinated by contributing to the achievement of the subsystem's function. What contributes to this co-ordinated achievement of function constitutes the values of each system. So, for example, within the legal system, whose function is conflict resolution, the roles of participants such as judges and lawyers are structured by ideas of justice that allow the resolution of disputes to represent something more acceptable, and successful, than the application of naked coercion. This version of law as a system is challenged by empirical experience. Law in many instances not only fails to resolve conflicts but by producing new laws that clash with established expectations it also creates conflicts that would not otherwise arise. And any attempt to claim that the legal system has any set of functions that are sufficiently specific to orientate the roles of its participants falls foul of the fact that other systems can be seen to carry out some of the functions attributed to law, and vice versa. Law is not the only mechanism for resolving conflict, and, with the political system, seems to share the role of setting standards, goals, or other normative expectations.

If one accepts these kinds of arguments one could, or perhaps should conclude, like Sampford, that law is not a system, or is not best understood as operating as a system. And there are alternative formulations of this conclusion, for example, that law is at best a relatively autonomous system.[15] But to call law a relatively autonomous system is simply to concede that what you have identified as its structure does not account for the

[12] Parsons, 1951, especially ch 2.

[13] See Parsons and Smelser, 1956, 46–50.

[14] See Bredemeier, 1962.

[15] Such analysis is put forward by Beck, 1994, as a criticism of Luhmann's analysis of law as a system. Van de Kerchove and Ost, 1994, engage in a similar exercise of exploring the meaning of what a system is (ch 1) in order to question seriously its systematic qualities, preferring to see law as operating through an oscillation between order and disorder.

whole of law. Only some of law, albeit that part which might include most of law, or the most important parts of law (depending on the basis of assessment used for such judgements) is accounted for by the structure in question: hierarchy of rules; standards or reasons for action; justificatory principles; actions attributable to a dominant function; etc.[16] If one accepts that law is a relatively autonomous system, yet continues to regard law as something that can be described as a whole by reference to a particular set of relationships, one is either being inconsistent, or claiming that a particular attempt to describe law as a system is, despite its inadequacies, superior to other ways of attempting to understand law. To explain how law can be a system, despite the above arguments, we need to re-examine our idea of a system.

A system cannot be a mere collective or aggregate of phenomena. We need to keep the 'interdependent' character of the parts, as set out in Dewey's definition, in mind. Namely, there needs to be a relationship between its parts. Unrelated matter does not amount to a system, even if the future configurations of that matter (such as a cloud of gas molecules[17]) are quite predictable. We need to move from the Aristotelian idea of a system being a relationship between a whole and its parts, an understanding that leads one to look for fixed and given structures, to an alternative understanding of the nature of a system. The jurisprudential debate over claims that law operates as a system has been a kind of quest for the Holy Grail. What structures are sufficient to determine what can belong to law rather than another social phenomenon? What interrelationship of parts and whole explains law at both the micro-level (what single elements can belong to law) and at the macro-level (how can law be understood as a whole). Instead of this focus on the idea of a whole constructed by, and in turn constructing, its parts through fixed and given structures, can we consider the possibilities for a system to exist without a fixed structure? Can a social system, such as law, exist and evolve with structures that are contingent and open to change? By what processes could this occur? To begin to explore this idea, to move beyond an attempt to identify specific structures that account for the whole and the parts of a legal system, we need to re-examine what it means for something to be a system and focus not on the idea of structure, but that of boundaries.[18]

Systems exist by distinguishing themselves from their surrounding environment. This does not mean that systems are isolated from their environment, and that nothing enters and nothing leaves. All systems,

[16] According to Brian Tamanaha, Luhmann's theory is functionalist (with a small 'f'). Such functionalism falls foul of Barnes's definition: 'A functionalist account mentions *only* those operations, and those consequences thereof, that help us understand the equilibrium of the system.' *The Elements of Social Theory* (1995) 40, as quoted by Tamanaha, 2001, 188.

[17] To give Sampford's own example.

[18] See Luhmann 1995, especially 194–97 and the analysis of '*meaning-constituted boundaries*'. This is autopoietic systems theory's '*leitdifferenz*' (guiding difference).

social, biological, psychical and physical, are open to their environment, in the sense that some things enter and others leave. The key question is how systems determine what can enter and leave. What, within the system, restricts its interaction with its environment? Without any such restriction we do not have a system. We just have a particular part of a more general environment. To think of a system as something with a totally open environment is actually to abandon the idea of a system. And to think of a system as something totally isolated from its environment is, as we have just stated, to hypothesise about an entity that does not exist as such, even though it might be so constructed for the purposes of logical or other forms of thinking or conceptualising.[19]

Terms such as 'open' or 'closed' systems have been developed within both the physical[20] and social sciences to refer to particular kinds of restrictions on what may enter or leave a system. Rather than repeat and adopt these terminologies here, we prefer to focus on the more general point that systems develop boundaries, not in the sense that nothing passes through those boundaries, but in the sense that the system closes itself to its environment by establishing restrictions on what can enter or leave. Only by doing this can a system differentiate itself from its environment.[21] This in turn is the basis of the system's identity – what separates it from what surrounds it. Statements like 'the open rests on the closed',[22] which may seem paradoxical or merely playful, are actually quite logical and appropriate. Finding out how a system establishes restrictions on its openness to its environment, its closure, *is* the basis of its openness to its environment.

From this new starting point, we can begin to describe how law exists as a system. What differentiates law, as a system, from its environment? What is the basis of its closure (which is also the basis of its openness)? In his discussion of Luhmann's version of functionalism, Sampford, relying on *Social Systems*,[23] did not feel that Luhmann had moved sufficiently far from Parsons' functional systems theory. Luhmann accepts that subsystems duplicate each others' performance (for example, law is not the only conflict resolution system) but still insists that law carries out an overall function that is peculiar to itself: 'establishing and stabilizing normative

[19] Kelsen's 'pure theory of law' captures this kind of construction, at least in its form up to 1960, and its reliance on neo-Kantianism.

[20] As an example of the importance of the relationship between closed and open systems in comprehending the physical world, see von Bertalanffy, 1976, 39–41 and 121–25.

[21] 'The environment is a system-relative situation. Every system removes itself from its environment. Therefore the environment of each system is different. And thus the unity of the environment is constituted by the system . . . The environment is simply "everything else"' (Luhmann 1995, 181). For further elaboration on the relationship between system and environment, selection as an internal response that reduces the complexity of a system's environment and thereby increases its own complexity, see ch 5, 'System and Environment'.

[22] L'ouvert s'appuye le ferme' (Edgar Morin).

[23] 1995.

expectations'.[24] This was interpreted by Sampford as a claim that this function generates and maintains law's existence as a separate system.[25] Whilst society needs normative expectations, the idea that this need could structure the behaviour of individuals throughout the legal system, through the creation of roles and the generation of values and commitments likely to fulfil this general function, is implausible.[26] However, this is not the kind of functionalism, or system, that we need to consider. The function of law, within Luhmann's theory, is not something that orientates and separates it off as a separate social system. It is merely something that we can observe. If we consider what law does within society, by contrast with other parts of society (mass media, science, economy, etc.) we might agree that it generates and maintains normative expectations in the face of counterfactual examples.[27] Attribution of function is an observation about the contribution which a system makes to the continuation of society.[28] One is able to observe systems, sociologically or scientifically, and make assessments of their function.[29] The description of law as a system that contributes normative expectations distinguishes it from the economy as the system that manages expectations about the future availability of scarce resources. This does not mean that law never allocates resources or that the economy never generates normative expectations. By contrast, science creates 'truthful' knowledge, and the mass media generates information. But the claim that law is the primary supplier of something a society needs in order to function should not be translated into a claim that this need structures the behaviour of all individuals who participate within the legal system.

To understand the existence of law as a system we need to begin, not with how it may function within society, but how it establishes a boundary between itself and the rest of society, and to comprehend how this may be

[24] Luhmann, 2004, ch 3, 'The Function of Law'. This statement is made at numerous points throughout his book; a useful example that clarifies its meaning can be found at 151–54.

[25] Tamanaha (2001, 36) adopts a similar interpretation and critique of Luhmann's systems theory.

[26] 'Luhmann has abandoned many of the more systematic aspects of Parsonian structural functionalism but his retention of function as the key relation between the elements and the use of institutions (or 'decision sets') as the supposed fulfillers of these functions is fatal to the acceptability of his system' (Sampford, 1989, 132).

[27] Crucially, in *Law as a Social System*, Luhmann is clear that a system's function is the surplus value that it creates for other systems, and not a guiding distinction within the system itself.

[28] The functionality of differentiated subsystems is due to their role in providing society with meanings. To hypothesise society without any systems is to imagine a society which has no meanings, which is the equivalent of imagining no society. However, from a systems theory perspective it is precisely functional differentiation that is the basis of the complexity of modern society; see King, 1997.

[29] That said, according to Luhmann only the science system adopts 'functional analysis' within its 'system reference'. Thus, for general systems theory 'functional analysis' needs to 'address the problem of complexity instead of the problem of maintenance continuances' (1995, 52–58).

possible without the presence of fixed and given structures. Society, for Luhmann, consists of its communications.[30] Inanimate objects are not part of society – they do not communicate. Nor are the biological, chemical or thought processes that operate within human beings – these things may motivate communication, but are not themselves communications. These objects and processes form society's environment. Law's existence as a system operates as a subsystem of communication within society, and society consists of the sum total of communications. It is relatively easy to see how society, as the totality of communication, establishes a border with its environment. Society is open to, and influenced by, what occurs in the physical world, and what takes place within the minds and biological processes that constitute human beings. But there is no possibility for communication to become the same as its environment. One can communicate about the physical world, or about the human beings that inhabit it, but those communications remain separate from these objects of communication. The medium generated and carried by communications is meaning.[31] Only what is meaningful can form the content of a communication. And this allows human beings, motivated by their thoughts, to make communications that allow them to participate within society. But communication cannot be reduced to thoughts, motivations or attitudes. Thoughts remain thoughts until they are communicated, and once they are communicated they are not just thoughts, but communications.

There is a vast literature on whether or not the possibilities of what can be communicated are established through structures, and what form those structures might take. Fortunately, we do not need to explore this here. If the reader can understand what is meant by the claim that communications remain separate from (closed to) their environment we can move on to the more controversial and relevant question: how can law exist as a separate system within society? We cannot point to an obvious separation such as exists between communications and other phenomena (such as objects in the real world, or processes of cognition). Everything that explains why and how communications are separate from their environment fails to explain this particular separation. Legal communications are not thoughts, or physical matter. Like other communications they have the potentiality to transmit meanings. The vast bulk of legal communication uses language, and the language (English, French, etc) is the same language used within the mass

[30] For background, see Luhmann, 1995, ch 4, 'Communication and Action'. For an unequivocal statement: '. . . my point of departure is the systems theory of Niklas Luhmann. Here, society is viewed as consisting of communication and nothing but communication. The fundamental event in society is seen as communication rather than action' (Andersen, 2003, 153).

[31] See Luhmann, 1995, ch 2, 'Meaning'. For an explanation of Luhmann's understanding of meaning (which operates between actuality and potentiality) and semantics (which involves condensed meaning), see Andersen, 2010. This understanding is particularly relevant to our discussion of legal pluralism in Chapter 4.

media, science, politics, morals, religion, and the economy. The same structures of syntax and grammar apply, and whilst there may be some unique terms within law, these are insufficient to justify a claim that law is in any significant way separate from the rest of society. Communications are not limited to language (images – including images of silence – communicate meanings as well as speech) but again relatively little of law is communicated through images and symbols that are unique to it (albeit that some of its symbols may be important).

With all the common features of legal and other communications, how can law establish a border between itself as a system of communication and other communications? What stops communications from politics, morality, science and the economy entering into law, leading to the conclusion that there is nothing systematic about law that separates law from these other parts of society, and gives it a distinct existence and identity? The answers provided within legal theory have been sketched at the beginning of this Chapter. That provided by Luhmann is based upon the difference between codes and programmes.[32] Luhmann claims that social systems (subsystems or function systems) separate themselves from each other through their existence as separate systems of meaning. Legal meanings are the result of the relationship between legal communications. What establishes that a communication is a legal communication, one that connects to other legal communications and generates legal meanings, is the code that is being applied. Legal communications code the world in terms of a binary opposition: legal/illegal. Other systems code the world using different binary oppositions: true/false in the case of science; government/opposition in the case of politics; payment/non-payment in the case of the economy; information/not information in the case of the mass media; and so on. These codes are distinctions, but they are not structures. They are meaningless in and of themselves. To be told that there is an undefined state, 'x', that is legal, or true, or a payment, or information is only to know that the other side of the distinction does not apply: that it is not illegal, not false, etc. Meaning is generated through the constant process of communicating about the application of these distinctions. Communicating on the application of the code, a process Luhmann calls self-observation, generates programmes. The term self-observation is appropriate here, because the communications which seek to explain the application of the code are applying the same code as the communications which applied the code before. Here one has legal communications (communications applying the code legal/illegal) communicating about communications that applied the code legal/illegal. Thus observations on the application of the code are generated within, and by, the system itself. The boundaries of the legal system

[32] This becomes much clearer in Luhmann's later works, and especially in his analysis of law – see Luhmann, 2004, ch 4.

are reconstituted with every legal communication. Every communication that has a legal meaning forms part of the legal system. Legal meaning is coterminous with communications that are applying the code legal/illegal. All communications applying this code form part of the legal system, and all communications that are not applying this code form part of its environment.[33]

The idea that a system is differentiated by a code (a distinction that has no necessary relationship with any structures) seems a rather unpromising basis from which to establish and maintain something as complex as a modern legal system. If Dworkin's structures of justifications fail to account for the legal system's identity due to differences between judges as to what constitutes a good reason for a legal decision (let alone differences between lawyers and non-lawyers, and between non-lawyers), then surely the problem is multiplied immeasurably once we accept that the distinction legal/illegal refers to nothing outside of itself. But here we need to consider the role played by programmes. Programmes are generated through communications that account for the application of the code. This would include both ex-post rationalisations and hypothetical future applications of the code. These programmes stabilise the process of coding, but they do not determine its application. By accounting for the application of the code (this situation is legal because . . .; this situation constitutes a payment because . . .; this situation is information because . . .; etc) a system creates a body of communications that represent a resource (a system's memory) that make the application of the code meaningful. To account for the application of the code in a manner that is meaningful, participants in a system have to draw upon existing communications that account for the application of the code. These communications are not isolated from each other, but on the contrary, they are systematically connected with each other. The minimum but essential connection is that they all apply the same code: legal/illegal, or they all have the same trajectory moving toward or away from that code. But they also relate to each other in the sense that prior communications are the raw material from which to produce new ones. The complexity of the system's memory increases as the process of self-observation continues. We end up with something as complex as the modern legal system, which has a vast collection of procedural and substantive provisions, rules, institutional processes and structures, which constitute its programmes.

An example should assist at this stage. One that will be familiar to many readers is the case of *Riggs v Palmer*,[34] explored repeatedly by Dworkin in many of his writings, most notably in his debate with Hart and his followers.[35] Dworkin uses the case to illustrate his claims that law consists of

[33] The analysis of binary codes, and in particular the legal code, is developed more fully in Chapter 4.

[34] (1889) 22 NE 188.

[35] Especially 1977, ch 2; 1986, ch 1, in particular 15–20.

principles as well as rules, that the possibilities of what can become law are not limited to rules as recognised by a rule of recognition, and that law has an irremovable moral element. The facts of the case are that Elmer Palmer, grandson of the testator, murdered his grandfather in order to prevent him from altering his will to cut Elmer out of his inheritance. Following his conviction for murder Elmer sought to claim his inheritance under the will. This was contested by Elmer's aunts, the testator's daughters, who were named in the will as the persons who would inherit if Elmer failed to meet various conditions surrounding the bequest: die before his majority, unmarried, and without issue. As Elmer had reached his majority, these conditions did not apply and, if the will were applied according to its terms, Elmer would have inherited a sizeable fortune. In a majority decision, the Court of Appeals of New York decided that Elmer could not inherit, relying on a principle: 'no one shall be permitted to profit . . . or take advantage of his own wrong'. In addition, in the face of a statutory duty to give effect to the intention of the testator, the majority asserted that whatever the legislature intended by passing the relevant statute, they would not have intended that a person should be able to inherit when they had murdered the testator. What makes this decision part of the legal system? The crucial element is the code. The case applies the code legal/illegal. The case did not decide that the inheritance was moral or immoral, or efficient, or the expression of some truth. It decided that inheritance by Elmer would not be legal. Had the case gone the other way, it would still be part of the legal system. The judgment would be no less of a legal communication if it had decided that the inheritance was legal.

We need to explore the case further in order to comprehend how the code operates to construct a barrier between the legal system and its environment, which includes moral communications (which does not mean that on the surface there are not many legal communications that are, at the same time, moral communications). We need to consider the communications that led to this decision, and those that followed it, and see how a code that links these communications to each other also serves to place severe restrictions on the ability of other communications (here moral ones) to operate within the legal system. The decision was that of a court. The issue was that of the right to inherit under a will. The dispute was that between beneficiaries of the will, one of whom was a convicted murderer. The case arrived at court following a civil trial court decision, and an appeal. The trial would have followed procedures which included pleadings and discovery. The appeal would have involved time limits and grounds of appeal. These are all recognisable legal communications that are difficult to typify as moral ones (despite ubiquitous phrases such as the rule of law appearing to offer some attempt to conflate them).[36] More importantly,

[36] See Chapter 6 for our analysis of 'the rule of law' from a systems theory perspective.

they will have operated to constrict the ability of the parties to raise moral arguments. Think about the arguments that are *not* open to the parties in this dispute. Whatever their opinion on the legitimacy of the New York legal system or the merits of court procedures, it is only by accepting the authority (legality) of this appeal court, and the authority (legality) of the court below to make its decision (an authority to make a wrong decision which can be corrected on appeal), that enables these parties to have this issue decided by the Court of Appeals. Similarly, whilst either party may have views on the legitimacy of inherited wealth, it is only by accepting the applicability of the New York law on wills that these parties can have this matter resolved in this court. Since they are both claiming under the same will, neither party can raise arguments about the legality of this particular will, let alone wills in general. As all of the legal communications that lead to the moment of decision will involve communications that utilise ideas of statute and precedent, there is no possibility of an outright assault on the status of statutes or appeal court decisions as law. It is in this restricted context, established by legal communications – communications which establish at every stage what is legal – that the court had reference to what appears to be a moral communication: that 'no person should profit from their own wrong'. The huge numbers of interconnected communications that establish this context also make it clear that this principle has no general application within the legal system; a vast number of legal rules operate to allow persons who commit acts which others might regard as moral wrongs, but nevertheless to benefit from them. Of more particular relevance, the law of inheritance, which provides a facility whereby the owners of property are allowed to distribute it as they see fit, rather than by reference to individual or social ideas of need or merit, drastically curtails any ability to raise issues of morality.[37] Only by disturbing large amounts of the communications which stabilise the application of the code legal/illegal to the distribution of property following someone's death, can the court give an expanded role to the moral maxim here. In systems theory terms, the court would have to alter a major part of the system's memory. Of course, the court did not do this. Instead, it drew on the moral maxim to justify an exception to the law of wills, and an exception to what would appear to have been its more usual approach to statutory interpretation. People who murder testators in order to inherit under their wills are not allowed to inherit. This principle does not introduce general issues of merit or need (as operate to a greater or lesser extent in other legal systems), or even a need to enquire whether a beneficiary's inclusion under a will was the result of some personal wrongdoing so, for example, provision for mistresses remained undisturbed.

[37] Other legal systems operate different rules which may correspond to a greater or lesser extent to different conceptions of moral acceptability representing need, merit, etc.

There is no denying that a communication with a moral form – 'no person should profit from their own wrong' has been used here, within a legal case, to construct an answer to the question: is it legal for Elmer Palmer to inherit under this will? And, within any system which seeks to code situations in terms of what is good or bad, the conclusion that it would be wrong for Elmer to inherit might be connected to other communications which coded in a similar way – if it is wrong for Elmer to inherit, in what other situations would it be similarly wrong? This may even arise in another court decision. But one can also see how a moral philosopher could re-open the decision in *Riggs v Palmer*. Elmer is punished for his crime by imprisonment. Should he be doubly punished by this loss of civil rights? The purpose of the testator in leaving his farm to his grandson, cutting out his daughters, was to create or continue a patrimony. Should the fact of the murder defeat this purpose and, if it does so, is the testator also being punished? These interconnected moral communications could make a fascinating seminar on law and ethics, or even lead to a moral critique of the reasoning in this case (a phenomenon that occurs in response to all areas of law where moral communications are utilised or thought to be utilised to justify legal decisions, as Dworkin so aptly demonstrates by using this and other seminal cases). But they will not disturb the legal system, which will continue[38] as the connection of communications that bond on the basis of the application of the code legal/illegal, and not the code good/bad. If the executors pay the inheritance to Elmer it will be illegal. If the daughters seek to sell the inheritance it will be legal. Whether these actions will be good, or bad, is not something that will concern the legal system, unless legal communications again generate a situation, or issue, where moral communications can be applied (or one might say re-applied or re-used) within the legal system, to account for the application of the legal code.

We have used the example of Elmer Palmer's case, and the utilisation of moral communications within the legal system, but one can repeat this analysis in other areas of law, where communications from other systems (law's environment) are used to justify the application of the legal code. For example, one can explore the utilisation of communications from science in the law of evidence, or the utilisation of communications from the economy in so many areas of commercial law. Issues arise which make these 'non-law' communications relevant, but they have to be inserted within chains of legal communications that have been generated as answers to the application of the legal code that did not draw upon the same kinds of communications. We might say (using a moral system's account of communications to communicate about the legal system) that the legal system utilises incommensurate values.[39] So, for example, whilst one might find

[38] At least in the context of the functionally differentiated societies that we live in, namely, for the time being, as the contingencies of these arrangements remain.

[39] See Seung and Bonevac, 1992.

areas of law where the application of the code can be explained in terms of the value of efficiency, attempts to account for all of law by reference to this single value are implausible, because there are some communications within the legal system that cannot be explained as expressions of economic reasoning.[40] But the incommensurability of the values utilised within law do not prevent legal communications from connecting with each other, because the essential basis of connection is not a coherent or consistent application of reasons for applying the code, but simply that the communications are applying a common code and not the code of another system. Thus, what might appear to be 'the problem' of incommensurability, from the points of view of other systems, is diffused within the legal system through its utilisation of legal communications.

This analysis is not unique to law; indeed that is its strength for those who use it to study the interrelationship between law and its environment, most particularly other subsystems of communication. For one encounters similar codes and programmes operating in the same way in other systems. In our discussion of *Riggs v Palmer*, we have pointed out that the connections that can be made within a moral system of communication[41] are not the same connections that can be made within the legal system. One can also look at the relationship between the law and the mass media, or law and politics, analysing the different possibilities of connection, and therefore different meanings which arise, even with communications which have an identical form (syntax). To use another example, consider a Green Paper that was published by the previous government on criminal appeals, which sought to prevent the legal system from quashing the conviction of persons on 'technical' grounds.[42] One might describe this, without reference to systems theory analysis, as an example of politicians, responding to newspaper stories that persons who are 'guilty' are 'getting off' on appeal, and wanting to remove this possibility. But systems theory analysis can illuminate the many difficulties of offering adequate descriptions of this situation. Whilst newspapers have generated programmes to stabilise the application of the media code, distinguishing information from non-information (news/not news), which include expressing outrage at the legal system's apparent willingness to accept that a person who may be factually guilty should nevertheless remain unpunished, and this can be expressed within political communications as a reform proposal, there are no equivalent communications within the legal system. The legal system constructs convictions through procedures that would not be acknowledged by sci-

[40] We make this statement despite the attempts made by Richard Posner in his many writings to suggest that they might be. Dworkin's critique in its many forms (for example, 2006, ch 3, 'Darwin's New Bulldog') is, we believe, persuasive.

[41] For a systems theory analysis of the code of morals, see Luhmann, 1992–93, and our later discussion in Chapter 4.

[42] Quashing Convictions 2006: http://www.nio.gov.uk/quashing_convictions_report_of_a_review_by_the_home_secretary_lord_chancellor_and_attorney_general_sept_2006.pdf

ence as an appropriate basis for the establishment of a truth, and the legal system deals with this deficit by justifying convictions after a 'fair trial'.[43] These aspects of trial, the ones that compensate for the legal system's inability to 'know' the truth or at least explore it using the methods of testing and proof to a scientific standard, cannot be acknowledged, within the legal system, as 'technicalities'. Whilst any particular breach of a legal procedure may be regarded as not sufficient to justify quashing a conviction, there is simply no way that all breaches of these procedures can be treated in this way, or even a class of such breaches. To acknowledge a class of breaches as 'technical' is to indicate that the procedures being breached are an unnecessary part of the trial process, a concession which invites a reform removing them. Whilst such internal reforms are a routine consequence of the appeal process (alongside the converse situations where omitted procedures are declared to be essential to a fair trial) there is no scope for the legal system to eradicate what the media are complaining about: the presence of procedures whose breaches justify quashing the convictions of people who may still be guilty of the offences charged. Whatever procedures are left in place, a successful appeal based on their breach can always be reported in the press as the release of a person solely by reason of a breach of procedure, and therefore 'technical'. Under these conditions, the Green Paper proposing the abolition of 'technical appeals' cannot be given commensurate meaning within the legal system. In systems theory terms, the legal system is (in its current configuration of programmes) closed to this reform proposal.[44]

To recap, the existence of the legal system is simply the connection between all of its communications, which interconnect through the use of the same code, which is different from the codes of the systems in its environment. This does not mean that communications from another system cannot be re-used within the legal system. But to be re-used within the legal system they have to be separated from their existence within their originating system, where they take their precise meaning from their network of interconnected communications within that system. The selection and use of communications from other systems is established internally, though the interconnection of law's own communications. And by connecting communications from other systems to its own existing state of communications, it gives them its own legal meanings, and establishes (on an ongoing basis) the possibilities for future extrapolation. This process of interconnection through a distinct code also constitutes the legal system's

[43] See Nobles and Schiff, 2006a; also, see analysis of these issues in Chapter 8.

[44] And in practice, after considerable criticism principally from lawyers (see, for example, the response of the Criminal Cases Review Commission: http://www.ccrc.gov.uk/CCRC_Uploads/QUASHING_CONVICTIONS_RESPONSE_FOR_WEBSITE.pdf) most of the proposed reform was not enacted. http://www.nio.gov.uk/response_to_quashing_convictions_consultation_paper_october_2007.pdf

boundaries with its environment – that which at any given moment restricts what, from another system, can be utilised within the legal system.

At this point we need to introduce an important distinction within systems theory, as to what constitutes a system's boundary. There are two senses in which systems involve boundaries. The first is the sense in which we have been discussing it so far: boundary as the outer perimeter of a system. A system cannot reach beyond itself – so its environment remains inaccessible to it. A boundary in this sense can also be described as a 'horizon'.[45] To understand this idea of boundary, and how social systems respond to it, it is useful to return to reconsider society as a system which consists of the sum total of communications. Everything that is not a communication forms the environment of this system: the physical world, including human biological processes, and the consciousnesses of human beings. None of these things can *be* communications in themselves; rather they can only become the subject of communications. In this sense, the borders of society are whatever lies outside of (is not) communication. But society deals with its environment by making it the subject of communications, and in so doing, creates a border inside communication. We have communications about society's environment, and communications about society. Thus the boundary between the system of society and its environment is recreated inside the system of society. And it is this distinction inside society which forms the basis of society's responses to its environment. The manner in which society constructs its version of itself and its environment inside society is the basis of society's responses to that environment.

As before, once we can understand how this distinction operates at the level of society, we have to apply the same understanding to its differentiated social subsystems. Each of society's social subsystems has to create its environment, using its own communications. In the case of law, these are communications which are coding in terms of the binary code legal/illegal. Using these communications, law will communicate about its environment (the physical world, society as a whole, human consciousness and each of the other social subsystems, including organisations and interactions). And in the process of constructing this environment it will also, using its own communications, attribute some parts of its own communications to that environment, and others to itself. Thus just as society has to construct itself as something separate from the rest of its environment, within its communications, in order to communicate about that environment, so too law has to construct something as itself, distinct from its environment, within its own communications.

These secondary, internal boundaries, constructed by and within communication, are important to understanding the basis of systems' relationships

[45] See Philippopoulos-Mihalopoulos, 2010, for a fuller discussion of the relationship between boundaries or borders and horizons.

with their environments. The possibilities of what can be recognised and reacted to by communications that are coding legal/illegal depend on the programmes of law. But these programmes will always refer to both law and its environment. So, for example, when the Theft Act states that dishonestly taking property belonging to another with an intention permanently to deprive is illegal, there is both a self-reference to the law, and an external reference to an outside environment that will be identified by reference to legal constructions of property, intention, permanence and dishonesty. Whilst the legal system, like society, can never reach beyond its border, where that involves reaching beyond its own communications to something other than its communications (here its border is a horizon), it can operate on both sides of the border that it creates inside itself, through its own communications. And this is the basis of each social system's orientation to its environment. Unable to reach the environment which lies beyond its communications, each system constructs a version of its environment internally, and generates a dynamic whereby communications assigned to its environment form triggers (conditions) for the programmes which orientate the application of its code.

This understanding of the processes through which law, in common with other social subsystems, maintains its separation from other systems, gives us a different understanding of systems, and the role played within systems by structures, from that explored by Sampford. There is no doubt that law develops structures; its programmes – rules, principles, procedures, sources, etc., for the application of the code are structures. But the processes by which these structures are generated, self-observation within the system on applications of the code, ensures that these structures cannot determine or account for all applications of the code. They are also themselves open to change, since the same processes which generated them can also change them. What is important about these structures is how they limit the possibilities of what can, in any particular context, consist of a legal communication. To refer back to our analysis of *Riggs v Palmer*, none of the parties would be able to have a court rule on their disputed will whilst maintaining that legislation and appeal court decisions were not a source of law. This is a typical experience for anybody seeking to generate any dispute capable of being decided by a court. It generates, within legal theory, positivist accounts of the legal system that attribute the identity and boundaries of what can be law to a restricted list of legal sources. But, as Sampford notes, sources of law fail to account for all of the possibilities of what can belong to the legal system, and do not explain how the sources of law and their relative priority alter within the legal system. The typical legal positivist response to the incomplete account of law afforded by sources of law is that these structures account for the bulk of legal decisions, but leave 'gaps' or penumbras of uncertainty, where decisions have to be reached on other grounds, but having been reached thus, form part of the legal system thereafter by reference to the authority of the institution which makes that decision, an authority understood by that institution's status as a source of law. This approach leads to communications that systems theory would include in the legal system, by reference to the code applied, being excluded by other theories. For example, Raz demotes the status of decisions within the penumbra through a distinction between applying and making law, and between the deliberative and executive stages of action.[46] Where the source-based norms of the system have not achieved a stability of interpretation that dictates how the code should be applied, we do not have law, but a situation in which one must wait for law to come into being. Thus all the communications that may be brought to bear to decide a hard case are still, for him, not legal.

By contrast with Raz's analysis, communications that construct decisions under conditions of uncertainty (contingency) are part of the legal system because of the code that is being applied. There is, however, more that can be said about this. Self-observation leads to programmes, and these will be different within different systems. Attempts to describe the system by reference to the programmes that stabilise the application of the code have led to theories, like those of Hart and Raz, whereby what cannot be stabilised is not part of the legal system: the system's contingencies (its hard cases) lie outside the system.[47] But systems theory does not require us to accept that where the application of the code is not stabilised by programmes, one has nothing but the arbitrary application of the code. There are structures, in addition to programmes, that restrict the possibilities of what can form part of a system. In addition to applying different codes, systems have different kinds of communication to deal with contingencies. Luhmann calls these their formulas for variety. In the case of the legal system, the principal formula for variety is 'justice'.[48] What come within a system's formulas for variety are the kinds of communications which allow a system to recognise its own contingencies. Each subsystem recognises them in its own manner.

It is useful here to use Raz's positivist theory as a contrast. If legal systems are only established through structures that give predictable stability to the application of their codes, then there is something suspect about claiming that communications made under conditions of uncertainty belong to the system. For Raz, this marks the boundary of what can be law. At this

[46] For a brief statement, see Raz, 2009, 90–97; more generally see Raz, 1994, Part II, 'Between Law and Morality'; Raz, 2009, Part II, 'The Nature of Law and Natural Law'; Raz, 2009a, Part II, 'Law, Authority, and Morality'.

[47] Although we have not come close to presenting the tightly reasoned arguments that Raz employs to situate carefully his 'source-based' thesis about law (as distinct from Hart's), we believe that it is appropriate to draw out these differences in approach to contingency in law because of the specific role attributed to contingency within systems theory. See Luhmann, 1998, ch 3, 'Contingency as Modern Society's Defining Attribute'.

[48] Luhmann, 2004, ch 5.

point the legal system can only wait for things that lie outside itself (politics, morality, self-interest, etc) to eliminate the contingency and bring new law into being. If the communications that accompany the applications of the code under conditions of uncertainty are called law – suggesting that they form part of the current legal system prior to decisions which eliminate the uncertainty – this is an error. Here Luhmann's analysis is nearer to the kind of position outlined by Dworkin. If the system has its own kinds of communications for dealing with its own contingencies, and if those communications are different from the communications used by other systems to deal with what those systems recognise as their own contingencies, then we are still inside the system. Within law, the communications that self-consciously address the need to make selections under conditions of uncertainty are referred to, at the most general level, as justice.

But then, is justice an 'empty formula'? If it were truly so then anything could be presented within the legal system as justice. This would be the equivalent to admitting that any form of communication could justify the application of the code, so that, at moments of contingency, the legal system has no boundary – any and every kind of communication can become a legal communication. The same arguments apply in respect of the formulas which operate within other subsystems to deal with their contingencies. So if, for example, anything can be presented as appropriate to a judgement of 'scarcity' within the economy, then at moments of contingency the economy has no boundary separating it from other systems. But, whilst these formulas are necessarily loose, are they empty or meaningless? And more importantly, can they establish any distinction of meaning from each other, based on their operation and location within different subsystems? To explore the possibilities of difference between different formulas for contingency, consider the following question: is it appropriate to justify decisions dealing with contingencies within the legal system, ordinarily, by reference to willingness to pay? Despite the efforts of economic analysis of law scholars to demonstrate that the articulation of legal doctrine is compatible with decisions made by reference to considerations of scarcity and allocation according to willingness to pay, the fact remains that this is not the form in which legal doctrine is, in nearly all instances, articulated. Allocating legal entitlements in response to contested legal claims by reference to arguments of efficiency (allocation in accordance to willingness to pay) is no problem for the legal system if this remains a motive (in the mind of the person making the decision). But if this basis of decision were articulated as a justification it would normally be incompatible with the arguments put to that decision maker. In the case of that decision maker being a judge, those arguments would be contrary presentations/interpretations of legal doctrine.

Formulas for variety or contingency have to process their contingencies in a manner that allows the system's communications to continue – business as usual. But justifying the application of the code of one system in situations of uncertainty using communications appropriate to another does not allow for this. Raz, in his theory of 'law as authority',[49] puts a heavy onus on the concepts of precedent and legislation to transform communications of unlimited variety from other systems into legal ones. Whilst legislation seems able to transform all kinds of communications into legal ones, adjudication is far less open (a feature exploited by Dworkin). A judicial decision reached without reasons, or by reference to reasons that are incompatible with the communications that have created the opposing alternatives that have to be chosen between, does not resolve the contingency at the level of evolution – 'what follows from this'. For example, deciding between two alternative versions of doctrine by reference to the solution which was most efficient (allocating resources to those who value them most in terms of willingness to pay) would not tell one which of these two versions of doctrine was 'right', or thereby adequately allocate 'legal rights'. Instead, it would communicate that both arguments of doctrine were wrong, or irrelevant, and should themselves be re-formulated as economic arguments. This is not something that the legal system can build into its operations while continuing as a legal system. Raz (and before him Hart) places too much reliance on the 'authority' of courts to decide a legal contingency, and too little attention to the limited range of communications that can be used to resolve a legal contingency, and the manner in which the system itself structures what can be used.

The need to resolve doctrinal disputes using communications that are a continuation of doctrine gives content to one of the maxims which is central to the 'justice' of any legal decision: treat like cases alike. As with the even more formulaic references to 'justice' in law (generally grouped under the heading of the 'rule of law'),[50] the notion of treating like cases alike seems to be without content, allowing any decision maker to assert what he/she finds to be similar within any two situations, and thereby do 'justice' according to their own subjective assessments. Whilst the possibilities of alternative selections cannot be eliminated by systems (that is what is involved in systems having contingencies)[51] it is the system's ability to construct the alternatives, and to require selection between alternatives by reference to formulas that structure what communications can be drawn upon from another system to make that selection, that ensures that the boundaries between systems do not disappear, even at the moments of the resolution of a system's contingencies. It is not 'just' within the legal system to

[49] Law must have authority or at least 'claim[s] . . . legitimate authority' (Raz, 2009, 30).

[50] See our discussion of the rule of law in Chapter 6.

[51] And it is for this reason that Luhmann is able to observe that 'the function of system differentiation can be described as *intensifying selectivity*. . . . The main function of the system of society, then, is to enlarge and reduce the complexity of external and internal environments to the effect that other systems will find enough structure to support boundaries and structures of higher specificity. Any experience and action in such a society has to rely on a complex network of selective boundaries that reduce open contingencies' (Luhmann, 1977, 31).

ignore the manner in which legal communications build 'cases' to be adjudicated upon, when deciding what is alike to what. And it is not possible to replace this idea of justice, which operates all over the legal system, with the formulas for contingency that operate within the economy (efficiency) or politics (the common good).

Treating like cases alike is a most significant communication associated with justice under the law. To the extent that all references to justice in law may appear to be empty formulas, the important thing to understand is that such references to formulas to deal with contingency are different from the equally 'empty' formulas that orientate communication about selections under conditions of uncertainty within other subsystems. For example, as already mentioned, within the economy the formula for contingency is management of scarcity. Every decision within the economy can be described, within the economy, as the management of scarcity. Jokey statements like 'there is no such thing as a free lunch' make the same point – all decisions which allocate resources move those resources from alternative uses. Advocates for the economic analysis of law want this insight to be applied to legal decisions. In other words, they want the formula for variety within the economy, the management of scarcity (that is, concerns with efficiency) to be applied to the legal system.

In their debate with those who advocate economic approaches to legal decisions, legal theorists like Dworkin[52] point to the 'injustice' of reaching all legal decisions using economic criteria, such as allocation in accordance with willingness to pay. In addition, they can point to the corrosive effect on established areas of legal doctrine, if legal decisions can be re-examined by reference to economic criteria. And they can point to the inability of the economy to allocate resources by reference to willingness to pay, in the absence of legal rights, such as property and contract rights that are not allocated in this manner. These arguments point towards the differences between communications about justice, law's principal formula for contingency, and those of the economy. Law communicates not only about the contingencies of the present in terms of justice, but also those of the past. The legal system can produce understandings (self-observations) of its past decisions in terms of justice, which indicate, at the most general level, how future decisions should be reached. The most important of these is that identified by Hart: to treat like cases alike.[53] This requirement may, in terms of various philosophical critiques, appear empty, as it requires decisions on what constitutes a like case, before it can operate. But nevertheless, as a formula it describes exactly what has occurred in the building of law's programmes – a constant process of accounting for the application of the legal code. If situation A is legal, what distinguishes it from situation B

[52] Dworkin, 1980, and more recently, Dworkin, 2006, ch 3.

[53] See, for example, 1958, 623–24.

which has been coded illegal? And when applied in situations of contingency, it requires communications which compare the alternate possibilities of coding – legal or illegal – and it produces reasons that are compatible with existing reasons (the system's memory) to account for the coding applied. The apparent emptiness of the formula does not prevent it from operating differently from the contingency formulas of other systems. So, for example, treating like cases alike cannot help looking backwards, to past applications of the code, even if there are also forward observations: what happens in other future cases if this is found to be legal/illegal. By contrast, the economy does not treat the past as something that has any general claim to be repeated.[54] As such, managing scarcity does not require treating like cases alike, or at least not in the same manner as the legal system. We could, like Dworkin, say that law is principled, and does not allow for 'chequerboard' solutions, whereby rights are allocated to individuals only if, and in so far as, they achieve goals. But systems theory gives a less celebratory account of the reasons for these phenomena: the communications of the legal system cannot carry out the operations of the legal system (which include making decisions in situations where there is no good reason to decide one way rather than another) without communicating about those decisions in a manner that is compatible with the communications through which it has constructed its other programmes and structures. If there is one way to carry out this particular operation which allows the legal system to continue to carry out its other operations, and another way to carry out this operation that threatens to undo the ability to continue with these other operations, the legal system is unlikely to select the 'costly' communications in place of the 'less costly', easier ones.[55]

The argument being made here is not that particular decisions could not have been made or justified by reference to other kinds of communications: ones which refer to democracy, or efficiency, etc. Or even that the motivation behind a particular selection will lie outside of communication in self-interest, altruism, emotion or desire. It is that, when communicating within a system about the reason for a selection, each system has developed different general communications to justify its own selections, and that the differences between these formulas alter the nature of the possibilities for dealing with contingencies.

To recap: the legal system maintains its boundary against the communications of other systems being able to enter into itself (except on terms that are compatible with itself) through the need to connect legal communications to the application of a different code from other systems, the complex

[54] See our analysis of law's construction of time in Chapter 5 below.

[55] Those who find this description too anthropomorphic, in its reference to the legal system making less costly selections, are asked to reserve judgement until they read the next Chapter: 'Why do judges talk the way they do?', which links this process of selection to the motivations of individuals.

memory of interconnected communications that it has generated through self-observation on the application of the code, and the different formulas for variety which it applies to deal with its own self-generated and self-observed contingencies. If we relate this account of law's existence as a system back to those analysed by Sampford, we can see that it is compatible with the structures which he discusses. Law does, at its current stage of development, rely heavily on sources to stabilise legal meanings. It also involves a process of selection in which communications (including communications about values) from other systems can be utilised, but the contingencies of the system (what is open to argument and what it is possible to argue) are established by the communications (including self-observations) of the system itself. In making selections the legal system has regard to general forms of communication which are routinely self-observed within the system as 'justice'. So law has both source-based *and* content-based structures which restrict but do not determine the possibilities of legal meaning.

The inability of structures generated through legal communications to determine what can be communicated within and by the legal system should not surprise, given our description of the manner in which these structures are generated. Self-observation will not eliminate the need for decisions about the application of the code, and applications of the code provide the basis for new observations that have the potential to replace earlier ones. This includes even the most important structures within the legal system, such as the nature and scope of constitutions, statutes, and precedents as sources of law.[56] It is generally acknowledged that sources change both in their content and relative hierarchy over time. Within the UK, the law of precedent altered in the nineteenth century, as part of changing understandings within the legal system as to the nature of legislation. The legal doctrine of parliamentary sovereignty (a principle of statutory interpretation) has altered as a result of entering the European Economic Community in 1973 and then the European Union in a manner that could not have been predicted with any certainty, from the passage of the statutes which affected that entry. Similar changes in the lists and hierarchies of sources can be identified in other nations' legal systems. Systems theory alters our understanding of these changes. The status of structures within the legal system is established by the operations that they enable. As we pointed out in our discussion of *Riggs v Palmer* the centrality of the main sources of law (statutes and court precedents) is re-affirmed through the difficulties of making a legal claim or argument of any complexity, whilst at the same time seeking to deny that these are sources of law. Similar difficulties inhibit claims that the authority of these sources of law is synonymous with their status as moral communications. This is part of a

[56] We discuss these matters more fully in Chapters 5 and 6 of this book.

more general restriction: making legal communications requires one to draw upon the existing store of communications that have already been utilised to generate legal meanings. Communications are a continuation of the legal system from its current state of existence. This is also systems theory's answer to the definitional question identified at the beginning of this Chapter. Does law have a relationship between its whole and its parts, which justifies it being considered as a system, or do we have to accept that law is not a system, as described by Dewey, on the basis that, without structures that can determine all of the possibilities of its elements, there is no relationship between the whole and the parts, and therefore there is no system?

The relationship between the whole and the parts is the process whereby individual legal communications constitute continuations of the system. Just as the possibilities of continuing communication in general (society) are dependent on the communications that are available to be continued, so too the possibilities of continuing legal communication are dependent on the total legal communications available to be continued. In this way, from moment to moment, the whole does determine the possibilities of the parts whilst, at the same time, the parts (each new legal communication) are altering what constitutes the whole. This is a reflexive relationship, both at the level of society as a whole, and within each of its subsystems. Executed through millions or even billions of legal communications, this has transformative possibilities which can exist alongside extremely stable structures. Whilst almost every conceivable legal communication within a legal system may seem to confirm a stable understanding of the nature and hierarchy of legal sources, there is always the possibility of building up bodies of legal doctrine that will challenge and alter those understandings.[57]

This explanation of law's existence as a system alters our understanding of the basis of human participation within law. In *The Disorder of Law* Sampford constructed much of his challenge to the possibilities of law existing as a system on the nature of interaction and the problems of subjectivity. He points to the asymmetrical nature of most human interaction, whereby each party experiences a different understanding of the meaning of what has occurred. Alongside imbalances of power, which leads to different understandings of relationships (e.g. what those with power regard as authority, those without power may understand as coercion) there is also the different set of experiences and perceptions that any individual brings to an interaction, which provide a different basis from which to interpret what occurs.[58] Sampford's conclusion is that both society and law represent

[57] As we describe in particular in Chapter 4 by reference to the ideas of legal pluralism and legal globalisation.

[58] Luhmann recognises the same problem, which he calls 'double contingency'. He explores how individuals can mutually reconstruct their own understandings in the course of interaction in response to each other, thus achieving co-ordination – a process he calls interpenetration

a mêlée rather than a system. He argues that what has been described as systems are, at best, simply the overlaps of individual understandings and commitments. Systems theory, as we have described it in this Chapter, explains how individuals can participate in systems despite these differences. And, in the next Chapter, we go on to explore that 'whole' even further. In particular we describe the nature of individual 'commitment' to the legal system, especially by looking at the role of the judge within the legal system.

(Luhmann, 1995, ch 6). But in modern societies in which so much communication does not allow the addressee to respond directly to the addressor, interpenetration cannot explain how society can be constructed with any degree of stability.

2

Why Do Judges Talk the Way They Do?

> The workings of the judicial process [are] conducted upon the tacit assumption that the common law (we are not concerned here with statute) always provides an answer to the matter in issue, and one which is independent of the will of the court. Put differently, the conventions of legal argument embody a belief in the theoretical possibility of a comprehensive gapless rule of law. It is as if lawyers had all been convinced by Dworkin, though none of them have. (Simpson, 1986, 9)

> There is no doubt that the familiar rhetoric of the judicial process encourages the idea that there are in a developed legal system no legally unregulated cases. But how seriously is this to be taken? . . . it is important to distinguish the ritual language used by judges and lawyers in deciding cases in their courts from their more reflective general statements about the judicial process. (Hart, 1994, 274)

> When we recognise that respected judges, like Cardozo, whose opinions resemble those of other judges, write off the bench about judges' legislative functions, and we note that their views are often not challenged by other judges, we should pause in concluding that judges who write typical opinions either do not believe in discretion or are hypocrites. (Greenawalt, 1975, 384)

> In many areas – politics, society and law – where value commitments are unavoidable, the thing to do is not to try to hide them, but to be as *explicit* about them as possible. Maybe if judges have developed particular theories of morals, politics, and society they should say so up front, and incorporate them explicitly into their decision-making. (Waldron, 1990, 123)

These four quotations are directed on their surface towards the issue of whether or not judges exercise discretion. But they raise a wider issue too. Why should there be a divergence between what judges say and what they believe? The extent and nature of this divergence is central to much jurisprudential debate. Hart admitted to the existence of conditions that might lead to rhetoric, namely the inevitability of penumbral or hard cases, without discussing the reasons why judges might continue to speak in such cases 'as if' they were finding law, and not making it. Dworkin took the manner of judicial speech in such circumstances as evidence that, even in hard cases, judges were indeed finding and not making law (or at least only exercising weak discretion). Various realist and critical theories identify disingenuousness in claims to apply rather than make law not only in hard cases, but in all cases. Alongside different views as to the extent to which judges fail to acknowledge what they are in fact doing, when deciding law, there is also a range of views as to the reasons for these potential failures. Judges lack the political authority of legislatures and, as such, could expect to be criticised for undertaking a legislative function. Parties who lose in such cases might expect to be particularly aggrieved. As well as avoiding criticism, judges gain authority, and prestige, by claims that they primarily exercise a technical function in identifying the law. And, on a more positive note, a judicial reluctance to admit to making law can be seen as part of a judicial reluctance actually to make law, which can in turn be seen as a commitment to various constitutional principles, such as democracy, the rule of law and the doctrine of the separation of powers.

Investigating the scale and nature of this divergence between what judges say, and what they know to be the case when making decisions, has taken many forms. Much of the debate between Dworkin and his critics has not been empirical so much as analytical. The practical and linguistic difficulties of presenting any claim of there always being 'right' answers to making legal decisions led Dworkin to back down from his earlier more absolutist position. And of course there is empirical evidence, in that judges, off the bench, have been willing to admit that they make or have made law, though they have tended to stress the exceptional nature of this. Deconstructing or 'trashing' judicial decisions has seemed both to confirm the fact of judicial law making, and challenge judicial claims that this is a rare occurrence by demonstrating the alternate possibilities within any court decision. Those who accept that legal sources fail to explain the decisions of judges have looked to external explanations for the construction of judicial choices, with Feminist, Marxist and Critical Race theories making significant contributions at this point.

So, the issue of judicial failure to acknowledge the 'real' possibilities of choice is not a minor one in so much jurisprudential discussion. Communications by judges which fail to acknowledge such choices in their judgments can be contrasted with their willingness to do so at other times. It appears that self-observation by judges operating within the legal system is not the same self-observation, even though made by the same person, when not operating in their adjudicative capacities in courts. By looking at these different self-observations, from those who appear to operate at the heart of any legal system, we might shed some new light on the substantive issues that are being addressed in these communications. Perhaps it might even allow us to see the prior debates about these issues in a new light? We can ask, why is there a divorce, on at least some occasions, between what judges say at different times in different forums, and why might the repeated exposure of this divorce leave their communications unaltered, at least to the extent that their legal judgments consistently continue to fail to recognise this divorce?

As we hope that our introductory Chapter has demonstrated, the communication of judges that represent their self-observations of the roles they play in the legal system provides a central focus of many legal theories, and the starting point for others. In seeking to apply Luhmann's systems theory in considering these self-observations, we face a challenge in explaining the nature of Luhmann's distinction between psychic systems, and social systems. What motivates us as human beings is different from the social systems in which we participate as addressors, and addressees. A clear analysis of what communications consist of, within Luhmann's theory, will potentially not only increase our understanding of exactly those aspects of a legal system that are represented by judicial self-observation, but also explain the limits of an individual judge's ability to exercise choice when participating in social systems (including the legal system). The question 'Why do judges talk the way they do?' is an opportunity to explain the nature of this participation.

In the next section of this Chapter we provide a brief introduction to one of the explanatory concepts of autopoietic systems theory, that of redundancy in forming a link between the social and the individual. In the following two sections we apply the insights available from this analysis to judicial communications and the commitments that they represent, and the character of judicial discretion.

Social Systems, Psychic Systems and Redundancy

The social, within Luhmann's theory, is communication.[1] We cannot per se experience another human's thoughts. Until thought is communicated, which may be by speech, gesture, writing, and even on occasions by inaction and silence, we cannot claim to 'know' what is in another person's mind. And, of course, even communicated thought is, if we consider it carefully, only a communication. We never actually experience the other person's thought. Similarly, we can communicate about, or think about, another person's body. But that person's body remains separate from ours, and indeed even separate from its own thoughts.[2] In this sense, humans lie outside of communication. This may strike the reader as specious, or unnecessarily complicated, but legal theory, and legal doctrine, is full of communications about these unreachable aspects of a human being that

[1] This involves a radical understanding of communication and its relationship to action that is distinctive, and which we try to explain in this section. For a terse statement of Luhmann's understanding of communication and the 'restructuring of theory' that this entails, see Luhmann, 2002, ch 7, 'What is Communication?' As an example of how the nature of communication as understood by Luhmann and Teubner (see particularly Teubner, 1993) has generated debate with specific reference to law, see Bankowski, 2002 and Paterson, 2002.

[2] 'The mind thinks what it thinks and nothing else' (Luhmann, 2002, ch 8, 'How Can the Mind Participate in Communication?' at 174).

seem to belie the fact that they are unreachable. So whenever you read or hear words like 'inclinations', 'motives', 'purposes' and 'feelings' you are engaging with communications about something that itself lies outside of communication. The consciousness of an individual, the thoughts and feelings that they experience, are, within Luhmann's theory, a system, but he terms this system a psychic system[3] and carefully distinguishes it from social systems, which consist of communications.[4] Thus, for systems theory the human is outside of systems of communication (as regards human minds and bodies), but from this premise it is not correct to conclude that systems theory has nothing to do with the reasons that judges give for their decisions or the manner in which legal cases are framed, as these reasons are communications (the central ingredient of this social theory).[5]

Individuals communicate (as do corporations, and computers).[6] Luhmann has drawn on communication and information theory to delineate carefully what this involves, and what in turn constructs the possibilities of communication. In particular he makes use of two distinctions: redundancy[7] and information, and redundancy and variety.[8] These two distinctions are interrelated. Information (meaning that is new) can only be conveyed against the background of redundancy (meaning that is unchanged). What within any communication is redundant, and what is information, is not static and given.

[3] 'By excluding minds and bodies from society, systems theory establishes three main types of systems: systems of communication (social systems), systems of life (bodies, the brain, and so on) and systems of consciousness [psychic systems] (minds)' (Moeller, 2006, 9, and see ch 1, 'What is Social Systems Theory').

[4] It is not necessary as part of this introduction to demonstrate how systems theory is able to accommodate the distinction between these different systems whilst at the same time maintaining this distinction. However, it is relevant particularly to the focus of this book on 'self-observation' to point out that the key to this operation is indeed that of observation: 'The interaction between systems of the mind and systems of communication is not realized in the creation of a supersystem that could accomplish operations integrating the conscious and communicative operations according to the structural determinations of both systems. Instead, systems of the mind are capable of observing communicative systems, and communicative systems are able to observe systems of the mind. In order to be able to say this, we need a concept of observation that is not psychically conceived, that is, related exclusively to systems of the mind' (Luhmann, 2002, 179).

[5] The careful distinction between social and psychic systems that systems theory adopts (and in relation to which difficult epistemological questions arise) is necessary in order to avoid misunderstanding built on the confusion arising from what social and psychic systems share: 'Social and psychic systems do not only share language as a common medium, they share the "universal medium" (*Universalmedium*) "sense" (or *Sinn*). Minds make sense of the world and themselves, and so do social systems.' Moeller, 2006, 65, and see ch 2, 'What is Real?'

[6] Consider Teubner, 2006a, 499–502.

[7] Redundancy is a concept that has a special meaning in systems theory, as derived from its use in information and communication theory, being more concerned with what is a necessary precondition to successful transmission of communication, than what is useless communication, as we go on to explain. Other concepts that systems theory adopts with specific meanings from information theory include those of information, noise and entropy.

[8] See Luhmann, 2004, 316–30; on the relation between redundancy, information and variety as applied to legal argumentation, see Luhmann, 1995a, 290–94; see also King and Thornhill, 2003, 49–52.

But the meaning generated by a communication is always the difference between the two. The first of these distinctions is best understood by considering a single communication. The information provided by a communication is what is new. But in order for a communication to provide information other communications must remain the same. Redundancy in communication is a necessary background to information. We experience this distinction on an everyday basis without thinking about it. Road signs take a standard form. The symbols used, by their very homogeneity, make it possible to extract information from them easily: 'Expect – deer/bends/junctions, etc.' Time is another classic example. When we are told that the time is 9.25, this makes sense against a background of communicating time in terms of 60 minutes to an hour. Timetables represent a further refinement. Not only do these rely on the limited number of ways in which we record time, but by setting out information in standard arrangements they make it easy to extract what is different (information) from a background that remains unchanged (redundancy).

Whilst the distinction redundancy/information goes to the actual information generated by a particular communication, the distinction redundancy/variety goes to the potential information that could be communicated. Against any given background of unchanged communication, what is the range of new information that can be generated at any given moment? In the case of our timetable, there are any numbers of times that can be given for the services being timetabled. So we have a lot of variety. But, on the other hand, there are not a lot of ways in which time itself can be communicated within that timetable if the communication is going to be successful.

The example of communications about time and timetables may suggest that redundancy and variety have a linear relationship, whereby things that begin as variety become redundancies, creating new variety (new possibilities) – standard time creates the possibilities of timetables – developing timetabling creates increased possibilities for communicating about the organisation of events, etc.[9] And quite a lot of society's systems of communication (including law) evolve in this manner. But this is not always the case. The information that can be generated against the background of any given redundancy includes the possibility of creating new redundancies that can challenge, and displace, previous ones. However, it is impossible to make a communication that immediately deconstructs the communica-

[9] Within systems theory, time is a more complicated matter. Whilst systems of communication use common signifiers for time, time has different meanings within each system. For example, to give a flavour of this kind of analysis, in relation to Luhmann's analysis of risk: 'Although time itself cannot be bound, it can bind by giving events structural value. To put it more precisely: events pass as soon as they come into being. They have no duration (otherwise we would speak of states, however brief these might be . . . the concept of time binding shall indicate the generation of structures in the autopoietic process of continuous self-renewal of the system, thus not simply the coming into being of factual states . . . of some duration' (Luhmann, 1993, 52–53). We develop this analysis of time in relation to the legal subsystem in Chapter 5.

tions that constitute the background redundancy that generates the information contained in that communication. So the process by which variety can lead to new redundancies that displace earlier redundancies is constrained. Instead of such instantaneous deconstruction of prior redundancies, variety has to lead to the establishment of new redundancies from existing ones. Only on this basis can rival redundancy, and the displacement of earlier redundancy, occur. What we have here, as Luhmann rightly observes, is an evolutionary process;[10] one can only evolve new communications from the communications that are already available, even ones that will replace those which currently exist.

Redundancy represents a real constraint on communicative possibilities. We have to use redundancy to convey information. And the costs of abandoning redundancies are often considerable. The example of changing the basis for telling time makes the point very well. Should we decimalise time? Well, not for those communications where this would require new clocks, the re-programming of all computers, the translation of large amounts of existing technical and non-technical literature, and the alteration of vast amounts of general social communication. Dispensing with what is the redundant background to information always requires that information (if we still wish it to be communicated or transmitted without entropy, or random errors) be generated through a new redundancy. Not only will this require a cost in terms of creating information in new ways, but one cannot assume that attempts to generate new ways of conveying information will be successful. They are only successful if they succeed.

Now consider the position of human actors. To communicate information, humans have to make use of the store of available redundant communications. As individuals, they cannot successfully communicate (transfer or receive information) without utilising redundancy. Of course one can imagine setting up new ways of communicating between pairs of individuals – along the lines of a private language – but think of the constraints. Not only would those individuals have to utilise existing social redundancies to construct their new communications, but they would not be able to use them with others without a process of initiation. And what is going to motivate all these other individuals to adopt this new system, given the presence of an alternative and in the short run lower cost alternative. Of course if, like the changing of a currency or driving on a particular side of the road, these new communications have to be simultaneously introduced to a large number of persons all at once, then the costs of change are enormous.

[10] 'The conditions for evolution are a product of evolution. This applies also to the difference between text and interpretation . . . But further amplification of the conditions of evolution, of the impact on elements (variation), the impact on structures (selection) and integration in the autopoiesis of the reproductive context of complex systems (restabilization), also comes about as a product of social evolution' (Luhmann, 2004, 243, see also 243–62). For a more extended discussion in relation to art, see Luhmann, 2000a, ch 6.

How much of a restraint does redundancy place upon what can be communicated? The examples used above, most particularly that of time, suggest that redundancy *can* be a major constraint. But the use of the particular example of time also points by contrast to the fact that little of our communication seems quite as rigid as this. It may be convenient to communicate in the same manner on lots of occasions, but does not the vast store of communications available to us as background give us a substantial ability to vary what can be said? If we regard our store of communications as an undifferentiated mass, then this seems pretty much the case, even allowing for such central co-ordinating communications as a common basis for identifying time. But if instead we accept (or at least engage with) Luhmann's description of modern society as consisting of functionally differentiated and constantly evolving subsystems of communication,[11] then we can see that redundancy may provide significant and systematic constraints on what can be communicated in particular contexts. The claim, that society consists of separate systems of communication (the legal, political, economic, mass media, scientific, etc),[12] necessarily involves the claim that redundancy is system-specific. Luhmann's theory of society as made up of autopoietic systems of communication requires us to consider not only that redundancy is necessary for information, but that redundancies are not identical within the differently functioning systems or subsystems of society.[13] What constitutes redundancy at any moment within legal communication is different from what constitutes redundancy within other subsystems of communication. Thus what can be communicated within the medical system as a subsystem of science is different from what can be communicated within the political system or the mass media about medicine.[14] Science has generated communications that provide background redundancy to all sorts of scientific information, as has politics for political information, mass media, and law, with respect to the information that they generate in turn. And Luhmann's combination of an understanding of society as separate systems of communication together with the concept of redundancy not only leads us to conclude that redundancy is system-specific, in the sense that different systems can employ different redundancies on a routine basis, but also requires us to accept that the redundancy that can be utilised within a system, at any particular moment, is established by that system.

[11] For the classic background, see Luhmann, 1982; as an example of a more recent statement of the character of horizontal differentiation, rather than hierarchical differentiation, charactering modern society (but according to Luhmann, using the form of horizontal differentiation as the key element, now inappropriately described as post-modern society), see Luhmann, 2000b.

[12] For a succinct statement about autopoiesis as relevant to the focus of this Chapter, see Luhmann, 1995, 34–38 and 218–21.

[13] Luhmann, 1995, ch 1, 'System and Function'.

[14] For a concrete example, see Nobles and Schiff, 2004.

Returning again to the human actor, communication requires participation in a system of communication. Successful communication requires the utilisation of redundancy in order to communicate information. And that redundancy depends on the system that the individual is seeking to participate within, and the operation within that system which the individual is seeking to affect. This does not reduce the individual to an automaton, whose communications within a system are entirely determined by the system. But it does create a situation in which the actor is severely constrained in how and what they can communicate. And it also provides a link between the system of communication and the actor. If the actor is motivated to communicate, the terms of that communication are dictated by the system in which they participate. The redundancies of that system and its variety (what can be successfully transmitted at any point in the system's communications) are given by the system. Human actors, through participation, learn to recognise redundancy, and to utilise it in the construction of their communications. And, on the negative side, there is a cost to any human actor who fails to identify redundancies, which is to fail successfully to make the communication, and to achieve the operation that they would have wished to achieve. This has implications for many of the claims made about the nature of individual actions and beliefs.

These observations help and indeed require one to understand that individuals can and do participate in more than one subsystem, and are able to communicate different things within these different systems. So, for example, we should not presume that everything that judges communicate is a legal communication just because they are judges. Judges who make press statements are attempting to have their communications selected by the mass media. As such, there is no reason to expect that these communications will generate further legal communications. Whilst such communications are likely to use the words legal/illegal (the code of the legal system)[15] the aim of such communications, if selected by the mass media, is for them to be coded by the mass media using its code (information/non-information, or more colloquially, news/not news).[16] Similarly, when judges give public lectures, or publish law review articles, their communications will be selected in different ways (applying different codes and programmes) and generate different further communications, in different systems: education, politics, mass media, law, etc.

Utilising the distinction redundancy/variety not only refers to what can be communicated at a particular moment, but allows us to describe the process whereby new possibilities of information are generated. We can attempt to track communications that generate new redundancies, and new variety. Like Luhmann, we regard this distinction as an important medium

[15] See Luhmann, 1992.
[16] See Luhmann, 2000.

to allow one to describe and analyse the evolution of systems. And, if we take on board the notion of separate systems of communication, and the ability of systems to determine what redundancy is available for the next communication, then we also have to recognise that the ability of individuals to communicate about their 'internal' feelings will vary from system to system, and within systems. This leads inevitably to a considerable inconsistency in the correlations between individuals' consciousnesses and their communications. We can surmise from the fact of an individual's communications that they were motivated to communicate. We can further surmise that they were motivated to identify and engage with the redundancy present at the moment of communication. But we cannot read off from their communications exactly what those internal feelings might have been. In particular, as in the case of law, where those communications take a normative form, and implicitly communicate an internal commitment to the legal system, or particular legal norms, we cannot assume, from the fact of communication, anything more than a desire to execute a particular operation.

Applying our discussion of redundancy, we need to examine communications, including judicial communications, in terms of the operations which they affect, and the variety of communications that are open to judicial actors given the presence, at the point of their participation in the legal system, of redundancy. In the next two sections we take two issues, central to much legal theory, and explore them using this analysis. The first is the claim that public officials, most particularly judges, must have a greater commitment or more committed internal attitude to the legal system than other actors. The second is that referred to in the introductory quotations to this Chapter: the issue of judicial discretion. We will investigate what operations are enabled via a redundancy represented by 'conventions of legal argument [that] embody a belief in the theoretical possibility of a comprehensive gapless rule of law', that would not be affected otherwise.

Judicial Communications and 'Commitment' to the Legal System

Let us begin with the position facing judges involved in adjudication on substantive legal issues. The context for these issues is a mass of legal communications. For a start judges are judges, appointed as such to courts, with jurisdiction to decide the issues before them (if their capacity or jurisdiction is not accepted, then *these* background questions will themselves become legal issues). Cases will not arrive in courts by themselves, but only as a result of originating instruments, discovery, etc. The substantive issues must themselves be identified by reference to statutes, precedents, etc. These communications will typically have a normative form, and the legal information which they generate will have normative meanings. Judges are called upon to adjudicate, which, in our legal system, requires them to identify who is entitled to decisions in their favour. This in turn requires judges to identify which legal norms are available to them, and how they direct them to decide the legal issues before them. Our legal system requires judges, in nearly all instances, to give reasons for their decisions. Whilst this can be justified by reference to various values, an important consequence of these kinds of communications from a systems theory perspective is that they facilitate the evolution of the legal system. Without reasons being given in the past, judges would not have the enormity of resources (redundancy) available to convey information now. And with these reasons in turn, further resources are created for further legal communications. Reasons are also important for appeals, which in turn generate resources for further legal communications.

At the moment of decisions, judges can make a variety of determinations, but they do so against a background of considerable redundancy.[17] And they are not alone in this. For the parties before them to have reached courts with legal issues there will be an enormous number of further potential legal issues which either have not been raised, or have been resolved. In this sense, the issues which judges have to decide have been framed by the communications which lead to those points, and the store of redundancy available to judges, at those points, to make successful legal communications. As human actors participating within society, many different kinds of communication are open to judges. They can declare their beliefs that the legal issues in the cases before them ought to be decided in particular ways not suggested by the law, or even declare their agnosticism. They can similarly communicate their opinions as to the legitimacy or otherwise of the legal system as a whole, and any reforms they may wish to recommend. But for judges undertaking the legal operations of adjudication, the task facing them is to make legal communications. They have to reach decisions that are recognisable as decisions, within their legal systems. And if they want to make decisions that are likely actually to dispose of the issues before them, they have to make decisions that are either unlikely to be appealed, or likely to be upheld on appeal. As we have just described, the situation in which they find themselves to be judges, is created through a vast number of legal communications. It is a context created by the system of communication in which they operate, through conducting trials/appeals and making decisions to participate in it or not. As human actors they can always fail to communicate, either wilfully or not.[18] But if they are going to

[17] At times, this can make the only communications open to judges ones that would appear to be recognisably correct legal communications as a matter of deductive logic (see MacCormick, 1978, 19–37).

[18] The failure to speak by others involved in legal processes will often generate legal meanings (communication). For example, a criminal defendant who fails to respond to the request

communicate,[19] then the legal information that they are able to communicate is going to be a function of the redundancy that provides a background to their communications.

Assuming that our judges continue to participate in their legal systems, what choices are open to them? Can they decide that the normative form of legal communications, expressed for example in terms of legal rights and duties, is inappropriate, and adopt a different 'detached' form of communication? How can they express their authority to decide the matters before them as judges, without accepting the normative communications that have put them into the position of being judges, establish the previous proceedings as trials or appeals, and frame the matters they have been asked to decide as legal issues? This is neither to say that these legal communications could not be re-phrased in a different form, nor that these judges, within different systems of communication (mass media, education, politics) could not do this themselves.[20] But, at the particular moments which require decisions that can be recognised as legal decisions, none of these options are open to them. It is not just that judges might have sworn oaths, or that they might feel that it is prudent or right to do what others expect of them. The expectations of others, expressed in terms of redundancy, lie in the fact that the redundancy which judges can utilise to generate the legal information which they wish to put into communications is the same redundancy open to their legal audience in identifying what, within their communications, represents legal information.[21] Indeed, it will include the same redundancy that enables judges to understand why they are judges and not ushers, why their courts are courts and not theatres, and what the parties have argued before them and what it is that they are called upon to decide.

How should one describe judges' positions: the fact that the redundancy available for them to make communications that are likely to dispose of their cases is the same body of rules, principles, etc, that will be used by their intended audience to decode their communications and identify the information within them? One can if one likes call this a 'practice theory of rules',[22]

to enter a plea of guilty or not guilty will, under current UK law, be considered to have responded with the plea of not guilty. This is not inevitable – it could be the opposite.

19 Or even, as illustrated in the previous note, communicate by failing to speak or respond.

20 So, for example, there is nothing which prevents judges imitating Oliver Wendell Homes from giving lectures or writing essays describing the 'bad man's perspective' on law. But if these judges applied this perspective to themselves, within a decision, and confessed to making decisions solely on the basis of participants' suffering detriments or securing benefits, their legal communications would either not be recognised as such, or trigger corrective legal operations.

21 This can be described in terms of conventions. The use of a particular language 'is something [done] in conformity to a convention: something everyone in *P* does because he expects his conversational partners in *P* to do it too, and because a common interest in communicating leads him to want to do his part if they do theirs' (Lewis, 2002, 177).

22 As Hart recognises his jurisprudence has come to be called; see Hart, 1994, 'Postscript', 254–55. The implications of what such an understanding of Hart's theory involves leads to substantial disagreement within traditional jurisprudential debate: see Perry, 2001.

but the practice in question is communication within a system of communication. There is no practice outside of these communications. And the fact that the 'practice' would have no normative force if it were not followed by others has no separate existence or manifestation apart from its existence within these communications. If others do not utilise normative communications in a particular way, then you cannot utilise those communications in order successfully to communicate normative meanings. If they do, you can. Of course, one can also talk about legal standards being adopted as guides to appropriate behaviour, but with judges, the behaviour in question is the making of communications.[23] Therefore, there is actually no need for judges to make statements confirming that the rules which they are proposing to adopt are being followed by other judges. If the parties which these judges' communications are directed towards were not constructing their communications using the same redundancy, then these judges would not have the ability to make successful communications. To phrase this in the terms of one of Dworkin's arguments, judges operating within the legal system cannot refer to the standards which they apply as having their validity because of their common application by other judges. They must communicate as committed vegetarians would talk about their own decisions not to eat meat. On these communication menus, there are no non-vegetarian options. Judges cannot sensibly communicate that legal standards are not appropriate guides to their behaviour. Since the behaviour in question is legal communication, the only way in which that behaviour can occur is through the application of these standards to their behaviour. If judges wish to make legal communications (ie to continue as judges making their decisions) they will have to apply existing legal standards to their own behaviour. They have no other resources open to them.

This is not a claim that judges applying the law always approve of what they are communicating. Nor is it a claim that they will not, outside of actual adjudication, criticise the decisions that they and other judges might have taken in the course of litigation, or criticise the character of the law in some of its particular branches, or even question the legitimacy of the whole legal system. Still less is this a claim that judges cannot make legal communications in terms of legal rights and duties whilst believing, that is, thinking, that the standards that they are applying are actually completely inappropriate, or simply do not or cannot determine the issues before them. The beliefs of judges, except to the extent that these are manifested by communications, remain unknown to anybody but themselves. But what we can say is that such critical options are not open to them as legal

[23] At the level of judges, disobeying law (see our Chapter 3) means not communicating law as others might expect them so to do. The position with other practice-based rules is more complicated. As communications reach beyond language, it can become tautological that practices are inseparable from communication. The claim that rules are based on common compliant practices requires the fact of compliance to be communicated.

communications at the moment of their legal decisions. Then what, you might say, of judges who make legal decisions and insert a note of reluctance regarding what the law requires them to do?[24] Are they not expressing a different, less committed attitude towards the law? And is that not also a legal communication? A bold answer here would be 'no'. What legal meaning is communicated by such statements? They do not in any way alter these judges' communications of what they find the law to be. Indeed, a divergence between what they find the law to be and what they would like it to be is exactly what they are communicating by their expressions of reluctance. Nor can such statements represent a refutation that the law as found represents an appropriate guide to these judges' behaviour. Again, as the behaviours in question are the decisions which have been communicated, it would be operationally self-refuting for judges to claim that the considerations that led to their expressions of reluctance actually outweighed their reasons for their decisions.

If the judiciary, when giving judgments, are unable to escape from utilising communications that have a normative form, and an implicit meaning that the authors are committed to the law as a standard for action, what can we conclude, from the mere fact of those communications, about judicial beliefs as to the legitimacy of the legal system? The correct answer is nothing. And that answer requires us to reconsider much of the legal theory that has been devoted to claims about the internal commitments that are required from legal actors in order for a legal system to exist. Starting with Hart, there has been a long-standing debate on the 'internal attitude' that must be evidenced by public officials, and in particular the judiciary, for a legal system to exist. If the premise of this debate has been that judges, when acting as such giving judgments, could exhibit (which means communicate) any other attitude, then that premise is simply false. And in replying to various predictive theories of law, from Austin to the American Realists, by pointing to their failure to acknowledge the forms of communication which he gives as examples of an internal attitude, Hart was doing no more than taking particular legal operations (such as the making of legal arguments in courts, or the giving of legal judgments) and pointing to the impossibility of such operations being achieved by different forms of communications than those actually employed. Judges communicate through communications which have a normative form: rules and other standards.[25]

[24] 'It is time that the legislature considered this law and its reform . . .'

[25] Of those who have developed Hart's theory, Raz probably comes closest to consistently acknowledging the separation between psychic systems and systems of communication, by claiming that judicial speech implicitly affirms the existence of some person (whom he calls the legal man) who has a positive internal commitment to all legal standards, and wills compliance with them. Raz appears to accept that this person need not in fact exist, recognising the purely 'justificatory [and practical] tenor of the statements whereby officials invoke legal obligations' and never confusing 'a claim-to-legitimacy with legitimacy itself' (see Kramer's analysis of Raz, 1999, ch 4 at 89 and 90). On Raz's analysis of how legal authority can be

If Hart's major contribution to legal theory was an important recognition of something that is inescapable (judicial actors have to use rules, and the meaning of judicial communications that take the form of the application and identification of rules have an implicit meaning that the actor regards those rules as appropriate standards for the resolution of the disputes before them), what follows from this? Well, for a start, it makes it more difficult to talk sensibly about a judicial commitment to the legal system, if this is taken to assume the possibilities of judicial non-commitment to the legal system. By acting as judges, which means by making legal communications within a role and situation constructed by other legal communications, judges daily make statements whose implicit meaning is that they accept the legal system as a normative order. Indeed, they cannot carry out their jobs, making judicial decisions, without expressing such commitments as they go about these tasks. We can reason that if judges found that their daily legal communications caused them intolerable psychic discomfort they could be expected to resign, and find other occupations, so that every judge can be presumed not to be in such a state. But above this threshold, it is difficult to draw conclusions from legal communications about the inner motivations and feelings of judges (that is, such motivations and feelings cannot simply be imputed to them as part of the process of decoding their legal communications). Indeed, it is even difficult to agree how to describe these internal feelings. At a common-sense level, it seems to make sense to claim that judges who mentally regret the operations carried out through their communications are less committed than those who do not. And if they take the opportunities, within other systems, such as the mass media, or politics, to express that regret, might we be inclined to describe them as less committed to the legal system than judicial actors who do not make such extra-legal communications? But is it more accurate to describe such judicial actors as actually more 'committed' or less committed to the legal system than their more silent colleagues? Are actors who can demonstrate that they have 'overcome' their political or moral reservations and still given effect to the law less committed to the legal system than colleagues who, as far as we know, have experienced no such reservations about the moral or political implications of parts of their judicial role? And whilst such conflicts of commitment, or their expression outside of the legal system, may have their casual effects, they will not prevent the legal system from continuing; for what level of commitment does the legal system need, in order to continue, except the willingness of its actors to continue communicating?

Our analysis here is not completely different from what has gone before, particularly the work of Neil MacCormick. He acknowledged, in *Legal Reasoning and Legal Theory*, that judicial actors can find themselves, at least

communicated, and who it can be communicated by, see Raz, 1994, ch 10, esp 215–20; for a strong criticism of Raz's analysis of 'law's claim to legitimate authority' see Himma, 2001.

on some occasions, in situations where the legal communications available to them are severely constrained, appearing to require one solution as a conclusion from deductive reasoning. And that once such a situation has occurred, whilst the next operation (an order in favour of the 'winning' party) does not follow as a matter of logic, but only if the actor chooses to make the requisite communication: 'Given the institutional pressures within the legal system – the opinion of the profession, the possibilities of appeal, etc, and given the external pressures of adverse press publicity and Parliamentary comment and the like, it would be *so strange as to be barely imaginable* that a judge having established the justifiability of one decision by logical argument from sound legal premises and findings of fact should then issue some diametrically different order.'[26] But observations encouraged by systems theory invite us to take the implications of such examples much further. For a start, if the ability of a judge to fail to give appropriate effect to an easy case is 'so strange as to be barely imaginable', how much more strange is a failure to adopt normative forms of communication when undertaking a judicial role, at any point. And what makes a communication 'so strange as to be barely imaginable'? MacCormick includes the actor's awareness of the communications of systems in which s/he is not participating, and may never participate: the mass media and politics. But the starting point for identifying what is 'strange' in a judicial communication, and one that operates regardless of the judge's awareness of the communications of other systems, or the likelihood that other systems will produce any critical communications, is the same redundancy that generates all legal communications at those points in the legal system. If judges make communications that the legal system identifies as 'so strange as to be barely imaginable' they will be identified, within the legal system, as errors.[27] And an awareness of what constitutes error in this sense will have guided actors' selections of communications at every stage in the processes that have led to these particular decisions.[28]

[26] Our emphasis. MacCormick's analysis also raises questions about the practical significance of the judge's duty to apply the law. If the moments that can be identified with this duty are also situations where communications incompatible with it are 'so strange as to be barely imaginable', then how much causal influence is left to the moral communications that might make this duty a moral one? This does not stop MacCormick from claiming that the reasons which individuals might offer for acting in accordance with this duty 'have an importance which cannot be overlooked' (MacCormick, 1978, 64).

[27] Even judges in the highest courts, from which there is no apparent legal appeal, have to avoid errors at the level of communications that are 'so strange as to be barely imaginable'. If they did not, appellants would be encouraged to argue cases that were equally strange/erroneous.

[28] MacCormick also describes the moment when a judge has to make an order in response to a decision and in response to propositions that lead to only one correct outcome as one of duty – a duty to apply all of the legal systems' rules. This is correct in terms of the relationship between the rules of the system, and this moment can be described in these terms by actors within the system (advocates, appeal judges or the judge her/himself) if this judge ceases to participate in the legal system at this moment. However, this same 'duty' (the need to utilise the system's redundancies to make legal communications) is not experienced by this judge solely at the point when an order is granted, but at every point when she/he has utilised legal communications.

MacCormick has also anticipated some of this analysis in his attempts to refine Hart's distinction between internal and external attitudes. He has argued that the internal attitude comprises a cognitive element (understanding the presence and nature of rules) and a volitional one (wishing those rules to be applied). With this further distinction, MacCormick has attempted in turn to identify three positions open to those engaging with social rules: the insider who accepts rules by wanting them to be applicable to their behaviour and those of others (whether enthusiastically or simply to avoid the disadvantages of disobedience by others); the moderate outsider (the 'hermeneutic approach') who understands the meaning of the rules to insiders but has no desire for her/himself or others to comply with those rules, and the extreme external observer who can identify regularities of behaviour but has no concept that these regularities are related to the presence of a rule.[29] We believe that our analysis, using Luhmann, can take this further. First, the rigour of Luhmann's separation between systems of communication and psychic systems avoids the slippage from analysing statements which have an implicit point of view, to ascribing that point of view as a necessary (internal) fact for the making of those statements.[30] And second, MacCormick fails to analyse the conditions that establish when these different kinds of communication can be used. So, for example, he asserts that the legal scientist and social theorist *can* make statements that do not purport to reveal anything about their own commitments, critical morality or group membership without considering the difficulties facing judges, who *can't* make statements that do not purport to reveal commitment. MacCormick, following in the Hartian tradition, seeks to analyse language, and categorise the kinds of statements that can be made, and the actions that they can perform. Luhmann, through his theory of systems, requires us to consider how the context of communications is established through communications, and how that context (redundancy) structures the possibilities of what can be communicated at that point. Using Luhmann to go beyond MacCormick, we have to examine how redundancies within systems restrict the choice of forms of communication available to the actors who participate in those systems.

A further implication of this analysis is that one needs to question the use within legal theory (and social theory) of the concept of conventions.[31] The

[29] This discussion is now clarified in MacCormick, 2008, ch 4.

[30] For example, with the writings of Finnis, who argues that the presuppositions inherent in both insiders and outsiders' points of view (that someone wants the rules to be applied) necessitates a belief system shared at least amongst the judiciary that legal rules are for the common good: see Finnis, 1980, 9–19.

[31] So much detailed analysis within legal theory relies on some understanding of conventions as foundational to law's practices. See, for direct analysis of law's autonomy as resting on a particular understanding of social conventions, Marmoor, 2001. Conventionalism is, of course, one of the conceptions of law analysed by Dworkin, 1986, ch 4, but using an understanding of conventionalism that has been seriously questioned; see Simmonds, 1990.

judicial contribution to the existence of law as a system has been described in terms of judicial conventions about the use of appropriate sources of law, the correct manner of speech, etc. These 'conventions' point to something outside of the system itself, as the mechanism for the legal system's ability to maintain its autonomy, and evolution. If conventions mean widespread acceptance, common positive commitments internal to the relevant actors (or common perceptions of criticism from other systems) then one can sensibly talk about the legal system changing when its conventions change. A shift in conventions allows for a change in what can be communicated. For example, changing commitment to parliamentary sovereignty, and an increasing acceptance of European integration, might explain developments in the treatment of sources of UK law. By contrast, redundancy would invite one to consider, at each moment in the system, what communications were available to the actors in question. These communications *are* the conventions. There is nothing outside of them which limits the possibilities of communication. And the possibilities of communication (the conventions) alter as those communications occur, in that those communications can generate new redundancies, and new variety. To ask about the strength of a convention using systems theory is to identify what operations cannot occur at present without utilising the particular communications in question. The cost of abandoning conventions is the cost of abandoning particular kinds of redundancy, which is the need to find other ways to carry out the same or similar operations using different communications, and the risk, in any attempt to do so, of failure.

Following on from this, there is also a tautology in Hart's claim that the judiciary must accept a rule of recognition as a common basis for identifying what counts as a rule of the legal system. Without here entering into the extensive controversy of exactly what counts as the rule of recognition (rules, principles, standards, etc) the need for a judiciary to utilise a common basis for what is capable of identifying a legal communication is simply a re-statement of the basis for communication: redundancy. Judges cannot communicate with each other without utilising the redundancy that is available to them.

In keeping with Luhmann's theory, we must also advance our observations on the basis that systems of communication need to be identified separately from institutions. Thus judges, giving legal judgments, make legal communications. But senior judges, for example, giving public lectures[32] or writing law review articles are not making legal communications.[33] And it is their different ability to make communications as they participate in different systems of communications that supports the claim that the

[32] www.judiciary.gov.uk/publications_media/speeches/index.htm.

[33] An institutional approach, which looked at 'the judiciary', the roles they play, or their position within a hierarchical institutional structure, is less likely to keep these different kinds of communications separate.

beliefs of judges differ from what, within their judgments, they say.[34] In addition, although the focus of this Chapter is on judicial communications, it might assist our understanding of the limited options open to adjudicating judges, to consider the communication options open to other participants within the legal system – lawyers and lay people.

Whilst the ability of lay people to make legal communications, generating legal information, is more limited than that of judges deciding cases, moving through our society without making legal communications is virtually impossible. What lay person is going to fail to claim under contracts, or assert property claims, let alone fail to express the legal position when their car is obstructed by illegal parking, or they are assaulted? Whilst these events may be acknowledged as harms or wrongs, they will also be recognised as involving legal rights and crimes. Which individual is not going to communicate that they have rights as a tenant, or owner-occupier, or have the ability to leave their property to people on their death via their wills? Imagining an individual who never utilised legal communications, even in order to construct a position from which they could make other kinds of claims within other systems ('Leaving all your property to my sister is wrong')[35] is very hard. Even tramps are likely to communicate thefts and assaults, let alone recognise the signs that indicate when they are likely to commit a trespass. And again, this leaves those individuals in a position that can be described as operationally self-refuting. What does it signify when someone makes an appeal to the law?[36] By making this form of communication they are not communicating that an event is uniquely illegal. They are drawing on a redundancy that overlaps with much of what is utilised by judges and lawyers. Lay people do not expect everything that they would like to be the case to be the law. They generally know that legal rights derive from gifts, contracts, transfers, and that law is made in Parliaments, courts and town halls. They also generally understand such constructs as rights, that is, not just predictions of the likelihood that harms or benefits will happen in particular circumstances. By participating in the legal system through making legal communications, these lay people will exhibit Hart's internal attitude. But what they will not exhibit when making such communications is the state of their beliefs, whether these represent

[34] The beliefs of judges (if this means their conscious thoughts) can never be known, except as they are communicated: for background, see Luhmann, 2000, ch 8. So the claim that judges do not believe what they say is most commonly a claim that what they communicate on one occasion contradicts what they communicate on another, plus the assertion that only one of these communications reflects their conscious thoughts and feelings. Other bases for this assertion tend to be rooted in argument: that what judges say is factually implausible, or incompatible with a claimed necessary element of a legal system.

[35] Lay persons find that pivotal aspects of their lives are constituted by law, and in turn use law to orientate themselves in their claims as to what is right or wrong (see Postema, 2008, 45–65).

[36] We ask this question here, as opposed to the more systematic meaning of appeals in law, which we consider in Chapter 8.

approval or disapproval of the standard to which they are referring, or approval or disapproval of the legal system as a whole.[37]

Moving on to lawyers, when individuals seek legal advice, the communications that result draw on a redundancy that overlaps with that used by judges, and generates legal information of a similar complexity. And, as with lay people, some of what is then communicated will take the form of a prediction of what might occur, rather than a statement which simply has a normative meaning. The so-called 'bad-man' approach to legal advice tells clients not what the law requires, but only what is likely to befall them from the activities of legal authorities if they proceed with particular courses of action. Legal advice, unlike judicial decisions, can take this form. Judges cannot express their own decision as a prediction of what others will do. They express their decisions as a conclusion on the law, even if they concede that another court might take a different view. By contrast, lawyers can express vicarious opinions, in terms of what the courts are likely to decide. And they can further distance themselves from judicial communications by expressing views on the likelihood of judicial outcomes in terms of predictions of alternative decisions, and the likely consequences that will follow from them. But even here one needs to recognise the limited ability of lawyers, when giving advice, to abandon the normative form of legal communications. Indeed, if lawyers deconstructed every legal communication that they utilised in order to reconstruct legal advice into predictions, it would be impossible for that advice to be given. What lawyers in fact do is engage with legal communications in their classic form, in order to construct narrow issues, and only at that point reconstruct communications that have a normative form into predictions of consequences that do not. Having given advice in that form, they then have to re-engage with normative communications in order, like judges, to generate the legal arguments that will need to be presented to the court. These arguments will not duplicate the predictive elements found in the advice, not simply because lawyers can be expected to be partisan but also because such communications will not be recognised by judges as legal arguments. They will not offer them reasons that can form part of their legal judgments. Thus it is not that detached, vicarious normative communications cannot form any part of the legal system. It is rather that the legal system establishes where and when such communications can form part of itself by reference to the information that needs to be generated in order to carry out particular legal operations.

What we can conclude from the above discussions is that whilst there are detached and committed participants (whether these are judges, lawyers, or lay people), if that means that some participants in the legal system experience internal approval when making legal communications, and others wish

[37] Further, a range of questions that can be grouped under the title of 'legal pluralism' arise – we deal with these questions in Chapter 4.

that what was available to be communicated was different, this does not result in detached and committed communications.[38] The legal system, especially in connection with adjudication, is not made up of committed and detached communications. Adjudication can only be carried out through committed communications. Detached communications would either fail to carry out the adjudication, or would be identified by the system as reasons why the decision should be regarded as an improper one. Successfully carrying out adjudication involves only committed communications, which have normative meanings, because these provide the background redundancy which enables one to generate legal information – a legal decision justified by legal reasons.[39]

A lot of jurisprudential discussion of the internal attitude, including that by Hart himself, addresses the question of what motivates individuals to make legal communications, that is, what internal commitment or desire is necessarily coupled with the kinds of expressions (calls to comply, criticisms for deviation, etc) that constitute the manifestation of the internal attitude. Arguments commonly take the form of identifying what is either necessary or sufficient for those communications to generate the meanings (information) that they do. Hart himself was quite an agnostic in regard to this question: '. . . both this general obedience and the further use of and attitudes to the law may be motivated by fear, inertia, admiration of tradition, or long-sighted calculation of selfish interests as well as by recognition of moral obligation. As long as the general complex practice is there, this is enough to answer affirmatively the inquiry whether a legal system exists. The question of what motivates the practice, though important, is an independent inquiry.'[40] In our opinion this agnosticism is appropriate, as Hart is correct to assert that the question is not what motivates individuals to make legal communications, but what they communicate when they are so motivated. In making legal communications individuals communicate legal information, and the information that they communicate does not alter its form (ie cease to be normative) because of the motivation that has led them to make the communication in question. Of course if they communicate their beliefs at the moment of making such communications, then this may deprive the subsequent communications of their normative form and meaning. But first, this will not be a result of the existence of motivations as

[38] It is the legal system itself that identifies when a statement can be regarded as detached, ie as a disingenuous and therefore improper legal communication. The legal rules dealing with competence and bias identify cases from which judges must disqualify themselves, and deal with the competence of individuals to deliver legal judgments.

[39] If the legal system contains what observers might describe as a moral element this will also not be located in the beliefs, motivations and commitments of its participants. These too will be found in the system's own communications, and will be exhibited where the system includes operations that cannot be carried out except by the inclusion of communications that also have moral meanings.

[40] Hart, 1958a, 92–93.

beliefs or commitments, but because of their manifestation and existence as communications. And secondly, such manifestations raise the issue which we have been discussing: are the communications which represent manifestations of belief compatible with, or do they add anything to, the legal communications that the individuals in question are motivated to make? In some circumstances, communicating a commitment or motivation at the same time as making a legal communication will undermine the ability to make the communication one is motivated to make.[41]

If detached forms of legal communication are not available to judicial actors participating in the legal system, what other restraints might be described usefully in terms of a system's redundancy? The other example we wish to explore here is the judicial failure to acknowledge that they are making law, at the moment of its making, in their judgments.

Judicial Discretion

Systems theory does not regard human beings as simply robots, participating in systems of communication without exercising elements of choice. One choice is not to participate, although as we have indicated, never participating in the legal system is extremely difficult. Other choices go to the making of communications. This is not a free choice, as we have tried to show in our previous discussion. There are lots of communications which, whilst they may bear a close resemblance to the beliefs and commitments which motivate individuals to make legal communications, cannot form part of what is communicated without preventing the desired communications from being made as effective communications. But choices remain. Lawyers choose what arguments to make in order to produce the decision which favours their clients. And the choices here will not only go to the substantive content of the arguments, but the manner of their presentation. And likewise judges will have to exercise choice in the construction of their judgments. All this is fairly uncontroversial. But what remains a major issue in jurisprudence is the extent to which judges exercise choice in establishing what the law is. And a major part of this controversy, as illustrated by the four quotations which introduced this Chapter, is the manner in which we should understand the judicial failure to admit whilst adjudicating that their decisions are, on at least some occasions, the result of individual choices rather than the application of pre-existing standards.

Before we proceed to explore the judiciary's failure to admit changing or making law in their judgments, we need to make a few remarks on the nature of this phenomenon. There is plenty of evidence that judges change

[41] Speech act theory recognises, for example, that insinuation cannot be combined with explicit statements. One can also talk of 'insincere' speech acts, such as manipulation. See generally Strawson, 1971, ch 8, especially at 163.

law. Not only were judicial decisions the primary source of English law from the twelfth century to the second half of the nineteenth century, but they were also the means by which that law altered from its original customary content. And, whilst legislation has taken over as the major mechanism by which law is both established and changed, the amendment of law through judicial decision has continued. Judges, in articles, books and public speeches, have felt no need to deny the alterations in the law which their brethren, or even themselves, have affected to the law. One can even find examples of decisions in which the subject of discussion, and the issue to be decided, is how to respond to a change in the law. Thus, for example, in *R v Cottrell*[42] we are told: 'It is artificial to pretend that the law was not changed, or to dress its impact in the jurisprudential disguise that the law had, in Blackstone's word, been "discovered".' *Cottrell* was a Court of Criminal Appeal decision on the right of defendants to appeal against their convictions on the basis of a change in the law, which had to deal with the consequences of the House of Lords decision in *R v J*[43] to alter 50 years of settled law on the right to prosecute for indecent assault where the time limit for unlawful sexual intercourse with a child under 16 years of age had passed. Whilst the Court of Appeal in *Cottrell* dismisses the artificiality of a pretence that law is 'discovered', the House of Lords judgments in *R v J* contain no awareness, either in the majority judgments, or Baroness Hale's strongly critical dissent, that any of their Lordships are involved in an exercise in changing the law.[44]

Whilst *R v Cottrell* contains an admission that it is 'pretence' for judges to deny changing the law, *R v J* is an example of the communications that generate such criticisms.[45] Their Lordships presented judgments that explored what the law was, rather than admitting that their decision would establish or change the law. They also failed to acknowledge that a hard case, which could generate divergent views of the law, must necessarily involve the exercise of some choice or discretion. And lastly, in the exercise of that choice, there was no recognition that factors such as their gender or biography (and in other hard cases their race and class) could operate as factors influencing their judgments. How do we explain such, to quote

[42] [2007] EWCA Crim 2016, para 25.

[43] [2005] 1 AC 562.

[44] The judgments, on both sides, attempt to 'discover' the appropriate law on the right to prosecute for indecent assault contrary to Sexual Offences Act 1956 s14(1) (which contains no time limit) in light of s6(1), dealing with unlawful sexual intercourse (which does). It is a case of statutory interpretation, and whilst both sides describe the consequences of their particular interpretations, there is no suggestion on either side that their conclusions are anything other than what the statute requires. For the majority, as much as the dissent, the basis for the construction of each judgment is that the statute requires, and has always required, the interpretation offered.

[45] To those readers who do not accept that *R v J* is a hard case that changes the law, we simply invite them to apply our analysis to whatever case they would recognise as such, from any area of law that has evolved through judicial decisions.

Hart, 'rhetoric[al]' omissions? Hart also talks about 'ritual' language, and the quote from Simpson at the start of this Chapter speaks of 'conventions of legal argument [which] embody a belief in the theoretical possibility of a comprehensive gapless rule of law'. What is the nature of this ritual or convention?

One can offer various normative or functional explanations of the judicial failure to acknowledge what they do (establish or change law) when they do it.[46] As with MacCormick's explanation of the judicial duty to give effect to clear law, one can attribute this to various sociological or political factors: a desire to increase their own, and their profession's, social standing; or the need for unelected officials to avoid political criticism. And one might also hope, perhaps through academic critique, to expose this element of law making, and all the unacknowledged elements that contribute to judicial decisions, and thereby help to produce different outcomes in the future. In keeping with Luhmann's theory, and the forms of autonomy which his theory recognises, we prefer to begin with an exploration of the operations which are carried out by legal decisions, and to consider how these would be made more difficult, or impossible, for judges, if they did not utilise the redundancies currently available within the legal system. In so doing, we hope to identify the costs to such actors of ceasing to utilise that redundancy, and to consider how such costs, which operate at the moment of each communication, might structure the participation of judicial actors within the legal system to a greater and more predictable extent than theories that rely on those actors' awareness of, and response to, the anticipated consequences of their actions in terms of gender, class, race or professional interests.[47]

Let us begin with those explanations of judicial communications which seek to demonstrate their self-serving qualities. A convention amongst judges to hide their law-making function at the moment of legal decisions is difficult to reconcile with a willingness of judges, in law review articles and public speeches, and even, as in *R v Cottrell*, in some decisions, to admit that their decisions make, and don't simply identify, the law. And it is their willingness to admit that they make law which provides evidence that at least some of their communications have a disingenuous quality that can be described as 'rhetoric'. Why hide in one moment what can be revealed, in public forums, at others? Of course these public admissions are usually accompanied by claims that law making by the judiciary is of a different quality from that of the legislature, that it is more incremental, or interstitial. Some will see rhetoric not only in the failure to admit to making

[46] It is not necessary to show that the judiciary *never* admit to making law when they make it in order to justify a discussion of the many, nearly all, or virtually all (depending on one's critical stance) occasions when they do this.

[47] In doing this, we do not deny, any more than Luhmann, that law can be shown to operate in a manner that advances class, gender and race interests.

law when doing so, but also in these further claims that judicial law making has a limited character. For whether one focuses on acknowledged 'landmark' decisions, or simply seeks to expose the alternatives that are available in more ordinary cases, it is easy to show that the changes in law affected by the judiciary are, on at least some occasions, as politically significant as much of what is carried out through legislation. So the convention, interpreted from this perspective, is to admit to the fact of law making (but not at the time when it occurs), and to disguise its extent, and the political nature of the choices which accompany it. By what mechanism is such a finely balanced self-serving convention maintained in place against the vagaries and judgments of individual judges, who might be expected to hold different views as to the likely consequences, whether in the mass media or politics, of its infringement. What would be a systems theory explanation?

We cannot overcome the separation between psychic and social communication and know what is in the minds of judges. But we can begin this enquiry into the restrictions on the possibilities of communication open to judges by asking what restraints hypothetical honest judges might encounter (our version of Dworkin's Hercules!).[48] Honesty is subjective, which creates a situation in which the more learned our imagined judges, and the more self-aware they are, the more difficulties they may have in articulating all of the factors within their consciousnesses (or even their unconscious motives) which have influenced their decisions. Think of the enormous difficulties. Within moral philosophy there is an extensive debate between cognitivism and non-cognitivism; this debate raises the possibility that it is not values but desires that motivate human choices, with reason operating only as a mechanism to increase our ability to achieve desires. Closely allied to this are debates about ethical relativism, which raise the question of whether values, or desires, are the result of culture, class, race or gender. And for those who believe that the acquisition of values or desires is more individualistic, one might look to psychology or biography. So honesty about the nature of choice, if this means identifying the reasons why judge X chose to make decision Y, could take us through moral philosophy into anthropology, sociology and psychology, with little or no certainty of a definite conclusion. This leaves our honest judges in a difficult position, and the more self-conscious and widely read they are, the more difficult that position could be. The 'nightmare' level of honesty would be judges who adopted the style of some post-modern writers, attempting to deconstruct their decisions at the moment of deciding, by attempting to identify, with total honesty, what has brought them to believe that X rather than Y is the appropriate outcome for the case at hand.

[48] 'An imaginary judge of superhuman intellectual power and patience who accepts law as integrity' (Dworkin, 1986, 239).

We can dispose of this 'nightmare' scenario by reflecting on what is involved in 'making law' within our system of precedent. Higher courts do not simply announce their decisions. They give reasons. And the reasons provided will be intended to persuade others (judges, lawyers and sometimes even politicians and lay people) that their decisions are appropriate. This is a significant constraint. It will take us well away from our 'nightmare' scenario. Rarely will judges' self-conscious observations on the basis for their moral values persuade other judges of the correctness of their decisions, whether those decisions are presented as a conclusion of law, or a deliberate attempt to make new law. If judgments are intended to persuade, then the communications chosen to construct them must be appropriate to that task. But what is it that makes particular kinds of reasoning appropriate to that task? We can call the standards of legal rhetoric a convention, and just accept that 'they are because they are' amongst sufficient members of the judiciary. But systems theory invites us to go further, and examine what operations these reasons facilitate that would not occur, or not occur in the same way, if different reasons were given.

First, we need to remember that the giving of reasons by judges operates within a system of precedent. As such, the reasons provided have to guide the making of further decisions. This provides a filter against all kinds of 'honesty'. Confessions of an idiosyncratic kind that reveal why particular judges reached particular decisions make no contribution to this process. In effect, as precedents, they leave matters undecided, as there is no reason for persons with different histories/gender/class to reach the same decisions. In order to operate as precedents, judges have to remove themselves from their judgments, whatever their beliefs as to the manner in which their own personal experiences might have shaped their decisions. This is the beginning of a process that can, from outside the legal system, be described negatively as 'dishonesty', 'hypocrisy' or 'rhetoric', or positively as 'impartiality' and 'objectivity'.

Second, as pointed out by Hart, when judges are called upon to choose between two legal solutions to a legal issue, part of their task is to integrate their chosen solution into the existing law.[49] Again, this is part of the system of precedent. Law evolves by each new law fitting into the existing law. We might call this an examination of the 'legal consequences'. It involves a consideration of the implications for existing law if the chosen solution *is* the law. One solution may lead to one configuration of legal relationships, whilst the other leads to a different one. In making this comparison judges are involved in a contemplation of redundancy: 'What possible differences to future legal communications follow if these matters are decided one way rather than the other?' And from the perspectives created by these alterna-

[49] Hart alternatively suggests, in relation to 'a system where *stare decisis* is firmly acknowledged, [that] this function of the courts is very like the exercise of delegated rule-making by an administrative body' (Hart, 1994, 135).

tive configurations of hypothetical future legal communications, judges have a limited ability to view the implications for the rest of society. To some extent this description of alternatives involves an element of persuasion, showing how judges have chosen the better outcome. But restricting this persuasive element is a communication that is a necessary part of the evolution of law: what might it mean to establish this precedent?

A third factor in this assessment of judicial communications is the nature of the procedures through which judges establish the existing law. When identifying settled law judges make communications that do not differ in form from those used to establish new law. (Indeed, that is what leads to accusations of 'rhetoric'). In other words, the processes which are necessary in order to choose between alternatives are not different from the procedure involved in identifying what alternatives are available to be chosen, including those cases where a judge might conclude that there are no alternatives, that is, that the matter is disposed of by settled law. In a case of settled law we might expect literal meanings and purposeful interpretation to coincide, principles to support this, minimal disturbance to other areas of law from adopting this interpretation, and whilst the legal result might not be able to be presented as reasonable (in the sense that it is beyond criticism) at least it would not appear wholly unreasonable (in the sense that it is indefensible). But if this is what constitutes settled law, then the difference between finding law and making law is not a difference of kind, it is a movement along a continuum. Elements of what constitute settled law may find themselves located on each side of a choice between offered alternatives. This means in turn that there is no clear demarcation between areas of law that are settled and those which are not. What then would it mean for judges to exhibit honesty when they move along this continuum? One envisages a situation in which judges who feel that they are involved in the making of law should offer one of two kinds of admission. Either that there is no settled law, and so the decision represents an addition to law, or that there is settled law, but the judges in question regard the existing law as so unsatisfactory that they are going to have to change it.

What are the problems with such additional elements of honesty? To put this in systems theory terms, how would the adoption of such communications change the nature of legal communications and the operations that they carry out? Would adjudication continue as adjudication with this small change? Or would the introduction of such 'honest' communications block or impede the making of communications and the operations they carry out (which participants are currently motivated to achieve).[50] And if these impediments to future communications represent the costs of such

[50] The discontinuity in communication at this point has already been discussed in terms of law's formula for contingency in Chapter 1.

admissions, what exactly are the gains (remembering that the participants in the process have to be motivated to make these new forms of communication)?

There are penalties for this kind of honesty. Judges who are not self-conscious in their judgments as to what represents settled law will have a distinct advantage over those who are. These judges will simply not have to make such honest admissions, or at least not make them at the same point on the continuum as their less self-aware colleagues. Of course if the admission that one was making law had no adverse implications for our judge (as is the case, for example, when statutes expressly give discretion to individual judges) then there might be no immediate disadvantages from making such confessions. But our judges have to decide on their communications by reference to the legal system as it currently is, and not as they might wish it to be. And given where we presently are, judges who admit to making new law other than as authorised by statute or precedent are at a disadvantage in deciding the cases before them, and judges who go so far as to admit to overruling settled law because they do not regard it as appropriate ('the law is currently x, but we think it ought to be y') are at an even greater disadvantage.[51] The most obvious disadvantage is not the external one of political, media or academic criticism, but the internal one of failing to achieve a successful legal operation; actually to dispose of the cases before them. Such statements are, within the legal system as it currently exists, going to communicate information that is decoded as an 'error'.[52] In the case of lower court judges, it is going to produce a version of the easy case: the easy appeal. In the case of a supreme court, such communications are not apparently open to correction by appeal. But one should not assume that this makes a significant difference. The techniques of legal argumentation that identify errors in a lower court judgment (a contemplation of legal consequences that includes a sense of what can no longer be decided if this communication were accepted by one's audience) apply to lower and higher court judges alike. Whilst the error would be less easy to remedy, contemplation of what it represents to the legal system (in terms of a loss

[51] Hart's reference to rhetoric (at the beginning of this Chapter) gives us one clue, if rhetoric here is intended to refer to the intention to persuade. If a judge's intentions are to persuade that the appropriate legal decisions should be those chosen by them, then they are severely handicapped in achieving those results if they admit, within their judgments, that they are not establishing the law, but instead deciding what the law should be in the absence of settled law. An admission: 'There is no law here, but we personally think the law ought to be x' will, within our existing legal system, lead to an appeal. Under our system, judges are authorised to establish what the law is, they are not authorised to establish what the law ought to be. Here, as in the previous discussion of detached/committed communications, communications that admitted to the exercise of discretion to make law may represent the judges' beliefs, but they will undermine the intended outcome (and thus work against the motivation to make 'legal' communications).

[52] Systems theory analysis supports classic positivist claims, namely those of John Austin that nullity is a sanction, at least in the case of judges, even though the communications of the system do not acknowledge this.

of redundancy) is still present. One example of this is the former House of Lords unwillingness to abandon its practice of regarding its own decisions as binding precedents, evidenced by the delay in introducing a practice direction allowing overruling, and the limited number of times it has been used since being established in 1966. There are huge costs in terms of a lack of redundancy if the Supreme Court makes communications which acknowledge its willingness to change law solely on the basis that it is no longer satisfactory. And the practice direction only deals with the ability of the House of Lords, and now the Supreme Court, to change its mind about what the law has always required, that is, to find the law to be different, not openly to make different law. This further move, especially if it involves an abandonment of the techniques of statutory interpretation, would amount to communications that were truly, to quote MacCormick, 'so strange as to be barely imaginable'.[53]

If honesty is not rewarded, then it will in practice be discouraged. Judges will not be prompted to make admissions that will almost certainly undermine their attempts to make the law into what they might like it to be, since honesty will tend to work to prevent their desired outcomes from occurring. However, could there be an institutional change to achieve this result – to remove the penalty for honesty and the reward for 'hypocrisy'? Well, this would require a change in the legal system. What communications within the legal system could alter it to allow this to happen? We cannot say that such a change could never occur – systems theory, with its limited scope of understanding systems in terms of communications, can never predict how a system might change itself over the long term. But we can see why, at present, such a change would be quite difficult. The most flexible instrument for changing the legal system that we currently possess is legislation. But this gives us a problem. If judges were told in legislation that they could make new law whenever they felt that the law was not settled, or even that they could make new law whenever it was settled but they disagreed with it, then 'rhetoric' or 'hypocrisy' would cease. But this would be because the range of discretion that has already been expressly handed to judges in areas like sentencing and matrimonial settlements would have been extended to the whole of the law. And not only is such a mandate unlikely to be enacted, but it would not actually do what those who want an end to hypocrisy are asking for. They want judges to be honest, that is, to admit that they make new law despite the absence of a statutory authority to do so. They are not asking for judges to be given such monumental powers that the need to be 'hypocritical' will never arise.

[53] A legal decision that judges were authorised to decide what the law ought to be in areas covered by statute without reference to the techniques of statutory interpretation is even less believable, given how many routine decisions are made possible by the background redundancy of the doctrine of parliamentary sovereignty.

Assuming that the legislature is not going to grant judges an express general power to alter the law, we find ourselves in one of the situations of inconsistency, if not paradox, that systems theory leads us to expect to find within all systems of communication.[54] Whereas the legislature cannot or would not give judges a blanket power to make new law, nevertheless it needs judges to carry on with the task of applying the legislature's law. And it also needs judges to interpret and alter their interpretations of law to take account, to quote Hart, of 'our relative ignorance of fact . . . [and] . . . our relative indeterminacy of aim'.[55] And with this last 'need' we can say that, in effect, the legislature needs 'hypocrisy'. To be effective, the legislature needs the judges to carry out operations that it cannot expressly authorise. Judges must make law, in the sense of dealing with the inevitable contingency within a system that cannot provide in advance for all situations, by using communications that do not admit that law, in this sense, is being made. These particular examples of 'hypocritical' communication facilitate a workable version of what is commonly referred to, within the legal and political systems, as the doctrine of 'separation of powers'.[56] Whilst the need for judges to make law is inescapable, their inability to proclaim that this is what they are doing, as they do it, leads to different forms of law making than would occur if judges could utilise communications that confessed to their law-making role as they were doing so.[57] Whilst there is undoubtedly a creative element in making new law through the development of precedent, it is still a continuation of the techniques involved in 'finding' settled law; most of the redundancy remains the same. And as such, it does not provide the same opportunities as would be present if a judge could simply say: 'At this point I have run out of law, so the best law I can create in this situation is . . .' (let alone, say 'Here I find the law so

[54] Luhmann identifies this particular paradox as 'the third question': 'the paradoxes of the changing interpretation of law which has to, but cannot, refer to itself as some kind of legislation' (Luhmann, 1988, 155). See further, in relation to decision making in courts, Luhmann, 2004, 280–96; and more generally in relation to the legal system, Perez and Teubner, 2006. See also our review of the latter book, Nobles and Schiff, 2007.

[55] Hart, 1994, 128.

[56] Other key doctrines that inform the legal and political systems, such as 'the rule of law', are considered at length in Chapter 6.

[57] In keeping with systems theory we are not claiming that the current situation has been rationally constructed, but that it has evolved. That evolution was achieved by the judiciary continuing to perform those same operations within the common law (and on the continent within the civilian tradition) that they had performed for hundreds of years prior to legislatures developing a radical ability to change law. Within the natural law tradition, by appealing to higher levels of generality, law was constantly evolved through communications that failed to acknowledge that it changed. Increasing use of legal communications around themes of authority increased the role of legislatures, but did not remove the need for a different (and one might say older) form of communication necessary to achieve some kinds of law making through adjudication: see Nobles and Schiff, 2006, ch 3; see also the underlying theme and its representation in the essays in Loughlin and Walker, 2007.

inappropriate that I am going to change it to . . .').[58] And this form of communication (their inability to proclaim that they are making law as they make it in the course of their judgments), rather than any personal political commitment held by one judge, or by judges in general, results in law making that can be described as 'incremental'. By contrast, if judges could communicate 'honestly', and admit to making law within their judgments whenever they felt that their decisions were not dictated to them by prior standards (or felt that those prior standards were inappropriate), then the content of the doctrine of separation of powers would depend on different communications, namely those expressing each judge's assessment of the deference appropriate to Parliament.

So, the conventions which allow discretion whilst failing to acknowledge it are not something which judicial actors have to accept in the sense of a consensus within their consciousnesses about the practices that they must commonly perform, or the political or professional reasons why such practices might be a good thing. They are first and foremost the experience of carrying out legal operations (generating information) against a background of redundancy, which enables routine decision making to occur. The individual actor who attempted to break with the 'convention' would be unlikely to find that their 'novel' communication was absorbed within the legal system rather than being recorded as an error, still less that it could generate a new redundancy for the making of routine legal decisions. There is no obvious way (at least in the present) for the judiciary to decide both easy and hard cases on a routine basis except by using communications that fail to distinguish clearly (from the perspective of at least some academics) between the finding of law and the making of law. However much their power may resemble that of Parliament (in terms of the significance of the legal changes produced by their operations) the communications which they use have to take a different form, one that fails to recognise that law is 'made' by judges who make decisions, but one that takes the form of a discovery of the existing law.

Conclusion

This Chapter has sought to indicate the reasons why judges, and other actors within the legal system, or indeed any system, might need to utilise communications that do not reflect their own (or perhaps even any human's) understanding of what is occurring.[59] Attempting to explore why

[58] The point can be illustrated simply by contrasting this open form of law making with the techniques described in books such as Twining and Miers, 1999.

[59] Or, as others might say from other perspectives, the legal system needs hypocrisy, just as, it has now become clear, do many institutions and organisations: see Brunsson, 2002, especially 27–39 and ch 9; and, in relation to law in particular, Philippopoulos-Mihalopoulos, 2006.

this might be a necessary part of any system's operations, and then identifying the operations which this makes possible, provides us with a radically different insight into the nature of judicial communications. Debates which are informed by ordinary language philosophy, speech act theory and other forms of linguistic philosophy, and focus on language and not systems, fail to identify the constraints placed by systems on actors' use of language. Arguments about the construction of meaning which limit themselves to language and its use, but ignore the restraints which arise from law's existence as a separate system of communication (with its own redundancies) have produced a series of irresolvable disputes about what truly occurs within legal systems. Systems theory offers legal theorists a new direction, with new insights. This is a journey which has implications for more schools of jurisprudence than analytical positivism. To call communications 'rhetorical' or 'hypocritical' draws attention to something important. But without analysis of why such communications occur, one is left uncertain as to the possibilities for things to be other than they are. Those who see hypocrisy as a personal failing might hope for more 'honesty'. Those who see 'hypocrisy' as a political strategy, intended by its users to maintain the legitimacy of the legal system in the face of possible criticism, will expect changes in the political or legal spheres that diminish the need for deference to lead to immediate changes to the frequency and nature of 'hypocritical' communications. Systems theory, by focusing on the operations that communications make possible, identifying the need for new communications to replace former redundancies if the possibilities of communication (variety) are to alter, and acknowledging the evolution of systems into ever more complex forms, offers a powerful alternative explanation for many of legal theory's central concerns.

Understanding how redundancy constrains the possibilities of what can be said, including the ability of an individual to make statements about their internal states, and how these constraints are system-specific, so that they vary between systems and between different points in the same system, offers a hermeneutic approach that can be applied not only to law, and the particularities of its 'rituals' and 'rhetoric' but to other subsystems as well: science, politics, mass media, the economy, etc. For, in the resistances which social systems of communication offer to psychic systems, with which they can only loosely 'structurally couple',[60] individual actors are constrained. Understanding the constraints of judicial communication

[60] 'Structural coupling' is a key concept of systems theory, including but also going beyond the coupling between psychic and social systems, that represents the stability with which different social systems recognise each other's communications, but without those communications expressing the same meaning. For a succinct statement of this concept, see King and Thornhill, 2003, 32–33. We offer a more 'systematic' account of the structural coupling between the legal and political systems in Chapter 6, and to some extent the legal system and other subsystems, including psychic systems, in Chapters 7 and 8.

mirrors the participation of other actors within their systems of communication, and helps with our understanding of the autonomy not only of law, but of these other functioning systems in contemporary societies as well. More significant, we offer an understanding about self-observations made by even the same people (such as judges) having different meanings according to the different contexts of the system's communications within which they currently form their network of meaningful communications.

3

Can One Have a Right to Disobey a Law?

In this Chapter we move from the communications of those who appear to operate at the centre of the legal system, judges and other legal officials, to those who appear to operate at its periphery but in circumstances in which they offer a challenge to the core of the legal system. At its core, law makes a claim to legitimate authority (and judges, as we described in the previous Chapter, communicate in terms of their commitments to that authority), while those who engage in civil disobedience make claims that it is right, or that they have a right, to disobey the law. Applying the understanding of systems theory, we analyse those claims. The Chapter explores how such claims might operate as communications within the legal system and the political system in order to evaluate whether it is possible for either system to incorporate such claims into their routine operations. This exploration leads to some appreciation of the apparently contradictory practices that can be shown to result from those who engage in the form of protest of civil disobedience as part of their campaigns.

The question in this Chapter's title allows us to explore an issue that is central to political theory – the nature of legality and its relationship to the distribution of political power. A systems theory approach to it requires us first to consider the ability of the legal system to recognise such a right. How would such a right, if articulated within law, affect law's operations? Our conclusion is that a right to disobey law is not something which law can actually incorporate into its operations. The recognition of such a right serves only to make whatever aspect of law's environment it previously referred to as illegal, as now legal. Law's resistance to the incorporation of such a right into its own operations has, in turn, implications for the political system. This is the subject of the next section of the Chapter. Here we introduce the reader to Luhmann's sociological understanding of the manner in which political power is distributed through 'legitimate' collectively binding decisions, with the parameters of those decisions routinely established through legality. This is a relationship of structural coupling between law and politics (explored more fully in Chapter 6). What we seek to show here is that politics gains a technical basis on which to distribute power through utilising (re-using, or having its own communications 'second coded' by) the communications of another system, the legal system, that will not itself recognise a right to disobey law. This creates a situation in which the articulation of power within the political system cannot incorporate a right to disobey law into its own operations without creating a loss of redundancy. The other way of looking at this is that the routine articulation of the distribution of political power in terms of legality provides a constant stream of communications within everyday political administration whose implicit meaning is that legality establishes the legitimacy of collectively binding decisions. In the face of these redundancies within the political system, a right to disobey the law is a form of communication that can only exist, in any systematic form, within the periphery of the political system, a subsystem which Luhmann called 'protest movements'. These difficulties go some way towards explaining the apparently contradictory behaviour of human actors who use arguments of civil disobedience in order to express resistance and seek tolerance whilst engaging in protest movements, and who then fail to express acceptance of a right to disobey law once in government. In the final section of this Chapter we consider a case study of civil disobedience which exhibits the difficulties faced by the legal and political systems in recognising a right to disobey the law: the current campaign for the legalisation of assisted suicide, and the case of Debbie Purdy.

What can a theory that understands society as a social system made up, together with its structural conditions, institutions and organisations,[1] of a network of meaningful communications, but society as including functionally differentiated subsystems (with their own network and distinct sets of meaningful communications), tell us about civil disobedience? Most of the informed and extended discussion of this subject is part of political philosophy.[2] This is hardly surprising since the self-observations of so much political discourse in modern democratic states is organised around ideas of legitimacy; with civil disobedience and conscientious objection being counterposed against those of legitimacy within such discourse.[3] Theoretical

[1] We engage, but only briefly, with systems theory's understandings of organisations in Chapter 7.

[2] See, for some of the classic essays, both theoretical and more practical: Bedau, 1991; Pennock and Chapman, 1970; Edmundson, 1999; Benewick and Smith, 1972; Walzer, 1970.

[3] Luhmann's analysis of the political system claims that since the eighteenth century legitimacy has operated, in many of its forms, as a key to the self-understanding of the political system as a constitutional system organised under law, and in terms of democratic principles (see Luhmann, 1990a, especially chs III, VI and VIII; see also Thornhill, 2008). This internal construction of legitimacy is part of the modern political system's ability to co-ordinate its complex organisation, including the elements of politics, administration and public. We will explore the character of legitimacy as an external referent of the political system, and at the same time an internal referent for that system's co-ordination, later in this Chapter, but should begin such a discussion by drawing the reader's attention to a systems theory analysis that understands 'legitimacy' (which may have some relevance to all subsystems) as being as significant in its relevance to the political system as 'validity' is to the communications of the legal system; and how legitimacy might play a similar role as a formula for contingency in the

ideas that identify the conditions which bestow legitimacy on bodies that promulgate the standards that regulate social life, inevitably also identify the conditions that undermine that legitimacy, and in turn reduce or terminate the obligation to follow those standards. In doing so, these ideas also offer justifications for the practice of civil disobedience.[4] The assumption underlying much of this literature is that a better understanding of the theoretical and philosophical arguments surrounding questions of legitimacy will equip people with a greater ability to react to conditions of injustice, through being able to articulate claims that they have a right, or that it is right, to disobey unjust laws. This is the point at which systems theory can make a contribution. If society has separate subsystems of communication, then the opportunities for communication open to participants within these different systems should also differ. This will include the opportunities to make communications about civil disobedience. The issue which we will explore is the respective ability of actors within different social subsystems (protestors, but also politicians, prosecutors, judges, juries, etc), to make these kinds of communication. We consider this issue by examining the scope for the legal and political systems to acknowledge that it is right, or that one can have a right, to disobey the law.

Many of those who claim to practise civil disobedience may experience gross forms of oppression (assassination, torture, disappearance, imprisonment without trial) or other lesser forms. These experiences make it costly for human beings to articulate their resistance to or defiance of political and legal regimes. But our focus is not on these forms of abuse, but the difficulties of communicating that defiance. Is there anything to be said about the ability of political and legal systems to incorporate civil disobedience communications into their routine operations? Are there any significant operations that could not continue if such incorporation occurred? How much of the current complexity of each system would need to be sacrificed, or need to be extended? And most importantly of all, if these communications were to play a larger role within the political and legal system, how might the process of evolution develop? This is not an approach which belittles the difficulties of civil disobedience for those who engage in it. Rather, it presupposes that actors will find difficulties in making particular forms of communication, arising from the limitations of the system of communication in which they might wish to participate, even if they do not face physical or other threats. This raises the possibility that

political system, as does 'justice' in the legal system (see our later analysis in this Chapter, our analysis of justice in Chapter 1, but also our analysis of the rule of law, constitutions and human rights in Chapter 6).

[4] For example, as a treatise in moral philosophy, such as Greenawalt, 1989, or as part of one in political and economic theory, such as that by Rawls, 1971, ch VI, or one in jurisprudence, such as Dworkin, 1977, 'Civil Disobedience', ch 8, and Dworkin, 1985, 'Civil Disobedience and Nuclear Protest', ch 4, or one of radical political philosophy, such as Zinn, 1968.

communications about civil disobedience may meet resistance which takes a different form from the kinds of control that can be exercised through actual or threatened application of physical force, or loss of status, as a means of motivating human action.

In light of the fact that the literature on civil disobedience is closely related to the issue of state legitimacy, and political theory, one might expect our enquiry to begin with the political system. However, we start with the problems generated by civil disobedience claims or arguments in favour of a right to disobey law within the legal system.

Civil Disobedience within the Legal System

As Raz has correctly observed, the legal system's demand for obedience is absolute, in the sense that the system acknowledges no basis for identifying exceptions to its own duties outside of itself, namely absolute in no other sense than the exclusivity of law to determine what one's legal obligations are. Raz states that 'the law assumes the right to determine in what conditions legal requirements are defeated by other considerations'.[5] This 'right' is nothing more than the legal system's closure. The legal system determines what is legal and illegal, not the mass media, or science, or even politics.[6] To communicate that someone is under a legal duty, and for that communication to form part of the legal system, it must be linked to law's own conditional programmes, which establish the basis on which law's code will be applied. One cannot utilise the legal system's communications in order to determine that a legal duty can apply in a particular situation, and then utilise the communications of another system in order to show that no such legal duty arises. The communications which construct the duty, and those which remove it, must both be indicated by the legal system itself.[7] To allow the conduct prima facie coded as illegal to be re-coded as legal requires a new legal communication.

[5] Raz, 2009, 236.

[6] These other systems can include communications that something is legal, or illegal, but these are conditional programmes for those systems, not their codes. (See Chapter 4 for a full discussion of this.) Politics can only pronounce on legality when this can be connected to the application of its code: government/opposition. There are few resources within the political system to establish legality. Instead, the political system is dependent on the legal system for the routine establishment of what is legal or illegal. (See the next section of this Chapter.)

[7] This analysis does not conflict with that offered by Dworkin (see especially 1986), in which the programmes that determine legal duties involve 'interpretive practices' and allow much more room for the incorporation of broader ideas than simply rules to such determination. Dworkin also recognises that legal programmes can offer such a balance of considerations that even the highest court might, within a short time, change its mind. Neither does Raz's analysis contradict the 'realist' contention that the specific determinations of individual judges might well be better understood as personal or political preferences, rather than rule-bound decisions.

If there were to be a right to civil disobedience recognised by the legal system, what form would this right take, and what difficulties would this present for the legal system's self-construction? What would it mean for something to be illegal, under the criminal law, or a tort or breach of contract within civil law, yet still be a right within the legal system, by reference to a concept of civil disobedience? To consider the resistance of the legal system itself to such a right, we have to ask ourselves what are the implications for the legal system itself, from creating, via a legislative act, or some court precedent, a right of civil disobedience, namely one not only to dissent from but to disobey law?[8] Could such a right operate as an exception to all of the laws' duty imposing rules, or at least some of them?

The first point to note about such a right is the difficulties that the legal system would have in recognising a right in these terms. Exceptions to conditions of liability, whether civil or criminal, are not articulated within the legal system as rights of disobedience. Rather, they operate as restrictions on the scope of the primary provision. One talks of a right of self-defence that makes one's aggressive response legal, not a right to disobey the laws of assault or murder when one is faced with a threat of violence. Necessity, self-preservation, and other matters that cause the law to use forms of communication that circulate in moral philosophy have not traditionally caused the law to articulate these exceptions as rights to disobey the law. Rather than generate rights to disobey, the utilisation of moral communications within the legal system has generated changes to law's obligations.

According to Luhmann, this aspect of the legal system is fundamental to its evolution. In 'The Third Question: The Creative Use of Paradoxes in Law and Legal History'[9] he analyses the need for judges to offer right answers. He does not here refer to the possibility of a single correct answer based on irrefutable premises. Rather, he brings attention to the manner in which decisions can be shown to be incompatible with each other, and the inability of judges to accept this incompatibility. Whilst a teacher or therapist might be able to acknowledge that incompatible positions are both right, because there is some truth in both, or some therapeutic value, judges have no such freedom. This is a consequence of their duty to decide the matter brought to them by the parties. They are not free to compromise, either over the issue brought to them, or the arguments brought to them by

[8] Hence Raz finds it straightforward to recognise that laws may be useful, and 'a legal system good or even perfect while denying that there is an obligation to obey its laws' (2009, 249). This conclusion is consistent with what is often called a 'hard positivist' understanding (see Penner, 2002). However, the German constitution (its Basic Law) might be understood to create such a right, via either the right to assembly, which might include public protest, or other rights. But these rights will then be subjected to interpretation which follows the pattern represented in the arguments which follow here (see Quint, 2008 for detailed analysis of the relevant provisions in the German courts). Equivalent provisions operate in other legal systems including the constitutional rights of freedom of religion and conscience, which equally require interpretation.

[9] 1988.

each side in support of their claim. They have to decide which of the parties should win, and why. And in justifying their decisions, they have to decide on the arguments presented to them. These legal arguments will invariably refer to earlier legal decisions, that is to earlier answers to earlier legal questions. In giving their decisions, judges have to decide which of these earlier answers are correct, and how they apply to the case in point. And their judgments, in turn, provide the basis for legal arguments in some future case, which again have to be judged as correct, or not.

For Luhmann, this process suppresses a central paradox, which is the lack of any foundation which establishes, under all conditions, how the legal binary code (legal/illegal) is applied. There is only the endless application of the code, and the ever more complicated justifications of its application, which generate what he calls law's conditional programmes.[10] But within this process, the evolution of courts, and their central role in generating communications justifying the application of the code, has played a key role in allowing law to develop a complexity that is in keeping with its environment (to evolve in response to developments in the political, economic, scientific, religious, mass media systems, etc). One example of the central paradox, located within judicial reasoning, is 'the changing interpretation of law which has to, but cannot, refer to itself as some kind of legislation'.[11] A brief examination of how this particular paradox has operated within legal reasoning will illustrate why it is so difficult for a legal system to react to arguments about the injustice of a law, in terms of a right to disobey that law.

Within the forms of legal reasoning that dominated both the civil and common law systems prior to the development of modern positivist theories of law, moral communications formed part of what it meant to identify the law.[12] Natural law, as practised by civil law system lawyers, assumed that the particular rules of a jurisdiction took their legal force through being the expression of a higher law (the Justinian Code) which had a greater moral force. Whereas for common law system lawyers, the existing law represented remedies for social wrongs, and a guide to what further wrongs should receive remedies in future.[13] Thus, within both these systems, treating the positive law as the expression of a higher law both facilitated the identification of the law and formed a basis for its reform. Starting from the

[10] See Luhmann, 2004, ch 4, particularly parts IV and V. We describe in more detail the relationship between codes and programmes in the next Chapter.

[11] Luhmann, 1988 at 155.

[12] See Nobles and Schiff, 2006, ch 3, 'A Sociological Understanding of Natural Law and Common Law Theory: Constructing the Conditions for Legal Positivism' and sources cited therein.

[13] Barden and Murphy's understanding of natural law suggests that its existence on the Continent was closer to that of the common law than this opposition would suggest, involving not only an appeal to higher law, but an attempt to base decisions on entitlements that have their basis in custom, which the authors call 'living law' (2010).

presumption that the local positive law merely expressed something which was superior to it (Roman law, the *Volksgeist*, English custom, etc) lawyers could argue for changes to the local positive law as 'better' expressions of the superior source. Within this form of argumentation, a finding that a particular law did not express the superior source formed a basis for its amendment or reform. So, for example, within the common law, where the decisions of judges were treated as the identification of remedies for customary wrongs (custom being the 'real' unwritten law), a finding that a particular judgment was not in keeping with the wrongs identified in surrounding judgments undermined the status of that judgment as an expression of the true law. In this way, mistakes could be rectified, and reforms introduced in response to social change when new wrongs were considered analogous to those already recognised.

Thus, within a legal system that understands itself as the expression of something superior to itself (a natural law self-description) the acceptance that a particular law is unjust (not in accordance with that superior source) does not generate a right of disobedience to law, but an acceptance that the law which infringes the superior source is not truly law at all. If a law so described ceases to be law for any purposes (as with the future status of court decisions found not to be in accordance with the justice represented by the surrounding common law), there is no law available to be the subject of a right of disobedience. Where the incompatible provision retains a reduced status within the legal system (as with the common law's tolerance of statutes that were felt to be in conflict with the reason of the common law), the legal system will itself articulate the degree of obedience appropriate to the law in question. Again, the law does not need to articulate the nature and extent of the obligation appropriate to an irrational or unjust law, and then articulate a right of disobedience to it.

This form of legal reasoning has continued with the evolution of constitutions at the end of the eighteenth century. Here the higher source of law is itself a posited law: constitutional law. Incompatibility between constitutional law and the lower law has resulted in the potential for a lower law to be declared unconstitutional, that is, having no force as law. There is no need to talk of a right to disobey a provision that has been found not to be truly law. And this position does not alter if the constitution is itself given a natural law interpretation, as the expression of higher values that have to be re-interpreted in light of contemporary social conditions. One still ends up with findings that lower laws, being unconstitutional, do not carry legal obligations, rather than a finding that they do, but are subject to a right of disobedience. Where the laws in question are found to be constitutional, whether on the basis of a positivist or natural law understanding of what gives the constitution its legal force, there is no room for a right of disobedience, since the law will not articulate both obligations and a right to disobey them.

Within the UK legal system, the reasoning of the common law continues to have natural law elements. Whilst the common law is no longer considered unwritten, but is self-consciously contained in court judgments, and these have legal force based on the authority of a court within the system of precedent, rather than the quality of the reasons contained within judgments, there is still no ability to identify what a court judgment will contribute to the law except by reference to its reception within the legal system. And that process allows for judgments to be narrowed or expanded, distinguished and overruled, a process that involves the consideration of surrounding court decisions. So, whilst the law within the common law is a creation of the courts, it is not the creation of any particular court, and no court, no matter what its authority, can necessarily determine fully what the law is. As with earlier common law reasoning, a court generally declares what the law is by reference to its coherence with the surrounding law, and does not undertake an explicit act of legislation.[14] Within this process, arguments that a particular legal conclusion would be wholly unreasonable, irrational, or particularly harsh (that is, unjust) do not lead to a conclusion that there is a right of disobedience; instead, they may point towards an interpretation of the law that avoids this conclusion. Where this occurs, one does not have a right of disobedience, but a defeat of the interpretation that leads to the unjust results. Where such arguments are not sufficient to defeat an interpretation which leads to these results, one has an affirmation of the harsh interpretation as law, and where this involves a legal obligation, an affirmation of the duty in question. So again, there seems no room for a right to disobey law.[15]

These difficulties in developing a right to disobey law in legal reasoning are reflected in legal theory (or what we prefer to call law's self-description). The existence of a legal obligation alongside a right to disobey appears to represent an example of contradiction. Contradictory laws are possible, but not as part of the same operation. Thus, as Kelsen acknowledged, one can have contradictory laws, in the sense that the norms which give objective meaning or validity to legal acts (such as court decisions or legislation) can give rise to norms that contradict each other.[16] An example would be if different panels of the Court of Appeal reached opposite conclusions on a particular point on the same day.[17]

[14] As we have illustrated in the previous chapter.

[15] Legislation reveals a similar treatment of claims based on injustice. On the one hand, appeals to the authority of the legislature serve to shut out moral and political arguments, leaving no room for a right of disobedience. On the other hand, pointing out the injustice of particular results helps to steer a court in its choices between possible interpretations of a statute, but this results in a finding that the unjust interpretation is not valid law, rather than a finding that it is law, but one need not obey it.

[16] Kelsen, 1967, 26.

[17] Kelsen, at least before the new analysis he undertook in his later writings post-1960, thought such happenings would result in the contradictory laws being politically ineffective.

But one cannot have a single legal communication that communicates both a legal obligation and a right of disobedience.

The right to disobey a law also seems to create a law for which there can be no 'legal' sanction. According to the archetypical positivism of Bentham and Austin, laws that contain no provision for the application of a sanction are incomplete laws, or in some other way imperfect laws or inadequately described as laws. Every law, properly so called, creates at least the risk of a sanction applied by the law-making authority. So, a person who could break a law without any risk of a sanction is not really breaking a 'law' at all. Hart's attack on this position in *The Concept of Law* invites us to view laws as meaningful, even in the absence of sanctions. One can have a legal duty, in the sense that the law in question is a standard utilised to make critical statements calling for compliance with the law in question, even in the absence of sanctions.[18] This critical reflective approach evidences the fact that, where sanctions are applied, it is the breach of the legal duty in question that justifies their application. Where sanctions are not applied, or not even provided for, the legal duty, as a standard of what ought to occur, remains meaningful. But a right to disobey a law takes us a stage further. Not only does the law that is being disobeyed lack sanctions, but its existence as a legal standard of a type that could justify sanctions, if any were provided, has to be reconciled with a law that would make the application of any sanctions something that was wrong.

When one looks at the actual form of criminal law provisions, the removal of the ability to sanction appears even more difficult to reconcile with its continued status as law. Criminal provisions do not strictly provide for legal duties, and then stipulate the sanctions which will follow from their breach. Instead, they typically take the form of a statement of the penalties that a person will face if they carry out a particular act. For example: 'A person who dishonestly appropriates property belonging to another shall be liable on conviction to a term of imprisonment not exceeding five years.' If there is a legal duty not to do the act that leads to the sanction (here theft) then, as Kelsen correctly claimed, it is not something that is expressly stated, but is implied or attributed to a law that only stipulates penalties (what Kelsen called its primary norms). Thus, if the legal duty only arises from a law that states that a person is liable to sanctions on carrying out a particular legal act, how is this duty to be implied in the presence of a legal right not to be punished for doing that same legal act?

The difficulties of generating a right to disobey within the legal system are also evident in the writings of those who have explored the issue of civil

[18] The 'critical reflective attitude' to rules operates irrespective of whether there is, or is not, a sanction attached to the particular rule in question. In other words it applies to those rules which are facilitative and do not obviously impose legal duties as correlates to sanctions, as well as those which clearly do as they have definite sanctions attached for non-compliance.

disobedience. Dworkin, in his early essay on 'Civil Disobedience',[19] points to the benefits to law from the disobedience of those who regard a particular law as unjust. These benefits arise from the ability of courts to revisit earlier interpretations, and find the law to be different from that previously supposed. For Dworkin, the benefits are more just laws.[20] But the manner in which these benefits are secured is not through an acknowledgement that the persons charged with offences have a right to disobey law, but that the law they disobeyed was not in fact a valid law.[21] Zwiebach concludes his book *Civility and Disobedience*, which argues for a right to disobey laws that contravene political rights, by examining how such a right might receive institutional support.[22] He acknowledges the need for public tribunals to assess when such rights of disobedience would arise, and ends by admitting that these public tribunals would amount to courts whose role would be declaring the laws transgressing political rights to be invalid. So again here, we find in fact a process which declares unjust laws invalid, rather than an acknowledgement that there is a right to disobey a law.

Raz has explored the merits of introducing a right for those who claim to have a conscientious objection to obeying a particular law to be excused from punishment or civil liability for their disobedience.[23] He discusses the possibility of a special and unified doctrine, granting a right of conscientious objection which can be invoked to obtain exemption from liability for any number of laws. He sees three drawbacks. The first is that the legal system has no access to the consciousnesses of human beings,[24] and must establish the genuineness of claims to conscience by reference to evidence. He thought that 'the word of the person invoking the right is almost invariably the only direct evidence', and that 'the opportunities for abuse are countless'.[25] Another of Raz's objections goes to the use of such indirect evidence of individuals' internal states. He feels that this will result in an

[19] 1977, ch 8.

[20] For Luhmann, the increased justice represented by a new interpretation of a law is an inevitable feature of the legal communications that effect such changes. Law does not evolve through communications that proclaim the results more economically efficient, or more politically expedient, whatever the underlying pressures on the judiciary. And by having to use communications that justify change in terms of justice as an overarching value, and not these alternatives, judges are inhibited in what they can present as a more 'just' interpretation of the legal system.

[21] Where the legal system fails to declare the law infringed invalid, Dworkin urges restraint on the part of those responsible for its enforcement, so as not to discourage future challenges which may be successful.

[22] 1975, 223–29.

[23] 2009, ch 15, 'A Right to Dissent? II. Conscientious Objection'.

[24] What systems theory analyses as the closure of a human's psychic system.

[25] 2009, at 287. This argument fails to engage with the manner in which law routinely forms views on individuals' intentions and their motivations, which it does by examining the record of those individuals' communications (spoken and unspoken – the meaning of their actions), against a background of assumptions which include a scepticism towards those who claim internal states that are self-serving.

inquiry into individuals' moral lives, to see if they can be confidently separated from those individuals who simply claim conscientious objection without more. His final objection is that such defences will encourage introspection, by forcing individuals to consider the relevant importance of moral reasons in their decision to disobey the law.

Whatever one's view of Raz's claims as to the ethical and practical difficulties of administering a doctrinal defence of conscientious objection, what he does not consider is the implications of such a doctrine for the evolution of law.[26] For a law that is formally still law, but incapable of enforcement, is exactly what has occurred in the past, in the development of equity and equitable remedies. The formal law, being unenforceable, ceases to be regarded as unjust, and is no longer subjected to legal challenges. Instead, the subject of legal challenges, and the demand for correct answers, becomes focused on the conditions of unenforceability, leading to the development of doctrine. And as such, exemptions based on moral considerations will inevitably 'evolve into a system of definitions and rules – and what else could a jurist do with them . . .'[27] One can expect a similar development with any attempt within law to acknowledge a right to disobey law.[28]

This brief consideration of forms of legal reasoning, and the evolution of equity, also illustrates the role played by justice within the legal system. Luhmann calls justice a formula for contingency, which description may seem to present justice as no more than an empty formula.[29] And it may also seem contradicted by the number of occasions when judges recognise a divergence between justice and what the law requires, but nevertheless uphold the law. But justice has a role in articulating the law which cannot be replaced by communications in terms of political expediency, or efficiency. Within the legal system, choices between indeterminate alternatives are articulated and justified through communications about the justice of a chosen outcome.[30] Justice does not give determinate outcomes, but it does provide law with its own communications for affecting its own choices. And thus it reduces the ability of other communications (political, economic, scientific, etc) to operate at these moments. Understood in this way, justice also has implications for a right of civil disobedience. Identifying an

[26] Raz's assessment of his own arguments is that it is better to avoid laws that challenge people's consciences rather than introduce such laws and then attempt to reduce their impact by a general exemption.

[27] Luhmann 1988, 157.

[28] And see our discussion of Debbie Purdy's case below.

[29] Luhmann 2004, ch 5; see our discussion in Chapter 1, which we apply here.

[30] This is not to deny that these other forms of communication cannot feature in an argument about what is just. The point is one of hierarchy. A judge who says that the 'law' requires something that is unjust, or that justice establishes which of two legal alternatives should apply, makes a communication that is likely to be accepted within the legal system. A judge who says that he prefers efficiency to the current law, or that in choosing between two legal alternatives s/he prefers the one that is efficient, over the one that is just, is likely to find her/his communications regarded as errors, within the legal system.

interpretation of a law as not just forms part of the process whereby alternative interpretations are chosen. Thus a right of disobedience does not simply create difficulties for the legal system because it creates contradictory communications about a particular legal act. It also asks the legal system to apply communications already used within the legal system to guide selections between indeterminate choices (communications about justice) for a different purpose: to acknowledge a right of resistance to law.

Is there any space within the legal system where a claimed right to disobey might operate? The answer to this is already familiar to us: within the parts of the legal system which the system identifies as areas of discretion. If a legal system contains no positive obligations to prosecute, it can leave it to politics to decide whether to enforce laws that will be disobeyed for reasons of conscience. And where it establishes discretion, for example, rather than fixed rules about sentencing, it can leave it to judges to decide how to react to particular acts of disobedience. Discretion, as an alternative to rules, allows law to have a different relationship with its environment. Legal discretion identifies categories of events to which the legal system will not have to react. The creation of such insensitive zones means that law's environment will not be subject to the uncertainties of doctrinal developments. The discretion not to prosecute keeps all kinds of legal issues out of the legal system.[31] They remain unresolved, in the sense that the courts are not called upon to answer them, and in not being provided with the opportunity to provide answers, the courts are also denied the opportunity to experience new versions of Luhmann's third question: the compulsion constantly to develop further doctrine by attempting to reconcile earlier answers to legal questions with new answers and with each other.[32] In Debbie Purdy's case we will see how difficult it is to remove the prosecutor's discretion to prosecute without altering the scope of the criminal law. But, before this, we need to consider how communications about civil disobedience operate within the political system. Can rights, or a general right to civil disobedience, exist within the political system, when it cannot in practice (namely in law's operations as they are communicated) exist within the legal system?

[31] For example, in our case study of Debbie Purdy's case below, Lord Hope's view of the scope of Suicide Act 1961 s2(1) being only provisional, pending a final determination of the matter following a prosecution; further, Lord Phillips' observations on the possibility that assisting someone to commit suicide abroad might actually be murder. Without prosecutions, these matters will remain unresolved legally.

[32] If one regards the ability of courts to re-examine the law to be valuable, perhaps especially if, like Dworkin, this is because it offers the opportunity for law to become more just, then it is counter-productive to urge officials not to prosecute those who break the law. The appropriate place to exercise discretion would be at the sentencing stage.

Civil Disobedience within the Political System

Given the legal difficulties in acknowledging a right to disobey law, a political right to disobey law requires us to consider the possibilities of something being a 'right' within politics that can only be a 'discretion' (not to prosecute) within the legal system. If the political right to disobey the law in question is based on an acceptance that conduct proscribed by law should be allowed, then one would ordinarily expect the political system to react by introducing legislation removing the illegality, and with it, the political right to disobey the law in question. In such situations the political right is only transitory. Nevertheless, there have been situations in which conduct is regarded as acceptable to a degree that makes it meaningful to talk about a political right to undertake the action in question despite the presence of a legal discretion to prosecute. A typical example might be the criminalisation of types of sexual conduct in one century, which have remained 'on the books' when sexual mores have completely changed.

But whilst it may be possible to have a political right to disobey a specific law, albeit that this right would ordinarily be expected to be removed through permissive legislation, a general right to disobey law on moral grounds is far more problematic for the political system. Legislation and constitutions operate, within the political system, as an enormous resource for legitimacy within modern states.[33] They provide a relatively clear, stable way in which to identify collectively binding decisions on a routine basis. To borrow again from Raz, they move politics from discussion about what is to be decided to a stage in which matters have been decided.[34] A political right, based on moral communications, to disobey law, threatens to destabilise this routine basis for establishing collectively binding decisions.

A systems theory analysis of the political system must start from the position that the political system generates legitimacy internally, simply through the stability and predictability of its own operations.[35] Legitimacy within the political system plays the role of justice within the legal system: a formula for contingency.[36] In building new conditional programmes for the making of collectively binding decisions, and generally when making selections from alternatives (contingency) the political system orientates itself using communications which present its decisions to itself as

[33] See our analysis of constitutions and rights in Chapter 6.

[34] In claiming that law which relied on moral communications for its conditional programmes could not really be law, Raz is observing on what the law provides to the legal system, and claiming that this is what makes it law. Soft positivists, who point to examples of law conditioned in exactly this way, are observing that the legal system does not limit what it will recognise as law to what achieves this function for the political system.

[35] See Thornhill, 2006, ch 4, especially 82–88.

[36] Thornhill, 2006, 82, and see Luhmann, 1967.

justified.[37] This obviously involves the utilisation of communications that would be recognised within the education system as moral and/or political philosophy. But the claim that these norms do not simply bestow legitimacy on the political system, like the claim that similar communications cannot bestow justice or legality on the legal system, is a reference to the fact that the selection of such communications is made internally, by the political system itself. This should not lead one to the conclusion that, within either politics or law, such 'moral' communications have no more than an ideological role, that they represent some second order of communication that is somehow less 'real' than other kinds of communication. These communications are used to create conditional programmes, and orientate selections. They also form part of what constitutes an operation (a vote, a resolution, an election, etc) within the system. So, whilst one finds communications that are recognisable within moral philosophy all around the political system (and indeed the legal system), and can observe the operations which such communications execute, one cannot conclude that the system as a whole is the expression of a coherent moral scheme, or that the legitimacy of the political system as a whole, or any of its parts, can be measured by the extent that it expresses particular moral values.[38] Even within conditional programmes that appear to express specific moral values, for example elections as an exercise in democracy, the internal constraints on contingency[39] are always the ability of the system's communications to continue. So, for example, if periodic national elections have become an operation upon which vast numbers of other political communications are premised, then what constitutes the legitimacy of those elections is not the objective value of democracy, but the difficulties of reconfiguring all of the communications that are connected to the communications that constitute those elections. What makes elections 'legitimate' is the fact that they provide the platform for the communications which follow.[40] They decide how the formation of a government will be decided. This does not render the 'democratic' communications around elections irrelevant or meaningless. These communications form part of what makes

[37] 'Legitimacy in the political system is thus a formula with which the political system can consistently and persuasively talk about itself to itself, and then provide itself with a coherent account of what it does and why it does it.' Thornhill 2006, 82; see also King and Thornhill, 2003a, 72–76.

[38] 'The political system does not obtain and utilise legitimacy by conforming to externally deduced norms or obligations. Rather, it secures legitimacy by conferring upon itself a differentiated and contingent form, which allows it to establish a level of predictability *in its own communications*, and so to gain acceptance for itself and, more broadly, to establish its political processes through society as valid and plausible sequences of operations' (Thornhill, 2006, 82).

[39] See Luhmann, 1998.

[40] 'The specific function of politics is fulfilled at the level of concrete interaction because these decisions are made *binding*. A decision is binding whenever, and for whatever reasons, it succeeds in effectively restructuring the expectations of those affected and thus becomes the premise for their future behavior' (Luhmann, 1982, 145).

the results of those elections the 'legitimate' basis for the communications which follow. But one cannot start from an acknowledgement that elections are self-observed within the political system through communications which make reference to democracy and conclude that an exposure of the limited opportunities for the expression of choice represented by national elections renders those elections illegitimate, or even 'less' legitimate. An illegitimate election is one that fails to decide how the government will be decided.

This understanding of the nature of legitimacy poses problems for moral and political theories that seek to ascribe the legitimacy of legal and political systems to the presence or absence of particular values. Consider, for example, a theory like that of Rawls,[41] who seeks to locate the justifications for civil disobedience within the values of a 'nearly just' society. Examined from a systems theory perspective, the political values of a nearly just society are an internal construction of that society's political system; through what communications, referring to what values, does that society's political system seek to describe itself as a totality? Self-descriptions are not merely 'ideology'. They orientate selections made within the system. But having identified the values expressed within a political system's self-description, one cannot then conclude that a critique of that system's operations, based on these values, will change any particular operations within the system. For a system to change its self-description, and the same applies at the lower level of self-observation, it must find alternative ways to communicate about itself that still allow its communications to continue. What then are the problems for a political system of communications which acknowledge a right to disobey law?

Once again, Raz's writings are useful here. Raz discusses the impossibility for a 'liberal' society of recognising a political right to disobey law.[42] For Raz, this forms part of the logic of political rights within such a society. He distinguishes claiming to do something which is right from claiming to have a right to do something. The latter is different, since the scope of action covered by such a right must include the freedom to do what is in fact wrong. So, to give his example, the right of freedom of speech is not simply the right to say what is correct, but also what is incorrect. This is what makes the right meaningful when asserted against those who disagree with what you say. He concludes from this that the right to disobey law cannot be a political right. The existing political rights establish one's right to do wrong, and one cannot then claim a right to do further wrongs outside these parameters. In the alternative, if one regards the current collection of political rights as incorrect, one can disobey the law, in order to put pressure on the political authorities to amend political rights to achieve a

[41] 1971.
[42] 2009, ch 14, 'A Right to Dissent? I. Civil Disobedience'.

correct configuration.[43] But one is not in this situation claiming a general right to do what is wrong, one is simply claiming the specific political right, or rights, that currently exist are wrong, and ought to be reformed.

Whilst Raz articulates this problem in terms of the nature of political rights and liberalism, systems theory suggests that the issue goes much deeper. The first problem for the political system, like any functioning social system, is to maintain its differentiation from the rest of society. Thus, for example, if we describe everything which is contingent within society, and which requires choice, as 'political', then there is no distinction between politics and economics, law, etc. The political system, like any other system, has to identify which communications, and which choices, belong to itself. In modern societies, the political system has identified the communications, and choices, which belong to itself through the application of its code: government and opposition.[44] Through the application of this code the political system constitutes the alternatives that it is able to select.[45] Many different kinds of phenomena are coded in this manner: parties, persons, and policies. The political system thus creates both its own choices, and the manner (votes, referendums, prerogatives, delegation) by which those choices are made. Law has played a central role in this process. Not only is a large part of the political system involved in selecting which laws shall apply to the rest of society, but the political system has also selected which laws shall apply to itself.[46] This results in many of the bases for its own further selections being grounded in legal communications. For example, the details of elections can be given permanence, and predictability, through being enacted within a Representation of the People Act. The most dramatic example of this process is the creation of written constitutions and Bills of Rights. But mundane examples, such as the ability of legislatures to create institutions, and to allocate power to them

[43] Zwiebach, 1975, for example, argues for civil disobedience as a legitimate response to a state's breach of one's political rights.

[44] Luhmann identified the first code of the political system as governing/governed, which served to identify those entitled to exercise power and make collectively binding decisions. This code was superseded, within democracies, by the code government/opposition. Government makes its decisions between the status quo and change (no reform/reform). Its rejected alternatives constitute opposition. Within democracies, the application of this coding has both generated and been stabilised by political parties, which define themselves and their policies in contradistinction to each other. Elections are a conditional programme for identifying which party henceforth constitutes government, and which opposition. (See King and Thornhill 2003, 70–72 and 117–20.)

[45] 'This code is a binary matrix through which the political system decides which elements in its environment are relevant to politics, and then communicates with itself about its decisions over these elements' (Thornhill 2007, 504).

[46] This statement is not an assertion that politics determines law's selections. Politics generates communications that it can expect the legal system to select. This can also be described as a second coding of political communications by law: see King and Thornhill, 2003, 109. For our more extended analysis, see Chapter 6.

through statutes, are just as important.[47] Thus at the same time as the legal and political systems become differentiated from each other, they also mutually support each other's operations; a relationship which Luhmann described as structural coupling. This does not mean that the two systems simply duplicate each other's communications and meanings. So, for example, it does not mean that political rights and legal rights have the same meaning. Whilst written constitutions with Bills of Rights may increase the correspondence of legal and political rights, the two operate in different manners. Both orientate system communications. As Raz notes, political rights organise communications about the acceptable limits of political action. Meanwhile legal rights, to the extent that they are more than the accumulation of legal decisions, orientate the making of further legal decisions. And they can obviously diverge so, for example, the scope of what, within the political system, might be understood by reference to a right to freedom of speech, can be compared to the bundle of legal rights that restrict speech and publication.

To contemplate a political right of civil disobedience, we have to examine two sets of possibilities. First is the ability of the political system to recognise alternatives outside of those which it has already constructed for itself applying the code government and opposition. Can there be an alternative to the alternative? Secondly, can the political system both legitimate itself using the legal system, and communicate about politics in terms of a right, for political reasons, to disobey law? We will begin by looking at the second question. Legitimacy, as argued above, is not something that is externally bestowed on the political system, but rather something that it generates through its own operations. So this second question requires us to consider the political system's ability both to construct itself, through operations that rely upon legal communications (as in the earlier example of Representation of the People Acts) and to acknowledge a political right to disobey the law.

From a systems theory perspective, the problem for the political system of acknowledging a right to disobey law is primarily an issue of 'redundancy'.[48] If legality has come to form part of the communications that bestow legitimacy on collectively binding decisions, then the political system cannot acknowledge the right to disobey the law with regard to such decisions with-

[47] Luhmann claims that the modern political system (particularly those of welfare states) creates a triadic internal division of itself into politics, administration and the public, so that its responses to itself (eg politics reacting to the public) become more complex, and thus more suited to its more complex but unreachable external environment. Within this division, administration is the subsystem which most completely transmits its decisions through the medium of law (see Luhmann, 1990, also Thornhill, 2006, 89–93).

[48] To refresh the reader's memory following the discussion in the previous Chapter: this is a term within systems theory that has a technical rather than a literal meaning, referring to communications that stay in place and provide the necessary context for more complex meanings (and, at times, changes or variety in meaning).

out finding alternative communications which allow its operations to continue. This is not a claim that legality determines the legitimacy of a political decision. To claim this would be to confuse the political system with the legal system. The fact that something is coded legal (it is legally valid) provides a platform for other legal communications which depend on this coding. In a similar manner, the fact that something is legitimate (that it is collectively binding) forms a platform for further political operations. There is a fundamental difference between legality as a code, and legality as a communication which is utilised to account, within another system, for the application of another code. There can be no third value between legal and illegal within the legal system. By contrast, within the political system, self-observations (communications) about the application of its code (government/opposition) can draw on legality to account for its decisions. This raises the possibility that decisions within the political system will not automatically be legitimate even though they are coded by the legal system as legal, and that that they will not necessarily be illegitimate even though they are coded by the legal system as illegal.[49]

To acknowledge these possibilities does not establish how significant they are. For a start, one has to remember that the coding of these two systems does not necessarily coincide temporally. So, for example, a coding of a political decision as illegal may take place many months, or years, after the decision occurred. In the meantime, many political communications may have occurred on the basis of the legitimacy of the now imputed operation. One cannot presume that the coding of this decision by the legal system as illegal will be capable of reversing all of the operations within the political system that have followed from it. And, in that sense, the legitimacy of the political decision cannot be determined by its current status as legal or illegal within the legal system. One needs to accept that acts of civil disobedience, and even revolution, may convey legitimacy upon operations within the political system. But this kind of possibility does not address the issue of civil disobedience as a right within the political system. For rights, as communications within the political system, are self-observations. Starting from the premise that the code of the political system, like that of any other system, is simply a binary distinction,[50] the system constitutes itself by the application of this code and communications which account for that application. Rights are such self-observations. As such, when one asks about the possibilities of existence for a general right of civil disobedience, one is asking whether the operations of the political system can generate self-observations that take this form. Will such self-observations

[49] So the state, which Luhmann argues is the self-description of the modern political system (its communications identify the state as itself, and the objects of state action as its environment), cannot be limited to what is legal. This is in contrast to the analysis of a legal theorist such as Kelsen.

[50] We explore this more fully in the next Chapter.

provide a stable basis for further observations (thereby contributing to the system's redundancy, as well as adding to its variety), or will they rather undermine the ability to make considerable numbers of routine political operations? If the latter situation applies, then whilst there may be plenty of occasions when actions that are illegal may provide a legitimate basis for political operations, this will always remain as 'exceptional', and will not generate self-observations that take the form of a political right to act illegally for good moral/political reasons.

Political rights can, normally, become exported to and reconstituted within the legal system as legal ones. With all the usual qualifications necessitated by an understanding of politics and law as separate systems each of which recursively selects their own communications and establishes their own meanings (which are never therefore the same), we can see, for example, that a political right to free speech can exist as both a political and a legal right. As a constitutional right, with a dual existence within the legal and political system, free speech has an existence within each system that supports its existence within the other. Law constrains what can be said in contravention of free speech within the political sphere. It gives stability to the political right and gives that right additional concrete expression to that which the political system, left to itself, could produce. Within the legal system, the right to free speech represents a version of politics that the legal system is able to process. Unlike so much of the political system, a constitutional right, like the right of free speech, is something that the legal system can use to organise its own version of the political system – the legally relevant part. Like other constitutional rights, this right brings the political system into the legal system to be organised as a limited and inter-related set of decisions, arguments, and values.

There are some who regret the reconstitution of political rights as legal rights, regarding the stabilising and concretisation resulting from this process as an undesirable stultification of the political process.[51] Other reservations relate the consequences of increasing the ability of unelected judges to influence the political system, through the interpretation of legal rights in general and constitutional rights (which can trump legislation) in particular. But a more usual approach to rights, and certainly that exhibited more generally within the political system, is a desire to see political rights enacted as legal ones. Following Luhmann's own analysis of the political system, as a system that produces collectively binding decisions, one can see how the legal system, through the device of legislation, offers the political system a hugely important basis on which to stabilise its own opera-

[51] See Griffiths, 1979 and Poole, 2007. For a more recent example, see Christodoulidis, 1998. Christodoulidis takes his standpoint in response to an autopoietic analysis of politics and law. In addition, radical feminist theorists such as MacKinnon question the benefits of incorporating women's political demands into law, given their view of the legal system as inherently male (see our analysis of social movements below).

tions, and motivate its actors. Whilst the political system is not limited to institutions such as legislatures or the executive, but operates wherever collective decisions are made via communications that code in terms of government (what has been collectively decided) and opposition (the alternatives), legislation provides the political system with a particularly important aspect of its self-constructed environment. For the political system, legislation is an output – the creation of something outside itself (simple recognition that the substance of legislation will be applied and interpreted in a process that is not in itself political, but rather legal). As such, it gives meaning and motivation to large numbers of political actors who wish to effect change in the world. One can so easily list all the disappointments that face such actors.[52] Those who look beyond the symbolic values of changing the law to the further effects which such changes might induce within other parts of society face all the problems debated within the huge literatures on regulation (and its failures), law in action (and its unintended effects), etc. And even symbolic gains can be reversed after short periods, especially within democracies with finely balanced political parties. But one still has to consider the consequences of decoupling politics from law. Whatever the level of disappointment associated with political communications aimed to reform the world via the medium of legislation, the alternative position, to reach collectively binding decisions without seeking to incorporate those decisions into law, seems even less likely to motivate political actors. And alongside the motivation factor there is also the issue of redundancy (as described above). Legislation provides enormous redundancy to political communication, at least at the present. So much of our political communication is organised around the process of gaining access to offices which allow the incumbent to, among other things, change the law.

Recognising that some rights, such as constitutional rights, have come to have an existence in both the legal and political systems, does not mean that all political rights operate within both systems to the same extent. Those which do not would include aspirational rights such as rights to health and education. Whilst some of these rights have been incorporated into documents that legal systems will take cognisance of, such as charters,[53] the effects of such incorporation within national legal systems are generally limited to aids to interpretation of domestic legal provisions.[54] Nevertheless, the political system can process communications that take the form of assertions of aspirational rights, and, at least to a limited extent, do so by

[52] And, for further analysis, see Chapter 7.

[53] For example, the UN Covenant on Economic, Social and Cultural Rights adopted in 1966, and 'in force' since 1976, which has set the parameters for these aspirational rights.

[54] And there are rights claimed within political systems, such as a right to general equality in the ownership of property, that have no counterpart in the legal system, and limited existence as communications within the political system too.

having them recognised, in turn, as legal rights. Thus, for the moment at least, much of the effort of the political system will be taken up with attempting to turn political interests, values and rights into legal rights.

It is against this background of what might be termed the 'normal' relationship between political and legal rights that we need to consider the nature of the right to disobey law. Whilst all rights have a different existence within the political and legal systems, the right to disobey law, if acknowledged as a political right, could not be exported into the legal system. Our analysis of the legal system suggests that when the legal system acknowledges a stable right to disobey a particular legal provision the status of that provision, as law, becomes problematic, leading to a reformulation of the law which dissolves the right to disobey. A general right to disobey law, framed in terms of ethical and moral considerations, would operate as a formula which destabilised a great number of legal communications initially, and generated litigation, leading in turn to juridification and a more complex understanding of the law which again would dissolve the right of disobedience. The only place within the legal system where a political right of disobedience is able to operate is in executive discretion, in particular the discretion to prosecute. A right, within politics, to disobey law on moral grounds could only exist as discretion not to prosecute within law. This means that the political right is exercised not with the permanence of legislative change, but with each decision not to prosecute. As discretion, the legal system will not restrain a contrary decision to prosecute. Thus, the content of this political right cannot be stabilised by the reaction of the legal system to behaviour that conflicts with it.

Does one conclude from this analysis that a political system which has an intense dependence on legality cannot incorporate communications which claim a right to disobey the law, and that this inability is not contingent on the ability of that system to be described, or to describe itself, as liberal, authoritarian, etc? Before reaching this conclusion one has to have regard to a distinction which Luhmann has drawn between official power structure and more informal communications. The former 'normally flows from the voter, across political processes, through the administration, to the recipient of these decisions'. This power is exercised 'legally on the basis of competencies'. But there is a countervailing communication process in the opposite direction. The 'eventual recipient of the voters' decisions energetically makes his wishes known through interest groups, the bureaucrats work out the possible decisions for the political realm, and the politicians try to persuade the voters to give their support'. These communications are not expected to reverse or deconstruct communications in the 'dominant' direction. The power which such communications carry is 'exercised informally on the basis of overburdening officials with complexity'.[55] What

[55] All the quotes in this paragraph are taken from Luhmann 1982a, 155–56.

Luhmann is pointing to in these quotations is the difference between the routine manner in which power is carried out through the political system using communications which rely on legality to establish legitimacy and the existence of other communications that challenge the results of the decisions which carry this power, and the fact that these other communications do not operate in the same manner. Can one have communications that cannot be incorporated into the 'official' circulation of political power, which do not provide a routine basis for the making of collectively binding decisions, but still have affects on the political system? And does civil disobedience provide one such example?

Social Movements and Civil Disobedience

> Protest differs from the format of political opposition within a constitutionally ordered democracy. In the latter, opposition is from the start part of the political system. This is exemplified by the fact that it must be ready to take over the government, or to participate in its running, and this has a disciplining effect. One may well engage in rhetoric and electioneering tactics . . . but ultimately one needs to be prepared to represent one's opinions and carry out policies as a government. Those who are protesting refer to ethical principles; and if one has an ethic, the question whether one is in the majority or the minority is of secondary importance. In all these respects, protest does not have to make any concessions. It purports to represent society against its political system. Thus it is not wrong to see the reason for the emergence of new style protest movements within the differentiation, and relative lack of vitality of the political system. The constitution serves to constrain the political system to itself. Protest movements consider this a provocation to provoke.[56]

Apart from the nature of civil disobedience as an operative communication within the political and legal systems, we need to consider a third system, but one which is less easy to describe[57] as a system. The individual who protests does so as an individual, but often as part of a social movement. Such social movements have had significant effects in the modern world.[58] The psychic motivation that might lead an individual intentionally to disobey the law, or challenge the law to conform to their interpretation of what is legitimate or morally acceptable to them, has regularly been incorporated into a social movement, such as the 'civil rights movement', the 'green movement', the 'feminist movement', or the 'peace movement'. Such movements operate through communications that postulate alternatives to

[56] Our translation of Luhmann 1982b, 206.

[57] Such external description is not the necessary condition for the system itself; internal distinctions, distinguishing systems from their environment, its code and programmes, self-observations and self-description, and ways of dealing with time (the relationship between the present and the past, and the present and the future) are such key ingredients.

[58] See Roberts and Garton Ash, 2009; Sunstein, 2003.

current practices. But what are these alternatives? In each case the communicative code upon which the various programmes of the different movements appear to be built is that of alternatives to the status quo (an alternative to the present, which present has generated the conditions that the alternative wishes to differ from).

Here we need to explore a distinction which is usually made at the beginning of analyses of civil disobedience. This distinction suggests that since those who engage in civil disobedience accept the legitimacy of the political system, their motivation is not that of the revolutionary who does not accept that legitimacy. Rather, they are committed in their disobedient activities to a change in law and/or political programme in a particular respect. They are proposing an alternative. However, it is not possible for such movements to distinguish the form of the protest, some particular act of disobedience or direct action, and the conditions that generate what is being protested about. For what they are protesting about is the failure of the political system to have selected the issue which informs their protest in a manner which they find acceptable. As such, their protest is inevitably not only for their issue, but also against the political system. The political system generates alternatives, which it codes as government and opposition. Social movements (if not espousing revolutionary goals) express a paradoxical claim: they wish for an alternative to the alternative.

Protest involves more than disagreement. It communicates resistance. It has to communicate this both to the individuals who need to be motivated to join the protest, and to the subsystem (politics, law, mass media, or the economy) that it is protesting against. One can see that in communicating resistance to the political system, social movements rely heavily on the mass media. The mass media provide the political system with communications through which it can construct its version of 'the public', and then respond to it: 'what the public want', 'what the public understand' 'getting our message across', etc. This ensures that the mass media have effects upon the political system, even though there is no direct and predictable correlation between media reporting and political reactions. In turn, the presence of the mass media influences the nature of protest. Events are created for news coverage which would not occur if the media did not exist. Resistance can be communicated within the media through drama, via the presence of large numbers, or by undertaking exploits which involve high personal risk. It can also be communicated though conflict.

Civil disobedience represents conflict and thus allows disagreement to be communicated as protest. In order for this to succeed, the acts of protesters have to be understood as breaches of the law. As such, there is an element of contradiction in the communications involved. For those protesting, civil disobedience is a claim that their acts of law breaking are justified by the cause which they are protesting about. But, to achieve civil disobedience, they need subsystems of communication, most particularly law, not to accept this claim. If the legal system accepted that the actions taken were justified, and concluded that they were not illegal, then the acts undertaken would not amount to civil disobedience. This does not mean that those committing civil disobedience will not engage lawyers and may seek to avoid punishment, but it does mean that, at the moment when the acts chosen are undertaken, the protesters must have some confidence that they will be coded as illegal within the legal system, or they will not communicate resistance by undertaking them. Similar considerations apply to the political system. As we have argued, the legal system makes space for civil disobedience through the creation of discretion. At this point, it can export the decision whether to prosecute or not to the political system.[59] In order to commit acts of civil disobedience, and communicate resistance, those who commit such acts need the political system not to orientate itself through communications that accept the protesters' claims, or at least not immediately. For example, it is difficult to communicate resistance to the political system through the media by choosing to breach a law which is known never to be enforced. The expectation that breaches of the law will be investigated and prosecuted, and that sentences will follow, is part of what, within the media, makes a deliberate breach of the law a communication of resistance. Protest would be undermined should either the political or legal systems adopt the communications of civil disobedience within themselves. Within law, it would result in the act of disobedience ceasing to be illegal, that is, disobedient. Within politics, it would no longer be legitimate to commence a prosecution. Both developments would undermine civil disobedience as a form of protest. Conversely, it is clearly demonstrable that, since neither the legal nor the political system has responded to civil disobedience communications by incorporating these communications into their own operations, that is what has allowed civil disobedience to communicate protest.

This is not an argument that civil disobedience has no effect on the political system. Clearly, we have many examples of civil disobedience campaigns contributing to political change, such as the civil rights movement in the US, the Suffragette movement in the UK, and Gandhi's campaign of civil disobedience in pre-independence India. But protest, as part of what Luhmann identifies as an informal countervailing system of communication, cannot be incorporated into routine operations by which the political system constructs legitimacy for the enormous number of technical decisions which make up the modern state.[60] Neither the ethical argument on which civil disobedience is based, nor the fact that it is communicated as resistance, provides an alternative basis for the legitimacy

[59] In particular, the subsystem within the political system of administration.

[60] Or rather, which make up the subsystem of administration, within the political system; the 'state' being a self-description of the political system whereby it describes itself as an entity distinguishable from the rest of society.

of these decisions. In that sense, the alternative that the protest movements offer, an alternative to the alternatives constructed within the political system, remains something to which the political system cannot respond. Instead, this countervailing form of communication operates as pressure on officials. Officials who have decisions to make (such as whether to prosecute or not) can have regard to the communications of civil disobedience in making their decisions. But what they cannot do is justify such decisions by adopting the same communications as the protesters. It is, for example, legitimate for a prosecutor to prosecute, or not. Legality establishes the discretion and at the same time the terms under which it must be exercised, such as 'in the public interest'. This allows decisions not to prosecute to be legitimate, on the basis that they are legal, without the necessity of recognising or incorporating the ethical arguments of protesters as part of the basis for the decision. This allows civil disobedience to affect the particular decision, as countervailing communications, without disturbing the role played by legality, as a basis for legitimacy within the political system.

The other place in which 'protest' can be incorporated into the political system is, as we have argued, in that system's construction of 'the public', and its reliance on the mass media for this construction. Positive reporting on acts of civil disobedience puts pressure on political parties to consider whether or not to accept the reforms demanded by those committing such acts, or other forms of protest, without their having to adopt the communication of civil disobedience, the latter being incompatible with the operations by which those reforms will be put into effect: legality.

Civil Disobedience within the Legal and Political Systems – A Case Study (Debbie Purdy's Case)

Euthanasia is a controversial issue, which generates communications in many systems. Within the legal system, the basis for prohibition is (relatively) clear: killing someone for good moral reasons (mercy killing) is (normally) murder, which often carries a mandatory life sentence, or manslaughter (in cases of diminished responsibility, provocation, or other defences) which carries no mandatory sentence, but for which one can often be sentenced for up to life imprisonment. Assisting someone to kill themselves is an offence in the UK under section 2(1) of the Suicide Act 1961, for which one can be sentenced for a term of imprisonment of up to 14 years. In his excellent book, *Euthanasia, Ethics and the Law: From Conflict to Compromise*, Richard Huxtable documents the apparent inconsistency between the condemnation of euthanasia which these legal provisions represent, and the treatment of those who engage in, or assist, 'mercy killing'. There is no recognition, from the principal actors in the legal system (most notably judges) that these offences are anything other than serious, and certainly no admission that the condition of the victims, or their relationship to the defendants, could generate a right to carry out the actions which have brought them to the attention of prosecuting authorities. But, at the same time, acts of 'mercy killing' are routinely responded to by a failure to prosecute, or the acceptance of a plea of diminished responsibility[61] on the basis of evidence that would not be acceptable with other kinds of intentional killings, and where conviction results in 'punishment' which is commonly either a suspended sentence or a short sentence or none at all. This seems to us to represent exactly the kind of pressure on officials which Luhmann identified with social protests. Here we have behaviour that is altered in response to moral arguments about the 'right' to carry out acts which are illegal, without those involved officially adopting the communications to which they are so obviously responding.

These kind of discretionary practices cause no particular problem for the legal system. The legal system identifies 'the law', with the prohibition. The practices of non-enforcement, charging with lesser offences, or giving small or no punishments can be absorbed. In some of these situations no justifications are given, whilst in others the justifications refer to the particular circumstances of the defendant (their emotional state, etc) rather than an acceptance that they had a right to disobey the law. The attempt to present the routine as an exception, and the failure to articulate what appears to be the underlying reason for these decisions can be observed from outside the system (as Huxtable has so clearly demonstrated) without causing the legal system itself any great difficulty. But can one go the next step, and recognise that those who commit these offences have a right not to be prosecuted or punished, because of the moral reasons for their actions?

This was the issue in the *Purdy* case.[62] Debbie Purdy, suffering from multiple sclerosis, a terminal and increasingly debilitating disease, has a devoted husband, Mr Puente, who is willing to assist her to commit suicide at a time of her choosing by helping her to travel to a country where assisted suicide is legal. She was concerned that, if he provided this assistance, he could face prosecution under section 2(1). Ms Purdy wished to assert that she had a right, based on considerations of personal autonomy, to call on others to assist her in terminating her life at a moment of her choosing. Whilst this right did not mean that she could require someone to assist her if they did not choose to do so, it should, she argued, allow those who are willing to assist her to die to do so without punishment or fear thereof.

[61] On the relation between diminished responsibility and prosecution for manslaughter rather than murder, see Mackay, 2004; and on the new diminished responsibility defence in the Coroners and Justice Act 2009, see Mackay, 2010.

[62] *R (on the application of Purdy) (Appellant) v Director of Public Prosecutions (Respondent)* [2009] UKHL 45, on appeal from the Court of Appeal [2009] EWCA Civ 92; [2009] 1 Cr App R 32.

The House of Lords judges who heard Ms Purdy's appeal could point to no basis on which it was authorised to overturn the statutory provision, or to insert exceptions into an offence which appeared to them to have been drawn up with the deliberate intention of allowing none. So it seemed that if he assisted his wife to die, Mr Puente would be breaking the law. But the House of Lords judges, relying on observations made by the European Court of Human Rights when dismissing a similar earlier application by Diane Pretty, shifted their focus from articulating whether his actions would amount to a breach of the law, to a consideration of his right to learn whether he would face prosecution for disobeying the law. The House of Lords judges ordered the Director of Public Prosecutions (DPP) to issue a statement of guidance, appropriate to persons in the position of Mr Puente, stating what factors he would take into account when deciding whether or not to prosecute.[63] In reaching this decision, the judges in the House of Lords held that the current general guidance was inadequate.[64] While their Lordships were not proposing to draft the DPP's guidance themselves, they were applying what might be called a 'fitness for purpose' test, the purpose in question being the ability of persons in Mr Puente's position to have a clear idea of the risk they face of being prosecuted if they choose to disobey section 2.

The DPP's practice of not prosecuting those who accompany persons to Switzerland to commit suicide had already indicated that Mr Puente only faced a low risk of prosecution, so one might view the requirement to issue specific guidance on the factors which he takes into account when exercising his discretion as no more than a device to make this information more available. But what the DPP is required to publish is not simply information, but guidance pursuant to a statutory power, which is, as the House of Lords recognised, a form of law. And, if guidance is meant to guide, it will be difficult for the DPP to issue it and then not to follow it. So, for example, where a person's situation exhibits all of the factors which point against prosecution, and none of the factors which point in favour, can the DPP

[63] The justification for this was first their acceptance that Ms Purdy's Art 8 human rights under the European Convention of Human Rights required that she know with certainty the risk involved, for persons in her husband's position willing to accompany her to Switzerland where she could lawfully be assisted to die, as to whether he could expect to face prosecution for his role, and second the duty of the DPP, under the Prosecution of Offences Act 1985 s10, to issue guidance to the Crown Prosecution Service on how to exercise the discretion to prosecute.

[64] Certainly there are some statements in the judgment which seek to avoid this conclusion. Lord Hope, for example, having written a judgment criticising the inadequacy of the current code of guidance to assist persons in Mr Puente's position, included an assertion that the DPP not only has the task of deciding exactly which circumstances will be an exception to liability to prosecution under s2(1), but that the decision whether or not to prosecute must ultimately be a matter for him. This sounds as if the discretion of the prosecutor remains unchanged: she/he can prosecute or not as she/he sees fit, and the DPP can issue such guidance to the CPS as he sees fit. Lord Hope also insisted that the law, by which he meant s2, had remained unaltered by this judgment. However, these statements are rather belied by the rest of his judgment, and those of the other Law Lords.

simply assert that, nevertheless, he favoured prosecution? Or will such cases require him to identify what particular circumstance make this prosecution acceptable, which will represent an amendment to his guidance. And what will such developments represent except yet another example of the process described by Luhmann, which we quoted earlier: a doctrine of exemption based on moral considerations which will inevitably 'evolve into a system of definitions and rules – what else could a jurist do with them?'[65]

The *Purdy* decision has the potential to disturb political communications about the right, or rather the absence of any right, to assist a suicide. The House of Lords in its parliamentary capacity had only recently debated whether the law should be altered to allow this, so that relatives and friends could assist those who might wish to commit suicide to travel to Switzerland without committing an offence, but the tabled provision which would have had this effect was defeated. Those in the majority wished to maintain the illegality of the practice in order to avoid any suggestion that some forms of human life are less worthy of protection than others. But at the same time, none of those who spoke against legalising this form of assistance wanted any of those who have provided it to be prosecuted. For these political actors, the unqualified legal prohibition against assisting suicide operated as a communication that there cannot be any right to take life. For them, an unqualified prohibition could co-exist with an acceptance that none of those who committed this offence in order to relieve the suffering of their loved ones 'ought' to be punished. Through this parliamentary procedure, and despite the radically different views that had been expressed (and the radically different views that could continue to be expressed after the debate), it had nevertheless been 'decided' that there was no 'right' to assist in the intentional taking of life. Deciding the legality of the matter was, as is quite normal within so much of the political system, treated as synonymous with deciding, collectively, what exists as a right. But the matter could not so easily have been treated as 'decided' if the legal system was expected to allow the issue to continue to be re-argued, through a doctrine which acknowledges a right to disobey law generally, or even just this law, on moral grounds.

The *Purdy* decision raises real doubts as to what has been 'decided' by Parliament regarding assisted suicide. The judges recognised that there were implicit categories of cases which were not being prosecuted by the DPP, and required him to make them explicit, in the form of guidance, which they recognised as 'law'. This addition adds something to the situation contemplated by those debating the amendment. It provides a legal category, or doctrine, which may operate to turn the practice of non-prosecution

[65] Luhmann, 1988. The need for the DPP to justify these exceptions, and the existence of such justified exceptions as reformulations, meets this description, aside from the possibilities of judicial review, and claims that prosecutions which conflict with the guidance are an abuse of process. See Nobles and Schiff, 2010.

(something the political actors approve of) into a legal right not to be prosecuted. As the judges deciding the earlier case of Diane Pretty were aware, allowing prosecutors to develop specific categories, based on moral or other criteria, in which they will not prosecute, undermines the ability of Parliament to 'decide' the law and, within the political system, to collectively determine what is 'right'. (Paradoxically, allowing them to operate using broad and undefined communications, such as 'public interest', does not prevent Parliament from determining what is legal, and right.)

Within the legal system, and assuming that the courts are at some stage called upon to decide on the right of a defendant who complies with the guidelines not to be prosecuted, we can expect one of two possibilities. If the court recognises that any person could have a right not to be prosecuted, then it will begin the process of articulating when that right will, or will not, arise. What was formerly a matter of discretion has now become juridified. As this occurs, then the understanding of what it means, within the legal system, for conduct to be criminal will, we suggest, become an amalgamation of the statutory provisions and the DPP's guidance. Within the political system, one can expect an increase in the complexity of parliamentary procedures. Just as the momentous decision of *Pepper v Hart*[66] led to a constant process of attempting to get ministers to make a statement about the intended effects of legislation, the development of doctrine which creates rules about the exercise of a prosecutor's discretion can be expected to become part of what is taken into account, within Parliament, when it attempts to use legality in order to decide what is 'right'. With these developments, the right to disobey the law opened momentarily by the decision in *Purdy* will quickly close. The alternative, which involves less change (and more redundancy) is that a future court decides that the DPP's specific guidelines do not establish a right to avoid prosecution, as they do not exclude the DPP's general power to prosecute whenever he feels that this is in the public interest. This development would restore the DPP's ability to decide how to respond to persons who give moral reasons for disobeying the law. But this will be an ability to respond to civil disobedience which does not require him to engage with the moral communications that generate that disobedience.

Conclusion

This Chapter has explored the difficulties and complexities of the communications set out in moral and political philosophy on civil disobedience from forming a stable part of either the legal system or the political system,

[66] [1992] UKHL 3. Momentous in terms of the consequences for the way in which subsequent legislation would be interpreted.

viz, the difficulties for both systems in acknowledging a right to disobey law. Within the legal system, the move from discretion to prosecute to a situation of no right to prosecute recognises the justification to disobey law but only as part of a process which will dissolve the ability to convey a legal meaning that the action complained of is illegal. Within the political system, the use of legality as a means to communicate what is legitimate results in a paradoxical situation in which illegality is being utilised to communicate that something is wrong, whilst the legality of prosecution is treated as insufficient to legitimate decisions to prosecute.

Individuals can exhibit attitudes towards law that might be called partial respect, in which they treat some legal duties as reasons for action but not others. But as our discussion of a right to disobey law shows, they have considerable difficulties in making legal communications in keeping with such attitudes. Whilst an individual's respect for the legal system may be partial, in that they can pick and choose which parts they regard as providing reasons for actions, their participation within the legal system is not. To make legal communications individuals have to utilise the store of communications currently available within the legal system to carry out the desired legal operations. If the legal system does not offer communications which allow a claim to a right to disobey to be acknowledged, so that it instead constantly translates such communications as claims to re-interpret the law, or admissions that an action is illegal which exclude the possibility that it can also be legal, or requests that those charged with discretion over prosecution, sentencing and conviction exercise that discretion so as to avoid the claimant suffering penalties, then we can say that there is no right to disobey the law. And this restriction covers both those who administer its courts and those who appear before them. Whilst one might expect at least some judges to be familiar with moral and political theory, and thus to be quite capable of understanding claims that some legal duties are morally wrong, there is no way for this 'knowledge' to be translated into a recognition that disobedience to law could be legally correct.[67]

[67] On the general difficulties facing judges who wish to incorporate their personal beliefs into their legal judgments, see Chapter 2.

4

Understanding Legal Pluralism

Whereas, as we have shown in the previous Chapter, it is highly problematic for individuals to claim that they have a right to disobey the law, there is an alternative way in which claims about legal obligations can be thought to represent different understandings of what the law demands. The modern form in which such claims are exhibited is through the notion of 'legal pluralism'.[1] This notion approaches directly the question of what law is, which is implicit in most self-observation about law whether articulated within courts, in political forums, or other settings (including those representing different cultural priorities). In this Chapter we consider whether systems theory has any potential to increase our understanding of legal pluralism and, briefly, the complementary notion of legal globalisation.

As with the idea that one might have a right to disobey the law, the notion of legal pluralism (and that of legal globalisation) is also problematic. Why might this be so both for socio-legal studies in particular and jurisprudence in general? Those who have developed this notion are motivated by the need to move beyond essentialist and functionalist conceptions of law towards a socio-legal concept of law unencumbered by the limitations that might arise from its associations with the nation state and the activities of legal officials, but to do so without losing the ability to study law as a separate social formation. Indeed, legal pluralism seeks to extend the study of law beyond state and inter-state legal orders to include non-state sourced forms of law.[2] In so doing, it raises the spectre that law ceases to be identifiable as a separate social formation, as the border between the legal and the social is dissolved. Phrases such as 'law from below',[3] 'an oppositional postmodern understanding of law',[4] 'law between

[1] There are alternative phrases for similar notions, such as 'legal culture', that explore similar issues; see, for example, Chiba, 1993.

[2] Early motivation for such extension reflected criticism of the exclusion of forms of law from the 'imperialism' of Western state-centred approaches (for background, see Fitzpatrick, 1984; Merry, 1988; Chiba, 1993), while recent motivation (perhaps a second wave of legal pluralists) also reflects the need for inclusion of forms of law that processes of 'digitalisation, privatisation and globalisation' seem to entail (Teubner, 2004, 3; for an earlier statement of this more recent motivation, concentrating on *lex mercatoria*, see Teubner, 1997; for a later and more extended statement, see Teubner and Korth, 2012).

[3] Merry *et al*, 2010.

[4] Santos, 2002, ch 5.

the global and the local',[5] or 'legal hybridization'[6] tend to reverse the hierarchical assumptions implicit in much legal practice and scholarship, and phrases such as 'the more the merrier'[7] or those applying the distinction between 'law as one' and 'law as many'[8] imply that law can only be captured in a combination of conceptions rather than a single conception, and in a range of linguistic forms rather than any single form.[9] A concept of law unencumbered by its associations with the nation state and the activities of legal officials can easily lose the ability to understand and thereby study law as a separate formation (as occurs when law is identified with multiple social norms, general accounts of social control, strongly held commitments, cultural conceptions, etc). Indeed, once one moves beyond the study of law as state law, what prevents each observer, or each system, from identifying different criteria for what constitutes law, according to their own observational standpoints, research objectives, or system priorities? The problem that then arises, which appears to be a feature of legal-pluralism-motivated studies of legal orders, is that these studies tend not to build into anything like a coherent and integrated body of knowledge, and are subject to system-specific observations.[10]

In his essay 'Two Faces of Janus: Re-thinking Legal Pluralism'[11] Gunther Teubner claimed that modern systems theory could be used to inform our understanding of legal pluralism including non-state forms of law[12] without suffering from the problems identified above. But, as he admitted himself, this is a surprising claim to make. The features which systems theory attributes to the legal system – that it is autonomous, reflexive, and self-productive – have some instructive plausibility when one accepts that law is restricted to state legal systems; but the one tenet which unites those who argue for legal pluralism is the insistence that state law is not the only form of, or model from which one can establish, legality. However, Teubner recognised this, and was directly seeking to address the slippery slope

[5] Goodale, 2007.

[6] Santos, 2006.

[7] Melissaris, 2004.

[8] Davies, 2005.

[9] Chiba, 1998.

[10] Thus, for example, Griffiths' classic statement of what legal pluralism is disputes all of the general definitions and theoretical understandings from those who had engaged in substantive analysis that appear to have been motivated by legal pluralism concerns: Griffiths, 1986. There is certainly neither one concept of legal pluralism, nor wide agreement about its value, or the value of the 'legal pluralists project' or how the empirical studies that it is engaged with are linked to a common theoretical understanding. For a full discussion of these background debates, see Benda-Beckmann, 2002; and for an introduction to the collection of papers by the 'Project Group Legal Pluralism' that try to move this linking forward, see Benda-Beckmann, F and K, 2006.

[11] 1992.

[12] For an earlier formulation described by Teubner as 'social law', see Teubner, 1991. Teubner has more recently offered a number of alternative formulations that reconceptualise legal pluralism issues, for example: 2002; with Fischer-Lescano, 2008; 2012; with Korth, 2012.

which faces legal pluralists when they insist that law is not limited to state law. It is difficult enough to observe and thereby construct an account of the relationship between law and the rest of society when one starts from the assumption that law is indeed limited to state law, or even that state law is the paradigmatic example of law, but once one abandons this position legal pluralism has additional difficulty in identifying any criteria for the legal which can distinguish what is legal from what is not within society, or as others might argue, from studying society as such, rather than law.[13] And seeking to identify law by reference to its functions (social control, dispute resolution, ordering social relations, etc) or its structures (institutions, personnel, norms, rules, etc) has not proved satisfactory.[14] Even where there is consensus on the criteria which should be applied, there is little accord on what follows from their application.

To address these problems, Teubner offered systems theory, which abandons structure or function as the explanation of how society might organise itself to include a distinctly legal subsystem, in favour of communicative codes. This autopoietic version of systems theory views law as one of modern society's functionally differentiated subsystems with each social subsystem characterised as operating through differentiated codes.[15] In common with society's other subsystems, law generates and maintains its separate identity through the application of a unique code: legal/illegal. The economy, the political system, science system, the mass media, and the legal system are distinguished from each other by the different binary codes each is applying. The code of law is legal/illegal;[16] that of the mass media is information/non-information,[17] for science it is true/false, for the economy payment/non-payment, and for politics government/opposition.[18] Teubner claimed that this approach 'delineates clearly the "legal" from other types of social action':

[13] This is explicitly stated by Kelsen as his criticism of Ehrlich's notion of 'living law': 1945, 28.

[14] This critique is fully developed in Tamanaha's non-essentialist legal pluralism, 2001; for a shorter account, 2000.

[15] Crucially for this version of systems theory, differentiated codes are what maintain subsystems' separate identity, not their functions. Function arises only at the level of society as a system, as a modern differentiated society depends on separate subsystems carrying out their respective functions in order for that society to maintain itself. Whilst a subsystem will include an internal reference within the system to society as an encompassing system, and its role within society, this will not maintain its separate identity. In the case of law, its function at the level of society is the generation of normative expectations (see Niklas Luhmann, 2004, ch 3), in the sense that this is what modern society needs from law in order to maintain its differentiation and current levels of complexity. But this does not mean that law is the only system that generates normative expectations, or that an internal reference to this function would maintain law's identity. On the difference between function, performance and (self) reflection, see Luhmann, 1977.

[16] See Luhmann, 1992, 145.

[17] See Luhmann, 2000.

[18] For a short account of the coding of each of these systems respectively, Luhmann, 1989a, chs 12, 10 and 13.

> *Legal pluralism is then defined no longer as a set of conflicting social norms in a given social field but as a multiplicity of diverse communications processes that observe social action under the binary code of legal/illegal.* . . . It is the – implicit or explicit – invocation of the legal code which constitutes phenomena of legal pluralism, ranging from the official law of the state to the unofficial laws of markets and Mafias.[19]

In this Chapter, we explore the nature of the legal code, and how it can be used to observe and study state, inter-state and non-state legal orders with a view to forming a view on Teubner's assertion that systems theory could both clearly delineate the legal from the non-legal within society, and engage with what motivates legal pluralism studies. We start by considering the criticisms of systems theory of one of the leading theorists of legal pluralism in order to understand its potential clearly, and having done so then address the question of how one identifies a subsystem code. Following on from this we have selected a number of issues that illustrate how systems theory might be deployed to engage in legal pluralism study, but recognise that we will only address a few of the many issues that could be considered. We will focus on how systems theory treats the relationship between law, particularly state law and violence (the link between law and the state being, as we have illustrated, a key concern for legal pluralist study); we will consider how systems theory approaches normative pluralism; we will then consider the issue of translation (particularly since legal pluralism confronts very different legal orders operating with their own terminology); finally we will examine how systems theory constructs the differences between modern and pre-modern societies. Each of these issues is of significance to legal pluralism and each, we suggest, can be illuminated by systems theory observations.

Brian Tamanaha's Criticisms of Systems Theory

In his book *A General Jurisprudence of Law and Society* Tamanaha offered what he called a non-essentialist approach to legal pluralism. He set out the case for a conventionalist approach to the identification of the social practices which should be treated as 'law'. He suggested that one should treat as law whatever actors, in sufficient numbers, themselves describe as law.[20] From this starting point, legal pluralism could take the form of comparisons and analyses of different manifestations of these phenomena, recognising that these phenomena often occupy 'the same social field'.[21] As part

[19] 1992, 1451.

[20] '. . . *if sufficient people with sufficient conviction consider something to be "law", and act pursuant to this belief, in ways that have an influence in the social arena*' (Tamanaha, 2001, 167, italics in original).

[21] *Ibid*, 172.

of his argument for this approach to legal pluralism, Tamanaha considered alternatives, including autopoietic systems theory,[22] as developed by Luhmann and Teubner. Tamanaha contended that Teubner had specifically offered systems theory as something which could address two of the major weaknesses underlying much writing on legal pluralism: the inability to distinguish legal norms from other kinds of social norms, and the difficulties of attempting to attribute any unique functions to law. But, whilst recognising that systems theory could offer 'interesting insights', Tamanaha felt that it contained several debilitating drawbacks, which he outlined and criticised.[23] He did so by introducing a hypothetical conversation,[24] and then proceeding to consider how systems theory would analyse it. The conversation addresses a situation that might arise in relation to state law. We reproduce that conversation here, both to begin to explain what is pluralistic about systems theory, and to assess the strength of Tamanaha's objections to it.

> Smith: 'The value of NEWCORP's stock will increase by at least 50%, and perhaps by 100%, when this takeover bid is made public tomorrow. If we buy now we will make millions.'
>
> Jones: 'You're right, we could easily double our assets. But it's illegal, and we might get caught. We could go to prison.'
>
> Smith: 'Sure it's illegal, but the risk of being prosecuted is small. We'll be rich if we do it, so it's worth taking the chance.'
>
> Jones: 'Okay, we probably won't go to prison, but it's still illegal, and furthermore it's immoral. It's wrong to break the law, and even if it weren't illegal it would be wrong and unfair to everyone else to use this information. Crime and immorality never pay.'

Systems theory considers modern society to contain separate subsystems of communication: the economic system, the political system, mass media, science, the education system, the legal system, etc. Each system is autopoietic: it forms its elements (communications) from itself (those of its communications which are available). Each subsystem's communications apply a code unique to that subsystem. In the case of law, the code applied is legal/illegal. Tamanaha assumes that systems theory would treat this conversation as part of the legal system, or rather, that it would treat parts of this conversation as part of the legal system: those communications that are creating legal meanings through the application of the code legal/illegal. He is also able to diagnose the other systems which are being drawn upon (or

[22] Systems theory was the only non-essentialist alternative discussed. Boaventura de Sousa Santos' approach was used to demonstrate the problems with 'essentialist, function-based approaches' (*Ibid*, 181–85).

[23] Tamanaha rehearsed these arguments in 2000, and even earlier in 1993.

[24] 2001, at 189.

participated in) by these two individuals. The opening sentence he attributes to the economy. Smith is anticipating that his payment for shares now will lead to a considerable profit. Jones's response is legal, he is identifying the action as illegal, and identifying possible consequences. At the end of the sequence, Jones is making claims as to the morality of their actions, drawing on communications that are neither legal, nor economic, but are recognisably moral.

Having used his understanding of systems theory to analyse this exchange, Tamanaha questions the benefits of such analysis. First, he believes that systems theory complicates a simple situation: 'What appears to be a rather simple conversation is extraordinarily complex when analysed from an autopoietic standpoint.'[25] Second, one may have difficulty identifying exactly which code is being applied (is Smith's second statement legal, or economic, or both?), which leads one 'to wonder what legal pluralists would gain by travelling down this path'.[26] Third, he believes that the theory is over-inclusive. By identifying the legal system with the application of the code legal/illegal systems theory ends up including communications 'which most people would not consider "law"'.[27] And lastly he feels that systems theory is under-inclusive, at least in relation to state law, as its focus on communication 'eliminates raw physical violence from within the law – thereafter it may at most be considered an effect or consequence of law as communication, or a part of law's environment'.[28] Tamanaha argues that, at least as regards state law, systems theory's approach is deficient if it fails to include 'an analytical apparatus which would include the material power of law as central to its existence while excluding' (in a reference back to his previous objection) 'such marginal phenomena as the private conversation between two individuals contemplating a criminal course of action'.[29]

Starting with Tamanaha's first objection: is this really a simple conversation? The only simple factor is the number of people involved: two.[30] But the complexity of meanings involved is significant. How can someone make a meaningful claim that shares bought today will double in value by tomorrow, except by drawing upon a network of communications concerning the stock market and share prices (the economic system). How do they assert that using their knowledge of those economic communications (including communications about facts relevant to those communications) will expose them to liability to prison for insider dealing without drawing upon a

[25] *Ibid*, 190.
[26] *Ibid*, 191.
[27] *Ibid*, 191.
[28] *Ibid*, 191.
[29] *Ibid*, 191.
[30] Tamanaha's use of this conversation, in which he invites us to allocate the different parts to different social systems, indicates that he is seeking to observe the participation of these individuals within social systems, rather than observing the social context of the conversation itself, which is an interaction.

network of legal communications? And how is the claim of unfairness made without reference to moral ideas of freeloading? This hypothetical conversation is anything but simple, and its complexity reflects the complexity of modern society, which requires individuals to participate in many systems of communication.

In order to explore Tamanaha's understanding of the application of systems theory to this conversation, we first need to consider his claim that this is a 'private' conversation and that systems theory would treat such 'marginal' phenomena as part of the legal system. Within systems theory, a conversation of this kind is itself a system: an interaction. Whether it also has an existence within a functional social subsystem such as law or the economy is not something that can be determined with any finality by an outside observer who observes no more than this conversation. The role of functional social subsystems in this situation is complex, but we can make it simpler by asking ourselves a question. How can this conversation have an existence beyond itself (that is, after the conversation ends, and including more persons than Jones and Smith)? One possible and indeed likely answer is that it may not. It may exist only as an interaction. But an alternative possibility is that it does have an alternate existence within functional social subsystems. But we have to wait and see whether this is the case, whether the legal system recognises this conversation as a conspiracy to commit a crime, or the economic system identifies it as an agreement to make a purchase, etc. The fact that this conversation between Jones and Smith may not in fact belong to any social subsystem does not mean that systems are irrelevant to the meanings generated within this conversation. Familiarity with social systems, and the manner in which they ascribe meanings to communications, allows the participants in such interactions to include far more complex and structured meaningful communications than would otherwise be possible. And this is what Tamanaha is actually discussing when he considers the difficulties (and successes) of allocating particular sentences within this conversation to particular systems. Consider his claim that this conversation might involve economic, legal and moral systems. He drew on those systems to construct his hypothetical, knowing that we too, as his readers, would recognise them as communications raising legal, moral and economic issues. Using the distinction between an interaction and a social system gives us our response to his claim that there is an ambiguity in some of the sentences as to whether they belong to the legal system or the economic system, or both. None of these communications will belong to a social system unless that system recognises them as belonging to itself, in which case they will have a dual existence, within the interaction, and again, within the social system. The best that can be achieved, by an observer of this conversation who is seeking to understand the meanings within it, is to observe which social systems the participants are alluding to, or seeking to replicate, within their conversation. This is systems theory's version of what is often referred to as a hermeneutic approach. One can do this with some success, and some ambiguities, exactly as Tamanaha does in his discussion. The point here is not that systems theory provides us with a means to break down every 'private conversation' (an interaction which has no further existence) into its constituent parts. Rather, it is that systems theory allows us to observe on the nature and existence of the systems which allow conversations, within a modern world, to consist of such complex meanings as does this hypothetical.

An observer of this interaction can observe how social systems are replicated within conversations, including aspects of their functional differentiation; and, we would suggest, how such conversations utilise the distinction between conditional programme and code which, at the level of social systems, maintains their autonomy. We might ask ourselves whether the reference to what is legal in Smith's second sentence ('Sure it's illegal, but the risk of being prosecuted is small. We'll be rich if we do it, so it's worth taking the chance.') operates as code or programme. Law is not the only system which makes reference to things being legal or illegal, but it is the only system which codes in terms of legal/illegal. If someone regards the risk of their conduct being found illegal as a cost against which to weigh the potential financial benefits, is this the replication of an 'economic' or 'legal' communication? We can answer this question by considering how the reference to illegality operates in the sentence. Does the acknowledged value of the illegal behaviour have any relevance to its illegality? By contrast, does the risk of going to prison for illegal behaviour have any relevance to the financial benefits? It is clearly one way – illegality is relevant as a cost to the financial benefit of insider dealing when deciding whether or not to buy the shares. The size of the financial benefit (they can double the value of the shares) does not alter the legality of what is being suggested. Having accepted the illegality of the proposed actions, Smith is replicating economic communications in which illegality is a factor relevant to the making of payments. Thus the fact that the legal system may not include this conversation does not mean that the legal system is irrelevant here. It is the presence of the legal system, and the economy, that structures the possibilities for expectations within this conversation. To make this point another way, if there were not pre-existing differentiated systems which transcended particular interactions, we could not recognise that this conversation *could have* separate 'economic', 'legal' and 'moral' elements.

This is not a claim that communications within any interaction could always be clearly identified by an observer as replications of particular social system communications. Indeed, the converse will more likely be the case, especially in interactions that function as part of what Habermas termed 'the lifeworld', or general social communication. To understand both the benefits and the limitations of using systems theory here we need to consider how social systems might operate to stabilise (rather than determine) the meanings generated within interactions. What Tamanaha introduces here as the 'legal' elements of a 'simple private conversation' is the application of state legal norms by individuals to their own contemplated behaviour.[31] What stabilises these meanings are the actual communications of the legal system, which occur when the system recognises communications as belonging to itself. In this conversation Jones and Smith are involved in a hypothetical application of the state norms of criminal law to their own contemplated behaviour. What stabilises this part of the conversation is the fact that the state legal system can recognise conversations such as this as evidence of an intention to commit a criminal conspiracy, and on rare occasions, actually does so.

To summarise at this point, Tamanaha's own position is in truth much closer to systems theory than he might suppose. Both might exclude this conversation from the ambit of the legal system. Tamanaha's objection to including lay communications about law within the compass of legal pluralism is not so much an argument as a simple re-statement of his own preferred position: our studies of law should be confined to what actors describe as 'law', and these actors would not apply this title to their own conversations.[32] Systems theory would not include interactions as such within the legal system, though it would recognise that some interactions' communications could also exist as social system communications. Tamanaha claims that the ability of such 'private' communications to become part of the legal system lies with the individuals themselves. If they, or at least a significant number of them, describe these conversations as 'law', then this is their status. Systems theory proceeds on the basis that the process of inclusion within a functional social subsystem is not established through consensus (the number of individuals who express a similar view) but through the operations of that system. The enormous numbers of systematically connected communications which circulate within the legal system of a modern society, creating ever more complex meanings,[33] do not represent a consensus of individual opinions. And these connected communications severely limit the ability of any individuals to declare, for themselves, what should be described as 'law'. Within modern society, such attempts by individuals to claim to define something as 'law' have to operate alongside a system that describes itself as 'law', in contradistinction to morals, or the economy, or politics, and maintains the separation of itself

[31] This is within the scope of the theory; a theory developed for the study of the social, and the social includes all communications not simply those which belong to functional social subsystems.

[32] Tamanaha believes that practical advantages follow from this approach, more recently claiming that extending legal pluralism to include 'day to day human encounters' leads to the conclusion that 'every form of norm governed social interaction is law', so that we end up 'swimming, or drowning, in legal pluralism' (Tamanaha, 2008, 393).

[33] Although always less complex than those within the whole of society. We explore this and other elements of 'complexity' in Chapters 7 and 8.

from those other systems by the application of a different code: legal/illegal. The communications of these individuals also have to operate alongside other functional systems, such as the economy, politics, and the mass media, which generate their own internal versions of the legal system. The communications about law within the economy, politics and the mass media will not correspond in a number of ways with the legal system's own communications. Nevertheless, the object of these other systems' communications will be the legal system, rather than whatever individuals, even in significant numbers,[34] might apply the label of 'law' to.

If both Tamanaha's approach and that of systems theory decline to recognise private conversations as part of the legal system, does this mean that neither approach can inform the study of lay communications, and what does this mean for legal pluralism? Do these approaches limit law to the communications of formal institutions: courts and 'officials'?[35] And, does this result in the only thing that can be observed as law being state law?

Systems theory, which concentrates on coding, can extend the study of what is legal beyond a focus on formal sources. Legal meaning occurs whenever the code legal/illegal is being applied implicitly or explicitly by the system to construct itself and its environment. It constructs both itself and its environment through its operations, and lay communications form part of this process. Whilst a discussion of hypothetical legal operations may remain at the level of an interaction, lay communications, no less than official ones, can perform legal operations. For example, lay persons who change their legal status through marriage, or alter the distribution of their wealth through gifts and contracts, utilise communications which transcend any accompanying interactions (conversations). Legal operations are not limited to what courts or officials regard as a valid application of rules, though it is difficult to envisage a legal operation in modern society that had *no* relation to the rules and norms recognised by courts, tribunals or some other such institution. So, for example, a marriage may be conducted according to norms recognised by courts (the registrar qualified to carry out the ceremony). However, the parties may be too closely related to be eligible for a valid marriage. Whilst the marriage may later be declared invalid, one cannot say that the ceremony had failed to perform a legal operation. From the date of the ceremony, until the flaws are recognised,

[34] 2001, at 167. Tamanaha seems to need 'significant' here to avoid recognising a subject's unique claim that something is law. He also includes a requirement that the use of the reference to law by participants should include an understanding that law here includes some notion of authority, thus removing references to scientific laws, etc (at 169) But this would still leave the 'laws' of grammar. Here he resorts to a pragmatic approach – we will recognise some references as those to law (socio-legal or jurisprudential) rather than others.

[35] 'Just as health is not found primarily in hospitals or knowledge in schools, so justice is not primarily to be found in official justice-dispensing institutions' (Galanter, 1981, 17). See also Tamanaha, 2007–08, where he argues for the necessity of going beyond the narrow focus of state law to study 'the actual behavior of the populace in relation to the legal rules . . .' (at 74).

the parties, for all sorts of purposes both inside and outside of the legal system, changed their legal status. For Tamanaha, the inclusion of the above examples within the legal system depends on whether the lay persons recognise themselves as 'legal actors'. Lay persons are likely to be sure that the personnel who staff institutions are legal actors, but less sure of their own status, even when they participate in such institutions (as defendants, contracting parties, etc). Applying systems theory, the inclusion of these communications within the legal system (as communications which constitute legal operations) does not depend on the participants' themselves recognising the nature of their own communications, or their own status as system agents.

Legal communications at the periphery are unlikely to make no reference to those at the centre.[36] Even without the involvement of legal professionals, lay people within modern societies understand that law emanates from parliaments, courts and town halls, and recognise certain formal documents, notices and street signs as communications about what is legal or illegal, which draw their authority from these sources. But neither does the centre ignore legal communications at the periphery. The work of legal professionals in constantly re-interpreting lay demands as contracts, trusts, debts, etc are communications which repeatedly generate a flow of communications back to the courts. And this flow is not limited to what is processed by legal professionals. Lay communications as to what is legal are an indispensible part of the legal system. If lay persons were unable to generate legal meanings, by what mechanism would they be able to make the communications that commence the processes which lead to matters being brought to solicitors, cases being brought before the courts, etc? And, just as one cannot judge the social importance of the contracts generated by lawyers just by considering those which end up in court, so too one cannot judge the social importance of lay legal communications solely by reference to which of these subsequently is processed by a legal professional.

Thus systems theory provides a method to observe lay communications in two ways. There are those lay communications which form part of legal operations and are part of the legal system. And there are those which are not part of that system, but are stabilised and structured through participants' familiarity with ones that are, and their experience of communications about the legal system within other systems (most notably the mass

[36] In place of a distinction between lay and professional communications, Luhmann used a distinction between the centres and peripheries of systems. In the case of law, the centre is the courts, with their peculiar responsibility for deciding what the law is, even when there are no adequate reasons for reaching a particular answer (Luhmann, 2004, ch 7). This responsibility, a 'prohibition on the denial of justice' (at 284–96), has led to courts developing doctrines with a level of systematic complexity that is beyond the capacity of most lay people to utilise. Lay legal communications, whether with other lay people or legal professionals, he located at the periphery. This spatial metaphor does not represent a hierarchy. All legal communications are just that – legal communications. Those within courts are no more legal than those without.

media). Inside the legal system, the possibilities for legal meanings are further stabilised by the manner in which communications at the periphery link to communications at the centre. In law, the centre is the courts. Other social systems also demonstrate this centre/periphery relationship: in the economy the looser meanings that develop in the periphery as to what might constitute a payment are stabilised when they become linked to communications located within institutions such as banks (as when money is deposited in accounts).

Systems theory not only addresses interactions and social systems, but also communications which occur inside institutions.[37] For example, it is a mistake to conclude that because a court is a legal institution, and a judge has a legal role, all communications that issue from courts and judges belong to the legal system. A recent development in the UK court system has been the increased use of press releases.[38] The fact that these are issued by Her Majesty's Courts and Tribunals Service, or even that they repeat statements made by judges in open court, does not make these communications 'legal'. They are offered as media communications, with the intention that they will be taken up and used by the media in the process of constructing stories about the legal system among other things. Thus, not only are 'private conversations' often complex, so are the communications of institutions. Both are sites in which different systems are drawn upon in order to generate different systemic meanings. Similar analysis applies to judges giving public lectures and even, though this is more subtle, when they issue homilies when sentencing criminals. Whilst some part of a judge's remarks may enter social systems, via media reporting, or appeals against sentence, much of what is said by a judge on such occasions remains at the interaction level.

How Does One Identify a Subsystem Code?

Especially when dealing with state law, within an English-speaking jurisdiction, it seems fairly easy to identify legal coding. The recognition that there are circumstances, actions or situations that are legal or illegal is something that is present throughout society, as is the general idea that everything that is not illegal is legal, and everything that is illegal, not legal. But despite this Luhmann insists that this code, which is represented in the binary distinction legal/illegal, is not 'logically deduced', neither 'did it [the legal system] come into being because it can be deduced from logical axioms', but rather 'the strict and unyielding distinction between legal and illegal is exceptional

[37] We consider the understanding of systems theory of institutions and organisations briefly in Chapter 7.

[38] And this has been developed even further in other jurisdictions; see Gies, 2005.

and not self-evident'.[39] That said, one finds plenty of communications that refer to things as 'legal' or 'illegal' and this can make the claim that law identifies itself through the application of its binary code of legal/illegal something that seems plausible and relatively unproblematic.

Problems, however, arise when one considers how codes operate,[40] and what distinguishes them from programmes. The presence of a communication which takes the form 'this is illegal' does not mean that we are in the presence of the legal system, a system that codes in terms of the legal code. References to something being legal or illegal regularly occur in the mass media, in politics, and the economy. But in these systems, these references will operate as programmes and not as code. What is the difference? With code one is looking for the primary distinction of the system – its basal distinction. Communications within a system generate meaning by accounting for the application of their primary distinction. Communications which account for the application of a code are observations upon coding, called within the theory secondary observation.[41] These communications (observations on the application of coding) build into ever more complex programmes which account for the application of the code in the past, its current application, and indicate how the code will be applied in the future. Systems other than law will utilise the distinction legal/illegal, but rather than as code, only as programme. So, for example, the economy will utilise the distinction between what is legal and illegal, and even the semantic 'illegal' or 'legal', but it will not code legal/illegal. Economic communications will not address their secondary observations toward the question of whether this legality is actually illegal, or this illegality rather legal. Indeed, rather than these concerns, whereby the legal system builds ever more complicated programmes, the illegality of some proposed action within the economy represents a cost, which in turn affects the ability to make a payment (as we described by using the interaction of Smith and Jones), as here the basal distinction or code is payment/non-payment. The trajectory of the communication of the legality of a proposed action is toward the cost of the action, and the distinction between what is legal and illegal as it is operating represents a programme within the economy indicating what might be more costly, and not as code, as it does within the legal system.[42]

[39] 2004, 177, and see further 173–80.

[40] To appreciate the character of a code and its operation as understood in systems theory, see the example of Luhmann's analysis of the code of art, 2000a, 185–96.

[41] To engage with Luhmann's analysis, one needs to appreciate the character of second-order observation and its difference and similarity to first-order observation. This is no simple task since it relies on a range of supporting (or self-supporting) arguments. A clear statement that represents well the form and logic of this analysis is presented by Andersen, 2010a. For Luhmann's own account of the difference between constructivist second-order observation and deconstruction, see Luhmann, 2002b.

[42] Teubner expresses the same argument informatively: 'The economy reconstructs the same course of events with its own fictitious distinctions and indications. If legal norms appear on the screen of the economy at all, then they are treated not as normatively valid, but as

So, one does not take a single communication, whatever distinction that communication might include, and allocate it to a system; one has to observe which system a communication belongs to by examining its trajectory within systems: what communications is it linked to in the past, and in the future, and what code is being applied by the system of which it forms a part. Only if the communication forms part of a social subsystem of communications, which is repeatedly applying the distinction legal/illegal, are we in the presence of the legal system.

To develop the sense of what we are looking for, let us take another example, and one which might be particularly important for understanding legal pluralism: that of morals (the third system referred to in Smith and Jones's conversation). We can ask the question of whether the moral norms that operate for a given community are 'legal', and such a question is implicated in many studies of legal pluralism (as of course it is for many other aspects of jurisprudential discussion). But, for systems theory, one has to ask the question of what the code of the moral is, and how that coding might operate within society. One asks this question knowing that the language of morals operates with distinctions: good/bad, good/evil, right/wrong, but that these distinctions will also operate in legal communication as they do in other communications.

Luhmann has concluded that the code of the moral in modern differentiated societies 'has become contingent', namely that it has lost its ability to organise itself systematically through a basal distinction, even though it still adopts binary distinctions such as good/bad, good/evil and right/wrong.[43] For these purposes, Luhmann argues that moral coding is 'always coding of communication. There are, in other words, no good or bad people, but only the possibility of indicating people as good or bad.'[44] Luhmann describes how the development of the 'interiorization' of the moral,[45] from the Middle Ages, has complicated the possibility of operating with communications that sharply divide themselves around a basal distinction, such as that of legal/illegal for the legal system. Under the conditions of modern differentiated societies, an order develops which reduces the functional operative capacity of the moral code.

> This order does not permit code values of function systems to be identified with moral values – neither with good/bad nor with good/evil. The government is not

entries in economic calculations. Economic communication builds an economic fiction of the law and uses it to condition its self-regulating programmes, for instance, those of cost minimization. . . . Where jurists get infuriated over violations and circumventions of the law, economists praise what they see as efficient economic behaviour – something which is admirably summed up in the notion of "efficient breach of contract"' (Teubner, 1992a, 466).

43 Luhmann, 1992–93, 1009.

44 *Ibid*, 1000.

45 This refers to the construction of what is good or bad about an action by reference to the subject's intention, or interior state.

> morally better than the opposition (but also not morally worse). The power holder is not morally better than his public. Whoever determines truths is not morally superior to whoever determines untruths. . . . Moral sinners, as well as the morally justified, must reckon with surprises, when on Judgment Day the true meaning of the code, 'transcendent/immanent,' will become manifest.[46]

Luhmann's account of the code of the moral can be described, as he recognises himself, as that of the cynic. His analysis is not aimed at decrying the application of the binary distinctions that form the basis of moral discourse, and ethics. But he seriously questions whether such distinctions can be studied sociologically in the modern world as providing any primary distinction that organises the operations, programmes and communications of a functional subsystem, as opposed to the selection of communications that can be used to commend or criticise the character of actions, behaviour and thoughts.

Law and Violence

Does understanding law as a system of communication eliminate raw physical violence from within our understanding of law? We can begin to answer this question by reminding ourselves that systems theory not only studies law as communication, it regards society as communications. It is true that raw physical violence, the kind of force that damages human beings in the same manner whether it comes from hurricanes, car crashes or executions is outside of communication. But what gives social meaning to this violence, and divides it into what is considered natural rather than intentional, as well as what is legal, political, or even sports violence, is communication. As such, just about everything that we mean when we refer to violence does come within the ambit of systems theory. With particular regard to state legal systems, it is clearly important to understand the links between the kinds of communications issued by legislators and judges, and the pain inflicted by wardens on prisoners. But again, this can be understood in terms of communications. As Cover pointed out in his seminal essay on the need to take account of the violence which accompanies legal communications, it is only because prison warders are willing to react to two rather similar forms of judicial communication (an order to execute and a stay of execution) in quite different ways, which makes it fruitful for opposing counsel on death penalty appeal cases to conduct their extensive arguments on the legality of the imposed sentence.[47] Applying systems theory, we must refer to the termination of the life of a prisoner, or not, in response to one of these two communications as an 'effect' of communication. The

[46] 1992–93, 1004–05.
[47] 1986, 1623.

chemical, physical and psychic processes involved in one person taking the life of another are not themselves communications and, as such, lie outside of society. But the institutional practices which have resulted in the predictability of such responses are constructed through communications and, as such, are open to observation through the application of systems theory. If the link between law and violence is built into our definition of state law, as occurs, for example, if we define state law as a monopoly of violence, or the infliction of evil in response to disobedience to a sovereign, we impede our observation of the manner in which power that leads to penal violence is distributed through communications (particularly political and legal ones) and the occasions when it is absent.

The ability to result in the infliction of physical pain is not only important to our understanding of the operation of state law, but the relationship between state and non-state legal orders, that is, pluralism in general. As Cover has observed, it is not the relative integrity of their respective interpretations that leads to state laws dominating over rival legal orders, but the greater likelihood that resistance to state legal norms will result in the infliction of physical suffering. The relative ability to avoid sanctions being applied to oneself, or to have sanctions applied to those with whom one has a dispute or grievance, provide motivations for communication.[48] As such, the manner in which state law distributes and utilises the ability to inflict physical and mental suffering will have its effects on the possibilities of co-evolution between rival systems of law. Legal theory has typically struggled with this issue in one of two ways. Theories like those of early English legal positivists Bentham and Austin, closely modelled on Hobbes' political theory, define law in terms of the ability to inflict sanctions, which not only neglects non-state forms of law but seems to ignore both the kinds of law which operate in the absence of sanctions, and the occasions when law which typically applies sanctions to a breach of duty will not be able to do so. Hart, building on the observation that legal meanings continue to be generated in the absence of sanctions, offered a replacement theory.[49] For him, obedience, at some unquantifiable level of significance, is a precondition to any claim by a group administering a system of rules to be legal officials, and for the system that they apply to be called 'law'. But once this level of obedience operates, the only acknowledgement of the role played by sanctions is that these will be understood as something that is 'deserved' by those who breach primary rules, and that those who administer punishments can explain their behaviour, to themselves and others, as acts taken in accordance with legal rules. Neither of these approaches – state law as sanctions, or state law understood without reference to sanctions – seems

[48] This forms part of what is observed when actors have access to more than one law – they act opportunistically.

[49] 1961, chs 5 and 6.

satisfactory for those who wish to compare state law with non-state forms of law, especially in those situations where the two co-exist.[50]

We should not describe a state legal system in terms of some fusion between law and some unspecified level of violence or effectiveness. Rather, we need to observe how other systems of communication develop (co-evolve) in response to different legal orders.[51] The particular system which is relevant to Cover's example of death penalties is the political system. What creates the wardens' level of attention to legal niceties is the manner in which legality (legal communications) has a second life within the political system (second coding) as legitimacy. Political power is distributed through a political system in which legality provides a way to distribute power, including the power to inflict pain and suffering, with technical precision. This is not the place to expand on this relationship (but we will do so in Chapter 6). Systems theory provides a basis for observing the manner in which political power, including physical violence, is delivered through law. Indeed, this structural coupling of the two systems, whereby the communications of law have a second existence and meaning within the political system, *is* system theory's account of the creation of what pluralists describe as state law.

The relationship between systems is contingent, and open to observation. The theory not only provides a means through which to study the relationship between the legal and political system, but also relationships between law and science, economy, the mass media, etc. As such, it can be used to consider non-state legal systems, for example legal systems whose communications do not have a second existence as political communications about legitimacy within the political system. Such legal systems may, for example, still achieve structural coupling with the economy. The ability of the economy to re-use legal communications in order to stabilise economic transactions is not co-extensive with the political system's re-use of legality (legal communications) to distribute political power. This is shown most clearly in the kinds of transnational agreements constituted by *lex mercatoria*. The economy does not give meaning to legal transactions in terms of the complex relationships between duties and rights which is their existence within the legal system. Instead, legal contracts are re-interpreted in terms of the likely profits and losses that may arise from different courses of action. But the role of legal agreements, and their ability to be translated

[50] If one describes this dilemma using terms commonly employed by William Twinning (see the index to his 2000 book, which gives various examples of this), another leading legal theorist who has written extensively on legal pluralism, there is a tension between 'law talk' and 'talk about law'. The improvement claimed by Hart over Bentham and Austin is based on the failure of the latter to describe law in a manner that would be recognisable to its participants – not enough 'law talk'. But the resulting theory can be accused of describing law only in the terms used by the participants of a state legal system – too much (state) law talk.

[51] We deal fully with the co-evolution of the legal system and the political system, and the implications of this for the use of force by the state, in Chapter 6.

into economic costs and benefits, is not limited to those which are created according to state legal rules, or enforced through state or regional government sanctions. In the study of non-state legal orders, we need to move from notions of a threshold level of effectiveness closely linked to the availability of state sanctions. Instead, we need to consider the effects of legal communications. Not, we stress, 'effects' in terms of any linear theories of legal cause and social effects, but in terms of the nature and extent to which the communications of a particular legal order are or are not reconstituted as communications within the economy, or religion, or even within culture, and vice versa.[52]

Normative Pluralism

In his seminal article 'What is Legal Pluralism?'[53] John Griffiths offers a theory of legal pluralism in place of what he calls 'legal centralism'. Legal centralism is the tendency to link all forms of law with the law of the nation state. This tendency is most closely associated with legal positivism, but Griffiths shows how it remains present even within approaches to law which are not positivistic and which even present themselves as pluralistic. He describes how the study of indigenous legal cultures under conditions of colonialism has commonly been reduced to a study of their integration, and expected assimilation, within a state legal system that 'recognises' them, though not in forms in which they would recognise themselves.[54] More radical forms of what can be described as legal pluralism (he focuses on the work of Pospisil, Smith, Ehrlich and Moore) stress the need to identify the norms which operate (and the manner in which they operate) within society, without giving priority to state legal norms. However, whilst each of these theorists, in their different ways, extends the study of norms beyond state legal norms, they fail to offer an adequate basis for the identification and study of law within society. Thus Ehrlich's 'living law' – the rules of conduct that actually operate within associations and families, are as much 'law' as the rules of decision which enable courts and officials to decide disputes.[55] Similarly, Smith's internal rules of 'corporations' (which include companies, clubs, and families), and the less inclusive legal orders which Pospisil describes operating within society (a hierarchy of increasing inclusiveness which rises from family, through lineage and community, to political confederacy) are all equally law. For Moore, all of the rules, customs and symbols which regulate behaviour within a semi-autonomous field can be considered

[52] See, for a much discussed pertinent example, Teubner, 1992a.

[53] 1986.

[54] Griffiths, *ibid*, calls these approaches 'pluralism in the weak sense', at 8.

[55] See Cotterrell's analysis of Ehrlich's ideas as part of his discussion of 'legal philosophy and legal pluralism', 2006, ch 2.

to be law.[56] However, the concept of a semi-autonomous field does not itself establish what constitutes law, nor is it necessary to label all of the norms within such a field as 'law'.[57] Self-regulation (via customs, symbols, rules and competitive pressures) creates and maintains whatever autonomy (and separate identity) operates within a given social field.

Griffiths introduces Pospisil, Smith, Ehrlich and Moore as examples of what he calls 'implicit' legal pluralism.[58] But what each of these theorists is identifying might better be described as normative pluralism. Each approach leads to the conclusion that what legal centralism identifies as law, nation state law, is, even within the nation, only one kind of norm. But if legal pluralism is understood as normative pluralism, then we probably abandon any claim to identify anything within society that is peculiarly 'legal'.[59] As Griffiths observes, the borders of the social are congruent with the borders of the legal. However, both when we expand the legal to cover every kind of norm, and when we dissolve the legal into whatever norms operate within a given social field, we not only abandon any claim that law has any peculiar role in structuring society, we do the same for politics, economics, religion, etc.

To show that this is indeed the case let us consider Moore's example of a semi-autonomous field. Moore offered this as the appropriate 'field of observation' for the study of law and social change in complex societies. A semi-autonomous field (SAF) has rule-making capacities, but it is set within a wider social field to whose rules and influences it is vulnerable.[60] A SAF is supposed to be something that is empirically observable. The observer will identify a SAF – a corporation, kinship group, profession, or institution – as something that generates internal norms, and identifies the groups which constitute the SAF and influences their behaviour. The acceptance that the field is only semi-autonomous requires one to accept

[56] Although Moore starts her 1973 article by discussing the benefits of moving to a position of normative pluralism (citing Malinowski), it is principally a discussion of the interaction of state legal norms with other norms which she does not label law. Only in her conclusion does she claim that one might consider both state law and other rule creations as equally 'law', and even here she is clear that this depends on the purpose of the analysis. If one is focusing on the bindingness of rules, it may be sufficient to call all types of binding rules 'law'. But in keeping with the structure of her own article, she insists that there are occasions when the source of rules, and the nature of the force inducing compliance to rules, needs to be separately identified. See her conclusion at 745.

[57] Indeed in this article (1973) Moore sees the only kind of norms recognised as 'law' as state laws (rules originating with, and enforced by, the state).

[58] While Anne Griffiths gives Pospisil and Moore as examples of what she calls 'New Legal Positivism' in her essay 'Legal Pluralism' (2002).

[59] A point made by Tamanaha, 1993.

[60] 'The approach proposed here is that the small field observable to an anthropologist be chosen and studied in terms of its semi-autonomy – the fact that it can generate rules and customs and symbols internally, but that it is also vulnerable to rules and decisions and other forces emanating from the larger world by which it is surrounded. The semi-autonomous social field has rule-making capacities, and the means to induce or coerce compliance; but it is simultaneously set in a larger social matrix which can, and does, affect and invade it, sometimes at the invitation of persons inside it, sometimes at its own instance' (Moore, 1973, 720).

that there will be external norms as well as internal ones. But once one has applied this internal/external distinction[61] (assuming that it can really be done – see below) with which categories does one describe and analyse the norms operating within the field in question? As happened to Moore herself, in her description of the New York garment industry, this involves the utilisation of categories such as the moral, the economic and the legal. Moore describes how those garment manufacturers who sought to enforce legal (state in this case) norms would face exclusion from contracts (economic sanctions) for their dishonourable behaviour (moral norms). Thus having described a semi-autonomous field in terms that amount to an undifferentiated normative pluralism, she was forced to reinstate categories of norms in order to describe what occurred within her chosen social field. And in the case of law, she was able to develop no alternative conceptual structure to distinguish the legal from the moral and economic, and thus fell back on an untheorised acceptance of state law as the 'law' within her chosen social field.[62]

Griffiths identifies what he sees as a contradiction between Moore's normative pluralism and her resort to state law in order to describe the elements making up the New York garment industry, but concludes that one should nevertheless stick with normative pluralism.[63] Law for him is the self-regulation that occurs within any given social field. All self-regulation is law. There are no features of self-regulation which allow us meaningfully to divide it into the classifications of law/non-law. Instead, he would utilise a combination of normative pluralism which is graded along a scale of 'legality': 'The self-regulation of a semi-autonomous field can be regarded as more or less "legal" according to the degree to which it is differentiated from the rest of the activities in the field and delegated to specialised functionaries.' Indeed, he admits that it may even be better 'to abandon the claim that there is any distinct activity which should be called law, and conduct analysis solely in terms of more or less specialised social control'.[64] But how is one to differentiate the 'rest of the activities' within a field from what is legal, having defined all self-regulation (or social control) as law?

Take the example of a hospital. If all the norms operating within a hospital are regarded as law, how are we to begin to describe the field? We can point to any number of norms: the technical norms of clinical procedure; the ethics of patient/doctor relations; the religious beliefs of staff and patients; the economic expectations of those who deliver medical supplies; the conventions of accountancy which produce budgets; etc. All of these

[61] Semi-autonomous fields 'resist' external norms, or they may internally 'co-opt' them, in which case they are not '(fully) external at all'. This account of the internal external division comes from Griffiths, 1995.

[62] For Moore, state law is an external influence on a semi-autonomous field because the source of the rules and the sanctions which could enforce them lie outside the field of study.

[63] Which he calls 'normative heterogeneity'.

[64] 1986, at fn 41. See also Griffiths, 1984.

norms are specialised, and many of them will involve specialised functionaries. One would also find norms operating which are general, both in the sense that they operate in all kinds of social fields, and are non-specialist. General standards of courtesy might be an example. All of these norms will operate, to different degrees on different occasions, on all of the actors within the hospital. But does normative pluralism, or normative pluralism graded as 'legal' according to the degree of involvement of specialist functionaries,[65] really assist our description of such a 'field'? How, for example, would we differentiate between medical competence as enforced by the GMC (General Medical Council), and medical negligence as administered by the courts? With a starting point that all forms of regulation are law, we can classify, or assess, the degrees of inclusiveness/formality/institutionalisation, etc of social control, and conclude, for example, that the GMC's disciplinary body and the courts are both law and similarly legal. And this approach allows us to make similar comparisons between these institutions and any other area of social life, in any society, which generates norms which regulate social behaviour. But how does this way of observing law assist any attempt to identify the relationships between the law and other parts of society? Or even the relationship between these apparently similar institutions?[66] Can one simply re-introduce classifications such as 'political', 'economic', 'religious', 'scientific', etc, as a second layer of analysis? And if one does so, is there a residue that is not a religious legal norm, an economic legal norm, or a political legal norm, but simply a legal norm?

Whilst normative pluralism starts by stressing that all norms are, as norms, equal to one another, and this certainly diffuses any claim that all law is state law, or all law is administered by officials, it does not provide a methodology for re-classifying the norms found in a particular 'field' thereafter.[67] In the absence of this, an observer is likely to fall back on an untheorised empiricism, which norms are classified according to what seems familiar – medical, religious – etc. It was this kind of empiricism which led to Moore falling back, as Griffiths saw it, into a form of legal centralism, whereby the 'legal' aspects of the New York garment industry were identified by her with contracts and statutes and their enforcement through

[65] This is Griffiths' suggested approach; see Griffiths, 1984.

[66] As institutions, the GMC and a court of law share the characteristic of institutions – they are social systems in which communications are attributed to the institution through the criteria of its addressor's membership. To compare institutions we need to assess the participation of their respective communications within different social systems. We therefore have to use criteria which can identify which social system those communications belong to, which moves us from membership to code.

[67] 'This approach attempts to make the best of an insoluble problem, but it generates confusion by doing violence to common understandings' (Tamanaha, 2001, 174). His examples of confusion are from the loss of distinctions between law and habits, customs, morals and table manners (ie no distinctions between kinds of social rules). But the more serious loss to common understandings, from a sociological point of view, is the inability to differentiate society into different social formations: politics, economy, science, etc.

courts. Systems theory offers a methodology for this process of distinction and description. Whilst the focus is on communications and not on norms (norms are only one form of communication) one can seek to identify to which system a norm belongs. Which code is being applied? Which system gives this particular communicated norm its social meaning?

We gave one example of this kind of analysis in our earlier discussion of the 'simple' conversation between Smith and Jones. Another is the question posed at the end of the last but one paragraph, concerning the difference, if any, between the nature of GMC enforcement of medical competence and medical negligence as enforced through the courts. If legal pluralism is simply normative pluralism – norms which are operating and influencing behaviour – then both bodies are equally applying 'law'. And if one is grading law according to the degree of specialisation and the use of functionaries then these two bodies seem as 'legal' as each other. But if one asks which code is being applied one can see that medical negligence, whether applied in the courts or being discussed by two doctors in a 'private conversation' is an application of the code legal/illegal. The doctors, or the court, are communicating, or replicating communications, in terms of conduct that is being classified by reference to the legal code and those communications that have legal meanings, that is, they are a continuation of the legal system, either at its centre or its periphery. By contrast, the GMC is usually not trying, or even able, to decide what is legal or illegal. Its responsibility for deciding whether a doctor is fit to practise medicine is a continuation of the health system in which the code applied is whether something contributes to patient's health or not (therapeutic/non-therapeutic). Even something as apparently distant from the application of clinical care as the question of whether a doctor who acts as an expert witness in court has brought the medical profession into disrepute is premised, however unconvincingly to an outsider, on the idea that having a 'reputation' is part of the process whereby doctors are able to administer medicine to patients.

Let us make our example more concrete. Consider the hearing before the GMC's disciplinary body, the Fitness to Practice Panel (FTPP) in which the eminent paediatrician, Professor Sir Roy Meadow, was struck off for serious professional misconduct in giving misleading statistical evidence at the trial of Sally Clark (convicted of murdering two of her infant children but later having her conviction quashed on appeal). The FTPP's decision to strike off Sir Roy from the medical register was appealed to the High Court, and overturned, and then to the Court of Appeal, who upheld the High Court decision, despite two of the Court of Appeal judges agreeing with the FTPP that Meadow's actions amounted to serious professional misconduct.[68] We can see that we are dealing with norms both in the court

[68] *General Medical Council v Meadow* [2006] EWCA 1390.

hearings and the FTPP proceedings. And the outcome for Professor Meadow (being allowed to practise medicine or not) are the same whether he wins or loses before the FTPP or the court. But what is the relationship between the FTPP and the courts in this situation, and the norms that each applies? From the perspective of the legal system the GMC's disciplinary body may be seen as part of the legal system, in that its cases are open to judicial review. But of course on this basis every decision in the public sector is also part of the legal system. And the sense that they are part of the same system increases here, where each body had regard to a norm which required them to consider whether Professor Meadow had committed 'serious professional misconduct'.

If we apply Moore's analysis, we would have to accept that the GMC is a semi-autonomous field. Doctors create their own norms, and the GMC seems the epitome of what we might mean by self-regulation. If, following Griffiths, we call its norms 'law', this does not really help us to explore the relationship between the GMC and the 'state' legal system as it is being played out in the Meadow case. There is also some difficulty in separating the internal aspects of this semi-autonomous field, its internal rules, from the external rules and influences. The GMC has a legal form, it enters into contracts, the need for a licence to practise medicine is reinforced by statutory provisions which impose penalties for practising without one, and as a look at their website indicates, the disciplinary proceedings are constructed with one eye to possible legal challenges. Thus the GMC is not simply influenced by or subject to the external rules and influences of the 'state' legal system, it is constituted by them.[69] What exactly is the basis of its 'autonomy'? Consider the following systems theory approach.

With the Court of Appeal, and this decision, we are dealing with the centre of the legal system. This court had to give an answer to the legal question of whether expert witnesses could be disciplined by their professional bodies for their performance in court as expert witnesses, or was this covered by an immunity? The court decided that there was no immunity. This was the part of the decision that is most likely to generate further communications within the legal system, since it is a precedent. The Court of Appeal judges were also clearly deciding what was legal – it was legal for a professional witness to be disciplined, even though it was not legal for this witness to be disciplined by the termination of his licence to practise.[70] Of course, the fact that this judgment consists of legal communications does not make every communication from the Court of Appeal legal. Just

[69] See our analysis of societal constitutionalism commenced in Chapter 6 and developed in Chapter 7.

[70] In their appeal against the High Court decision, which overturned Meadow's removal from the medical register, the GMC sought to re-establish the legality of their judgment that he had committed serious professional misconduct, although not to re-establish the penalty of erasure from the register.

as the GMC is an institution that is partially constituted by legal communications, so too the Court of Appeal is an institution that employs staff, issues press releases, etc. Not everything that is associated with the Court of Appeal as an institution is itself law. But the legal identity of this judgment seems beyond doubt.

Turning to the GMC, identifying all of its rules and customs and symbols as 'law' is unhelpful. Applying the pluralist approach of systems theory, we need to consider which communications within the GMC are generating legal meanings (through the interconnection of communications applying the legal code). As all communications which apply the legal code are part of the legal system, discussions within the GMC's FTPP as to whether their decision to discipline Professor Meadow was legal would form part of the legal system. But in having these discussions, the kinds of communications that are available to justify the application of the code give greater autonomy to the Court of Appeal than the FTPP. Within our society, as things currently stand, much of the extremely complicated justifications for the application of the legal code arise from the courts and their development of legal doctrine. Even lay persons, communicating without the aid of lawyers, know that claims about the legality of any matter are likely to involve references to what has been decided by courts. In the case of the FTPP, again as evidenced by the GMC's website, there is clearly an acceptance that issues as to the legality of the FTPP's proceedings can be 'decided' by the courts. Does this lead to the conclusion that the FTPP is simply subordinate to the courts? No, because there are other kinds of communications involved here than legal ones. In deciding what constitutes professional misconduct, some of the FTPP's communications form part of a social system that has to code in terms of what is therapeutic/non-therapeutic: the health system. As with all systems, the essential arbitrariness of this binary code does not prevent its application, observations upon the basis of its application, and the generation of complex programmes which structure but do not determine the application of this code. Scientific communications have a secondary existence within the health system, where their use to apply the health system code is also accompanied by, and connected to, communications that have little scientific content (that is, they would not be recognised by the scientific system as scientific communications). One such 'non-scientific' communication, relating to trust, forms the beginning of the GMC's code of conduct: 'Patients must be able to trust doctors with their lives and their health. To justify that trust, you must show respect for human life and you must . . .'. What follows is a list of considerations which serve to construct doctors as a profession. Alongside references to good clinical practice, which can be expected to link to (couple with) scientific communications via clinical trials, there are also references to politeness and consideration, avoiding discriminatory behaviour, and the need not to abuse individual or public trust.

A systems theory case study observes the manner in which these communications have been generated and applied by the GMC, and considers the respective abilities of the GMC's disciplinary body and the courts to process these communications. As with the potential of all appeals in law, a failure by law to construct some form of deference towards what the law understands as its environment can create a situation in which, whenever the remedies generated by appeals are attractive to parties disadvantaged by the outside bodies' decisions, those bodies' decisions will become an interim stage prior to final decisions by the courts.[71] Deference works to ensure that these outside decisions will not generate legal cases. There can be no certainty that a system or subsystem gets what it needs, but one can observe the features of the legal system that make it difficult for it to demonstrate something less than deference at this point. The legal system has little ability to present its own procedures and decisions as being capable of resolving scientific disputes. As such, there is every reason to expect that those communications that construct good medical practice by reference to scientific communications will be less open to being re-processed by the courts than those which do not. One must also have regard to the complexities of medical practice. A medical system, coding in terms of what is therapeutic or not, has to co-exist with some degree of stability alongside the economic system. And in forming a view of what is good medical practice, the GMC (as an institution) is a site where that co-existence is established. This will lead to judgements of what is equal and unequal in terms of poor medical practice by the FTPP which it will be extremely difficult to re-create within legal procedures.

An analysis of the respective abilities of these institutions to participate in different social systems allows us to form some view of the respective autonomy of systems, and the respective autonomy of each institution within each social system. Each social system remains closed to each other, in the sense that the codes (legal/illegal vs therapeutic/non-therapeutic) are different, and the meanings generated within each system cannot be reduced to the other. But from this starting point, autonomy becomes the ability of each system to re-use the other's communications as conditional programmes for the application of its own code.[72] How much of what constitutes good medical practice, leading to the application of the positive side of the binary code therapeutic/non-therapeutic, can be constructed through the re-use of communications developed within the legal system around the application of the legal code? This is not a question that is answered by

[71] See our analysis in Chapter 8.

[72] 'The internal constraints that render the mutual constitution highly selective must be taken seriously. . . . It is not just the local specialities of the diverse discourses involved, but basic requirements of their self-reproduction, including the resistance of presently existing structures, that lead with necessity to mutual misreading of discourses' (Teubner, 1992, 1456).

simply assessing the relative ability of each system to result in physical sanctions to individuals – though the presence of such sanctions will motivate individual participation in each system. The respective communicative possibilities of each system are more subtle than their respective general access to physical force. In our example, while the conclusion 'serious professional misconduct' is able to operate within both FTPP and court proceedings, the communications that can link to this conclusion are not equally available. The conclusions of the FTPP that a doctor's actions constitute serious professional misconduct warranting their being struck off the medical register are a continuation of communications which construct doctors as professionals, and the profession as the practice of medicine – communications whose common attribute is the application of the health system's coding. As such, these conclusions have a meaning that cannot be reproduced by the legal system, with its very different linkages of communications leading to a conclusion with the same semantic form. Attempts by the legal system to offer its adjudications as an appropriate mechanism to resolve such issues suffer from the difficulties of constructing routine decisions on this question without access to the communications which can give it a routine answer (or meaning).

From the starting point of this kind of analysis, we might conclude that, ordinarily, the decisions of the FTPP on the presence of 'serious professional conduct' justifying a doctor being struck off the register are not open to appeal on substantive grounds.[73] In this case, what does the Meadow litigation represent? Was it an exception to the general relationship of deference? It was an untypical case of misconduct, for it was triggered not by a complaint from a patient or medical colleague about the nature of Meadow's skills, but by a finding by a previous Court of Appeal (a criminal one) that Meadow had misled a court by giving evidence outside of his acknowledged area of expertise. Thus a court had already established that there had been a serious (that is, significant) error applying the legal system's own procedures for establishing which evidence might be taken to have influenced the outcome of a trial. Starting from this conclusion, the FTPP had to decide whether this accepted error constituted a serious professional misconduct, likely to undermine 'public trust' in the profession.

Whilst any court seeking to adjudicate upon the substantive merits of a decision by the FTPP might expect to have few communicative resources with which to construct a decision, this is not the case here. Those resources allowed the courts (the High Court, and then the Court of Appeal) to construct this as a question internal to the legal system – the probity of its own procedures. The different views of the High Court and the Court of Appeal show that the need to ensure the probity of legal proceedings could have led

[73] The legal system has more resources for forming views on the procedures of other systems, with the notable exception of scientific procedures, which are resistant to any claim that ideas like 'natural justice' are relevant to the production of facts.

to a decision either way. Whilst the judgments exhibit a concern that disciplinary bodies might exert pressure on experts which leads to bias in their evidence, this is countered by the acceptance that such discipline is part of the process whereby what constitutes expertise is created, and by the acknowledgement that where an expert's performance has been substandard, the expert's own disciplinary body is the only place where a court can refer the matter for remedy. The final decision opened professionals to a kind of discipline by their professional bodies that they might not have expected before and, as such, might be said to have increased the FTPP's autonomy. But the ability of professional bodies to identify serious professional misconduct in these circumstances is severely hampered in the absence of any finding by a court that the mistake, in legal terms, is a serious one, that is one that might be expected to have a significant effect on the outcome of any proceedings. And as such, the loss of autonomy, if any, is slight.

This brief case study reveals something of the potential of systems theory to enable analysis of normative pluralism. There is no surrender here to the claims that law supposedly makes for itself to be 'direct in its operation'.[74] Indeed, it allows us not only to explore the limitations of law's operations in terms of its inabilities to have its own semantics replicated within other systems, but to see how the process is a double one. In order to have its own semantics duplicated within another system, law has to be able to duplicate the semantics of other systems within itself. To re-state this in the manner expressed earlier, each system has to re-use communications developed to orientate another system's coding within its own conditional programmes. The relationship between law and other social systems does involve what Peter Fitzpatrick has called a 'contradictory process of mutual support and opposition'.[75] But this process is not limited to the relationship between state law and other social systems because law is not limited to state law, but includes all communications which apply the code legal/illegal. This approach is compatible with Fitzpatrick's proposal of 'integral plurality', in which we are encouraged to examine the manner in which 'Elements of law *are* elements of other social forms and *vice versa*'.[76] But instead of the vagaries of 'other social forms'[77] and an indistinct 'law' which

[74] A claim explored by Fitzpatrick, 1984.

[75] Fitzpatrick, *ibid*, taking a Marxist approach, asserts that anti-discrimination legislation cannot 'displace the opposing practical rationalities of the immediate relations of production' (at 120). But this inability is not limited to law's relationship to the economy, it extends to other social systems.

[76] *Ibid*, 122.

[77] Fitzpatrick gives as examples 'prison, the workplace, the family, various therapeutic regimes, monitorial schooling, and state welfare regimes' (at 130). Thus both institutions and disciplines (in the Foucauldian sense) are social formations which can share or fail to share elements with law as the counterposed social formation. These elements are communications, and to follow the process of sharing or rejecting, we have to have some basis for identifying which communications belong to what system, and to be shared they have to have a social meaning which requires them to move from institutions through society.

has state and non-state norms, the focus of observation and analysis is social systems of communication and their interpenetration through semantic replication. Among other benefits, this avoids confusing performance with code. In his article introducing the concept of 'integral plurality' Fitzpatrick claims that 'law is supporting that which supports it' citing the example of the way in which the workplace deals with much crime on behalf of the state.[78] But this performance (crime reduction) like more general performances (social control) is undertaken by both the economy and law. On what basis does one say that a performance shared by two systems is an example of one system supporting the other?[79]

Pluralism and Translation

The question of whether 'law' exists raises questions of translation.[80] What allows us to say that a term used in one language has an equivalent in another language? Of course, there is never an exact translation of the terms of one language into another, as the respective terms will always have different possibilities of connection within one language than they would within another. The problem is 'doubled' within systems theory by the claim that meanings created by communications are a consequence of the connections between communications within systems, so that the meanings of even identical terms within identical sentences used by different systems cannot be the same.

How do we know that the participants who do not speak English are referring to 'law'? There is no such thing as a one-word 'literal' translation. Even words that represent physical objects do not translate unless those objects are used in a manner that the translator perceives to be the same, or similar.[81] Complex words like 'obligation' are not, as Hart stressed, reducible to objects, but take their meanings within complex arrangements of

[78] *Ibid*, 122.

[79] The underlying premise is a form of functionalist argument which is deconstructed by Sampford, 1989, ch 5. Systems theory's focus on codes also allows for a form of legal pluralism that examines the manner in which the legal system presents itself through its own communications, both at the level of self-observation and self-description, without having to accept that these claims adequately describe law's operations. This in turn avoids analysis which treats law as 'dying' when interactions between social systems result in forms of law that conflict with the manner in which the legal system presents itself in its most general communications. The evidence to date is that far from dying, law goes on, albeit that communications and operations which cannot fit within a current general self-description (the sort of description which, for example, Marxist analysis might label bourgeois legality) have the potential to generate new ones. Fitzpatrick rightly regards these obituaries as 'peremptory'.

[80] The same questions are succinctly explored by Arnaud, 1998.

[81] For example, the sharp instrument that we might initially call a 'knife' will not translate easily into a culture that never uses objects with the shape that we associate with this word for cutting.

words,[82] so that the translation of one such word requires a translation of accompanying words to see if a similar word game is being played in another language. If one is committed to a non-essentialist approach to identifying law one removes many of the tools whereby the translation of the word 'law' might be disciplined.[83] One cannot look to function, or essential forms (or translations of function, and essential forms) to justify what is considered to be the use of a word equivalent to 'law' in another language. Can one rely on the conventions of translators? One may be satisfied with this approach at the level of accepting that droit/loi and Recht/Gesetz are references to law, but is this due to the number of times this same translation occurs, or the fact that legal translators, like most comparative lawyers, are content to accept that whatever else might not be law, state-enforced rules certainly are?

How do these problems of translation affect the claim that systems construct themselves, and can be observed to construct themselves, through the application of codes. The identification of legal communications with the application of the code legal/illegal is an observation on the manner in which the legal system constructs itself. It is a distinction which is different from the code applied by other systems. In the case of the economy the distinction is between payment and non-payment. The application of the code provides the basis for the next application of the code. This use of codes is not captured by a conventionalist approach. There is no claim that each application of the code has the same semantic form. For example, the fact that the conviction of a defendant makes their continued detention legal is not a statement that any person needs to make at the time of the conviction, or thereafter. Similarly, within the economy, the fact that someone redeems a mortgage creates the conditions for further transactions: no-one has to utter the word 'payment'. Binary codes are distinctions with a positive and negative side.[84] Functional differentiation could not occur if every social system relied on the same mathematical symbols (+/–) to indicate this process of coding. Different codes are applied. But the semantics which represent the application of the codes are not immutable. As such, the claims that the code of the scientific system is true/not true (false), that of the media information/not information, or that of law legal/illegal does not amount to a claim that these words are used on every occasion when coding occurs. The claim that the code of law is legal/illegal is particularly

[82] Hart preferred to elaborate on a system of rules as a set of rules identified by a master rule, and legal rules as those rules applied by officials. The reliance on officials raises its own questions of definition. Do different cultures identify different roles as those of 'officials'?

[83] See Twining, 2003, 226–27.

[84] And there is no requirement that the distinction be applied to only one side of the previous distinction. One can consider the possibilities of what is legal versus illegal in what has been decided to be illegal (the robbery is illegal, but would shooting the robber be legal – the mortgage has not been redeemed, but if a sufficiently secure promise to redeem is given, it can be treated as if it has been). One can even return to situations and reverse the coding applied.

persuasive because, at least in the English-speaking world, these words are frequently used in the operations of the legal system. But if the theory is to operate as a theory of society, then one needs to understand how codes operate in each social system, not just the legal system. And such an understanding may in turn increase our understanding of the nature of the legal code.

If we start with the media, the code identified by Luhmann is information/not information, a code which unifies the mass media as a system which includes advertising, news and entertainment.[85] But if one considered what words represent this distinction within daily newspapers it might be 'news/not news' or 'story/no story', in that one can imagine the rejection of a submitted article in terms of the statement 'this is not news' and the typical journalist arriving at a location and asking: 'What is the story here?' One can apply a similar analysis to the manner in which scientific communications link. The claim that science codes in terms of true/not true makes sense as a description of a code which links scientific communications together, and makes them a system and not a random set of communications which have no relationship to each other, without the participants having to use the words true, or false, within their communications. And in our earlier case study of the GMC, one can understand that a medical system is not identical with the science system, and that the positive/negative coding that makes possible the connection of medical communications, and thus (since connection is what generates meaning) makes them meaningful, is itself understandable as therapeutic/non-therapeutic without these words being applied on each occasion when the medical system uses communications that apply negative or positive values. Thus attempts to articulate these codes can only partially be explained by conventionalism, if conventionalism is based on the semantics of the participants.[86] Teubner refers to the 'implicit or explicit invocation of the legal code'.[87] Codes can be

[85] See Luhmann, 2000.

[86] This understanding of codes can be likened to the first principles of speculative and practical reasoning, as discussed by Aquinas. The binary opposition to be, or not to be, is the basis for generating factual knowledge, and the opposition good/evil, the basis for generating normative knowledge; knowledge in each case being generated through communications that apply these distinctions, though the content of what is known changes. These oppositions are implicit in all factual and normative statements. Systems theory recognises that the range of binary oppositions is not limited to these two. Consider the following footnote from Luhmann's chapter, 'Coding and Programming' (2004, 186): 'it should be noted that the recognition of values of acceptance or rejection explodes the classical structure of binary logic. With it the connotation of an ontological and ethico-political world-view collapsed. This was built on a single guiding distinction, namely "to be" versus "not to be" and good versus bad, which did not on logical grounds alone provide the observer with structurally richer options. So one could not distinguish . . . between truth (code value) and correctness (conformity with programme).' With science, application of current norms for producing truth is the basis for the production of truth. This cross-over (re-entry within the theory of forms as articulated by Spencer Brown) through the application of normative distinctions to the world of fact, multiplies the possibilities of binary distinctions and with it the possibilities of system formation.

[87] Teubner, 1997, 14–15.

'implicit' because they are abstractions. If one had regard only to the 'news' industry, and sought the code that linked all 'news' items, one might describe it as 'news/not news'. But the 'news' is only part of the mass media. If one sought to describe and identify the 'implicit' code that allows communications to connect from advertising, news and entertainment it would not be 'news/not news' but 'information/not information'.

The issue is first whether one can identify the codes through which communications can be interconnected and generate system-specific meanings. One is looking for a way of describing how a particular system applies a negative or positive value throughout all its operations. One might do this in the English-speaking world, using the codes legal/illegal, information/not information, government/opposition, etc. One does this accepting that a modern society does have an economy, law, science, mass media, etc, and that these are in some way differentiated from each other. Looking for codes, and applying the distinction programme/code, is systems theory's answer or methodology for seeking to identify and describe this process of differentiation, and the nature of the relationships that are possible between these different parts of society. Michael King offers a useful example of how this process occurs in practice:

> A family in a remote village in Botswana watching the OJ Simpson trial on a television set understand that what they are seeing is law and that this makes it different in nature to health, religion, politics or any other kind of communicative event. . . . one does not need to go back very far to arrive at a time when the notion of legal as being quite distinct from other meanings would have been incomprehensible.[88]

King's example does not depend on the family speaking English. What will make any discussion of the trial by this family an observation on law and not religion, or even dispute resolution, is their participation in a society in which the differentiation between law, religion, science, etc is also present.

With this understanding of codes, one does not simply go to translators and ask them what word they might substitute for 'legal', 'information', 'true', etc. One starts, again with systems theory, seeking to identify how religion, law and economy are differentiated and interrelate within another national territory with a separate language, or regionally, or globally. A person who undertook this exercise and sought to describe it to an English-speaking audience could still use English versions of the codes, whilst a person who did this and sought to describe their results to a non-English-speaking audience might choose words from that language to describe the different codes which make it possible for an economy to be separate from a political system. Rather than look for a translation of law, or even of legal/illegal, systems theory would start with the assumption that the differentiation of law, economy, politics, mass media, religion, science, etc, are a

[88] 1997, 123.

feature of modern society, identify how that differentiation operates, and translate the results.[89]

This issue of translation is related to, and informed by, another topic of concern to legal pluralists: globalisation. The reductionist nature of codes – the fact that they exist only as negative/positive distinctions, but nevertheless manage to be different positive/negative distinctions within different social systems, allow for connections within a system despite changes in language. This is easiest to see in the case of the economic system, which is the system that is most widely accepted as a global one. Whilst each side to a global economic transaction may speak a different language, the positive/negative coding whereby economic communications carry out their operations and establish the basis for further communications occurs nevertheless. This coding, which Luhmann, as usually translated into English calls 'payment/non-payment', might be translated into any number of languages. But every language will recognise that something positive has occurred in terms of expectations of an increase in resources. To use a metaphor here, codes can travel where conditional programmes (which are generated in language, and thus explicit, not implicit) cannot. The ability to trade with people who speak another language allows economic communication to be global, but it does not mean that the conditional programmes created with each language can be exported to each other. This, unlike the coding, *would* require translation.

Exploring Legal Pluralism in Modern and Pre-modern Societies

One of the stimulants for legal pluralism has been the discovery that defining law in terms of state law results in the conclusion that pre-modern societies that exist without states are without law.[90] Similar conclusions

[89] There is a sense in which systems theory has to plead guilty to the charge of 'parochialism', in that it addresses the forms of law that exist within societies that exhibit functional differentiation. For such a charge of 'parochialism' addressed to Teubner, consider Roberts (2005, 20): 'On another level, by resort to the abstraction of neo-systems theory, and framing his discussion in terms of communicative codes located within autopoietic systems, Teubner tries hard to distance himself from any parochial context. . . . But here again the escape is surely illusory; the provenance of 'the binary code of legal/illegal' seems directly traceable to those venerable representations under which the 'pure form of power resides in the function of the legislator' [Foucault]. We listen here to the formal and imperative tones of kings, and ultimately the criminal laws of nation states. The apparently differentiated character of national legal orders in the contemporary West, indeed state law's native claim to systemic qualities, reflect quite parochial and, perhaps, transitory characteristics of a particular cultural assemblage.' Roberts here assumes that the positivism represented by a binary legal code that is *not* that of a religious or moral system is restricted to the conditions of its origin, and cannot survive where law develops across state boundaries. Despite the moral claims of those who see in law, especially human rights law, a 'new moral order', there is little evidence that law will lose its positivistic character as it becomes transnational.

[90] Griffiths, 2002, 293–94.

result from attempts to define law without reference to the state, but retaining the features associated with state law such as institutions, universality, formality, etc. Does the same thing occur when the legal system is identified as a system coding in terms of legal/illegal? The answer is 'yes'. Does this matter? The first point to note is that this conclusion is not reached through the application of an arbitrary classificatory scheme applied to normative phenomena, but arises out of a theory of society. As such, if one has objections to this approach to the study of law within society, one needs to take account of the explanatory potential of systems theory as a means to understand society and the interactions within it, rather than focus on the pejorative consequences of finding that particular societies may or may not have a legal system.

Following on from this, systems theory analysis of law is the application to law of a theory that understands modern society as consisting of functionally differentiated social systems.[91] If we accept Luhmann's claim that modern society has evolved from a relatively undifferentiated society, in which communications which we would today identify as religion, politics, science, economics and law do not exist in separate systems, to one in which they do, then there is nothing descriptively inaccurate in concluding that what anthropologists and historians identify and study as pre-modern societies lack autonomous legal systems. Law as a separate social formation is, within this theory, law as a social system whose separation from other systems is achieved through a binary code, and whose relationship with other systems requires one to apply the distinction between code and conditional programme. Other sociological approaches would seem to reinforce the descriptive accuracy of this understanding of modern society – for example Durkheim's focus on the division of labour and Weber's observation that modern society consists of competing rationalities both acknowledge differences between the modern and the pre-modern in terms of an intensification of differentiation.

This process of differentiation has also altered the nature of societies' hierarchies. Pre-modern societies were organised in terms of vertical segmentation (tribes) and horizontal classifications (classes and estates), with these hierarchies being understood as something natural, or given, within a society that is bounded and forms an organic hole. Functional differentiation fractures society, so that the possibilities of communication (opportunities for meaningful dialogue) are structured separately within each system. This does not mean that opportunities are distributed equally amongst all persons, so that the inequalities associated with tribe, kinship or class disappear. But because tribe, kinship and class do not form the basis of the communications which organise operations within these separate systems, the evolution of these separate systems and their colonisation of society make it increasingly

[91] See Luhmann, 1977; Luhmann, 1997, ch 4, 'Differenzierung'.

difficult for these vertical and horizontal hierarchies to present themselves as 'natural' and, as part of this, to maintain an organic and holistic account (self-description) of society.[92]

On the basis of this theory of the evolution of modern society, there is good reason to resist equating what anthropologists and historians identify as pre-modern forms of law with the law of modern societies. The societies where this common term is supposed to be applied lack the separation of social formation which allows one to identify something as 'law' in contradistinction to morals, religion, politics, etc. This is not an arbitrary classification scheme. We observe law in a modern society, utilising its distinctive code because contrasting phenomena with their codes actually exist – or at least exist within organised communication networks. And our observation that one can meaningfully distinguish law from science, politics, religion, etc can be made because law, in a modern society, manages to distinguish itself from these other phenomena, and vice versa.

If codes presume functionally differentiated social subsystems it is equally correct to say that social subsystems presume codes. The insistence that the code of law, as with any social subsystem, must be binary is not because alternatives are impossible – codes with a third value, or ones which operated like spectrums of colours – but because of the difficulty of joining together all the diverse communications of a subsystem with anything more complex than a binary distinction. Having only two sides to the code allows for an easy move from one side of the code to the other. For example, a state of affairs that has been coded legal, such as a lawful arrest, can be revisited. This might result in the arrest being re-coded as illegal, or some part of it being coded illegal (the arrest was lawful, but the amount of force used to achieve it was not). Compare the simplicity of this operation with an attempt to add even one further distinction to a code, such as would occur if one combined legal/illegal with good/bad. Then any coding of a state of affairs would involve four possible states. If one developed programmes to determine what was good from bad which operated independently from those which distinguished legal from illegal, one could manage the complexity, but that would be because two separate codes were being applied, not a combined code with four sides. A genuine four sided legal code would require programmes which could distinguish the legal good from the illegal good, legal bad and illegal bad without a separate assessment of legality and morality. Whilst this might be possible in particular situations, would it be possible to develop the ever more refined distinctions between the four

[92] 'Modern society has realized a quite different pattern of system differentiation, using specific functions as the focus for the differentiation of subsystems. Starting from special conditions in medieval Europe with a relatively high degree of differentiation of religion, politics and economy, European society has evolved into a functionally differentiated system. This means that function, not rank, is the dominant principle of system building' (Luhmann, 1982b, 131).

states which can occur with a binary code? A binary code allows the crossing over from one side of the code to the other to become ever easier, in the sense that the system can become extremely refined in terms of what can make something legal, rather than illegal. This allows a system to become ever more sensitive to its environment, as it is stimulated to develop its programmes to prevent the switch of coding being arbitrary.[93] The claim for the necessity of a binary code is that this process of ever greater refinement ('technicalization') cannot be achieved with anything like the same ease, with anything more than a binary code.[94] Luhmann distinguished the meaning of code for linguists, from the meaning of code within systems theory, calling the latter 'a special case'. For linguists, codes are symbolic instructions for the encoding of messages, ie rules for the proper use of language. With this more complex understanding of codes, the issue for communication becomes whether the sender and receiver of messages are employing the same codes.[95] But whilst codes for linguists determine the appropriate semantics for a particular meaning, codes within systems theory operate without a definite semantic.

Observing functionally differentiated social systems is not the case at the level of pre-modern societies. One can call the normative order of a society that does not distinguish between law and other communicative systems 'law' if one wishes, and thus avoid the unfortunate legacy of legal theories that associate the presence of law with progress and civilisation. But one faces considerable difficulties with this approach if one attempts to reapply it when undertaking ethnographical or studies of modern societies.[96] The acceptability of calling everything 'law' within a society which does not have differentiated social formations (social systems) provides an impoverished scheme of analysis when attempting to describe a society that does have these formations. It does not aid analysis to deny that the evolution of modern societies has resulted in the development of separate social formations which it, society, has constructed as 'law' in contradistinction to religion, morals, politics, etc.

[93] There is a significant difference between considering whether the switching of coding is arbitrary and whether, at its source, it is paradoxical or not based on a plausible foundation. Systems theory adopts the latter explanation and thus accounts for law's binary code of legal/illegal as paradoxical, but not thereby arbitrary. Many of the various issues concerning paradox (including its productive capacity) in law are explored in the essays in Perez and Teubner, 2006.

[94] Luhmann, 1992–93, 998–99.

[95] For this understanding of codes for linguists, Luhmann refers to Jakobson and Halle, 1971); they explain: 'If the listener receives a message in a language he knows, he correlates it with the code at hand. This code includes all the distinctive features to be manipulated, all their admissible combinations into bundles of concurrent features termed PHONEMES, and all the rules of concatenating phonemes into SEQUENCES – briefly, all the distinctive vehicles serving primarily to differentiate morphones and whole words' (16).

[96] This was exactly the problem faced by Moore when she attempted to use her understanding of law, within the 'semi-autonomous social field', in her analysis of the New York garment industry. See Moore, 1973 and 1978, ch 2.

Systems theory provides a sociological understanding of the difficulties of having a common referent, 'law', for both state law in modern societies and non-state law in pre-modern ones. But can it do more? Can it inform our understanding of the nature of each of these phenomena, and the relationship between them: to meet the kind of challenge for which Tamanaha has developed his 'General Jurisprudence'? When assessing the ability of systems theory to meet this challenge, one should not conclude that systems theory identifies the legal system with state law, in the sense that the characteristics of state law limit the possibilities of further legal evolution. Because systems are differentiated by their codes, and not by their current structures, the current structures can only stabilise the current applications of the code, they cannot determine the future evolution of the system. In the case of state law, this represents a stage in the evolution of the legal system within modern societies, but not its end state. The prevalence and central role played by national legislation within modern legal systems generates a self-description of law, or jurisprudence, which is an abstract and more general representation of these kinds of legal communications: sovereignty, national constitutions, etc. But systems theory does not require us to accept that the communications generated within the legal system at a moment in its evolution, including those whereby the legal system describes itself to itself as a totality, are essential, and that they determine the future possibilities of what can be legal within that system. Any attempt to insist that all law is state law denies the presence of law within pre-modern society, but as Fischer-Lescano and Teubner have aptly demonstrated,[97] it also disapplies this label to the ever expanding transnational legal communications which apply the code legal/illegal.[98] The assertion that pre-modern societies have no legal system (a system separate from politics, the economy, and religion) is a valid claim, if the modern is understood in terms of a transition to functionally differentiated social systems. But this does not compel us to accept that legal systems are unable to evolve beyond the forms associated with the nation state.

What then of non-state law within a nation state territory? Here there has been an important shift in one of the central assumptions that informed many of the classic case studies in legal pluralism, the tendency to treat these studies' communities, typically villages, as closed societies. It is now accepted that local communities, even in some of the most remote places in the world, are interpenetrated by elements of the wider societies which surround them.[99] More recent studies acknowledge and explore the manner in

[97] See, eg, 2004.

[98] And, applying Tamanaha's test, whose participants describe their operations as law.

[99] 'Since the mid 1970s, anthropologists have placed greater emphasis on economic factors, social inequality and forms of domination. Especially in research on brokerage, pluralism and legal change, they have also recognised that the village is not generally an appropriate unit of study' (Snyder, 1996, 149).

which these outside elements, which typically include state laws, impact upon the norms and negotiations of these local communities.[100] This change of assumption informs, for example, Moore's concept of semi-autonomous fields,[101] and de Sousa Santos' idea of 'interlegality'.[102] But this recognition also diminishes the strength of any argument that a social theory developed in order to explain the nature of modern society has no application to the kinds of societies and case studies that form the subject of legal pluralism. Participation within a wider modern society requires the members of a local group which may have identified itself by reference to a common religion or ethnic heritage to engage with social systems. They become patients within a health system, pupils within the education system, voters within the political system, consumers and entrepreneurs within the economy, and litigants or defendants within the legal system, etc. In particular, what pluralists might call religious or customary law becomes only one part of a life that is experienced through these other systems.[103]

This process has implications for the practice of comparing the strongly held commitments of local communities with the rules and practices of a state legal system. The threat to such strong local commitments is not limited to how state law might threaten the ability of a particular religious or ethnic group to continue to live according to its own norms. The ability of these particular communities to exist within a modern society, whilst still retaining a strong and widely distributed sense of a particular 'way of life', is premised upon their isolation from a wider society that exhibits functional differentiation.[104] The economy, the political system, the science system, medical system and education system all pose problems for this form of social life. It is undoubtedly true that the threat of violence, organised and administered via a state legal system, represents a particularly strong threat for any community that operates within modern society on the basis of a self-conscious insularity. Non-participation in systems is an option whose costs to the individual rise when the state imposes penalties for this. But there is a strong sense of legal fetishism in seeing the threat to such communities as something that comes solely from a state legal system,[105] rather than from the fracturing of community commitments and understandings that results from participation within all of these social systems. As part of this, one must also have regard to the extent to which different legal orders generate relationships of structural coupling with the economy, political system, mass media, science, etc. If for example, it is local custom and not state law that provides the norms that stabilise the economy at a local level, then

[100] See, eg, von Benda-Beckmann, 2006.
[101] 1973.
[102] Santos, 2002, especially 437.
[103] See King, 1995, and Luhmann, 1984a.
[104] See especially King, *ibid*, 112–13.
[105] For an analysis of the debates about the meaning of 'legal pluralism' which suggest that there is an over-emphasis on the state, or state-centred issues, see von Benda-Beckmann, 2002.

this provides a motivation for individuals to continue to utilise custom. But where economic transactions take new and dynamic forms, as for example where there is participation in global markets, a positive legal order is more likely to generate norms that incorporate the semantics of those transactions. In order to study legal pluralism within modern society, we have to consider the ability of different legal orders to generate their respective legal meanings and, as part of this, to examine their respective abilities to incorporate the semantics of other social systems.

To make these arguments more concrete, let us consider Cover's analysis of one local community with strongly held commitments; in his article 'Nomos and Narrative' he analyses law in terms of the commitments of participants.[106] This approach has echoes of Hart's description of law in a pre-legal situation, where rules that are backed by strong social pressure are considered to be a primitive form of law. Cover refers to laws created in such a manner as paideic laws, and contrasts them with the technical forms of law administered by judges and state officials. The latter kind of law he calls jurispathic laws, on the basis that they are likely to be enforced, through violence, against paideic laws, and thereby absorb and deflect the commitments of the members of the community which have generated paideic law. Whilst 'Nomos and Narrative' is not an avowedly pluralist article, the implications of these ideas for legal pluralism have been noted.[107] Commitment is not simply a psychological and subjective experience, unique to each individual, but is structured through narratives, which in turn construct a nomos, or way of life. The particular communities used as examples of this process are the Mennonites and Amish communities living within the US. Cover argues that the commitments of participants within these communities to their way of life can be threatened by the violence that is likely to accompany the enforcement of jurispathic laws which conflict with them. Such a conflict tests the importance of a particular paideic law within the network of narratives which forms the group's self-identity.

Does Cover's description of the interaction between state law and the norms of a group lend support to an approach to legal pluralism that focuses on groups and their norms, rather than social systems and the meanings which they generate? The groups which he uses to illustrate the nature of nomos certainly pose problems for any claim that all of society exists as autopoietic social systems. But does systems theory help or hinder our ability to understand the nature of the experience of such groups? The ability of these particular communities to exist within a modern society, whilst still retaining a strong and widely distributed sense of a particular 'way of life', is premised upon their isolation from that wider society. It is not only the legal system that threatens their ability to construct their lives

[106] 1983.
[107] See Melissaris, 2004, 15.

through a common over-arching narrative. For example, one of the cases which Cover analyses as a 'legal' threat to such communities, *Bob Jones University v United States*,[108] was a decision on the right of a university administered by a religious group to continue to receive tax relief whilst maintaining a racist admissions policy. The case having gone against them, the university removed the racist restrictions. Thus it was not the violence of state law that challenged the commitments of this group, but their ability to continue in the economy. And it was their participation in the economy prior to this decision that opened them to this threat. Whilst the Amish submitted an *amicus curiae* brief in this case, on the basis that they regarded any attempt to regulate the internal affairs of a religious group as a threat to the continuation of their way of life, the actual decision left them unaffected, not least because the Amish do not rely on tax reliefs to sustain their way of life. They do not participate to any great extent in the wider economy, or construct their own community through market relationships. This makes it difficult to tax members of the Amish community on the same basis as the rest of the US citizenry.

Cover offered the idea of a nomos constructed through narratives as a means which might be applied to understand the commitments of any institution, movement or community, not only those which, through isolation from modern society, can maintain a unity to all aspects of their lives. But in so doing, he raises the same issue that we have already discussed in connection with the nature of law within pre-modern versus modern societies. One can call the strongest commitments of a community that does not experience the fragmentation resulting from functional differentiation 'law' if one wishes.[109] And one can contrast this with the very different nature of a legal system within a society that has evolved in such a way that law is different from religion, economy, politics, etc. But how should these respective understandings of the nature of law be used to analyse what is occurring within modern society? Whilst systems theory may not fully describe what is social about a non-differentiated society, it at least explains the nature of the threat posed to such societies. And if one moves on to discuss the position of a group that has not maintained the isolation of the Amish, such as the religious group in the *Bob Jones University* case, calling all of their strongest commitments 'law' robs us of the tools whereby we might analyse and construct the nature of those commitments and the threats to them. Participation within wider society requires the members of a group identified by a common religion or ethnic heritage to engage with systems. As previously stated,

[108] 103 S Ct 2017 (1983).

[109] Melissaris believes that such commitments identify the presence of different legal orders: 'I am claiming that a legal order can be identified with reference to the *outer limits of the commitment of participants to their shared normative experiences,* that is, the combination of their experiences of the world and their ability to prescribe ways of transforming the world collectively' (emphasis added, Melissaris, 2005, 853).

they become patients within a health system, pupils within the education system, voters within the political system, consumers and entrepreneurs within the economy, and litigants within the legal system, etc. Participation in these various systems represents an experience for individuals which becomes increasingly difficult to communicate about in terms of an overall narrative, a way of life, of the kind that is generated by the Amish. In particular, what pluralists might call religious or customary law becomes only one part of a life that is experienced through systems. And whilst the self-observations and self-description of those systems will orientate communication within each system in a manner akin to Cover's description of narratives, and generate a resistance to changes to those communications which parallels his use of the term 'commitment', those self-descriptions and observations will not replicate the self-descriptions of an ethnic or religious community. Indeed, as Cover describes with reference to encounters with the state legal system, they can be expected to produce changes within religious and ethnic self-descriptions.[110]

Within systems theory, the threat to strong commitments described by Cover is not limited to how state law might threaten the self-identity of a religious or ethnic group. No system reproduces the self-identity of other systems. Each system can only continue or not, and it can only continue by making new connections to what is available (the system's memory). This is what leads to claims that systems are imperialistic – each system can only code the world using their code and programmes. The economy fails to have regard to what cannot be reduced to cost. The legal system fails to have regard to anything other than itself (its programmes, which can of course include all sorts of versions of other systems' communications) as a means to code what is legal, or illegal, etc. Thus pluralism, within this theory of society, extends to the possibilities of co-existence between systems, and the role that the legal system might play in this.[111] One might ask what changes in the medical system have followed from changes in the law, and how roles within the medical system have altered (for example, self-observations on expectations of doctors) in consequence. But in tracking these kinds of changes one needs to be aware, as in the Amish intervention in the *Bob Jones University* case, that law can open one system to another. To give a further example, passing legislation which requires hospitals to seek private sector finance opens the medical system to new relationships (forms of structural coupling) with the economy.[112]

[110] Cover stresses that narratives and the 'laws' that they generate are not utopian, nor are they merely descriptions of existing behaviour. They are meaningful so long as they represent an 'ought' expectation of what is possible. As such, they can be expected to be altered and disturbed by the communications of members of the community whose lives require them to participate in the communications of systems which generate incompatible self-descriptions and self-observations.

[111] See Teubner, 1997a.

[112] We develop this analysis further in Chapters 6 and 7.

Having reached this wider understanding of the nature of pluralism, we need to remind the reader of the fact that systems theory does not understand law to be limited to state law. The legal system consists of all those communications which code in terms of legal/illegal, not simply those emanating from legislatures, courts, or officials. Cover's own examples of this are the representations which the Amish made to the Supreme Court in the *Bob Jones University* case, on the interpretation to be given to freedom of religion under the First Amendment to the US Constitution; the interpretation given by abolitionists to the issue of whether the Constitution allowed the practice of slavery; and the interpretation given to the 14th Amendment (equal protection) by members of the Civil Rights Movement. The alternative, to attempting to reject the legal communications of officials, is radically to re-interpret the system's memory to urge a position that is compatible with the non-legal communications that individuals wish to continue making. Counsel for the Amish managed to construct an interpretation of the First Amendment that would allow their way of life to continue, and one that could be submitted to the Supreme Court. This would not have allowed them to deny the authoritative status of judicial decisions – since every part of the procedures whereby they made those submissions, and the issue in the case to which they were submitting an *amicus curiae*, would have been constructed through such decisions (see Chapter 2). Nevertheless, they were able to present their position as an interpretation of the Constitution itself. In the case of the abolitionists and the Civil Rights Movement, we encounter what Cover calls 'unofficial' and 'radical' re-interpretations of law. These communications may challenge what is understood as 'state' law, but that challenge does not take the form of an attempt to re-state the communications of another system, or group self-identity. They are a continuation of the legal system and they can be understood (observed) as such within other systems. So, for example, it can be meaningful within the political system to claim that those who advocate a particular interpretation of the Constitution (even one which is unlikely to succeed if argued before the current Supreme Court) are not denying the legitimacy of the constitution 'itself'.

Conclusion

In *A General Jurisprudence of Law and Society* Brian Tamanaha dismissed the potential of systems theory to offer a foundation for the study of law across national, regional, community and cultural borders, or globally, in favour of his own non-essentialist approach, based on conventionalism. Along with other similarly general approaches, he was offering only a method of identifying data to be studied, leaving it to each observing theorist to adopt whatever conceptual or classificatory scheme assisted their particular research. In this Chapter, we have attempted to demonstrate the potential for systems theory to meet the challenge which Tamanaha set for himself: to be able to study forms of law that are not restricted to the features associated with state law, but without moving to an acceptance that all forms of normativity or social control constitute 'law'. Whilst Tamanaha claimed that the weakness of a systems theory approach lay within Luhmann's wider theory of modern society as characterised by differentiated social systems, we have argued both that Tamanaha's presentation of this theory has flaws, and that studying law using this theory of society is its strength, and not a weakness.

Enabling recognition of the plural types and sources of law and offering a means of their observation and exploration via a legal code rather than a definite semantic, systems theory engages with the manner in which legal systems, within differentiated societies, distinguish themselves from other social subsystems. It avoids the legal becoming inseparable from the social, not through the use of definitions or conceptions, which can vary between researchers and across societies, but through observation of the process of coding which links a system's communications. The separation of social subsystems is a feature of modern society; attempts to reduce law to the study of rules, norms or commitments, whilst they may broaden the scope of what is observed as law, lose the ability to describe law in contradistinction to other social formations.[113] Attempts to account for the distinctions between these different formations in terms of what they do (performance or function) or what values accompany their operations, suffer both from the overlap between systems of whatever is attributed to them and the difficulties of explaining examples which contradict these attributions. Systems theory shifts the focus from all of these apparently fundamental and 'necessary' attributes of systems, by recognising them as programmes which orientate and stabilise but cannot determine the application of a system's code. With this shift of emphasis from programme to code, we have a basis for studying law which does not presume that law can only exist as state law, or that state law provides a paradigmatic example of law to which all non-state forms of law can only approximate. Alongside these benefits, we also have a means to overcome the problems of language and translation. There are no determinative rules for translation, just as there are no determinative rules for the use of language. The codes which allow for the transmission of information through language depend on context, in that successful communication depends on the common de-coding of the context in order to produce a common meaning between the person transmitting and receiving. Thus, in the end, this means that language is both

[113] And thereby to fail to study the phenomena associated with legal pluralism through 'the acausal parallel processing of different distinctions' (Teubner, 1992a, 466) which, as we have argued here, is an appropriate precondition for their adequate linking and potential theorisation.

embedded within, and a manifestation of, culture. Translation is an attempt to re-create the meanings of one culture using the language of another. This poses significant problems for the translation of words like 'law', which, within language, provides a symbolic reference to all of the conditional programmes which orientate a particular legal system's application of the legal code, and can include the conditional programmes of the other systems which refer to the legal system in the course of applying their codes. By identifying the legal as a system whose communications link through the application of a common code which is not economic, scientific, religious or moral, but still manages to produce normative expectations, one identifies a legal system at a level of abstraction that does not rely on a common culture. With this starting point, one can then focus on the actual application of this code, and the programmes which are generated through its secondary observations, and thus describe its operations. This approach may well not satisfy all of those who are motivated to address issues of legal pluralism;[114] nevertheless, the recognition that all communications which apply the code legal/illegal form part of the legal system, and not simply the communications of particular members of state institutions, moves us away from the assumptions associated with theories which identify all law with the state. This understanding does not lead to the conclusion that all norms, rules or values, no matter how strongly actors may be 'committed' to them, constitute law, whether or not they apply this term themselves, while it offers the possibility of what pluralist motivation has not yet produced – a common theoretical endeavour, not based on a common conception of law, but a sociologically informed understanding.

[114] For example, see Davies 2005 for a fuller statement of the nature and implications of legal pluralism.

5

How Law Constructs Time

Einstein made it clear why we need to orientate ourselves towards time: 'The only reason for time is so that everything doesn't happen at once.'[1] But, such orientation does not mean that only one understanding of time operates within society.[2] This Chapter discusses some of the roles played by time within the legal system, how law travels through time, and the mode of time's construction within law, namely law's observations on its own temporality.

What is the role played by time within the legal system? If one starts with a theory that understands society as communications, and the legal system as an autopoietic subsystem of a functionally differentiated society, then one is led to expect that communications about time within the legal system will not have the same meaning as they generate within the systems that make up part of law's environment: the systems of politics, science, economics, the mass media, etc. This is not an incidental aspect of systems theory, but a consequence of its central and necessary distinction, namely that between system and environment. If something has an instantaneous and mechanical/chemical reaction to, or relationship with, the medium that surrounds it, then one would be hard pressed to speak of that something as a system, if one could at all.[3] The concept of system in general, but certainly when considering social systems, involves a separation of something from its environment. This separation should not be understood in terms

[1] Einstein's statement is mirrored in many other statements that try to capture 'the enigma of time', for example: '. . . past, present, and future do not apply to physical events, and so they neither come into existence nor cease to exist – they just are' (Whitrow, 1975, 143, quoted in Jacques, 1990, 29).

[2] In philosophical discussion (which discussion we do not intend to concentrate on in this Chapter) there is certainly no agreed understanding of time, whether in ancient philosophy (see Callahan, 1979) or even more so in the present (see Adam, 2004; Widder, 2008). In this Chapter we restrict ourselves to the application of one sociological understanding of time's operation. We are encouraged in this by Elias' suggestion that there are weaknesses and gaps in writing on the sociology of time (see also Hassard, 1990, 'Introduction'), which are in stark contrast to the significant complexities of its discussion philosophically. 'One can present it [one of the most crucial aspects of the problem of time] briefly in the following manner: in the context of physics and, thus, of the ruling tradition of philosophy, "time" appears as a concept at a very high level of abstraction, whilst in the practice of human societies "time" is a regulatory device with a very strong compelling force, as one can readily see if one is late for an appointment' (1992, 45; see also Adam, 2004, 'Epilogue').

[3] So, for example, salt dissolved in water is not a system.

of a barrier.[4] The separation is simply the negation of total and instantaneous[5] reactions between the thing and the surrounding medium, and the substitution of internal reactions to that environment. If in place of such mechanical or chemical reactions one finds a process of internal reactions, then one can readily apply the distinction system and environment. The presence of such internal reactions raises the possibility of changes to those reactions, so that the system–environment relationship could alter. But it also raises the issue of time.

For something to have internal reactions to an external environment takes time. Time is an inevitable part of this separation. If we focus on the totality of meaningful communications as a system (namely the social system of society), separated from the physical world, then we can see that there is a delay between communicating about the state of the world and the existing state of that world. This delay cannot be eradicated; it is part of the separation of a social system from its physical environment, and therefore part of its existence as a system. This separation increases the possibilities of survival, for if a system has time to react, then it has the possibility of altering the manner of its reactions. Time increases the likelihood of a system's successful adaptation to its environment. But it also creates risks, for if a system's reactions to its environment take time, and its environment is not stable, then the difficulties of having a stable relationship with its environment are increased by the time taken for its operations, namely the time it takes to construct and reconstruct its reactions.

Society has to manage the separation between system and environment (communications and the physical world) within itself, that is, through communications. As part of this, it has to generate communications about time. This has led to differences in the form or modality of these communications. Within modern societies, which understand themselves as capable of intervening in the physical world, and controlling the future, communications about time describe the present in terms of decisions having been reached in the past (histories), with their links to decisions that can be taken in the future, and to expected states of the world in an ever more distant future.[6] Ancient and more primitive societies, which do not seek to manage their physical environments in this manner, do not exhibit the same kinds of communications about time.[7] For example, here time is

[4] The temptation to conceive of this separation as a physical barrier is a misleading metaphor, since social systems cannot exist if their 'barriers' are impermeable, as illustrated in Chapter 1.

[5] And if not instantaneous, then time is necessarily relevant.

[6] For a classic statement of the different time conceptions of modern society, see Koselleck, 2004.

[7] In Luhmann's writings, see for example 'The Future Cannot Begin: Temporal Structures in Modern Society' and 'World-Time and System History: Interrelations between Temporal Horizons and Social Structures', in N Luhmann, 1982, in which he links the changing meanings of time with the changing meanings of nature (that which lies outside human control). Whilst the changing understanding of nature in modern societies is generally accepted, its links to changing modalities of time has not been explored or accepted to the same degree.

associated with the regularities of nature, so that the present is conceived as part of a cyclical motion that is not essentially different from the past, or the future. This way of understanding time is not compatible with a society that understands itself as being in a constant state of change, which is irreversible, and substantially the result of human decisions and choices (science, engineering, etc). Thus, time does not have the same meanings within different societies.[8]

As always, the radical implications of systems theory analysis arise when we take the next step, and consider the implications of this analysis for a functionally differentiated society. If the problems generated by time for societies and their responses (altered communications which alter time's meaning) can differ between societies (ancient and modern), can they also differ between the social subsystems or function systems of a single society? Clearly the answer, from a systems theory perspective, must be yes, but how can those differences be understood? They can be understood by exploring the way in which the system's communications link together recursively. As with the example of the manner in which communications about nature have implications for understanding and communication about time, so the modality of time communicated within different subsystems alters in conjunction with other operating communications within those subsystems which are never 'given' as such, but evolve as that system evolves.

There is no suggestion here that the reality of time, as the changing state of the universe from moment to moment, differs between societies, or between the subsystems of modern society.[9] Time, as part of a reality that exists outside of and can remain unaltered by communication, is not what we are discussing. Our focus is on meaning, and the role played by communications which address time and organise the meaning of those communications within different systems. Thus, another idea of time that we need to distinguish is chronological time, or time as a series of dates. Whilst this clearly differs between societies (our calendars and ways of recording daily time were different in the past, and are still not uniform across the globe today),[10] one can argue that chronological time is more uniform across modern societies than it has ever been. Does this not indicate that time has the same meaning across all subsystems of a society that share the

[8] And there are, of course, significant cultural differences in relation to time: see Jones 1988, and Levine, 1988.

[9] This common experience of time Luhmann calls synchronicity, to distinguish it from the different understandings of time that can be generated within systems, which he calls synchronisation. The common experience of time allows an event to trigger different communications within different systems at the same moment (synchronicity), but this does not mean that terms like the past, present and future have identical meanings within different subsystems in response to that event (synchronisation). On these relationships, and their correspondence with issues of system complexity and selectivity, see Luhmann, 1995, 41–52 and 185–87.

[10] We experience this, of course, when travelling and moving from one time zone to another.

same chronology? However, the scope for differences becomes apparent when we move from chronology to the distinctions between past, present, and future.[11] What does a system attribute to its past, and its present, and its future, and how might these differ between systems?

In what follows, we intend to explore how the legal system attributes these states to its own operations, and what it constructs as its environment. But to give an indication of what we mean by a system creating its own meanings of time, let us take an example from science. What is the current state of knowledge about the nature of a disease? If our understanding of that disease is based on long-term cohort studies, then statements about its nature are based on events in the past, and projections of the expected states of affairs in the future. And this 'present' is both an outcome of operations, peculiar to science, which have generated these connections between these particular pasts and expected futures, and are open to change through similar operations. This example exhibits the features that arise from the central distinction between a system and its environment. In order to react to something in its environment (a pathogen) science has to carry out its operations, which takes time. Science has to manage time through communications which link past events to predicted future states in its environment. As part of this process, it also has to construct a meaning of what constitutes the present, and what will convert the particular present that is being identified (here the current state of knowledge about a particular disease) into the past. In this example, what allows the science subsystem to attribute part of itself to the past is not the moment-to-moment alteration of the state of the universe. Nor is it the sequence of times and dates, though this chronology will orientate communications so, for example, we might talk about this particular state of knowledge becoming 'past' at a particular date, or current between two dates. The particular meanings of past and present generated here by science do not deny that there is a moment-to-moment present, which is capable of being linked to a common chronology. But they are not an expression of either, or an immediate response to either. Rather, they are an internal construct of the science system.

The fact that systems determine for themselves what events mean results in turn to different attributions of past, present and future by different systems in response to the same events. We cannot separate the generation of meaning of an event from our understanding of when it begins and ends. This can be shown through a further scientific example: a surgical opera-

[11] These distinctions are self-reflective and can be applied to themselves. So we can talk about past presents and future presents. These more complex distinctions increase the capacity for differences in meanings of time across systems. In addition, as Melissaris' (2005) account makes clear, there are alternative vectors for time differentiation than past, present and future, and, in particular, normative commitments associated with different understandings of the relationships between law and time.

tion. If we understand an operation as a series of surgical movements and accompanying procedures (as it is taught to medical students) then we may have one set of chronological times that correspond to the operation's future (yet to begin), present and past. Yet if there were a statute making a particular person liable for all injuries arising out of the conduct of an operation, there is no certainty that the legal system would consider the operation to begin and end at these same chronological times. The operation, for the purposes of legal liability, might be taken to include medical and administrative procedures which precede the surgical incisions, and after-care.

The relevance of temporal meanings, within systems, is not limited to the expression of references to temporal modalities such as past, present or future, or the identification of when particular actions began or ended. They also arise when a 'communication is not sufficient in itself – whether as an expression or as 'praxis' – but is guided by expectations in a temporal extension of its meaning and expresses those expectations'.[12] Luhmann terms this as 'time-binding'.[13] This is not simply an attribute of certain kinds of communication, but within certain systems is crucially linked to the system's function within society.[14] Time-binding refers to 'the possibility of communicating expectations and having them accepted in communication'.[15] The economy has to manage scarcity by producing expectations that consumption forgone now can result in possibilities of consumption to be enjoyed in the future. Politics has constantly to establish what has been collectively decided and thereby establish the limits of what can be collectively decided in the future. And law provides normative expectations. Legal communications, those concerned with legal norms, have a temporal meaning that the application of law's code will be made in the same manner in the future as the present. Without such (indefinite) permanency, the law would lose the meaning that gives it its function. This expectation of consistency in the application of law's code is the meaning of what law identifies as and through its norms. This meaning is not lost when events occur that law has forbidden, for the law will give effect to its norms by coding such activity as illegal. Events that law has not forbidden can be coded legal. Law's normative expectations only change as its norms change, that is, as the application of its coding alters, and it observes on that change (which observations can become or are its new norms).[16]

[12] Luhmann, 2004, 142.

[13] In particular, see Luhmann, 2002a, ch 3, 'Time Binding: Material and Social Aspects'.

[14] What Luhmann also calls the system's reference problem. The analysis here is built on Luhmann, 2004, ch 3, 'The Function of Law'.

[15] Luhmann, 2004, 142–43.

[16] By expectations, Luhmann is not referring to psychic states: the various internal conditions that can give way to 'disappointment', but again, to meaning. Most systems produce what Luhmann calls cognitive expectations. These are communications whose meanings can be challenged by factual counter-examples. So, for example, a statement that it will 'always

The claim that law's normative expectations exist as part of the meaning which its communications create is subtly different from more conventional understandings of what constitutes law's expectations. The difference arises from the manner in which expectations can be disappointed. As described above, law's norms create meanings in terms of the expected allocation of law's code to events. As such, these meanings are not directly challenged when events occur that ought not, according to legal norms, to occur. Disappointments of this kind – for example, the reactions of those who suffer from theft – do not disturb the meanings of the legal norm. Indeed, in expressing reactions to the experience of theft, victims will have to utilise the same norms and recreate the same meanings that constitute the law of theft. How else will they communicate that they have suffered from thefts? With this understanding of expectations, disappointment occurs only when the law changes. Communications which indicate how the code will be applied in the future may not, in the future, be applied. But this disappointment does not directly undermine law's function. Because it is only by accepting the time-binding meaning of the new law that one experiences the disappointment. A normative expectation is only disappointed when a new normative expectation is created.

Law only loses its ability to create normative expectations when its communications lose the ability to bind time, that is, if its communications about the reasons for applying its code (doctrines, sources, precedents, etc) became meaningless as indicators of how the code legal/illegal would be applied in future. Thus, it is not the fact of disappointments that represents a diminution in the ability of law to create normative expectations which bind time, so much as the loss of the ability to disappoint. If current applications of the code become communications that provide no guide to the application of the code in future, then they cannot disappoint. It is difficult to envisage the situation where this would occur in total. Legal communications have continued even in the most extreme situations of conflict. The time-binding quality of law's communications as a whole would only cease if its communications ceased to be accepted. That is, if they failed to generate any meanings about the expected application of the code, both now and in the future. At its extreme, this would be a situation in which the application of the code created no expectations as to how the code would be applied in future. At this point, we could speak of legal communications being 'meaningless'. It is extremely hard to envisage such a situation occurring immediately without a total destruction of society. There are many situations where individuals may not be motivated to make legal communications (during civil wars, on battlefields, etc). But in the modern world

rain on a Tuesday' can exist within some systems as an example of poetry, irony, or nonsense, but it cannot exist within science in the face of repeated communications that 'it is Tuesday, and it is not raining'. In contrast to this kind of expectation, law communicates meaning into the future that can be sustained in the face of communications that report on contrary facts.

there are no situations where the legal system ceases to operate altogether, since not only are there legal norms applicable to wars (civil and otherwise) but during wars, communications about the 'legal' ownership of property, and contractual entitlements, continue.

This description of the nature of law's normative expectations is not necessarily a claim that the legal system understands its own communications in the same manner. There are communications about expectations within the legal system, particularly within legal arguments as to which of one or more interpretations of the law would be most appropriate. Arguments against accepting a new interpretation of law commonly include a reference to the need not to disturb settled expectations. Such communications involve more than the fact of time-binding, since whatever decisions are reached in these situations, and whatever reasons are given for those decisions, the assumption that like cases will be treated alike (a promise directed always at the future) will apply. Law's own references to expectations acknowledge that actors within law's environment invest in the meaning of its norms: individuals will have taken action on the assumption that the basis of the application of its code will remain unchanged (at least up to the date of decision). This is a claim for the continuation of previously settled interpretations of the law. Within the legal system this is articulated as a claim that it would be unjust to disturb these interpretations. They operate in a conservative fashion, in the sense that they preserve established legal meanings, and provide resistance to innovative ones that would disturb them.

Whilst all norms bind time, in the sense of creating normative expectations, some norms create law's own modalities of past, present and future. The need to do this is, as stated at the beginning of this Chapter, a consequence of being a system. The internal responses of law reacting to any event take time. And the time taken for law to respond will not be identical to that taken by other systems. If the responses of systems were synchronised, then their operations in response to common events would always finish at the same time. But clearly this is not the case.[17] A violent event may produce a newspaper story, a criminal trial, and a political response, but there is no reason to expect these operations to consume the same amount of time. The lack of synchronisation between systems is part of what it means for time (as part of a reality outside of the system) to continue while the system carries out its internal operations in reaction to an event. Other systems will take time to carry out their operations, and produce, through their communications, new meanings. In order to process an event, law has to be closed to its environment. It has to select and identify

[17] And the significance of this, according to Luhmann, is considerable: '. . . the differentiation of function, performance, and reflexion at the operative level will differentiate time horizons. It will increase the complexity-in-time and will put tension on temporal integration' (Luhmann, 1977, 37).

that 'event' as something separate from the rest of its environment. But during the period when it is processing that event, its environment continues to change (newspaper stories are printed, political debates occur, scientific discoveries are made, new conversations take place).

Time, Law and Politics

The need for law to manage time, and the difficulties that could be created by other systems which operate with different modalities of time, was a central concern for Luhmann in his writings on the relationship between law and politics. Politics, with its purposive programmes, creates considerable difficulties for law if it is to continue with its function of creating normative expectations (binding time in the sense that we have described above).[18] Law's programmes operate on the basis of 'if x, then y'. But there is a necessity, according to Luhmann, for this x to be a present condition (or allowing for the time taken for legal fact-finding operations to be the current assessment of a past condition).[19] Politics orientates itself, to a far greater degree than law, around possible future states.[20] Raising the gross domestic product (GDP), lowering child poverty or unemployment, improving transport infrastructure and so on are clearly forward-looking goals. And they lead to administrative programmes in which decisions will be orientated around changing understandings as to what the future is going to be.[21] And in carrying out these programmes, political administration will organise and direct power through legal structures, that is, it is dependent on legality.[22] But the concern, for Luhmann, was that politics, through its structural coupling with law (legislation), was introducing forms of law that attempted to match its own forward-looking orientation. For such laws, within the formula 'if x then y', 'x' refers to an anticipated future state. For example, within laws introduced pursuant to a child-welfare programme, the basis for the legality of an award of custody might be 'the best interests of the child'. This programme introduces a subtle but important change to the modalities of time operating within the legal system. The award of custody must be based on an assessment, through a legal procedure, of what, in future, is likely to be the best situation for the child. This makes it extremely difficult for the law to create normative expectations:

[18] We describe these difficulties further in Chapter 7 when dealing with problems of steering.

[19] Or a present past, in the terminology adopted by Luhmann to deal with these complexities.

[20] Or as Dworkin would say, politics is goal orientated. Though for Dworkin, the distinction is between individuated states and aggregated states, whereas we are examining future orientated and past orientated states.

[21] In Luhmann's terminology, present futures: '. . . it is necessary to draw a distinction between the present future (when the prognosis is made) and the future present (the point in time when the event occurs)' (Luhmann, 2002a, 73).

[22] We clarify the nature of this dependence in the next Chapter.

expectations that the code of law will be applied the same way in the future. This is not just a problem of standardising what is included within the goal in question. Goals can be more or less precise, just as any other standard. But, even assuming we have a precise understanding within the legal system of what is constituted by 'x', we have the inescapable problem that the future cannot be known, and can always change. As such, every application of the code based on this version of 'if x, then y' is open to re-assessment as conditions change. This is different from new evidence about past conditions or changes in the law applied to past events both of which cause their own difficulties (some examples of this are dealt with later in this Chapter). Changes in law's environment (here, evidence of the child's personal circumstances, changes in theories of child development, the willingness of expert witnesses to offer different testimony, etc) are all relevant to 'x', and none of them can be presumed to remain stable. In the language of systems theory, law is opening itself to its environment in a manner that threatens its normative closure and therefore its social function (to create normative expectations). Of course a court will make an order based on the evidence available to it at the time, in the same manner as it decides on the guilt of a person accused of a past action. And the order of that court will determine the legality of the child's custody until another court makes a different order. But from the perspective of creating stable normative expectations, the fact that something is legal because it has been decided by a court, and will remain legal until overturned by another court, is quite an impoverished from of normative expectation. Certainly this is not the manner in which most legal communications are constructed – those around transferring property, committing crimes, etc. The creation of normative expectations for these kinds of conditional programmes lasts, as we described earlier in this Chapter, until the law changes. But these future-orientated forms of legal communication do not result in the application of law's coding changing because there has been a change in legal norms, but because there has been an alteration in the anticipated future facts.

Is it significantly more difficult for law to carry out its function of generating normative expectations if its operations are conditioned by reference to anticipated future states, rather than past ones?[23] And even if it is, should the reduction in law's capacity to generate normative expectations be something to bewail, or applaud? As previously stated, the difficulties of gaining certainty as to whether the condition has been satisfied must partly be a question of the precision with which a condition has been defined, whatever the temporal modality of that condition. But this truism overlooks the reasons why politics structures its programmes in the form of goals, which affects the level of generality likely to be found. And one also has to look at

[23] This applies in addition to the risk associated with observing inherent to the operation of all social systems; see Luhmann, 2002a, ch 4: 'The Risk of Observing and the Coding of Function Systems.'

this change in the modality of legal communications from the perspective of the relationship between law and politics. To begin to explore these different levels of concern, let us return to the example of child welfare and the best interests of the child. There is some reason to believe that the routine nature of court decisions on child custody changes the apparent modality of this standard. So for example, if the possible future represented by a child's best interests is re-interpreted within courts as 'mothers without serious psychological problems who have adequate housing will normally be awarded custody', then the apparent future modality has been re-interpreted as a normal past one. However, if we presuppose that courts would entertain a wide-ranging enquiry into all the factors that could influence a child's likely future happiness, taking into account the state of all expert knowledge on the subject, then we would have a genuine future condition for the decision as to which custody arrangements would be legal. Any decision by the court would be temporary, since another court could, with any alteration of the indicators of this possible future, as well as differences of opinion as to how to interpret those indicators, make a different decision. And prior to any court decision, parents, and their legal advisers, would have difficulty in knowing which custody arrangements might be found legal, again, not only because of the difficulty of knowing what view the court might take of the evidence of that possible future, but also from knowing what those facts might be. This would represent an erosion of normative expectations (the inability to know what facts will lead to the future application of law's code).[24]

This situation within child welfare law does not seem to point to any clear implications for society. It may encourage estranged parents to engage in an exploration of the situation most likely to produce the best future for their particular child, instead of insisting on their legal rights. This may compensate for the inability of parents to be certain of court outcomes, and the opportunities for extremely estranged parents to repeatedly litigate their custody arrangements. The balancing of these outcomes within the legal system will be found through the process of litigation. If it produces more repeat litigation than the current court system can cope with, the legal system must either receive more resources or alter its procedures and interpretations, to reduce the number of court cases to a level which can be processed. As mentioned before, there is some reason to believe that apparently open, future conditions for legal decisions are routinely interpreted more narrowly, and in a manner that alters their modality to a past, an interpretation which makes the litigation burden manageable for the courts.[25]

[24] In the terms which Luhmann uses, we could say that the distinction between future presents and present futures engenders conditions of 'undecidability' that many of law's programmes constrain, but which are opened to greater risk when political programmes are made part of the conditions for law's operations.

[25] We refer again to this issue in Chapter 7 when dealing with the risk of what we describe as the over-socialisation of law.

The example of child welfare shows us that law can be open to purposive styles of legal decision making, and be capable of self-correction, but that the burden on the system may become too onerous. Thus one should not conclude that all changes in the temporal modality of law's conditional programmes, even those with imprecise definitions, have radical implications for the future of the legal system. But there are other examples where this change in modality has more significant implications, not only for law, but for systems which rely on law's normative expectations to provide a stable foundation for their own operations.[26] Within the economy, legal communications offer a platform for economic operations (payments, credit, etc). Property is formed through legal communications, and legal rights are not created by reference to who can pay for them. So law's normative expectations are productive in that they allow the economy to have a complexity and form that it could not create for itself. Within the mass media, law is a constant source of news. And that news overcomes two of the difficulties encountered within modern society: knowing what is wrong or right, and knowing what has happened. Trials and convictions routinely provide stories that particular wrongful things have been done by particular people. Again, law's normative expectations allow the mass media to have a complexity and form that it would not otherwise exhibit. But what about politics? Legislation allows politics to introduce statutes which alter the normative expectations within law. And a large part of politics is devoted to introducing laws that will serve its political programmes. But what happens if politics, instead of introducing laws that will serve its political programmes, introduces laws which take the form of its political programmes? What if, if you like, there is a short-circuiting of the process, in which the general aims of politics are introduced into statutes, so that the future-orientated goals of those political programmes become the conditions for legality?

As the example of child welfare law demonstrates, the future orientation of legal conditions can increase the burden faced by law in generating and maintaining normative expectations. Where this burden is not managed by law through the narrowing of the conditions for legality (which may effectively reverse the modality), there may be a reduction in the use of law's normative expectations to structure other system relationships. Within politics, this has implications for the ability of politics to organise itself. The political system, through legislation, introduces legal communications which it expects will 'steer' society (one example of which is child welfare legislation). But it also uses legal communications to construct itself, or to be precise, to construct that part of the political system that it identifies as 'the administration'. Here legal communications are used to distribute the formal power to make collectively binding decisions. Legality is not a

[26] What we call in Chapter 7 the risk of decreasing complexity.

sufficient condition for a collectively binding decision within the political system. Indeed, the function of legality is to indicate the outer limits of a politically acceptable decision. Within the parameters of what is legal, there will be a range of decisions that can be made, and here something other than legality must be utilised to justify them.[27] By introducing legislation which makes the legality of political action depend not on past events, but on anticipated future states, politics changes the nature of its own legal framework. The legality of a political programme will become dependent upon its anticipated effects. As such, as with our child welfare example, theories of causation (here what actions can be expected to have what effects) become part of the conditions of legality. Since politics is at least as much about assertions as to what causes can lead to what effects as it is about which effects should be pursued, the inclusion of future aims as conditions of legality places the legal system in a position in which legality becomes a political question. Or rather, a situation in which the legality of political programmes appears to require the legal system to take political decisions – to decide which beliefs as to the factors likely to lead to anticipated future states are more plausible.

One could argue that law, or legal actors such as judges, will shrink from deciding political questions of this kind, on the basis of constitutional values, such as the separation of powers. And within legal systems that have developed communications in this form, there is a resource which can steer the legal system away from deciding such issues, which are likely to generate criticism that its actors are acting outside their proper roles. But, as the example of child welfare law showed, there is also a question of the ability of the legal system to continue with its routine operations, most particularly litigation, if it attempts to address these kinds of questions. For example, knowing what economic or social benefits are likely to follow from the building of a major new airport or road or train line is the kind of condition for legality (if x then y) which cannot produce a normative expectation within law. Any judge who attempted to provide a substantive answer to this kind of question would establish the legality of the programme only until another court reconsidered the question. Through what resources available to the legal system is a judge able to identify why one casual belief about the likely future state produced by an airport, road or train line is more plausible than another? And even if the matter could be decided, within the legal system, by an authoritative ruling (that these particular circumstances are, at this time, considered likely/unlikely to produce condition x), how is the legal system to resist further litigation when one or more of these particular circumstances changes, and the casual relationship between a new present, and this anticipated future state, must again be decided.

[27] 'The state has the law at its command – but only in accordance with the law' (Luhmann, 1990a, 192). We explore this 'central paradox' of the constitutional and particularly the welfare state in the next Chapter.

With such forms of legislation, a legal system which is not to become overburdened through the endless re-litigation of questions to which it can give no stable answers must find ways of defining the legality of political actions which limits the need to consider future states. Within the UK legal system, this takes the form of judicial review. Where the condition of legality is an anticipated future state, the plausibility and predictability of judgments that the administration has acted in a manner that is illegal (outside what has been collectively decided as the basis for decisions, and therefore not legitimate) become restricted to decisions about the manner in which the administration has formed its opinion about what can happen in future. This retreat from substantive judgments as to which conditions will actually produce anticipated future states is also a formula for further retreat. The uncertainties of causation under conditions of complexity lead not only to differences of opinion as to what factors can lead to what futures, but also as to how one takes decisions under conditions of uncertainty – what resources should one put into finding out what information could be relevant to the outcome in question. Thus, the classic *Wednesbury*[28] formula of unreasonableness for challenging the legality of administrative decisions (relevant considerations have been ignored, irrelevant conditions considered, or a wholly unreasonable decision has been taken) not only creates a constant danger of criticism that the legal system is seeking to make decisions for which it has no plausible or predictable criteria but, more relevant to its own operations, it is in constant danger of producing considerably more litigation than it can handle, whilst at the same time failing to generate normative expectations.

The legal system can control the inflow of litigation challenging administrative actions through provisions such as short time limits,[29] and moving to increasingly deferential formulas for review. But these solutions to the problem which future-orientated communications produce for the legal system do not address the changing nature and role played by legality within the political system. The creation of an ever expanding subsystem of administration, which we call the welfare state,[30] distributes power in the political system through collectively binding decisions. Collectively binding decisions establish the basis for future collectively binding decisions and constitute the legitimacy of those further decisions. We examined this process in Chapter 3, in connection with the possibility of a right to disobey law. The important point here is that law, through its capacity to generate normative expectations that take the form of conditional programmes (if x

[28] *Associated Provincial Picture Houses v Wednesbury Corporation* [1947] 1 KB 223.

[29] For example, in relation to judicial review, see Part 54.5 Civil Procedure Rules. 'The claim form must be filed – (a) promptly; and (b) in any event not later than 3 months after the grounds to make the claim first arose. (2) The time limit in this rule may not be extended by agreement between the parties. (3) This rule does not apply when any other enactment specifies a shorter time limit for making the claim for judicial review.'

[30] See generally Luhmann, 1990a.

then y) creates a stability to the outer parameters of what constitutes a legitimate political decision with a certainty that politics would not otherwise be able to enjoy. Whilst politicians, challenged through the courts, will often express regret at the manner in which legal standards may inhibit political action, the evolution of the welfare state, which represents an enormous increase in the power of the political system to affect the rest of society, has been made possible through the constraining effects of legality. Exactness in what constitutes the legality of a political decision allows the power given to those who make political decisions to be closely defined. This process has allowed politics to evolve from a system that relied heavily on the application of crude physical sanctions and had little interpenetration into the detail of subjects' everyday lives, to generate the vast bureaucratic edifice it is today, even within 'under-developed' countries. But legal communications that purport to make political goals the basis of political action remove the exactness of the structuring of political power, through the loss in the normative meaning of such communications within the legal system. This, in turn, makes it more difficult for the political system to calculate with clarity what, in any particular collective decision, represents the outer parameters of legitimacy. The concern here is that politics, by introducing legal communications whose conditional programmes adopt the time modalities of its own communications, will decrease its own ability to distribute power within itself. By increasing the flexibility in the possibilities of legitimacy at each point in a chain of collectively binding decisions, one might presume that the power which can be exercised at that point in the political system will increase. But, if similar flexibility is extended to the possibilities of legitimacy for collectively binding decisions generally, then one cannot reach this same conclusion. Those who make a particular collectively binding decision will lose the certainty that they have established the parameters for the next collectively binding decision in the chain. And there will similarly be less certainty as to the power which those who take this decision can expect to have transmitted to them by those who take previous ones.[31]

For Luhmann, the implications of this loss of power within the legal system are that it will not be able to respond to its environment with sufficient complexity. The foundation for an increase in the ability of the political system to generate complex programmes which could react to problems within its environment (employment, pensions, education, etc) is a structural coupling between law and politics in which law provides politics with a clearer framework for the taking of political decisions than would otherwise have occurred. The co-evolution that has taken place with legislation that distributes legality by reference to anticipated future states diminishes the ability of law to provide that framework. Whilst the usual rationale for giving powers

[31] We develop this analysis further in the next Chapter.

to the administration defined in terms of the pursuit of future states of affairs is that this increases the ability of the political system to distribute power, Luhmann's concern was that it would produce exactly the reverse effect.

So far in this Chapter we have raised the particular concern expressed by Luhmann about the potential dangers of extending the modalities of time that operate within one system, to those that operate within another: how such co-evolution might develop, and what the costs might be. For the rest of this Chapter, we wish to move on to consider two examples of the manner in which time is managed within the legal system, choosing examples where this management of time is the subject of external critique, to see if systems theory can increase our understanding.

A Simple Example: The Presumption of Innocence

The presumption of innocence (that all accused persons are 'innocent *until* proved guilty') is a principle of criminal justice which influences many aspects of criminal procedure. But one of its functions is to recognise that law takes time to carry out its operations – in this case, for pre-trial investigations to be carried out, for a trial to be conducted and a verdict reached. The presumption of innocence is linked, within trials, to the issue of who has the burden to lead evidence. But the state of 'innocence', within any criminal trial and before, is a necessary condition prior to the verdict. Verdict marks the completion of the trial, when the condition of the defendant can be changed to that of 'guilty'. But prior to the moment of this decision, there is no state that the defendant can be in except 'not guilty'. The phrase 'innocent until proved guilty' operates both within and outside of law, as the statement of a value associated with justice. But the state of not being guilty is an inevitable result of the nature of a criminal trial: an operation of law that establishes whether a person is guilty of a crime. Once a person has been selected to be the object of a criminal trial, the onus of producing evidence is a contingency that can differ between legal systems, or between different kinds or stages of trial within a particular system. But the state of being not guilty prior to the verdict is not a contingency. It is the only state possible prior to the decision which is known as a verdict. As such, this not-guilty state is extremely resistant to any contrary external communication. A universally known person could be filmed on live television committing a crime, but they would still be 'not guilty' for the legal system until such time as their trial was completed. And their trial, and pre-trial procedures, would still have to be conducted according to whatever norms constituted a trial and other aspects of criminal procedure. These could not be dispensed with without the legal system failing to achieve what, within the legal system, constitutes a criminal conviction. Thus claims that it would be 'unjust' to allow a person to be sent to prison or executed on the basis of general opinion, or media stories, is a consequence of the necessity for law to take time to carry out its own operations. And what is a tautology within law (a person who is not in the state of being guilty is in the state of being not guilty) has significance outside of law. Law will resist trial by media, or condemnation by politicians, simply by the need to take time to conduct its own procedures. No matter how often these other systems communicate that a person 'is' guilty, the legal system will insist that she/he is not 'yet' guilty. Guilt must remain a future state, until the trial process is completed. (And so long as the legal system constructs a verdict as a 'decision', that future must include the possibility that the defendant would be found not guilty, whatever the evidence against them. For the meaning of a 'decision' is that the result is not determined, and must therefore be contingent). Communications that a person is 'guilty' can be statements of a present condition in systems outside of law; but within law, until the necessary operations have been completed, this cannot be anything other than a 'possible' future condition.[32] This is an example of lack of synchronisation between different systems, leading to different modalities of time operating in those different systems.

This particular procedural principle is but one example of Luhmann's claim that justice is generated as an eigen value. The need for legal states to be established by legal procedures, the time necessary for those operations to occur, and the impossibility of short-circuiting that process by adopting non-legal procedures (carrying out the operations of the legal system using the communications of another system) mean that the delay involved in making legal communications generates a value: justice. Persons lynched by a mob or executed by agents of the state have (from the perspective of the legal system) suffered 'injustice' not because they have experienced a different fate (death by hanging or gunshot) from what they might expect from the legal system, but because the legal system will never be able to establish their status as that of convicted persons who have actually been sentenced to death (and those deaths administered by the state authorities). Thus there are no communications available within the legal system whereby their executions can be right/just.

[32] Indeed, where other systems, such as the mass media or politics, produce substantial or dramatic communications which insist that a person is guilty, or even might well be guilty, prior to the completion of legal procedures, the legal system can decide that it is not possible to carry out its procedures, with the result that the defendant is left in a permanent 'not guilty' condition, regardless of the evidence against them. For a dramatic example involving politics and the mass media, consider the case that became known as the Winchester Three case. The former Northern Ireland Secretary, Tom King, was the apparent victim of a terrorist plot to assassinate him in 1998. Tom King made a statement in Parliament about the abuse of the 'right to silence' and the government's intention 'to abolish it'. The Winchester Three, who had been accused of the terrorist plot against Tom King and had relied on their right to silence, had their convictions quashed due to the possible prejudice to their trial, and were then made subject to exclusion orders from the UK and sent to Dublin. See: http://www.guardian.co.uk/uk/2000/jun/20/northernireland.comment.

Other systems (especially the political system and the mass media) can challenge the 'injustice' of the time needed for particular operations within the law. This can generate a story of 'scandal' within the mass media, or collective decision that the delay or uncertainty involved is 'intolerable'. But the operations of other systems cannot replace those of the legal system within the legal system. Nor can they provide a systematic alternative to the manner in which legal communications are routinely re-used within their own system. The mass media, or politics, may declare that someone has committed a crime, but they cannot generate even these communications in circumstances where there is no 'news' and the 'criminal' incident has no political relevance (and can rarely do so even where these conditions do occur). As such, any attempt by a system other than law to claim that its operations have the value of justice cannot be other than episodic. By contrast, the everyday operations of the legal system establish ownership, wrongs and convictions on a totally routine basis. Law can be reformed, but until such time as it is, the only basis on which these states can routinely be produced is through the existing legal procedures. The justice of legal procedures (which includes the time taken to complete them) is simply the legal system's inability to offer any alternative, and the inability of other systems to offer any alternative to the legal system.

A Complex Example

Retroactive Laws

The issue of retrospectivity in law, the application of law to events which occurred prior to the introduction of the law in question (also termed retroactive law) demonstrates how, within law, the communications available to communicate about time are generated within the system itself and, in consequence, are likely to generate criticism when viewed from outside perspectives. Statute law normally applies only prospectively (to events arising after enactment, or date appointed for the statute's operation) so that any retroactive application of a statute is likely to attract criticism and require special justification. By contrast, changes in the law arising from adjudication normally apply retrospectively, in the form of a statement of the law applicable to the events which led to litigation, which must necessarily have occurred in the past. This distinction in the modality of these two forms of law is, it has been argued, part of what creates the legal expression of a political doctrine: the separation of powers.[33] But this claim

[33] An argument made by Gustav Husserl, 1955, 63. It is also an argument that has regularly been made by judges in the course of adjudication who claim that abandoning retrospective effect would lead to greater judicial activism, and dissolve the distinction between adjudication and legislation.

raises many questions. Why should those who draft the communications which the political system expects the legal system to interpret as statutes seek to avoid their having a retroactive effect? And why, by contrast, should their re-interpretation in the course of adjudication lead to a normal consequence of retrospectivity? What keeps these different parts of the legal system (legislation and adjudication) orientated towards their own temporal attitudes?

The retrospective application of law arising through adjudication is made less visible by the general failure of the communications which affect this kind of legal change to simultaneously acknowledge that there has been a change in the law.[34] Custom, and the development of doctrine (both within the common law, and through the exegesis of codes within civil law systems) were, and largely still are, communicated about in terms of a continuous present. The law is, as it has always been. This is obvious with custom, which takes its authority from claims of its long duration down to the present. But it also operates with interpretations of codes, which add and amend that code through a process of articulating what the code requires in particular, including new, situations. An interpretation of what a code requires may alter legal practice, but those who can give authoritative interpretations are rarely authorised to amend the code, and as such, have to express those interpretations as statements of an unchanging and already-existing law, even as they change it. This is not only a feature of civil codes, as it also extends to the interpretation of statutes. And the common law exhibits similar features. When the common law was described by its practitioners as the expression of custom, the current state of the law inevitably arose in the past. Judges could declare what the law required, but could not acknowledge their own role in creating it, and therefore could not place any temporal limitation on its application. Bentham, in one of the most famous criticisms of this 'declaratory' theory of the common law, whereby judges always claimed to 'find' the correct legal result and never to create new law, described the common law as 'dog's law', likening it to beating a dog in order to teach it what the law required. But the retrospective application of judge-made law has survived the recognition, even within the legal system, that this declaratory theory of adjudication is a fiction, or 'fairy tale'.[35]

The resilience of the declaratory theory in legal communications can be understood in terms of the difficulties of communicating in law, and carrying out its current operations, in any other way. All kinds of legal communications may be involved in the resolution of a particular legal issue, and they all have to be directed towards the present: what is the appropriate way of dealing with this matter, at this moment? The declara-

[34] As we have demonstrated in Chapter 2.
[35] See Lord Reid, 1972.

tory theory of the common law (the claim that judges only find, and never make law) is a fiction, and that fiction can be recognised and described as such both from outside the legal system, and on occasions from inside. But it is a fiction that allows the legal system to carry out operations that it cannot otherwise manage and as such is not easily abandoned. Consider, for a start, the fiction that judges always only find and do not make law in respect of statutes. Statutes have to be interpreted, and different courts can adopt radically different interpretations. Where this leads to the interpretation of one court being replaced by another, the new interpretation has a retrospective application. Whatever the court finds to be the law because it is a requirement of statute must also be taken to have been the law since the date of the statute's enactment or operation. And this continues when later courts use this decision as a reason why the statute must be interpreted in this way. They can acknowledge that the law changed with this decision, but the change was from one law that operated from the date of enactment until its repeal, to another that operates in exactly the same way.[36]

Treating statutes as authoritative statements of the law applicable from the date of their enactment or other starting date generates a treatment of judgments that duplicates the earlier manner in which common lawyers used to speak of the common law. Then, judges claimed that their judgments were not themselves the law, but simply the best evidence of a law that actually existed outside of their judgments. Since then, the common law has developed a much stricter doctrine of precedent, in which it is possible to say that something is law because of the authority of the court that pronounced it to be such. But with regard to statutes, the interpretation of the applicable law by a court, even if that court's pronouncement has an authoritative status as a precedent, is still communicated about in terms of the interpretation of something which lies outside, and exists prior to, the court's decision: the intention of Parliament. Statutes, in order to operate as overriding authorities, have to be interpreted using communications that refer to them as if the legislature has communicated what is to happen from their date of enactment or operation. The fact that different interpretations can be offered to a court by rival counsel, or different judgments reached by different judges or different courts, provides cogent evidence that the legislature has not, in fact, provided clear direction. Choosing between these alternative interpretations gives us judge-made law: a standard generated by a court whose decisions have the status of precedent. But this fact, however obvious, does not allow those involved in statutory interpretation to abandon the fiction that the legislature has decided what is to happen. This fiction, and the necessity not to recognise it as a fiction

[36] See Lord Scott's judgment in *National Westminster Bank plc v Spectrum Plus Ltd and others* [2005] UKHL 41 (hereafter referred to as *Re Spectrum Plus Ltd*).

when one carries out statutory interpretation, is an inescapable part of what gives statutes their role and status as authorities.[37]

The law created by statutes is communicated about as something that exists as a continuous present. When courts alter their views as to what a statute requires, they give a statute its normal status as an overriding source of law by describing that requirement as 'the law', that is, the current law. This is not a statement that the interpretation has just, at that moment, become law, *because* of this court's decision. It is a statement that the law has always been such, since the statute's enactment, and is thus also a statement whose meaning is that the law was not something made by this court, but rather something identified, that is, found. Thus a major part of legal argument is locked into using communications whose meaning includes the fiction that courts always find, and do not 'make' the law, and a secondary effect of this fiction is that the law 'found' by the court existed in the past as well as the present.

One can construct arguments as to why limiting the interpretation of a particular statute to its prospective effect would be appropriate, utilising communications about the common good, national interest, national security, morality, or even justice (in the sense that the new interpretation will come as a surprise to those who will be subjected to it). But these arguments are incompatible with the status of statute as an overriding authority. Whilst they may form part of the matrix of communications used to establish what Parliament intended by a statute, once the conclusion as to intention is reached, they cannot be re-introduced as arguments which limit the operation of the statute without conceding that statutes do not, after all, operate as overriding authorities. Instead, they are only prima facie authorities, whose application may be limited by reference to morality, national security, injustice, etc. This represents a potential loss of a vast amount of redundancy within the legal system. Or, to use colloquial language – it opens a huge can of worms.

When one examines the retrospective elements of adjudication, and considers whether they can be reduced or ameliorated, it is not enough to point out that the declaratory theory of adjudication is a fiction and, having exposed the judicial role in making law, simply urge those involved to reduce or eliminate this element of retrospection. One has to consider the difficulties involved in continuing to use communications whose meanings *necessarily* include an assertion that the law has always been what has just been identified, in combination with others which recognise that assertion as a fiction, and seek to remove the retrospective consequences of the

[37] On what it means for something to be an authority, see Raz, 1999, 186–210. Our point here is that this idea of authority (what one interprets as law must be taken to have decided something – to have moved from a deliberative to an executive stage), when applied to statutes, has a necessary temporal modality.

court's decision. The difficulties of doing this are captured in the words of Lord Goff in *Kleinwort Benson*, who opined:

> It is in this context that we have to reinterpret the declaratory theory of judicial decision. We can see that, in fact, it does not presume the existence of an ideal system of the common law, which the judges from time to time reveal in their decisions. The historical theory of judicial decision, though it may in the past have served its purpose, was indeed a fiction. But it does mean that, when the judges state what the law is, their decisions do, in the sense I have described, have a retrospective effect. That is, I believe, inevitable. It is inevitable in relation to the particular case before the court, in which the events must have occurred some time, perhaps some years, before the judge's decision is made. But it is also inevitable in relation to other cases in which the law as so stated will in future fall to be applied. I must confess that I cannot imagine how a common law system, or indeed any legal system, can operate otherwise if the law is to be applied equally to all and yet be capable of organic change.[38]

Lord Goff here is not stating that it is impossible to limit the retrospective effects of judge-made law. This would require him to ignore the example of overseas jurisdictions that have introduced prospective overruling for some purposes, as well the arguments of the minority in *Kleinwort*, who wanted an exception to be made in the case at hand.[39] Goff's statement points to the routine manner in which adjudication involves communications which identify a law that exists in both the present and the past, and the difficulties in both using these communications and denying the meanings which they express. Having used communications which ignore the role of the court in establishing law, and found that someone has a statutory entitlement which has existed since the statute was enacted, on what basis is that entitlement to be denied to others in the same position? Like cases must be treated alike. This formula is not, within adjudication, something that is empty of content. The legal arguments that will have been made to the court, and normally used to construct its judgment, will not seek to identify the claimant or defendant as someone uniquely placed to receive an order in their favour. Rather, they will have been articulated in terms of the right of persons, in the circumstances facing these parties, to receive the order sought. As such, a case which establishes new law is constructed through communications which presume that the law found to be applicable in the case at hand is equally applicable to the rights of other persons who acted at the same time as the parties before the court. Finnis has called this a 'duty not to declare and apply a rule unless it can fairly be said to have been all along a legally appropriate standard'.[40] But it is a duty

[38] *Kleinwort Benson Ltd v Lincoln City Council* [1999] 2 AC 349 (HL), at 378–79.

[39] The minority judgments in *Kleinwort* wanted to isolate transactions conducted on the basis of earlier 'settled' law from the application of a new right to claim repayment of monies paid under mistake of law when that earlier law was disturbed by a new decision.

[40] Finnis, 1999, at 175.

to do what judges cannot easily avoid, since this is the meaning of the communications which they use to construct their decisions.

The example of statutory interpretation shows that the fiction of judges finding law, when it is abundantly clear that they are in fact making law, is still a current and presently inescapable feature of a legal system. This is not an argument that a legal system has no way to limit the temporal application of judge-made law. Time limits, both those found in statutes of limitation, and time limits imposed on the rights of appeal, serve to limit the retrospective effect of judge-made changes to law, a feature which is sometimes directly addressed within the legal system.[41] As an alternative to finding that an earlier precedent was wrongly decided, judges can simply affirm that circumstances have changed.[42] This creates a situation in which the new decision has current application and a retrospective application back until the date of the events which led to the particular litigation, but no clear time line for any earlier application.[43] (This device depends on the plausibility of any claim that circumstances have indeed altered in a material fashion.) These devices operate to cure some of the consequences of a system in which the retrospective nature of judge-made law is both routine and unacknowledged.

Bentham's attack on judge-made law as dogs' law was directed at all developments and changes in the law that could not be known to litigants in advance of a judicial decision. This is a view which attributes the title of 'judge-made' law, and the conclusion that law making has been retrospective, to any situation in which the law to be applied is not clear, that is, to anything except settled law. But this is not what causes the declaratory theory to be recognised and confronted within the legal system. All kinds of 'developments' of law, statute, common law and constitutional law, occur using communications that take the form of an identification of what the law *is*, rather than acknowledgement that what is being sought is a change in the law. As we discussed in Chapter 2, these forms of communication do not change structure when one moves from settled to disputed law. Nor do they change from counsel to judge. Arguments take the form of assertions of what the law currently requires, not what it ought to require. This form

[41] Much of the US case law on the prospective application of judge-made constitutional law arose from the implications for the finality of state adjudication if new constitutional rights were given retrospective effect. See Shannon, 2003, and *Linkletter v Walker* 381 US 618 (1965).

[42] See, for example, *Fitzpatrick v Sterling Housing Association Ltd* [2001] 1 AC 27 in which the meaning of 'member of the family' was held to have changed between 1920 and 1994.

[43] See Tur, 2002; the example cited by him is *Hall v Simonds* [2000] 2 All ER 637 (the legal immunity granted to barristers in *Rondel v Worsley* held not appropriate as circumstances have changed). Tur also claims that retrospective effect is similarly diminished whenever a court declines to follow an earlier precedent, rather than overruling it. This seems wrong. As long as the later decision is accepted to represent the current law, its application is applicable to all who can bring their circumstances within its scope, which will involve some element of retrospectivity, even if it does not go back as far as the distinguished precedent.

of argument suppresses recognition that any decision which results actually represents a change in the law, though there may be some acknowledgement that the decision, being a precedent, makes the law clearer. As with communications whose meaning includes an acceptance of the authority of statutes, it is difficult to construct a judgment through communications which treat the law as something that currently exists, *and at the same time* construct an entitlement which arises only in the future. This also applies to the communications which are used in connection with appeals. Appeal courts receive arguments that the conclusions reached by an earlier court, as to what the law *is*, were wrong. Where they agree with these arguments, they do not recognise that the lower court had a law-making authority that was poorly exercised. Instead, they find that the lower court made a mistake in their interpretation of the current law.

Amid the routine creation of law, through adjudication, which is retrospective but does not acknowledge itself as such, we find communications which acknowledge adjudication as an exercise in retrospective law making. This is where the decision overruled is a precedent whose overruling can be expected to have significant consequences. These may be consequences for the legal system itself, as when a retrospective change in the law will disturb the finality of criminal convictions and civil awards.[44] Or the consequences may be for law's environment, when it can be persuasively argued that large numbers of legal transactions have been undertaken on the basis of the law announced in the earlier precedent.[45] Whilst a successful appeal from the decision of a court whose judgments are precedents *could* be described as a 'change in the law', it normally will not be. The arguments given to the earlier court, which will have been in terms of what the law currently is, can be expected to be repeated at the appeal. The judge-made law created by the lower court does not exist, as law, in the appeal. Like the earlier forms of common law argument, it is reduced to evidence of a law that exists elsewhere (typically in the judgments of *other* courts). Cases which seek to acknowledge and limit the retrospective effects of overruling past decisions, represent exceptions to this normal form of communication.

As Tur has observed, consistency and coherence could be achieved by treating all overruling in the same way, that is by treating all earlier overruled precedents as never having been law for any purposes.[46] Then one would have a single temporal modality for all of the legal communications involved in adjudication. Statute, common law and constitutional law could all be used to generate interpretations of the law for a common present, in

[44] These were the considerations which led the US Supreme Court to adopt a prospective application for constitutional decisions (see Shannon, 2003).

[45] This recognition can also occur through arguments that require courts to consider such situations as hypotheticals – see Finnis, 1979.

[46] Tur, 2002, 467.

a form that discussed this present as a continuation of the past,[47] and generated the same entitlements for all those placed in a similar position (treating like cases alike).[48] And those interpretations would not separate communications of what rights parties enjoyed from communications about the appropriate remedy. All parties with the same substantive rights could expect the same remedies. This also makes it easier to unfold the consequences of any decision. By contrast, attempts to introduce discontinuities into this process are far more problematic. Consistency and coherence are not the only values recognised within legal communications, so that one will also have exceptions, justified by reference in particular to communications about injustice. But one cannot build these exceptions into stable elements within the legal system unless they too, within their governing area, can be applied in a manner that treats like cases alike, that is, they too must exhibit coherence and consistency. And if there is to be an area of the legal system that exhibits a different temporal modality, the border of that area must also be identified in a manner that allows for coherence and consistency.

These problems can be seen in the recent experience of prospective overruling. The House of Lords examined this practice as part of their decision in *Re Spectrum Plus Ltd*.[49] In this case they overruled an earlier first instance decision which had interpreted a statute to allow a company's book debts to form the subject of fixed charges. Under the new interpretation, the charges were not fixed but floating charges, and therefore, under the terms of the statute, had no priority over preferential creditors. The House of Lords was asked to apply this interpretation prospectively only, on the basis that banks had relied on the earlier decision in forming judgements on whether to lend on this security. The court took note of examples of prospective overruling by courts in other countries (Ireland, Canada, India and the United States), and the express authority which it had been given in devolution statutes to limit the retrospective effects of any finding that the Scottish Parliament or Welsh Assembly had exceeded their authority. They also noted that the European Court of Justice has, on occasion, specifically limited the retrospective effect of its judgments. In light of all these developments, they concluded that there was no legal or constitutional principle which prevented prospective overruling. They accepted that they could be as flexible

[47] Postema, 2004, has used the metaphor of music. Legal interpretation, like musical appreciation, involves an experience of the present as a continuation of the past.

[48] Pure prospective overruling only applies the new rule to facts occurring after the decision. This treats 'like cases alike' but also deprives the 'successful' litigant of the benefit of the law which it has just been decided should always have applied to her/his case. If this approach is generally applied, it eliminates the incentive for litigants to pursue any case that requires a precedent to be overruled. But once a court allows a successful litigant to enjoy the benefits of the overruling, excluding others on the basis of the accidents of when they commenced their actions (or how or when they reached the appeal court) is difficult to present with any plausibility as 'just'. See *Re Spectrum Plus Ltd*, n 36 above, at paras 26 and 27.

[49] See n 36 above.

as these other courts and, to use the words of Scott LJ, announced that they would 'never say never' to the possibility of a suitable case arising, even with respect to a statute, in which, even without express statutory authority (as with the devolution Acts), they would limit their judgment to a prospective effect. However, having reached the conclusion that no principle prevented their restricting the application of any decision to future cases, they announced that any such cases were expected to be exceptional, and that the claimed reliance of banks on the first instance decision which they have overruled did not meet this standard:

> There could be cases where a decision on an issue of law, whether common law or statute law, was unavoidable but the decision would have such gravely unfair and disruptive consequences for past transactions or happenings that this House would be compelled to depart from the normal principles relating to the retrospective and prospective effect of court decisions.[50]

Why are these cases likely, at least for the foreseeable future, to be exceptional, since the House of Lords (now Supreme Court) has decided that there is no law, constitutional or otherwise, which prevents a court from taking heed of claims that an overruling, if applied retrospectively, will cause injustice? We suggest two factors. The first is the effect of the form of communication within legal argument – which fails to acknowledge the judge as a law maker. Even in cases of overruling, the argument which leads to the change in the law is articulated in terms of the original decision being a mistake. Any additional argument that parties should not suffer from the mistakes of the courts has to be reconciled with a decision which has been articulated in terms which affirm that the law has always been in the form argued for by the winning party. Second, and the two are interrelated, having decided what the law has required since the date of the mistake, on what basis of authority is the court able to justify failing to apply that law for the period prior to the decision.[51] What, other than the law, can justify a court in limiting the effects of its decision?

The problem of asserting limitations on retrospectivity can be avoided by a court finding that the new law did not apply in the past. Confining statutes to events taking place after their enactment is an uncontroversial example of this. A further refinement, as already mentioned, has been to identify statutes which are intended to speak to current conditions, which allows them to be re-interpreted with only limited retrospective effect. And

[50] See n 36, per Lord Nicholls, para 40.

[51] Lord Nicholls in *Re Spectrum Plus Ltd*, n 36, paras 24–25, noted one circumstance when prospective application might not only be allowed, but required. This was in connection with interpretations of the European Convention on Human Rights, on the assumption that the convention was treated by the European Court of Human Rights as a document whose requirements evolved. But this is because the law to be applied has been interpreted not to have retrospective effect, akin to a statute in connection with events prior to its introduction, rather than a decision to apply retrospective law prospectively.

if the European Convention on Human Rights, or Community Law, is treated as having a similar ability to speak to current conditions, then it is not difficult for a court to conclude that a current interpretation of the law does not alter the law all the way back to an earlier precedent which took a different view.[52] Then the earlier precedent need not be treated as a mistake any more than an earlier statute which is displaced or amended by a new one is a mistake. These developments allow a court to limit the application of a decision, not because the court has decided that its decision 'should' be limited because of its impact on the affected parties, but because the law that has been identified does not have an application before an identifiable period or date.[53]

Finding that the law is not, in fact, retrospective is not a hard option for the courts. Hardness occurs when the law identified is articulated as having required something in the past, but the court wishes to avoid the consequences that follow from this conclusion. Here the courts are being invited to separate the right declared from the remedies that would normally be expected to attach to such a right.[54] The legal system has few resources available to it for making this separation. This lack may not immediately be apparent, as the Supreme Courts of both the United States and United Kingdom have claimed jurisdiction to limit the temporal effect of their orders. But, having claimed this jurisdiction, through which communications can its application be stabilised? What are the problems in identifying the 'substantive' law through communications which express court decisions as precedents in which like cases must be treated alike, and then at the point of remedies, switch to communications which express a pragmatic view in which the lawfulness of what is required has to be articulated as an assessment of the consequences likely to follow from the retrospective effects of overruling? If these remain ad hoc decisions, the court has to make a plausible case that the consequences are so significant that an

[52] These developments are discussed by Rodger, 2005.

[53] Of course, such developments increase the variety and hence the complexity of law. Which provisions are taken to speak to current understandings and conditions, and which should be contained by evidence of contemporary understandings? See, for example, the discussion in *Boyce v The Queen* [2004] 3 WLR 786. In an appeal against a mandatory death penalty, the Privy Council was invited to conclude that the 1868 statute (as re-enacted in 1994) which stipulated the penalty should be updated, in light of a constitutional provision outlawing cruel and unusual punishment (itself updated in light of modern views of the death penalty), to provide for only a discretionary application of the death penalty. Having regard to other constitutional provisions which expressly provided for changing laws which offended these standards, which would be difficult to give any legal effect to in light of the appellant's arguments, the majority of the Privy Council refused to apply this approach.

[54] See for example *Percy v Hall* [1997] QB 924 in which the Court of Appeal decided that policemen could not be sued for wrongful imprisonment for arresting someone under a byelaw that was subsequently found to be invalid, provided that they had reasonable cause to believe in its validity at the time of the arrest.

exceptional decision is justified.[55] The difficulties of so doing can be seen from the Supreme Court's discussion of the request to suspend the making of their order in *Re Ahmed*, in order to avoid its immediate effect.[56] There, the court was asked not to make an order quashing an ultra vires statutory instrument which had led to the bank accounts of suspected terrorists being frozen in order to give Parliament time to pass amending legislation to make the freezing lawful. The majority could see no basis on which it, as a final court of appeal, could decline to give the order sought, or how the banks could lawfully continue to withhold these funds once the order was made. They were not persuaded by the argument that a suspension of the order would be treated by the banks as authority to continue holding monies illegally, and that the national interest justified the Supreme Court in condoning that misconception. Lord Hope, in dissent, articulated a more pragmatic view. If he could assist the security authorities by delaying the making of the court's order declaring unlawful the relevant statutory orders for a few weeks, for reasons of national security, he would. The dissent in this case is evidence that a court can be asked to make an order (or at least not make an order) which conflicts with the rights that they have just articulated in a judgment which establishes 'the law'. But it also illustrates the difficulties. It is quite normal for courts to move from a discourse of legal rights to one of practicalities when proceeding from judgment to a discussion of how an order should be framed, and when it should take effect. Lord Hope's dissent is framed as a temporary delay, to achieve a practical result, and, even then, as this delay has been requested with the express purpose of defeating legal rights, he feels the need to justify it by reference to considerations of national security, which he equated with 'justice'. The dissenting judgment is defensive in tone. It is constructed in the form of anticipation of criticism if the order were to be given as well as if it were not. But the criticism anticipated if the order is granted is generated within the legal system. The Supreme Court has just established the law – the parties' legal rights. By what legal authority can they then make an order contrary to those rights? Of course they are the highest court, with the highest authority to establish the law. But where are the communications within the legal system that provide authority for this court to decide that the law should not be applied? The Supreme Court is authorised by statute to decide matters 'in the interests of justice', but such general authority is a very limited resource – as it cannot mean that the Supreme Court can dispense with the law whenever it decides that it is not appropriate without encouraging appeals to change from arguments which establish

[55] There are parallels here with our discussion of civil disobedience in Chapter 3, and the discussion yet to come of the nature of the rule of law in Chapter 6. Legality allows the 'rightness' of political decisions to be understood as legitimate.

[56] *HM Treasury (Respondent) v Ahmed and others (Appellants) v HM Treasury (Appellant)* [2010] UKSC 2.

the law, to ones that seek to have the law overturned or not applied. And any interpretation of this general authority has to operate alongside the everyday practice of litigation which, in its current form, operates as arguments about what the law currently is – ie it does not recognise any authority for a court to disallow the law, and communicate its judgments as law making acts grounded solely in pragmatic considerations.

As well as the problems of generating plausible justifications for ad hoc refusals to allow the remedy to follow from the communications that have identified the law, we should also consider the problems of the alternative possibility. What are the prospects for prospective overruling becoming a stable element of the legal system? Could a development which has its origins in pragmatic considerations nevertheless establish itself as a legal doctrine? Can the courts create a situation in which it would be meaningful to communicate in terms of a 'right' to have the application of an overruled precedent limited to its prospective effect?

Here it is useful to consider the experience of the United States Supreme Court, who 'experimented' with prospective overruling as a doctrine in the 1960s. The experiment began[57] with the US Supreme Court decision in *Linkletter v Walker*.[58] In an earlier case, *Mapp v Ohio*,[59] the Supreme Court had made new constitutional law by extending the prohibition on the use of illegally obtained evidence from federal courts to state courts. *Linkletter* had to consider whether the decision in *Mapp* could potentially disturb the finality of all convictions in state courts that involved the use of illegally obtained evidence. This was a problem that was eventually solved through a quite precise rule: that new constitutional rights could not be relied upon by parties when their rights of appeal before the state courts had been exhausted. This rule leaves the new right available to every potential litigant, and every litigant still going through the state legal system, and limits the need for new trials. So the disturbance to the legal system from overruling a precedent is minimal. But, prior to reaching this position, the Supreme Court went on a doctrinal ride that began when the court in *Linkletter* held that the *Mapp* ruling should apply only prospectively, and sought to justify failing to apply the *Mapp* ruling to all litigants who came within the rule in that case (ie retrospectively). In seeking to formulate a reasoned basis for prospective overruling (rather than simply announcing that the decision was ad hoc and exceptional) that court could not escape the consequences of its own status as a court whose decisions are precedents. Like cases must be treated alike, but what, having regard to the facts and reasoning in

[57] Only in the sense that this was the first Supreme Court decision announcing a general basis for limiting overruling to prospective cases. There were isolated examples of courts doing this prior to this decision, which are noted in the majority opinion.

[58] See n 41 above.

[59] 367 US 643 (1961).

Linkletter, did this require? Did it apply to civil cases? If so, does that not mean that losses of money might be a basis for limiting retrospective effect? If so, what level of monetary consequences, demonstrated with what evidence, from which parties, will suffice? Is it relevant that one court decided the applicable rule, and another court decided the issue of retrospectivity. Henceforth, should a court that overrules always have to consider whether to restrict the application of the new rule, by reference to the criteria announced in *Linkletter* and other cases that overruled prospectively, or can/should the consideration of the need for overruling always be taken by a different court from the original one? The purpose of the new rule was to guide *future* behaviour (deterring the state police from conducting illegal searches), so the failure to treat like *past* cases alike did not diminish the effectiveness of the new rule. What other kinds of constitutional rules could be taken to have a forward-looking purpose of this kind?

This doctrinal journey was accompanied by an enormous body of arguments, from both judges and legal academics, on the correct position.[60] These included claims that the failure of a court to acknowledge that it does anything but find law, the retroactive application of its precedents, and the consequent need to consider the effect on those who have relied on an earlier precedent, all form an essential part of what makes adjudication different from legislation. Systems theory analysis supports these claims, but not from the perspective of those making them. The arguments of those who opposed prospective overruling were that this procedure would allow judges to act like legislators, which went beyond what was legitimate in their role as judges. But prospective overruling, as practised by the Supreme Court, did not lead to the legal system processing those decisions in the manner in which it would process legislation. Statutory rules and rights can be interpreted as being both technical and unprincipled. But Supreme Court decisions which interpret the Constitution, even ones that assert a right of courts to make law using the temporal mode of the legislature, have to be integrated into the legal system as interpretations of the Constitution within a form of interpretation that generates legal meanings by an endless process of treating like cases alike. So, any claim that a judge, by adopting prospective overruling, acts like a legislative body has to be qualified in light of the fact that judges can only make law (achieve something capable of iteration) if their judgments are accepted as precedents: a status that provides a fixed point of reference for further legal claims. Thus when the Supreme Court claimed that it had power to engage in prospective overruling, it had the inevitable result of stimulating further litigation because the judgments of this court *were not* treated within that legal system as the communications of a legislator.

[60] See Traynor, 1999, for a description of the extensive debates that these US cases engendered (how the doctrinal ride in the cases was mirrored in academic writing).

The conclusion of those who offered normative arguments against prospective overruling by the US Supreme Court was and will continue to be that the 'better' argument succeeded in influencing judges into abandoning the experiment with prospective overruling. An alternative view, reliant on systems theory observation, is that whilst it was easy to begin the experiment with prospective overruling (the Supreme Court identified some common law cases where the remedy awarded was not given past effect, and asserted that constitutional law and their role as a constitutional court was a continuation of the common law) it was not easy to establish any stability in this operation. The legal system communicates about settled law, extensions of settled law, developments of the law, and the interpretation of statute law using a common temporal mode that allows arguments and conclusions on appropriate remedies to take the form of extrapolations from that mode. Within this system, prospective overruling has only one stable communication available to it: the legal system is able to identify what constitutes an overruling. But, unless the legal system moves to a position that all overruling operates only prospectively, the practice can only operate as a contested issue. It is difficult to make and sustain arguments that all overruling with retrospective effect is unfair, so the fate of the experiment, had it continued, would have involved a constant process of litigating on the basis and limits of the practice. This process offered the Supreme Court an asymmetrical experience. Cases upholding the practice failed to establish a stable doctrine. But potentially endless litigation on the limits of the practice offered the court repeated opportunities to end the experiment.

Prospectivity and Statute Law

The insistence that statute law should not, except exceptionally, have a retroactive application is understood, within both political and legal theory, as part of what constitutes the rule of law. The best-known account of the qualities that constitute this part of the rule of law is probably that of Fuller, who regards the prospective application of law as one of the necessary conditions for law to be able to guide human conduct.[61] For Fuller, providing guidance through rules gives law a moral character, with the consequence that lapses from the conditions which enable law to provide guidance to citizens lessen the overall moral obligation to obey law. We discuss the rule of law in more depth in the next Chapter. Nevertheless in this part of this Chapter, dealing with the manner in which law constructs time, we need to anticipate some of the arguments of the next Chapter to

[61] 'Law is the enterprise of subjecting human conduct to the governance of rules' (1964/69, 106).

show why the prospective character of most statute law is not a moral value imposed upon the political system from outside, but a value which the political system can be expected to generate through its own operations.

Politics, by limiting itself to a large extent to a prospective approach to legislation, has increased the complexity and effectiveness of the distribution of power, and thereby increased its ability to understand its own operations as a steering mechanism within society.[62] Attempting to create retroactive legislation seems, at first glance, to be an attempt by the political system to increase its power. But this depends on the ability of the legal system to process such retroactive communications, and the ability in turn of the political system to rely on the legal system to supply a normative framework for the political system's operations. Consider, for example, one of the most notorious examples from Nazi Germany of retroactive legislation: the retroactive authorisation of the assassination of Ernst Roehm and his followers.[63] Whilst this action resolved a power struggle within the National Socialist movement, and as such can be said to have immediately increased the power available to the surviving faction, it did not increase the power of the political system as a whole. To avoid reducing the ability of the political system to distribute power, acts such as this have to remain exceptional. If the political system systematically resorts to retroactive legislation, it loses the ability to re-use legality as a basis on which to allocate the parameters of legitimacy. From this perspective, it is worth noting that the survivors of this power struggle felt it worthwhile (and meaningful) for them to pass retroactive legislation in order to legitimate the assassination. This action reaffirmed that legality should be understood as a basis for identifying what has been collectively decided. But one has to contrast this individual use of retroactive legislation with a regular and routine resort to retroactive legislation, to legitimate acts that were at the time of their commission illegal. This threatens to makes every understanding of legality within the political system as a legitimate decision subject to other less precise communications, for example, what will find favour with the ruler, or further a broad ideological aim. The micro-management of power represented by the creation of agencies, the allocation of responsibilities, and the stipulation of acceptable means, depends on the political system incorporating values associated with the rule of law: one of which is the avoidance of retroactivity. This does not mean that retroactive legislation never occurs. Indeed, as just stated, its occurrence can be a reaffirmation that legality should be understood as something that bestows legitimacy. But if

[62] See Chapter 6 on structural coupling between law and politics, and Chapter 7 on steering (control) through law.

[63] 'Returning to Berlin, Hitler promptly arranged to have passed a retroactive statute converting these murders into lawful executions.' Fuller cites this example to contrast it with the reasonableness of 'curative' retrospective statutes that reaffirm the law to be what parties (reasonably but mistakenly) understood it to be at the time of their acting (1964/69, 53–55).

it should become a normal and routine communication, rather than an occasional one accompanied by communications confirming its exceptionality, then it begins to undermine the micro-management of state power made possible by the application of the rule of law to state administration.[64] To draw here on the work of Cover, it is only because the political system (especially in its administrative subsystem) pays such heed to legality that something like the death penalty can be micro-managed by reference to extremely complicated substantive and procedural requirements.[65] In contrast, assassinations conducted by reference to what, it is claimed, will please the ruler, or further political goals, cannot achieve anything so precise or complex.

This analysis should not be interpreted as a claim that retroactive legislation, along with other breaches of the rule of law, is avoided by political actors because of their individual understanding of its relevance to the future of the political system. It should, rather, be understood in connection with our discussion of the difficulties of communicating the legitimacy of civil disobedience from within the political system (as set out in Chapter 3). The creation of a separate subsystem of administration within the political system has involved the utilisation of legality to structure legitimate decision making. This requires administrators to understand, at the moment of making decisions, that legality constitutes the parameters of legitimate decisions. Those involved in legislation have to generate these meanings for those in administration. We have argued, in our discussion of civil disobedience, that it is difficult for the political system to combine communications that structure power through legality, and to incorporate communications that acknowledge a right to disobey law. The ability of legislation to adopt a different temporal basis is linked to this same phenomenon. Retroactive legislation directed to the behaviour of officials threatens to undermine understandings that legality structures legitimacy. But, more importantly, the vast outpouring of communications premised on this understanding of legislation (routine legislation intended to steer society) make it difficult to generate contrary understandings on any routine basis.[66] Retroactive legislation directed to state action, like the emergency actions it is likely to legitimate, can only be communicated alongside 'normal' legislation in terms of exceptionality. This can be seen to apply not only to legislation directed solely to officials, but also that directed towards citizens. If action is to be taken against citizens on the basis of retroactive legislation, it requires the involvement of administrators who must communicate that legality structures what is permissible for them, whilst it does not structure what is permissible for citizens. We might say that it is part of the very nature of law, as law is understood within the political system (or at least a political system that has evolved to structure power via

[64] We develop this analysis extensively in the next Chapter.
[65] Cover, 1986 – and see our discussion of Cover's analysis in Chapter 4.
[66] See Luhmann, 1990a, ch IV, 'Societal Foundations of Power: Increase and Distribution'.

legality) for it to be prospective in application. The fact that retroactive legislation is exceptional, regarded as inappropriate, and in need of special justification, is not the result of a moral critique imposed on political actors from outside the political system. Rather, it is what Luhmann calls an eigen value – a value generated by a system repeatedly doing what it does. The vast number of communications intended to organise power within the political system using legality generate values articulated as the rule of law, amongst which one finds a negative assessment of legislation with retrospective effect.

This analysis should also not be taken as a claim that it is impossible for modern political systems to develop alternatives to legality as a basis for the legitimacy of political decisions: rulers' wishes and ideological goals can become 'trumps' for a decrease in its ability to organise power, and to undertake a steering legitimacy of political action. But this, for Luhmann, was an example of de-differentiation, a diminution in the complexity of the political system, and its role in the rest of society.[67] Our argument is that the kind of communications that offer resistance, within the political system, to this kind of development, are themselves a product of the political system itself, and not a result of a moral critique imposed from outside. It is actually the positivism of modern law, and the consequent ability of the political system, through legislation, to allocate legitimacy to any number of technical configurations (agencies, goals, funding, etc) that generates the temporal aspects of what Fuller called the 'inner morality of law'. If legality is the normal basis for the distribution of political power via legislation, then retroactive legislation can only be introduced as an 'exceptional' event. And where it is introduced, there is a need to demonstrate exceptionality, both in the sense of the deviation being occasional and the result of a special justification, which puts a burden on those seeking to make such communications to find a basis on which they can be made in a meaningful way. In a political system that operates without a moral consensus, and which uses legality as a substitute for that consensus in deciding what is legitimate, the resources for demonstrating exceptionality are necessarily limited.

Observing the temporal conditions of legal communications has raised many issues concerning the relationship between the legal and political systems of modern societies. That relationship will now be explored more directly, rather than through the lens of time construction. The form of the ensuing discussion will describe that relationship through the medium of structural coupling and co-evolution, rather than what this Chapter initially discussed, namely the potential discontinuities of the meaning of time of these two differentiated subsystems.

[67] We continue this analysis of de-differentiation towards the end of Chapter 7.

6

Politics and Law: The Rule of Law, Constitutional Law, and Human Rights

In the previous three Chapters of this book, we have introduced systems theory observations and analysis which lay the foundations for the exploration in this Chapter of the relationship between the legal and political systems. In our discussion of civil disobedience in Chapter 3, we described how legality provides a routine, flexible and technical basis for the political system to establish what constitutes legitimate collectively binding decisions. In our discussion of pluralism in Chapter 4, we have shown how modern law can be understood in terms of functional differentiation, which in turn opens the way to understand other legal orders in terms of the different possibilities of structural coupling which exist between law and society's other social subsystems. And in our discussion of time in Chapter 5, we introduced the different temporal orientation of political and legal communications. Building on these discussions, we here consider what systems theory tells us about the nature of the relationship between the political and legal systems at a more general level and, in turn, what implications this has for three of the concepts that are central to political and legal theory: the rule of law, constitutional law, and human rights. We have no intention of providing a comprehensive review of, or commentary upon, the vast non-systems theory literature on these topics. Nevertheless, we hope that this exercise will reveal the potential for systems theory to illuminate our understanding of the role played by these concepts within society.

We begin this Chapter by examining the idea of the 'rule of law', reconsidered by reference to the dynamics and constraints which result from structural coupling between law and politics. Understanding the rule of law in terms of the possibilities for co-ordination and co-evolution between two autonomous systems points in turn to how much of what is normally discussed in terms of constitutionalism (most notably the doctrine of separation of powers) is a by-product of a political system that rules through law. The second section of the Chapter considers the evolutionary step represented by a legal system's internal distinction between constitutional law and ordinary law. The last part of the Chapter deals with systems theory's sociological explanation for constitutional and human rights in terms of the evolution of modern societies away from stratification (classes and estates) and segmentation (families and tribes) as the basis for differentiation to one of functional subsystem differentiation, and then uses that analysis to advance its observations on social constitutionalism.

The Rule of Law

The rule of law is often contrasted with 'rule by men', a distinction which relies on the ability of law to operate as a set of constraining rules which determine or severely constrain the choices open to those, particularly judges, making decisions on legal issues.[1] But in turn, most versions of the rule of law generate criticism for their attempts to justify legal decisions by reference to rules, criticism which exposes the actual choices made, and invites the conclusion that the rule of law operates only as an ideology.[2] Those who accept that legal rules provide a severe constraint on what can be presented as a valid legal decision face the difficulty that the rule of law may be reduced to a tautology. The rule of law is simply 'the law' – decisions made according to the existing legal rules, regardless of the content of those rules.[3] This tautology can be avoided by attempts to contrast the experience of law in the centre of the legal system – the courts – with the lay experience of law. The rule of law can be more than whatever the law happens to be if the rule of law is identified with the ability of law to inform lay expectations, to provide guidance.[4] This offers the rule of law as an ambitious ideal.[5] One can identify conditions necessary for lay persons to be guided by law (legal rules have to be known, comprehensible, stable, possible to meet and applied by those in authority),[6] and contrast this with the state of any modern legal system – highly technical and complex, inaccessible to lay persons without the assistance of legally trained personnel,

[1] We are well past the conditions and circumstances in which all law could be described as an exercise in reason, and government by laws equated with the constraint of government by pure reason, a possibility rejected before the 19th century by Rousseau (see his *Considerations on the Government of Poland and on its Proposed Reformation* (1772) in his *Political Writings* (1977) 177–260 at 179. For a description of the manner in which the legal system supported this possibility, prior to the introduction of modern forms of legislation, see Nobles and Schiff, 2006, ch 3. The issue that arises under modern conditions is whether government can rule through law, and what follows from this.

[2] See, eg, essays in Hutchinson and Monahan, 1987, especially Shklar, 1–16.

[3] This tautology is most obvious with positivist legal theories. With substantive natural law theories, the identification of what can form a legal rule gives a moral basis to the content of law, but this still leaves the tautology that the rule of law and the law are the same.

[4] See Raz, 2009, ch 11, 'The Rule of Law and its Virtue', also Fuller, 1964/69, especially ch 2, and ch 3 at 106.

[5] Compare Simmonds, 2007, especially ch 3.

[6] See Fuller, 1964/69, ch 2, and as a summary of Fuller's 'purposive' account of law, see Summers, 1984, ch 2.

and without that assistance being provided on the everyday, universal basis necessary for the law to provide the guidance required by the ideal. There are also attempts to claim that the rule of law involves something more than the conditions which are necessary for law to guide behaviour, and that this extra dimension adds a moral element.[7]

We have addressed in part, in our discussion of the nature of judicial communication in Chapter 2, attempts to claim that the rule of law is an ideological device, designed to cloak a reality in which decisions are the result of subjective preferences, or political dispositions. Systems theory does not deny that these factors play some role in an individual's attempts at communication. But they are not themselves communications and, as we have shown, the law itself restricts attempts to include them within its communications. Actors who want to trigger one of law's operations have to select communications which are capable of having this effect. In the case of legal judgments, this does not allow judges to acknowledge the role played by their own subjective preferences or political views, or even, in the vast majority of cases, the fact that they are creating new law as part of their judgments. As such, whatever contribution is made by subjective elements to the selection of legal communications, the legal system is unable to generate a description of itself as the outcome of subjective choices: a 'rule of men'. This communication can only exist as an external description of the legal system. The legal system's own communications, the only resource from which a self-description could be generated, do not provide the necessary elements.

The fact that all social systems require their participants to make selections that are not determined by the system does not undermine the autonomy of that system.[8] The separation of the system is manifested, as explained in Chapter 1 on the nature of systems, by the different choices that are presented by each system, and the different communications that accompany those choices. The issues generated by the legal system for decision are not the same issues as those generated by the political system, or science, etc. To give some of Luhmann's own examples, the issue of proprietary estoppel is unlikely to be taken up by the political system[9] and the timing and conditions for the unification of Germany cannot be decided by the legal system as a legal issue.[10] And whilst the political system explains

[7] See Fuller, 1964/69 and his analysis of the 'morality of aspiration', especially at ch 1; and see Loughlin, 2010, ch 11, '*Rechtsstaat*, Rule of Law, *l'Etat de droit*'; also Oakshott, 1983.

[8] For example, if politics were only understood as consisting of contingencies and the selection of communications by individuals who have subjective motivations for their selections, then law, art, science, mass media, etc, indeed the whole of society, would consist of politics. There would be no possibility of contrasting politics with other phenomena. Observations about the relationship between politics and law assume that these are distinguishable from the rest of society.

[9] Luhmann, 2004, 376–77.

[10] *Ibid*, 366.

its decisions to itself in terms of legitimacy, the legal system's formula for contingency involves communications through which it understands itself to deliver justice. It is here that the rule of law has an existence within the legal system which is not tautological. In deciding legal issues (choosing between alternative interpretations of what the law requires) law constructs its own images of its environment. One of these, already discussed in Chapter 5, is of Parliament as a subject with a unitary will (interpreting statutes by 'giving effect to the intention of Parliament'). Another is the lay person whose behaviour is assumed to be regulated by the provision in question. This is where the 'guidance' attributed to law, under the rubric of the rule of law, finds expression within legal practices. The assumption that law is intended to guide those subject to its provisions operates as a series of preferences.[11] Interpretations that give law a prospective application are to be preferred to those that are retrospective. Those that are easier to comprehend and expect are superior to those which are more complicated, or can be presented as a surprise. The necessity for consistency (treating like cases alike) operates throughout the process, both in the construction of alternatives and their resolution.[12] From an external perspective, as stated above, the claim that law's purpose is to provide guidance to those subject to its rules is belied by its byzantine complexity, as well as those provisions which are retrospective, unknowable, impossible to meet, and the amount and frequency of new statutory provisions and judicial precedents.[13] But this does not remove the need for interpretations of its provisions, or for the communications which construct those interpretations to take the form of an attribution of guidance as a central aim and concern.[14] This is also an aim that the legal system can attribute to Parliament, and thus include

[11] These preferences were articulated by Fuller, who claimed that they represent law's inner morality. The jurisprudential debate generated by Fuller's claim (especially his debate with Hart, 1958) is directed at the relevance of these criteria in principally assessing the 'law' qualities of legislation. Inevitably many other issues concerning these preferences remain unconsidered or barely considered in Fuller's writings or the Hart/Fuller debate; see, eg, Charlesworth, 2010, Waldron, 2010.

[12] Similar processes operate within the criminal law, where selections between interpretations can be justified by reference to the meanings that are assumed to be communicated through appellate judgments, to those subject to criminal provisions. The assumption that these 'communications' actually enter into the consciousnesses of lay persons seem to be immune to the evidence that very few if any lay persons are ever likely to be aware of these doctrinal decisions (see Nobles and Schiff, 2006a).

[13] Indeed the improbability that lay persons will know even the criminal law applicable to their actions has led one leading criminal law scholar to argue that the 'common law ignorance-of-law doctrine is theoretically and practically unsustainable' (Ashworth, 2011, 25).

[14] The necessity for self-observations within law that orientate its selections, and their resistance to external critique, can also be seen in the common lawyer's claim, prior to the development of modern forms of legislation, that law was an expression of custom (see Nobles and Schiff, 2006, ch 3). Some of what Fuller calls law's inner morality overlaps with the assumptions of the glossators – who approached the *Digest* on the basis that their text was capable of providing a coherent and consistent basis for the resolution of disputes within a community.

within statutory interpretation. The assumption that the passage of statutes is a mechanism for guiding behaviour is a communication common to both politics and law.

As a basis for formulating and choosing between alternative interpretations of legal provisions the rule of law operates throughout the legal system. But it has particular significance in connection with the relationship between the legal and political system. Here it forms part of their structural coupling. This is more than the fact that the rule of law has an existence as a form of communication in both the legal and political system. Communications within one system that have a second existence as communications within another system constitute operative coupling, but more is required for structural coupling.[15] Structural coupling occurs when a system 'presupposes certain features of its environment on an ongoing basis and relies on them structurally . . . the forms of a structural coupling *reduce* and so *facilitate* influences of the [system's] environment on the system'.[16]

We can begin to explore the nature and content of this relationship by reminding ourselves of the necessary limits of law's interaction with anything outside of itself. Law is a system which generates meanings through the application of its binary code: legal/illegal. As such, its reaction to any other system, or the physical world, can only take the form of this coding. Operations within the political system can only be recognised by the legal system in terms of communications that apply this code. Similarly, the political system exists through communications which apply its own binary code, a code that could best be described as governing/governed at earlier periods, but has evolved into that of government/opposition. The application of this code generates operations which establish what is collectively binding. There is a tension between these two systems, as there is between

[15] Luhmann distinguished operative coupling, when a communication in one system is an event (attributed to its environment) within another system, from structural coupling. Operative couplings take two forms. First, these are simply the coupling of operations of the system with other operations of the system. The second version of operative coupling occurs when the system couples its communications with operations that it attributes to its environment (Luhmann, 2004, 381).

[16] *Ibid*, 382. There appears to be a terminological confusion, which we should mention, between Luhmann's writings on structural coupling and those of Gunther Teubner, since it is illustrative of some relevant issues for this discussion. In 'Two Faces of Janus . . .' (1992) Teubner offers 'linkage institutions' as a supplement to structural coupling, on the basis that 'legal misreading' (the observation of communications from another system using the code legal/illegal) happens only randomly, and 'structural coupling' leads to only transitory structural changes. He offers linkage institutions as a concept appropriate to the evolution of 'epidemic' misreading. Teubner's description of structural coupling seems to cover what Luhmann describes as operative coupling. It does not follow that structural coupling as defined by Luhmann is the same as linkage institutions. One possible difference between the two arises if we assume that Teubner's concept of linkage institutions involves a common semantics (as with his example of bona fides as a Janus-faced concept – operating differently in two systems, and his reference to an 'identical nom propre' (at 1458), whilst Luhmann's concept of structural coupling does not. That said, it is difficult to envisage a sustained structural coupling (using Luhmann's definition) that would not lead to common semantics.

any two systems. What politics establishes via its operations as collectively binding is not necessarily legal.

Having regard to the history of Western European states, Luhmann identifies the period prior to the establishment of positivist understandings of law (that is the generation of a positivist self-description by the legal system) as one where law generated a right of resistance to political action.[17] While this is something that is still associated with the rule of law (law as a restraint on political power) it is also apparent that for law to have a regular and routine experience of coding political operations as illegal would provide a very different relationship between politics and law than that which exists today. To consider the nature of these tensions, and the possibilities for their absorption, let us consider the historical example of the common law. A legal system that constructed itself through the application of its procedures to the resolution of disputes, and regarded its remedies as the rectification of wrongs, was quite capable of generating norms which ran counter to what a monarch desired.[18] The pressure on actors within each system resulting from such tensions has implications for the possibilities of each system. The implications for the legal system can be illustrated by the example of *Shelley's case*.[19] This case is the origin of a doctrine of property law that lasted from 1581 to 1926 in English law, and was still operating in some jurisdictions in the United States as late as 1971.[20] According to the legal historian Brian Simpson,[21] this case arose out of a disputed inheritance between the Catholic and Protestant branches of a landed family, which led to Elizabeth I letting it be known to her judges that she favoured the Protestant claim.[22] Not surprisingly, the Protestants succeeded in the court. But their success was not communicated in the form of an acknowledgement of the Queen's request (and one may suppose that such a communication would not have satisfied that request – Elizabeth wanted the legal claim to succeed, not for the result to be understood as something outside the law). Instead, the judges responded to the monarch's desires by

[17] *Ibid*, 360.

[18] An example discussed by Luhmann is the dispute between James I and the senior judge Edward Coke. Neither system can surrender its closure – the political system's determination of what is political cannot be decided by law, while the legal system's determination of what is legal cannot be surrendered to politics (*ibid*, 362).

[19] *Wolfe v Shelley* (1579–81) 1 Co Rep 93b; 76 ER 206.

[20] See Simpson, 1995, 40.

[21] *Ibid*. Simpson's discussion of this case is entitled: 'Politics and Law in Elizabethan England: Shelley's Case (1581)'.

[22] Simpson relies on the report of this case by Edward Coke, whose account of the Queen's interest had to be diplomatically phrased. According to Coke, the Queen expressed her interest in the form of a direction to the Lord Chancellor to summon all the judges to hear the case, ostensibly 'to prevent long, tedious and chargeable suits between parties so near in blood'. In Simpson's view: 'It seems likely that the real reason for the intervention of the Queen and her Chancellor was to bring pressure to bear in favour of Henry Shelley', and 'We can be sure that the judges would all be perfectly aware of the politics of the dispute, and the wishes of the Queen and her Privy Council' (*ibid* 33–35).

re-working the common law.[23] The monarch had the individual result that she desired, but she also produced something in which she had no interest: a common law precedent which lasted hundreds of years. But the law had no way of achieving the result she desired (that inheritance by the Protestants would be found legal) without including these additional consequences. Imagine the process repeated on a regular basis. Daily requests that particular cases should have particular outcomes would be unlikely to produce doctrinal developments that could be integrated into the legal system without reducing the ability of that system to provide relatively stable and consistent outcomes in property disputes.

This example shows that the legal system cannot develop and maintain its complexity without finding an adequate means to respond to the political system. This is not simply a political problem – the possibility that law will generate resistance to political authority. It is also a need to prevent the political system from overburdening the legal system with its demands. The development of complex programmes for the application of the legal code has to find a compatible relationship with the distribution of power through the political system. Compatibility between systems cannot be achieved through shared meanings. Nor can co-ordination be achieved via the responses of legal actors to the immediate threat of physical force directed in response to political factors. Even our example of Shelley's case simplifies the problem here. The reign of Elizabeth I represents a relatively stable period in English political history, characterised by a near absolute monarch. History is replete with narratives of political power moving dynamically between families, court favourites, and individuals. To achieve co-ordination between the political and legal system, there have to be some stable structures, within either system, to which the other can respond.[24]

At this point we can return to the concept of structural coupling: a system presupposes features of its environment on an ongoing basis. The presupposition here is not entirely internal to the system. For two systems to structurally couple there has to be some operation or operations in one system which the second system can identify and to which it can respond. The presupposition refers to the meanings generated within the second system. The second system can attribute meanings to the operations to which it is responding which are very different to those attributed to those

[23] The assumption that the case was decided according to legal principles allowed Coke to formulate the rule in his report of the case, illustrating the point that the system creates doctrine, even when those who make decisions fail to do so. The rule, for those interested, was that a gift 'to A for life, remainder to A's heirs was a gift to A absolutely, which he could deal with as he liked'. This was sufficient, in the case, to defeat the Catholic claimant.

[24] 'As long as the legal system is directly exposed to the pressures of its environment within society, it cannot focus on particular disturbances. Then all possible pressures deform the law, either by ignoring it or bypassing it, or they make the system declare legality or illegality legal, as the case may be. Without structural coupling in the relations of the functioning systems of society with each other, law is corrupt in the modern sense of that term' (Luhmann, 2004, 385).

operations by the first. From the perspective of the first system, the qualities attributed to its operations by the second system can be described as a fiction, or presupposition. When the second system carries out an operation which involves the identification of a particular operation (set of communications) within the first system, the second system removes those identified communications from their context (the communications of the first system with which they can be connected) and reproduces them within a new context (the communications of the second system to which they can be connected). This is a process which can be described as a 'reduction' that 'facilitates' the influence of the second system's environment (namely, the first system) on the second system.

Now we are ready to address the problem of how the legal system and political system can co-ordinate their respective operations without the possibility of shared meanings. Can the political system develop in such a manner as to offer a stable set of operations (structures) to which the legal system can develop a stable set of responses (its own operations/structures). One is not looking for developments in one system, but for compatible developments in both. The systems theory term for this is co-evolution.[25] And the particular co-evolution that has occurred between the legal and political systems within modern society is what each can describe as the rule of law.[26] The difficulties created by Elizabeth I in seeking to influence the outcome of a particular trial can be compared with the social reforms (the Reformation) achieved by Tudor monarchs through their ability to influence the composition of Parliament. Parliament already existed within the legal system as a source of remedies for wrongs, albeit one that lacked the systematic qualities of the common law. It also had a status within the

[25] 'This is defined as the development of autonomous evolutionary mechanisms in closed systems and their reciprocal structural coupling' (Teubner, 1993, 52–53). See also Thornhill, 2008, at 173.

[26] Since structural coupling is a relationship between society's autopoietic subsystems, the use of the term in any historical context opens the debate as to when these systems became autopoietic, and the related issue of whether their autopoiesis can be partial. One also needs to take account of statements like the following: 'As long as the old class structures remained, no structural couplings were possible in the relation between the political system and the legal system' (2004, at 389). Luhmann's point here is that one cannot talk of social subsystems when society was structured through classes, castes and estates. In these periods law and politics operated within classes, castes and estates more than it operated across them, and as such, were subsystems of those classes, castes and estates, and not subsystems of society. In addition, Luhmann is offering structural coupling as an answer to the question of how society could co-ordinate itself once it had lost the ability to represent itself in forms appropriate to estates: centre/periphery, city/country, and relations of rank. Nevertheless, the manner in which law and politics 'structurally coupled' prior to the emergence of functionally differentiated social subsystems demonstrates a similar dynamic to its operation between social subsystems, and generates the conditions for a solution to the greater problem of co-ordinating social subsystems: 'We have outlined a hypothesis indicating relations between a transition from stratification to functional differentiation and the invention of new *or the reformulation of old mechanisms for structural coupling* during the transition period' (1992a, at 1439, emphasis added).

common law that reduced its ability to disturb the common law. It was treated within the legal system as a court whose decisions (statutes) had a higher jurisdiction than other courts, and thus had to be followed; but statutes were not treated as precedents. The communications which led to this situation were the common law's descriptions of judges' decisions as the embodiment of reason and custom. Parliament had a jurisdiction which required its statutes to be followed, but statutes were regarded as poor indicators that something was actually a social wrong that needed a remedy. Whilst a judge's decision provided a point of reference for arguments that other matters were sufficiently similar to be also treated as wrongs, statutes, unless endorsed by judicial approval (incorporated into the substratum of the common law) did not. Thus on the one hand statutes involved the exercise of power on a general basis, as they established rules: categories of wrongs that needed to be remedied. As such they made large changes to the legal system. But these were changes that did not automatically produce precedents[27] and, as such, did not disturb the maintenance and development of common law doctrine.

The common law's response to Parliament did not depend on Parliament's composition, or what influences had been brought to bear in order to pass particular statutes. These matters form no part of statutory interpretation either under the Tudors or today. This simplification of Parliament by the common law immunised the common law from having to respond to these other kinds of political communications.[28] This is not a one-way process. In turn it allowed Parliament to become a focus of the communications that distributed political power. Control of Parliament, however achieved, provides a stable means to effect changes in the law. The perceived necessity and benefits of controlling Parliament also operate to stabilise politics. Politics can evolve from a system that focuses on the formation and maintenance of rival armies to parliamentary politics, in which the focus is on the ability to introduce laws.

We can see the dynamics that produce the rule of law even in *Shelley's case*. The dispute which came before the court was triggered by an exercise of physical force. One branch of the family evicted the other from the disputed land by turning up with their men at arms. Elizabeth I had access to sufficient men at arms to have determined who should enjoy physical possession of the land. But one of the major mechanisms whereby English monarchs had gained power at the expense of lesser Lords was the creation of the King's courts. These courts provided little incentive to parties aggrieved at the behaviour of Lords to litigate before them unless they were

[27] They could develop such a status by being recognised as part of the 'substratum' of the common law, but this is a result of their integration within the common law on the same basis as judges' decisions (as good evidence of a wrong), not on their status as statutes.

[28] 'What [a system] couples with is an important as what it excludes' (Luhmann, 2004, 382). See also Luhmann, 1992a, 1433: 'Structural coupling organises decoupling.'

also a means to gain access to the physical powers of coercion which lay with the monarch. Thus even Elizabeth I faced a dilemma. The ability of the courts to increase the monarch's power over Lords depended on the physical force available to the monarch being applied in accordance with the decisions of those courts. Those courts had developed doctrines which structure their decisions which did not recognise the religious or personal preferences of the monarch over the outcome of a legal dispute as a legal argument. Going outside the courts and just lending physical force to the preferred party would undermine the power which the courts had generated for her as a monarch, and also represented a political risk. The risk arises from the political communications which have accompanied the creation of the King's courts – the claim that physical force applied as a result of legal decisions is legitimate, but physical force applied in order to avoid or resist the decisions of those courts is not.[29]

In this historical example we see the beginnings of what has come to be described as the rule of law. The political system perceives[30] an increase in its power by distributing that power through law, and this cannot be achieved without the political system being in turn restrained by law. Direct attempts to influence particular legal decisions via the application of political power to actors within the legal system cannot be other than exceptional if the legal system is to continue to offer a means to distribute political power which achieves that increase. The separation of powers can be understood in terms of the ability of two social systems to achieve a relationship of structural coupling, which increases the incentive for actors to participate in either system. Law gains incentives for litigation and the adoption of legal forms when politics channels the application of physical force through law. Law's stable reactions to the operations of those institutions which it recognises as sources of law, combined with law's failure to respond to much of the political system (everything that cannot be processed as a law-creating act), provides a stimulus for political communications directed at the control of those institutions. This is a situation where law's autopoiesis, the necessity for it to construct legality from the existing

[29] As Simmonds has observed, when examining the ability of 'evil' rulers to abrogate the rule of law, the restraint of violence between subjects is a precondition to the creation of effective political power, not least because the revenues necessary to finance rulers come from trade and markets, which do not function well when such violence is not restrained. The incentive to comply with a state regime that outlaws private violence is undermined if state violence is applied outside of that regime in support of private violence. Simmonds discusses the disincentive effects which arise if those who obey law are punished by rulers for such obedience. But the same problem arises if those who disobey law (by failing to put their disputes through the courts when summoned) are rewarded by the ruler through ruler-directed physical force in support of their cause outside of the mechanisms which have been set up to identify and punish illegitimate violence (see Simmonds, 2007, ch 3, 'Evil Regimes and the Rule of Law' at 103).

[30] This is a necessary qualification. The political system has no direct access to its environment, but can only construct its own version of its environment internally, and this includes its own perceptions of its own influence upon its environment.

state of legal communications, is both a restraint on politics and a means by which politics increases its ability to structure itself, and to perceive this increase as an increase in its ability to structure society.

These constraints, and the resulting increased possibilities for the political system to affect the rest of society, increase with the development of states. The origins of the state lay in forms of administration undertaken by rulers.[31] But the further development of those forms of administration has involved the use of legality to structure not only the relationship between those who rule and those who are ruled – rules directed at the behaviour of subjects, but to constitute the political system. These constitutive rules have allowed the political system to direct political power on a flexible and technical basis.[32] Political communications, through the techniques of statutory interpretation, are second coded as legal ones. Legality, in turn, is reinterpreted within the political system as legitimacy – a basis for understanding something as collectively binding. This has allowed the political system to use law to create state agencies, with staffs, budgets, mandates and powers. This reflexive application of political power – the use of political power to induce changes in the legal system which alter in turn the possibilities of the political system, has provided the structures that we experience as the modern state (the 'state' being the political system's self-description of these developments).[33]

The structural coupling between law and politics represented by Parliament, whereby law treats statutes as new law, has vastly increased the ability of politics to stabilise itself, and increase its ability to affect society. This coupling has also involved an immunisation – political communications structure the control of Parliament through operations to which the legal system did not react (or not in any substantial way). This meant that law offered no basis for resistance to the political communications which established control of Parliament. It is both elements of this particular coupling, the operations to which law has a stable reaction, and those to which it has a stable non-reaction, which increase the ability of the political system to direct power. If political power is directed towards the legal system other than through the structural coupling of legislatures, in an attempt to evade the political consequences of particular legal decisions, this can result in new couplings which weaken its ability to distribute power.

If one accepts that the political system gains in power through the co-ordination of its relationship to the legal system, one should not leap to the conclusion that politics determines what can be legal, and thus in turn,

[31] 'The institutionalization of political power and the establishment of rule-based governmental procedures are, in short, methods of maintaining and enhancing governmental authority. Constraints on power generate power' (Loughlin, 2010, 339).

[32] For a detailed historical account of this process, see Thornhill, 2011.

[33] 'By the year 1800 "the state" existed as a formula for the self-description of the political system' (Luhmann, 1990a, 135, and see especially ch III, section III).

what can be legitimate in politics by reason of being legal. Human actors who are regular participants in both systems (such as parliamentary draftsmen) can seek to devise statutes that give effect to political goals. And this process is assisted and stabilised in the knowledge that courts which interpret statutes are required to search for the intention of Parliament. But this cannot result in a process in which the legal system operates as a determined instrument for politics. One can observe that, even in a legal order such as that of the United Kingdom prior to the Human Rights Act 1998, when the statute was treated as the highest form of law, law did not only operate as an instrument for the channelling of political power, but also a source of resistance. There are several reasons for this. First, there is the sheer impossibility of any actor, however familiar with two systems, being able to predict with complete accuracy the meanings generated by that system in future. A statute's meaning within the legal system is an outcome of the context in which it is interpreted, which in turn is a result of the procedures, precedents, and factual circumstances which create the observational standpoint of whichever actor in the system is eventually called upon to communicate that meaning.[34] But the dynamics that produce resistance are not limited to the impossibility of predicting with certainty the meanings generated by interpretation within the legal system. This deals with only one side of the problem. The political system is also dynamic, so that what, at the moment of a statute's passing, might be considered as an appropriate goal or outcome, does not remain static, nor does the political system's understanding of the structuring of power represented by that statute. In this situation, political communications about the legal system, such as complaints that 'unelected' judges are offering resistance to legitimate policies and practices, are inevitable.[35]

The resistance which the legal system could offer to politics has been reduced, but not eliminated, through the co-evolution of both systems. When the legal system evolved primarily through the development of legal doctrine in response to litigation, it generated a natural law self-description. This self-description, and the interpretative processes which generated it, offered relatively high possibilities for law to be experienced (communicated about) within the political system as resistance. But the coupling of

[34] 'Since the system is determined by its own structures and can digitalize – namely, particularize itself only by its own operations' events in its environment regardless of which system they belong to – those events cannot intervene in the system in the form of 'inputs' for the purposes of their structural coupling. To put this differently, the system is not a transformation function, which always transforms inputs into outputs in the same way; nor does it do so when the system structures itself with the help of conditional programmes. As far as the system itself is concerned, structural couplings can only trigger irritations, surprises and disturbances' (Luhmann, 2004, 382).

[35] Hart dealt with this as part of his concept of law, in his admission that discretion could not be eliminated from the law by rules, due to their indeterminacy of aim and their unforeseeable relation to facts. But he did not explore the manner in which this contributes to law being experienced, within politics, as resistance to legitimate government.

law and politics through legislation, and the development of politics into a system which has sought to reform society through law, led in the eighteenth and nineteenth centuries to an outpouring of technical legislation in all Western European states. The communications necessary to integrate this kind of law into the legal system (that something is law because of its authority, not because it represents reason or custom) generated positivist self-descriptions within the legal system (displacing natural law ones). This has lowered the resistance which the legal system offers to politics but has not eliminated it.

This element of resistance can be regarded (even from within the political system) as something which increases the power of politics. It allows the political system to describe itself as more than a means to reconcile the competing interests of individuals and groups.[36] Law communicates about its own selections with its own contingency formula, that is, justice. As such, when applications of the legal code become the subject of political criticism, this is not a wholly negative experience for politics. Such criticism is the manifestation, within the political system, of what can also be described as a political achievement: the creation by politics of something different from itself – law. A system which relies heavily on instrumental forms of reasoning, and contentious claims surrounding sovereignty manages, through structural coupling, to produce communications in another system that are not instrumental, but constitutive, and whose meanings include a commitment to authority stripped of any particular political goal.[37] Law also reproduces, within its own processes, the belief that drives the political system: that politics can operate as a means to control society. Law makes selections using the assumption that laws are intended as guides to action. Whilst these interpretative techniques can be experienced (communicated about) within politics as resistance, they can also be experienced (communicated about) as deference. But the legal system cannot carry out all of its operations through communications which involve deference to authority. The communications which accompany its selections still involve communications which have their origins in moral systems. Although these communications may no longer generate a natural law self-description within the legal system, nevertheless, they still generate occasions when

[36] The philosopher Michael Oakshott argued that the rule of law is more than an instrumental form of association. He identified additional elements which he claimed are a moral form of association. In his discussion of Oakshott, Loughlin looks to the history of law to see if Oakshott's scheme is anything more than a logician's dream (Loughlin, 2010, 324–32). He argues that the justice necessary to make law a moral association has been lost with law's evolution from natural law forms of reasoning to positivist ones. We argue here, by contrast, that law's resistance to politics has continued to be communicated about within the legal system itself, and in the media, both as justice and as morality, and that these communications form part of the structural coupling which is the rule of law. Whether these communications would or would not be acknowledged by moral philosophers to add a moral element does not determine the ability of law and politics to ascribe moral meanings to them.

[37] See Oakshott, 1983.

what is experienced (communicated) as resistance within the political system is experienced (communicated) as a moral value within the legal system, alongside the legal system's constant observation of itself as an expression of justice. Thus in claiming to be the author of law, the political system also claims to be producing justice and morality. This allows the 'rule of law' to be claimed as a value, and not simply an instrument for the implementation of political objectives. Lastly, the resistance of law to politics can also be communicated about positively within the political system, in the form of an attribution of its own failures to control events outside the system: 'It's not our fault – it's the judges' fault'.[38]

The gain in power represented by the structural coupling of law and politics via legislation is, of course, not simply the result of a coupling between two systems. Were politics able to form a compatible relationship with only law, then we would have a situation in which two of society's subsystems had a stable relationship, whilst the rest of society experienced the direction of political power via law as pressure – the duplication of the kinds of reaction we have just discussed in terms of the legal and political systems. The ability to distribute political power through its second coding by law is in turn dependent on the ability of law to form relationships of structural coupling with other social subsystems.[39] From this perspective, a discussion of relevance of the rule of law to political power requires an analysis of whether political power second coded through law is more or less likely to form compatible relationships with society's other social systems than political power directed without reference to legality.

A systems theory analysis of the rule of law shares many of the conclusions of recent non-systems theory analysis of the topic. Politics increases the stability and complexity of its own structures by ruling through law. Maintaining this increase in power involves an acceptance of the doctrine known within law and politics as the separation of powers: that the political system will introduce legal rules through legislation, but will not seek to influence the interpretation and application of those rules at the point of adjudication. What systems theory offers is a different understanding of the nature and possibilities offered by this process. First, one cannot look to the political system to find the foundations of law. There is not a hierarchical relationship whereby one system determines the possibilities of the other. The process is an interactive one. The historical state of the legal system

[38] See Holmes, 2003.

[39] There is support for the claim that the structural coupling between politics and law has been more stable, and less of a restraint on law's ability to evolve its complexity, than the relationship between law and other social subsystems. See, eg, Teubner's article on the problems of regulatory failure – 'regulatory trilemma'. Teubner believes that the coupling of politics with law, and law with other social systems, should be studied empirically, and went so far as to suggest that such empirical studies might alter the political system's understanding of its own environment (Teubner, 1992a, 470). We discuss the issues introduced here, especially 'regulatory trilemma', more extensively in Chapter 7.

– how it constructs what is legal at any moment – is as much of a constraint on the possibilities of structural coupling between law and politics as the current manner in which the political system establishes collectively binding decisions. Secondly, one is directed towards quite different explanations of the processes which have generated and maintain co-evolution. This second point requires further elaboration.

Understanding the rule of law as the product of the structural coupling and co-evolution of the legal and political systems alters our perspective on the distinction between societies which exhibit the characteristics of the rule of law and those which apply political power (the threat of physical force or the distribution of economic resources obtained through the threat of force) to influence society without that power being distributed through legality. Where this involves the application of political power to alter the particular decisions of the legal system it is experienced by the legal system as a burden. The system may, as in situations like Shelley's case, respond to the political demand but continue to articulate its decisions in terms of general norms. Alternatively, such demands may result in legal communications which immunise the disturbance to its redundancy (see Chapter 2 to be reminded of the systems theory understanding of this term).

The infamous *lettres de cachet*, which operated in France prior to the French Revolution, can be understood as the antithesis of the rule of law. But another way of understanding this device is as an example of coupling between law and politics in which law is immunised from politics, rather than structurally coupled and stimulated to co-evolve. From this perspective, we can consider the implications (both for this device and its modern equivalents) of such couplings.[40] The *lettres*, by themselves, operated to make the imprisonment of their objects legal. In such political cases, no further justification needed to be forthcoming from the legal system. By contrast to the application of physical power to ordinary criminal proceedings, which might be expected to generate some response within the legal system, the use of these *lettres* immunised the legal system from having to respond, except to recognise the issue of the *lettres* as something which put the imprisonment authorised outside the jurisdiction of the courts.[41] This leaves the autopoiesis of the legal system undisturbed. But this form of structural coupling puts new responsibilities on the political system. By what means and on what basis are such orders/*lettres* to be issued? If they

[40] These would be operative couplings, but not structural coupling unless politics and law co-evolved through the generation of structures in each system in response.

[41] For an English example, one might take *Darnel's Case*, also known as the *Five Knights case*, 3 Howell's State Trials 1 (1628). When five knights refused to provide the compulsory loans required by Charles I under the royal prerogative, he had them imprisoned, by royal writ. The knights sought to issue a writ of Habeas Corpus, which Chief Justice Hyde denied, on the ground that: 'if no cause of commitment be expressed, it is presumed to be for the matter of state, which we cannot take notice of' (at 57). In this situation, as with the *lettres de cachet*, the legal system, even as it denies jurisdiction, finds the imprisonment *not illegal* ie legal.

exist as an 'arbitrary' experience this does not mean that they will be granted without any rationale, but that their legitimacy will not be established by their legality. If they are awarded as a result of bribery, or in response to family connections, or by reference to general political goals, this represents surrender by the political system of a relatively precise means for distributing the power to imprison, for one that is distributed on a much less precise basis. Whilst general criminal laws allow the legitimacy of the continued imprisonment of particular persons to be externalised from the political system to the legal system (actors within the political system can decline to address such a 'legal' question), procedures like *lettres de cachet* generate political communications which cannot be rejected in this manner. Petitions, the seeking of 'private' influence and 'bribery' can be expected to accompany this form of power. *Lettres de cachet* represent an alternative basis for the distribution of political power, in the form of physical force, to that of legality, but without the technical precision which (compared to general political aims and ideologies) legality brings. The absence of legal restraints in this situation is often equated with increased political power, on the assumption that physical force distributed directly through political communications allows less resistance than power which has to be second coded as legality. But such assumptions ignore the consequences for the political system itself from such developments. Physical power directed through general political communications is power dissipated. Power distributed by reference to communications about loyalty, whether to a leader or a political cause, may inhibit expressions of resistance, but it provides a relatively unspecific mechanism through which to direct the application of that power. To echo Foucault here, politics loses the ability to distribute power through itself with micro precision.[42] Such developments may increase the power of a particular political regime (especially if that regime faces immanent removal from office), but they represent an overall weakening of the power of the state.[43]

[42] As an alternative to applying physical force through political communications, the political system may structurally couple with the military system. If a positivist legal system was actually the command structure envisaged by the early legal positivist Austin, this might offer similar possibilities for the distribution of power. But if one approaches systems as combinations of operations and observation, in which the application of their codes is stabilised through structures arising from secondary observation (the system's own observations of itself and its environment), then neither the military nor the law are reducible to a hierarchy. We can only here sketch what it might mean for the military system to be structurally coupled with the political system. Such coupling takes place through concepts like national security. If political power has to be expressed in terms of national security this represents a contraction of possibilities within the political system. At the same time, it represents an increase in the burden placed upon the military system, which must now undertake operations which used to be undertaken by state agencies and legitimated through legality (extending the role of courts-martial extensively).

[43] One of the best examples of this process is the Soviet Union's attempt to utilise the political power of its Gulag system to generate economic resources. Failure to meet quotas was interpreted as political resistance, and punished. As such, from the bottom of the system

In constructing a systems theory account of the nature of the rule of law, one needs to go beyond an observation of the manner in which this structural coupling increases the political system's perception of itself as steering society to some explanation of the reasons why this evolution has occurred and what maintains it. Non-systems theory accounts are likely to focus on the values and interests of individuals, and seek an explanation based on the ability of individuals to recognise the rule of law as a human good, or a means for those who rule to achieve their interests or goals in an efficient manner. A systems theory explanation has to rely, like our Chapter on judicial communications, on an understanding of the manner in which individuals, as psychic systems, have themselves to structurally couple with social systems. They are restrained in what they can communicate by the redundancy of the subsystem in which they wish to communicate. In our Chapter on civil disobedience we observed the inability of the legal system to generate a right of disobedience to law, and the similar difficulties found within the political system. The vast number of political communications orientated to the control of legislatures, and the huge number of collectively binding decisions that operate to distribute political power through the parameters of legality, generate resistance within the political system to any communications which lay claim to a right to disobey law. This meaning provides the parameters of the collective decisions through which so much political power flows, leaving less precise communications with the task of fine tuning the exercise of that power.[44]

As with actors in the legal system, participation in the political system requires the individuals concerned to make communications which have implicit meanings. Here, the implicit meaning is that illegality is also illegitimacy. The meaning of these communications is not removed by the repeated example of state actors committing illegal acts, because the issue for systems is not whether normative expectations are belied by factual examples. Indeed, a normative expectation is distinguished from a cognitive one by the ability of the former to survive counterfactual examples. Rather, the issue for a system is whether it is possible to generate alternative normative expectations – alternative redundancies. Which political communications are capable of generating an alternative basis of legitimacy to that provided by legality? As we have described in our Chapter on civil disobedience, attempts by participants in the political system to recognise a right to disobey law, whether as members of Parliament, civil servants,

(prisoners who cut the end of the same felled trees again and again to meet their quota of felled logs) to managers who claimed to hold stocks that did not exist, the political system could not produce the information which it needed in order to understand itself to be 'directing' the economy. Rather than achieving the regularities of expectation represented by structural coupling, the political system was constantly 'surprised' by its environment (see Appelbaum, 2003, 326–29).

[44] Using John Searle's terminology (1969), the context of their communications is established by constitutive rules, which establish their authority.

leaders of political parties, or prosecutors, face the resistance generated by their constant need to utilise communications that constitute the political system (and their own particular position within it) on the basis that what is illegal is also illegitimate.

If we can understand the creation of the modern state as the result of a co-evolution stimulated by the structural coupling between law and politics involved in legislation, then we can use this to explore the resistance generated within politics to an abandonment of rule by law. Understanding that the restraint of law increases the power of the political system allows one to move away from explanations which rely on the ability of individual human actors to recognise the rule of law as a moral value and pursue it. As Martin Loughlin has observed, accepting that the rule of law increases the power of politics leads to an account which 'aligns the rule of law (*Rechtsstaat*) with the dynamic that drives the development of public law (*Staatsrecht*/*droit politique*).[45] One is no longer relying on an ideal mode of human association: a 'logician's dream'.[46] Loughlin offers an explanation based on the self-interest of individual actors: 'Governments rule by means of law because, by maintaining such rule-derived expectations, they foster the allegiance of their citizens, which is, in turn, power-generating . . . to the extent that rule of law values are maintained, it is because they are perceived as prudential necessities rather than universal moral absolutes'. But what is prudential is itself a consequence of the institutional arrangements which have evolved within a society. For it to be both practical and prudential for government actors to communicate their support of the distribution of political power through law, one requires 'an institutional arrangement with the potential to establish a system of countervailing powers such that it is able to function in a way that bolsters mutual respect for the rules'.[47] Loughlin's own explanation for the evolution of institutional arrangements which 'constrains and disciplines individuals' in these ways is a rich historical account of the development of an autonomous political sphere in which 'Constitutions are constantly evolving in the light of political necessities and, as a result of this evolutionary impetus, the meaning and impact of legal concepts and doctrines will similarly change'.[48] By introducing systems theory, and structural coupling, we offer an explanation for this evolutionary impetus in terms of the co-evolution of the two systems. The prudential elements of this evolution do not require a consensus amongst political actors that legal restraints operate to increase their power. If that were so, the process of evolution would be subject to the vagaries of opportunistic illegality, and the difficulties of establishing agreement as to which illegalities could, or could not, be tolerated without a

[45] 2010, 340.

[46] *Ibid*, 330 – Loughlin's verdict on Oakshott's account of the features which make up the rule of law.

[47] *Ibid*, 340.

[48] *Ibid*, 12.

diminution in overall power. Rather, the prudential elements of this process arise from the risks posed to individuals who seek to apply political power on an illegal basis. Because power can be exercised with relative precision when channelled through legality, political actors have been motivated to direct power through this mechanism. This has created a political system in which government is both constituted by, and operates through, communications which equate illegitimacy with illegality. This does not mean that the political system has no resources from which to articulate a claim that illegality is legitimate. The communications that accompany selections from between parameters of illegality (national interest, race or tribal values, class interest, the common good, the sovereignty of the people, etc) are available to be utilised by those who wish to claim that their illegal actions are justified.[49] But such claims have none of the technical precision of legality, nor do they enjoy the surplus value of generating communications within the legal system which are organised by reference to justice.[50] Their opponents, by contrast, can point to the illegality of their actions, and draw on the eigen-value generated by the everyday communications through which political power is constituted and transmitted: illegality is illegitimate. Therefore it is the combination of two elements which generates what can be described as prudential: the risk that illegal actions will generate communications of resistance, combined with the ability of political communications that are second coded as legal to distribute power without generating that resistance.

Systems theory may also throw some light on the debate between those who claim that the rule of law is a condition which is equally open to monarchies, dictatorships and democracies, and those who argue that there is some kind of connection between democracy and the rule of law. One can argue, using systems theory analysis, that the rule of law creates a potential for political power which is only fully utilised within democracies and, as such, provides an incentive for communications which can evolve the political system into this form. This argument goes as follows. The ability of politics to interact with its environment (the rest of society) is increased by its communications being secondary coded as law. This provides an incen-

[49] This analysis is compatible with theories which deal with the paradox of the political system whereby whatever communications are offered to justify a particular form of government always have the potential to subvert that particular form of government. For example, sovereignty based on the agreement of the 'people' to a particular configuration of government cannot explain why this agreement should be permanent. Even the restriction of sovereignty on a Hobbesian basis – the maintenance of peace and security – opens the way for claims that any current configuration of government institutions would need to be suspended in a situation where this was required for reasons of national security (on the complications of this, see Schmidt, 1922/2005, Agamben, 2005). This same paradox is present in civil disobedience literature, where the natural law reasons for claiming obedience to law also generate claims for a right to disobey law.

[50] This was part of the reason for Hitler eliminating Ernst Roehm and his supporters – controlling the agencies of the state offered more possibilities for power than the less directed violence of the brownshirts (*Sturmabteilung (SA)* – Stormtroopers).

tive for human actors, participating in politics, to make communications that seek to control what law recognises as legal sources. But it also can be seen to stimulate particular kinds of politics. As we pointed out earlier in this Chapter, the law's indifference to the basis of control of the legislature when carrying out statutory interpretation stimulates political communications which seek this control. But the potential of this structural coupling is not as great when politics organises itself on a non-democratic basis. The creation of a state apparatus that can seek to organise health, education, the military, economy, etc requires a political system capable of generating policies and programmes directed to all of these aspects of society. A military dictatorship organised around national security, or a monarchy which aligns itself with an aristocratic class, is not as able to develop the complex alternatives required to co-ordinate the political system with other social systems. The ability of politics to achieve structural coupling with social systems via law is increased if the political system can handle a wide range of alternatives. This is achieved in modern political systems by moving from demands of deference and loyalty to rulers, to the tolerance of opposition. The tolerance of opposition allows alternatives currently not chosen to remain available as future choices. This process operates, but in a more limited way, within monarchies and dictatorships. Here the distinction between government and opposition is expressed through factions seeking influence with the monarch/dictator. But the ability of politics to generate complex alternatives in response to the ever increasing complexity of a functionally differentiated society is much greater when politics evolves into party politics within democracies. (Here we are summarising Luhmann's writings[51] on the nature of politics in the welfare state.) Thus, whilst the structural coupling between law and politics which constitutes the rule of law is not limited to democracies, there are reasons to believe that the rule of law has made a contribution to the evolution of politics into democratic forms.[52]

Law does not have to achieve structural coupling with the political system in order to exist, as evidenced by the development of transnational forms of law, which can be created and applied without reference to political institutions. Nevertheless, the relationship between the political and legal system within nation states has historically been so close that state law has been treated as synonymous with law, or at least a paradigmatic example of what can be described as legal. This relationship has not been symmetrical. Whilst law has been treated as having a necessary relationship

[51] Luhmann, 1990a.

[52] 'The democratizaton of the political system and the positivization of the legal system have only been able to develop by conditioning and stimulating each other . . . this cannot happen without both the separation of systems and a mechanism for their structural coupling' (Luhmann, 2004, 380). For a full historical account of the manner in which inclusion in power, leading to democracy, operates to increase the power available to the state, see Thornhill, 2008 and 2011, and our further discussion in this Chapter.

with the state, states are not assumed to have the same relationship with law.[53] This asymmetry is captured by the concept of the rule of law. This concept gains importance in political theory on the assumption that there can be other forms of rule: rule through the application of physical force, or economic incentives, not themselves authorised by law, or even contrary to what law stipulates. Whilst the possibility for such rule cannot be denied, given historical examples, the functional differentiation of social subsystems, and their co-evolution in response to their structural coupling, provides a systems theory explanation for the creation and maintenance of the rule of law.

Constitutional Law

Understanding the relationship between law and politics as one of structural coupling increases our understanding of the nature of the rule of law, but what of Constitutions, constitutionalism and constitutional law? These too can be understood as an example of structural coupling. Indeed, the tenets of systems theory lead one to accept this as a matter of definition. If the political and legal systems are separate social subsystems, then they can only co-ordinate their operations through the development of compatible expectations, rather than shared meanings. This is, however, more than a matter of definition. The development of constitutional law is a further co-evolution of the structural coupling represented by the rule of law. We can see this if we take the example of the US Constitution.

The role of the US courts in interpreting the US Constitution has been subjected to sustained criticism. As well as pointing to the changes which occur when political communications are reinterpreted within the legal system as issues of constitutional law,[54] the judicial claim that they operate as the guardians of the Constitution has been challenged through the use of historical evidence which indicates that the framers of the Constitution had expressed no expectation, or desire, that it should become the subject of detailed textual analysis in the courts: 'The written Constitution is neither a lawyer's contract nor a layman's document: it is a political artefact.'[55] The claim that this Constitution was not expected to be the subject of legal interpretation draws further strength from the medieval understanding of the nature and distribution of political authority as 'fundamental law'.[56]

[53] Kelsen tried to reduce the state to its legal form. For a discussion of the difficulties of this, and the impossibility of excluding illegal state action, see Vinx, 2007.

[54] See Christodoulidis, 1998, for an excellent sustained systems theory analysis of the kinds of re-interpretation which law imposes on political communications.

[55] Loughlin, 2010, 298, echoing and citing Roosevelt's address on Constitution Day, 1937: 'The Constitution of the United States was a layman's document, not a lawyer's contract.'

[56] Fundamental law is distinguished from ordinary law by the claim that there is an area of politics that is not subject to legal review. But this places the legal system in a paradoxical

The fundamental law of a realm, as a development of custom, could only be described as a Constitution in the sense adopted by Burke, in his *Reflections on the Revolution in France*.[57] The idea that a Constitution could be contained within a written document[58] was, alongside the idea that the authority of that Constitution could be generated from the sovereignty of the people, an evolution of the political system. But there is no evidence that those responsible for taking this step intended for the written Constitution to be more open to legal interpretation than fundamental laws.[59] Against this background, the decision of the Supreme Court in *Marbury v Madison*,[60] which within the US legal system marks the recognition of the basic principle that the federal judiciary is supreme in the exposition of the law of the Constitution, can be understood (within academia and the political system) as an unwarranted usurpation of power by the judiciary.[61]

A systems theory analysis of this development needs to start with recognition of the co-evolution which had already occurred: the rule of law as a structural coupling through legislation. The background to the political dispute which formed the setting of the *Marbury v Madison* case, the first US decision which recognised the existence of constitutional law (or the constitutional legality of the Constitution), was a construct of legislation.[62] The outgoing Federalist-dominated Congress had passed a statute creating a new level of courts, with a view to their being filled by the outgoing Federalist President, John Adams. This statute also reduced the number of Justices who would sit on the Supreme Court by one, to come into effect with the next retirement, thereby preventing the incoming President from appointing the next Supreme Court Justice. The incoming Jeffersonian party dominated Congress passed a statute partially repealing the earlier one. That same repealing statute also altered the terms of sitting of the Supreme Court, in order to postpone any challenge to the repealing statute. Thus, the attempt

position. For, even as it denies jurisdiction to issues which come within the scope of fundamental law, it does so within the context of litigation, and that litigation has to identify the issue as coming within the scope of fundamental law. Thus not only cases where executive powers are upheld as legal, but even cases where the court refuses jurisdiction over matters of state, can be cited as evidence that the legal system does indeed decide issues of fundamental law. See Grey, 1977–78, 854.

[57] 1790. To those who would add natural law and reason as a source of fundamental law, we would quote Grey: 'The two sources were not seen as in conflict: the old was the reasonable and the reasonable was the old' (1977–78, 853).

[58] By contrast to the idea that an otherwise unwritten Constitution could include a document, such as the Magna Carta.

[59] More open, rather than not open, for the reasons set out in n 55.

[60] 5 US (1 Cranch) 137 (1803).

[61] 'The Founders expected constitutional limits to be enforced through politics and by the people rather than in courts . . . Their history, their political theory, and their actual experience all taught that popular pressure was the only sure way to bring unruly authority to heel' (Kramer, 2004, 91).

[62] This background is set out by Van Alstyne, 1969.

of the Federalist party to alter the judicial system during their last days of office had been thwarted by the passage of legislation. (Both parties were operating on the basis that political power could be directed through legislation.) The remaining problem (for the Jeffersonians) was that Adams had purported to make a large number of appointments to staff the new positions before leaving office. One of the new appointments was Marbury (appointed as a Justice of the Peace). However his commission was not delivered to him. President Jefferson took the view that commissions which had not been delivered were void. The commissions that had been delivered were accepted as valid.

If Chief Justice Marshall, in giving the judgment of the Supreme Court, had agreed with Jefferson that judicial appointments were not valid until they were delivered, the legal issue would have been decided without having to form any view on the status of the Constitution within the legal system. It would still have represented political power second coded as legality, but this would not have stimulated political or legal development. Instead, Marshall took the view that the judicial appointment did not require delivery to be effective. Having eliminated this solution, the next least radical legal solution was to hold that Marbury was appointed as a Justice of the Peace according to the provisions of a statute and that the court could make an order requiring his appointment to be honoured. Congress's activities were organised around its ability to make valid law, which included its ability to distribute judicial offices through statutes, an assumption held in common by both political parties in passing the legislative enactments which formed the background to the dispute over Marbury's appointment. The US legal system had continued the doctrine of parliamentary sovereignty, in which statutes were superior to the common law as a source of law, and conflicts were resolved through the process of statutory interpretation. The obstacle to this legal solution lay not within the legal system but with the political system (and is not even alluded to within the judgment). Any order upholding Marbury's appointment was already anticipated, within the political system, as a 'Federalist' decision, generating communications that questioned whether such an order should or would be enforced by officials of the new Jeffersonian Federal Government.

What further options are available within the legal system at this moment? How is the co-ordination between the two systems resulting from a structural coupling through legislation to be maintained? The mutual distrust between the two political parties cannot be re-expressed within the legal system in its political form, and settled through the kind of negotiated trade-off which is possible within politics ('we will accept half your current nominees'). And such a result would disturb the expectations of the political system, which is, like Queen Elizabeth in *Shelley's case*, waiting for recognition as something different from itself: a 'legal' resolution of the case, not a political one.

The judgment explores two further possibilities. The first is the possibility of including the disputed appointment within the category of executive discretion, a category of appointment which the Supreme Court would not seek to know the reasons for, nor enforce against the wishes of an incumbent Secretary of State.[63] What complicates this possibility is the use of legality to create the offices of state. There is by the date of this decision an assumption common to the political and legal system that the structure of government, at the level of awards of offices and commissions, is to be distributed through legality. Indeed, the ability to distribute judicial appointments through law is what has generated this dispute. So there is no possibility (without losing a lot of redundancy in both systems) of abandoning the assumption that the allocation of offices is normally enforceable through the courts. Could Marbury's appointment be likened to that of a senior member of a Secretary of State's department – a person whose role was not to give effect to government policy – but to create it? Such recognition would concede that judges were political appointments like any other – not at the level of politics where power had already been distributed through legality, but at the level where decisions on the distribution of power were made. Our Chapter on judicial communications has described the difficulties of generating self-observations on judicial decision making that acknowledge precedents as law-creating acts akin to legislation. And when one remembers that William Marbury was a mere Justice of the Peace and not a federal judge, it would be difficult for the legal system to incorporate such premises into its own communications without threatening an internal hierarchy which is maintained by communications which assume that lower court judges have to treat higher court judgments as authoritative pronouncements of law. So it is unsurprising that the *Marbury* judgment failed to interpret the doctrine of executive discretion in such a way as to admit that all judges, even Justices of the Peace, are akin to senior political policy makers. And there is no reason to believe that this discarded 'solution' would have seemed plausible within the political system. One of the premises of Congress as a focus of political communications is that the law directed at Justices of the Peace will control what they do in their courts (and in turn provide guidance to citizens).

The solution adopted within the judgment was to treat the appointment as valid, but to use the Constitution as the reason why no order could be issued by the court requiring Marbury's commission to be given effect. It is here that Marshall is credited with making a choice between two different kinds of Constitution: Constitution as fundamental law, which has a political existence that is not duplicated within the legal system, and Constitution as law, which has a dual existence within politics and law. One cannot give

[63] This deals with politics by immunising the legal system – identifying events to which it will not respond.

a systems theory answer to the question of why he made this particular choice. But we can explore the reasons why this was a possible choice at this time – why it is something which could form part of this legal judgment, and be taken up by the legal system as a legal doctrine. Some of the reasons for this have already been discussed under the heading of the rule of law. Part of what would, in medieval Europe, have been covered by 'fundamental law' had by the date of the *Marbury* decision already entered into ordinary law through the coupling between law and politics represented by legislation. The evolution of the political system into a series of nation states had been achieved through the second coding of political power as legality – the creation of government departments, allocation of budgets, and creation of offices had been achieved through legislation. This had even extended to the appointment of judges, as evidenced by the statutes passed by Congress. The idea that the Constitution can exist as fundamental but non-legal 'law' is not simply the result of restraint on the part of legal actors and deference to political action, it includes the restraint provided through the difficulties of litigating political issues as legal ones. But the use of legality as a means to distribute political power draws the legal system into the political system, in the sense that political issues about that power have a second life within the legal system. Marbury's appointment could not easily be treated by the legal system as a non-legal issue. It was treated, both by the court and by the President, as a matter of law. And having been recognised by the legal system as a legal issue, it was not something which the court could refuse to decide.

Another reason that this development was possible, which is quite mundane but nevertheless important, is the reduction of the Constitution to writing. The complaint made against the lawyer's appropriation of the Constitution (already quoted) is that they have reduced politics to something like contractual drafting. But the ability of a Constitution to form part of the legal system depends on it being open to be used to create recognisable legal communications. And this is exactly what Marshall's judgment does. He makes the radical claim that a Constitution is a body of laws in the context of a political dispute over the abuse of a power to appoint judges, but does so in the form of a technical dispute over the right of the Supreme Court to issue a writ of mandamus. A 1789 statute had granted the Supreme Court a general right to issue a mandamus. Marshall asks whether this power is constitutional. He looks to the common law to find the earlier basis of this right, and concludes that at the date of the Constitution's adoption it is a right only open to an appellate court. He looks to the Constitution to find the status of the Supreme Court, and finds the provision which stipulates when the Supreme Court acts as an appellate court, and when it has a general jurisdiction (acts at first instance). He treats this provision as an attempt to determine what powers the Supreme Court was intended to have at the date of the Constitution. He then asks what effect the 1789 Act has, and concludes that it is an attempt to give the Supreme Court greater powers than were provided for in the Constitution. Marshall goes on to assert that the Constitution is not fundamental law as that term as been traditionally understood (not law at all) but fundamental law in the natural law sense of a law that invalidates lower laws (here statute and common law). But most of the job of showing that the Constitution is law has already been achieved in the earlier analysis. Marshall has shown that the US Constitution contained provisions that, on at least some occasions, could be subjected to the same kind of legal analysis that generates disputes over contractual terms or statutory provisions.

Marshall was only able to extend the legal system to include the written Constitution because the Constitution provided him with the kind of document which allowed the legal system to take that step. This judgment is recognised, within the US legal system, to have established the principle that the Constitution is law, and that lower law which conflicts with it is not valid. But this recognition was itself a process of repetition – the recurrent utilisation of the Constitution as a legal document which could be integrated with other legal documents (statutes, precedents) to provide answers to legal issues. And through that process of repetition, the status of constitutional law provides an increasing redundancy within the legal system, such that it proves ever more difficult to remove it. The importance of this ongoing reflexive process, the evolution of the legal system through the constant application of the distinction between unchanging law (Constitution) and changing law (legislation), should not be underestimated.[64] Within the United States, it forms a central distinction utilised within both federal and state law, with each state having its own Constitution and constitutional law. With this development, it is difficult to imagine any US advocate or judge seeking to generate a legal argument which sought to reject the existence of constitutional law, or the appropriateness of that law being established through the process of adjudication within the courts. Any such rejection would represent an attempted deconstruction of the communications on which a recognisable legal argument would have to be based. For those communicating within the US legal system, the existence of constitutional law, and the power of the judiciary to declare statutes unconstitutional, is currently undeniable.

This systems theory analysis of the US Constitution – both the first step towards judicial review of statutes based on constitutional law and the increasing redundancy produced by the repeated application of the distinction applied in that first step – has implications for much of constitutionalism. Looking first at the legal system, it is a mistake to equate the restriction represented by Constitutions solely by reference to the formal provisions of

[64] 'It is not the "big decision", the mythical foundational act, that is relevant for the existence of a constitution, but rather long standing chains of communicative acts, bound to one another, of the successful anchoring of a constitution as the "highest authority".' Teubner, 2011, at 250, quoting, in translation, Vesting, 209, 613.

a constitutional document.[65] As with our analysis of the rule of law, what creates the difficulties of co-ordinating law and politics, and produces what politics experiences as resistance, is the redundancy[66] of the legal system. In order to respond to political pressure the legal system has to re-configure its communications. The more redundancy that needs to be sacrificed, and the more operations that cannot be carried out if that redundancy is sacrificed, the more any actor within that system is motivated not to make those communications, or to make counter-communications in response to those who do. This requires us to refine our understanding of the constitutional law found within different national legal systems, and even within the same national legal system over time. Whilst the legal system may describe *Marbury* as a case which 'established' the doctrine that the federal courts could declare statutes unconstitutional and legally void, it is the ever increasing use of the distinction introduced in that case within legal communications that inhibits the ability of any legal actor, no matter what opinions they may have expressed in other contexts, to deny or reverse that distinction.[67]

Turning to the political system, how does it respond to the evolution of a legal system beyond a coupling based on the distribution of political power through legality via legislation, to one in which legislation can be declared illegal? Any assessment of this response should start from an acceptance that much of what is understood as constitutionalism has its origins in the rule of law, rather than a written Constitution. The separation of powers is considered essential to a Constitution, and the rule of law, but this separation is a result of rule *through* law. The political system cannot rule through law without that law being applied. An application of law cannot take place without interpretation by the party applying it, within the system of communication which both generates and restricts the possibilities of interpretation. Put in more prosaic terms, the political system cannot distribute power through legality and at the same time deny that the outcome of legal issues is to be decided by the application of legal doctrine. An

[65] Comparing the constitutional legal provisions of different states, and reducing these to models of, for example, hard or soft review, or various other characterisations of such judicial review (see Gardbaum, 2011) cannot be based solely on a comparison of formal provisions. A nation state which offers what might be described as hard review of legislative or executive action is one whose legal system has evolved to the point where the abandonment of that form of review is no longer possible without putting the legality of a vast number of operations which presuppose the possibility of that review, and its historical outcomes, in question.

[66] If needed, see our analysis of this concept in Chapter 2.

[67] In this, the US legal system prior to the decision in *Marbury* can be likened to the UK legal system immediately after the passage of the European Communities Act 1972. Arguments about the effects of this statute on the doctrine of parliamentary sovereignty oscillated between no effect and significant effect. But with the development of community law as an important element of UK legal provisions, and the increasing redundancy within the UK legal system represented by the integration of community law and UK law, the ability to treat the European Communities Act as an 'ordinary' statute, such that any explicit or implicit conflict with its provisions amounted to its partial repeal, has become increasingly difficult to maintain.

ever increasingly technical distribution of political power through law generates doctrine of ever increasing complexity. From this position, the separation of powers is a self-observation, generated separately within the political and legal systems, which acknowledges the inability of the political system both to utilise legality to distribute political power and at the same time require legal operations to be carried out solely through political communications. That this occurs within the political system is an outcome of the political system's investment in legality. Even in cases like *Shelley* or *Marbury*, where the political system wants a particular result, it demands a legal result. But a legal result cannot be produced without reference to legal communications. The legal branch of the separation of powers is traditionally thought of in terms of a separate institution (the courts) or separate personnel (the judges). But one can also see it in terms of separate subsystems of communication. The distinction between politics and law is established through their existence as separate systems: the different meanings that each can generate (uniquely) through their own communications. The development of a separate profession, able to educate its members in the complexities of the communications needed to carry out legal operations, is both an outcome of the process of autopoiesis and a necessary condition for its continuation at ever greater levels of complexity. And by producing ever greater quantities of complexity, through legislation, the political system is constantly reproducing the conditions which generate what, within the legal and political systems, are described as a separation of powers.

The role of the courts within the doctrine of separation of powers is commonly understood as a restriction on the powers of the executive and the legislature, or rather, on the executive as it rules through a legislature. But, as with the rule of law, political communications generate this idea of resistance and, indeed, need to generate it. The premise of a legislature's existence is that making law makes a difference – legislation is a significant political act. As such, it is belied by communications whose implicit meaning is that legality provides no significant restraints upon those who exercise judicial office. If it was not, if all adjudication (including statutory interpretation) was simply the expression of political beliefs, especially party political beliefs, by those who held judicial office, then the appointment of judges would be a very important political act, but the activities of a legislature would have little relevance at all. In this situation, political communications surrounding the appointment of judges cannot but echo what is commonly referred to in the sociology of law as the *relative autonomy* of law. Statutes are passed on the basis that legislation creates something which restricts the freedom open to judicial and executive actors, insulating them from at least some of the considerations which led to the statute's creation.

As with legislation, the Constitution is not a single entity, but a relationship between two systems. The incorporation of the Constitution into the

US legal system, which began with *Marbury*, marked a departure from the political and legal idea of Constitutions as something outside of the legal system,[68] but it did not convert the Constitution into something that existed only through, and within, the legal system. The legal system can only recognise a Constitution generated through the application of its code and in response to legal issues, while political issues, even constitutional ones, cannot always generate legal cases. The meanings given to the Constitution within the legal system (the 'legalised Constitution'[69]) cannot control or determine the meanings, or the change in meanings, which occur within the political system (or vice versa). Some recognition that one is dealing with two autonomous systems, and not a single entity, is found in recent US writings into the nature of constitutional change, which apply an approach to political science known as American Political Development (APD).[70] A legal interpretation of constitutional change identifies this with the formal process of amendment, or shifting judicial interpretation of constitutional provisions. But more recent writings have sought to show how the political system is capable of both identifying particular issues as having 'constitutional' significance, and changing what is considered to be constitutional, without reference to the legal system. The 'legalised Constitution' has been contrasted with an 'informal' Constitution, or the 'Constitution outside the courts'.[71] The political Constitution has evolved through communications which echo legal ones: disputes over the purpose of constitutional provisions, treating decisions based on interpretations of constitutional provisions as precedents, and attempting to identify principles which restrain day-to-day politics. Despite the echo, this analysis accepts that the creation of these principles, precedents and purposive interpretations within the political system does not mean that they are also legal principles, precedents, and interpretations. Rather, this analysis identifies an interaction between the two, whereby transformations in the political understanding of the Constitution result in turn in changes to the legal interpretation of constitutional provisions.[72]

APD analysis shows us that understanding the Constitution in terms of the different meanings given to a common text within two different systems should not lead one to the conclusion that each system evolves without reference to the other. The process is one of co-evolution. This co-evolutionary process is illustrated in the account of constitutional change offered by Bruce

[68] As stated in n 55 above. The legal version of this separation involves a paradox, as it can only be expressed from within the legal system, through legal operations.

[69] See Griffin, 2007, 52.

[70] See Orren and Skowronek, 2004.

[71] Griffin, 2007, 58.

[72] APD focuses on institutions, and sees the development of the Constitution as an inter-institutional one, where 'different institutional rules and norms will abut and grate as a normal state of affairs' (Kersch, 2004, 8, cited by Griffin, *ibid*, 58).

Ackerman.[73] Ackerman has developed a theory of constitutional change based on the reciprocal influence of legal and political developments. He has sought to show how changes in the Supreme Court's interpretations of the US Constitution need to be understood as responses to developments within the political system. The US Constitution cannot be interpreted, inside the legal system, by reference to what that text might have meant in the historical circumstances surrounding its adoption. The legal system cannot reach judgments on the legality of political actions by reference to the state of the political system in the eighteenth century – one that had no party system, or federal welfare state. In order to maintain a co-ordinated relationship to the political system the legal system has to take cognisance of the political system's current understandings of itself, and what that system regards as fundamental (constitutional).[74] However, this cognisance has to take the form of an application of the legal code, and to be achieved despite the inability to recognise that every norm which the political system treats as 'constitutional' is also a legal norm.[75]

Ackerman's analysis can be criticised for its failure to recognise the full extent of the dynamic interaction between the two systems. There have been more examples of co-evolution than the three which he identifies.[76] His work has also focused on the manner in which changes to the political system have led to radical re-interpretations of constitutional law, making it a one-way analysis of the influences which lead to co-evolution (the political Constitution evolves, and law eventually incorporates these changes

[73] Ackerman, 1991.

[74] Ackerman uses the term 'We the people' to signify the constituent power of the US citizenry to alter the US Constitution. He argues that certain elections (notably those following political disputes over interpretations of the Constitution) constitute exercises of this power, whether or not the election is followed by a formal amendment. In this way he explains both the passage of the 14th Amendment and the reinterpretation of the constitution to legalise Roosevelt's expansion of federal powers under the 'New Deal' as amendments to the Constitution. See further Fisher, 1998, 237–47.

[75] Ackerman criticises the orthodox view that the judges of the middle republic (between the Civil War and the New Deal) reached a 'mistaken' view of the Constitution. He wants the reinterpretation to be recognised as an amendment of the Constitution, justified by the electoral mandate provided to Roosevelt and Congress. But in the absence of a formal amendment, what communications were open to the Supreme Court, in dealing with cases like *Lochner v New York* 198 US 45 (1905), except to declare the middle republic's judges to be 'mistaken'. Of course, as an external observer, he offers a persuasive argument that the legal system's internal reconstruction of these decisions as 'mistakes' is itself mistaken. But it is doubtful that the legal system could replace its own formal criteria of what constitutes a constitutional amendment with that offered by Ackerman, which would require legal actors to distinguish between normal and extraordinary elections, normal mandates and constitutional mandates, etc.

[76] Ackerman discusses the foundation of the Constitution (made necessary by the failure of the Confederation to anticipate the development of a federal government), its reconstruction (which in conditions of laissez faire and limited government could be interpreted as a limitation of state and federal rights organised around ideas of freedom of contract and protection of property) and the New Deal (which provided a constitutional basis for the Federal Government's welfare state programme). For this criticism, see Griffin, 60, quoting the historian Gordon Wood.

into its interpretation of the legal Constitution). This focus is an understandable correction to the internal legal understanding of the Constitution which identifies the Constitution with constitutional law, and only recognises changes in the Constitution when these are acknowledged within the legal system: formal amendments or decisions which overrule earlier interpretations of constitutional law. But there is scope, using systems theory analysis, to investigate also the role played by the legal Constitution inside the political system.[77] As well as a division between a legalised formal Constitution, and a political informal one, one can also examine how each is re-created inside the other. Such an analysis, using the concept of structural coupling, does not limit the idea of co-evolution to a process whereby changes in one system produce changes in the other (and vice versa). The immunities within each system are as important for the process of co-evolution as the responses. Just as the lack of legal responses to political communications surrounding legislation have provided a stimulus to the political system to focus political activity around the control of legislatures, so has the legal system's inability to respond to political communications about the Constitution directed by the political system's own understandings as to what is constitutional. Whilst many of the most important US constitutional issues have been decided within the political system without reference to the legal system (such as the military draft, the Louisiana Purchase, and the Federal Reserve System);[78] the legal system has, nevertheless, provided some stability to what, within the political system, is treated as 'constitutional', that is, power that is constituted and not open to change.[79] There is a sizeable literature on the paradoxical nature of Constitutions, dealing with the manner in which they purport to represent a final exercise of political power despite the absence of any coherent account as to how the body (the people, constitutional convention, or God) which has the authority to exercise this power (constituent power) can be prevented from re-exercising it to create a new set of governing institutions (constituted power).[80] This is a paradox which, within the political system, is defused through its operations. The resistance to constitutional change within the political system, like the resistance to change within any system, is a function of the social costs of that change, which are distributed through a system by operations that cannot, or are unlikely to occur, as a result of the consequent loss of redundancy. But this process is assisted by

[77] For a sustained example using systems theory, see Christodoulidis, 1998.

[78] See Whittington, 1999, 12. Wittington lists 87 examples of such changes.

[79] The particular example given by Griffin, 2007, 58–59, is the inability of the political system to reach any consensus on grounds for impeachment of a President which fall short of a crime, even though Article II, sec 4 of the US Constitution refers to 'high crimes and misdemeanours' and has been interpreted to cover abuse of power and incompetence.

[80] See the essays in Loughlin and Walker, 2007. Loughlin, 2010, provides a full historical survey of the evolution of ideas of both constituent power, and constituted power, and the problems of reconciling the two.

the coupling between the legal and political systems. The redundancy within the legal system represented by the extensive use of the distinction between constitutional and ordinary law provides a resistance to political power and, within a political system which distributes power through legality, an internal basis of resistance to the re-opening of the issue of constituent power. However, whilst there may be resistance, any suggestion that this power has been exercised once and for all is belied not only by the inability to offer any coherent justification for this, but also by the evidence that Constitutions, as a site of coupling between law and politics, continue to evolve.

One consequence of understanding Constitutions as a form of inter-system co-ordination achieved through structural coupling has been that constitutionalism has been given a wider application within systems theory than is normally the case within political or legal theory. Once one has understood political Constitutions in this manner, why should our understanding of the nature and effects of law be limited to the structural coupling which occurs between these two particular systems? Even when one considers political Constitutions, the claims of politics to rule through law cannot be properly considered without extending one's consideration of structural coupling from politics and law to that between law and whatever social system it is attempting to regulate. This invites one to consider, as we have done in our Chapter on legal pluralism, what possibilities exist for law to develop through forms of structural coupling between itself and other social systems which do not depend on the distribution of political power made possible by the structural coupling between law and politics represented by the rule of law.[81] Within systems theory, the phrase societal constitutionalism points towards these alternate possibilities. This development is discussed in the next section.

Constitutional and Human Rights, and Societal Constitutionalism

Constitutional and human rights[82] have been given a sociological explanation within systems theory by reference to functional differentiation. This categorisation has been introduced already in this book especially in the context of our discussion of legal pluralism. Modern society is viewed by Luhmann to have a different dominant basis for differentiation from that of

[81] See Teubner, 2010 and 2004.

[82] The clearest presentation of Luhmann's explanation of constitutional and human rights is that provided by Verschraegen, 2002, based in turn on Luhmann, 1965. This section relies heavily on Verschraegen's article. See also Verschraegen, 2006. For a particularly perceptive analysis that adopts a similar approach and applies it to US Supreme Court cases on racial discrimination, abortion, homosexuality and privacy, see Baghai, 2013.

earlier societies. These earlier societies had dominant differentiations based on tribes or families (segmentation) or estates and classes (stratification) rather than by 'function' (science, economy, politics, law, etc). The claim is not that these earlier societies were entirely constituted through segmentation or strata. So, for example, a society which was differentiated through dominant distinctions of strata (aristocracy, gentry, peasants, etc) would have internal distinctions within those strata based, for example, on family. Nevertheless, the dominant distinction generates self-observations and self-descriptions peculiar to each kind of society. Most importantly, the communications which accompany a society in which the dominant distinction affects a distribution of humans within that society, according to the status established by their births, generates a self-description in which the status of individuals within that society is part of a natural order. These distinctions, and the communications which create and support them, make human rights, as presently experienced, difficult to conceive or communicate about except as utopian ideas. Rights exist within such societies, but in the sense of the entitlements due to a person by reason of their particular status within that society. There is no, or very little, recognition of a form of rights applicable to all humans within that society regardless of their status. And rights, being tied to status (membership of a particular status group) are not understood as individual rights, there to protect individual interests and allow for individual choice.

The transformation of rights from a sense of what is appropriate in a given social situation (rights as *ius*) to rights as individual entitlements, some of which are available to all humans, is generally acknowledged as historical fact.[83] Systems theory interprets this evolution in the nature of rights as a consequence of the evolution which occurs at the level of functional differentiation. The changes in society collectively described as the Enlightenment (the creation of an autonomous political realm, independent of religion; the emergence of science, as a field which generates knowledge separately from religion or politics; the development of an economy in which transactional possibilities are structured by wealth, and not social position; etc) represent a new dominant differentiation within society. Society is differentiated through its social subsystems, into autonomous spheres – the religious, political, legal, scientific, etc. These systems establish which communications belong to themselves, by reference to each system's existing communications. And in establishing what constitutes an economic, political, religious or legal communication, these systems in turn establish who, under what circumstances, constitutes an economic, politi-

[83] See Barden and Murphy, 2010, 212–18. Though the transformation is accepted, dating the transformation depends on whether one looks to the first writings when the possibility of subjective rights were explored, attributed to William of Occam in the 14th century, or when they were incorporated into political discourse and revolutionary documents in the seventeenth and eighteenth centuries.

cal, religious or legal actor. Each system in its reflexive communications recognises only what is relevant about a human actor for its own operations. So, for example, the economy only recognises what allows a human to participate in an economic transaction as a consumer, or producer of goods. The political system recognises the human as a subject, or citizen.[84] This partial recognition of the human being – recognition and attribution of status within a system solely by reference to the attributes relevant to that system's operations, does not correspond with the treatment of humans under dominant societal conditions of stratification or segmentation. The birth status of the individual, their position as member of an estate or family, does not determine their position within politics, the economy, religion or law. Rather than being allocated a place within society on the occasion of one's birth, participation as actors within these various systems has to be established separately according to each system's criteria. The roles of scientist, pupil (within the education system), politician or consumer are constructed in ways that do not recognise the individual's rank within a stratified or segmented society as a relevant criteria (membership of the aristocracy provides no automatic basis for one's recognition as a scientist, lawyer, scholar, or political leader).

Prior to the development of autonomous functional subsystems, one's position at birth principally established one's social position. Altering that social position was not impossible, but nevertheless rare and, in keeping with the self-description of such societies as a natural order, could be expected to generate communications which identified such situations as abnormal, inappropriate or even unnatural. One's social position, as lord, gentry or peasant, was something which most of the population could expect to inhabit throughout their lives, with little possibility of change. By contrast, the partial recognition afforded to human actors within a society consisting of autonomous functionally differentiated social subsystems creates a situation in which participation within each system is not given by birth, and is open to change. An individual's statuses are contingent on their acquiring the attributes appropriate to each system.

Under conditions of functional differentiation, human rights gain a plausibility which is impossible under conditions of segmented or stratified differentiation. Consider first the idea of equality. As a claim that all humans should be treated identically it remains a utopian ideal. But as a demand that human actors should be treated in accordance with the criteria of relevance generated by each functional subsystem – that medical resources be distributed according to health needs, education according to intellectual ability, consumer goods according to wealth, etc, then it has

[84] Thornhill shows how these recognitions by the political system increased that system's power to affect society, through by-passing the private, local power relationships that constituted feudalism (Thornhill, 2011). For a short statement of the thesis of Thornhill's book, see Nobles, 2012.

meaning in terms of the eigen values generated by the communications of each functional subsystem. Similar processes operate with reference to ideas of freedom. Within a society in which one's social position is allocated at birth, the concept of individual freedom – a social identity constructed through individual choices – lacks plausibility as a description of the situation of the normal human actor within that society. But within a society composed of separate functional subsystems, possibilities of inclusion depend on the attributes which individuals acquire (wealth, education, etc). The social identity of all individuals becomes understood in terms of these acquired characteristics. Equality and freedom increase their plausibility in relation to each other – and in contrast to the values generated by the segmented and stratified differentiation which functional differentiation replaces. The equality represented by each system's application of its own criteria for participation and roles is also a routine and endlessly repeated denial of the relevance of features associated with segmentation and stratification. Attempts to impose or maintain these latter criteria (distributing system roles by reference to race or estate) represent an improper interference with an individual's access to those system roles (that is, they lack plausibility as communications within the respective systems) and can be expressed, politically, as a denial of freedom, and corruption.

Constitutional and human rights such as freedom of speech, religion, life, property and privacy[85] operate as inclusion rights, ensuring that humans can participate within the different functional subsystems that constitute modern society. At the most basic level, a human cannot participate in social systems without the security represented by a right to life, and freedom from torture. Individuals also need to be able to participate in more than one system, and not have their ability to do so restricted by either pressures arising from stratification or segmentation (restrictions arising from estate, race, family, etc) or by their participation in a particular system. Freedom of religion insulates the political system from dominant religions, preventing politics being used to impose religious uniformity. If achieved, it means that membership of a particular church is no bar to political opportunities. Property as a constitutional or human right protects an individual's ability to participate in the economy, etc. As claims to individual inclusion within systems, and as restraints on the use of political power to coerce individuals in their choices as to how and when they will participate in different systems, Luhmann considers them as mechanisms for protecting and stabilising functionally differentiated societies.[86] Human rights as rights of inclusion operate both to protect human beings from the risks of exclusion from society's subsystems (their inclusion within society

[85] See Baghai, 2012/13, essay 1.

[86] Natural law and natural rights do not offer an adequate basis for such self-limitation, as the self-description of society as a natural order, which gives content and plausibility to such rights, has been eroded through functional differentiation.

no longer being established through their social position at birth) and to allow each of the functional subsystems to increase the scale and complexity of its operations through their application to all human actors capable of meeting the system's own criteria for inclusion. In addition, as a human's participation within different social systems varies throughout their lives, and even from moment to moment (consumer, patient, church member, etc), human rights exist not as group rights, but individual rights.[87] Rights of inclusion are attached to the human subject – the subject who is outside systems – the subject who is not (yet) consumer, citizen, church member, etc, but 'merely' human.[88] They belong to a human subject whose identity is not given by the social position which they enter at birth, but which is created through their participation in various systems. As such, these rights are not rights in the sense of *ius* – a right to any particular state of affairs – but rights attached to the individual – explicable as means to give effect to an individual's interests and/or will, whereby they can create their own identity.

Luhmann argued that human rights were not only an outcome of the evolution of society from stratification and segmentation to functional differentiation, but that they also operated to protect that evolution from regression and de-differentiation. For him, it was crucial that human rights operated as political communications, introducing self-limitations to the political system. According to Verschraegen, Luhmann was mindful of the Nazi experience, seeing totalitarianism as an example of de-differentiation resulting from the over-ambitious attempt of the political system to control and regulate the other social systems, with enormous costs to those other systems, and humans.[89] Human rights offer a mechanism for the political system to avoid over-extending itself. Without such self-limitations, the political system is in danger of seeking to impose levels of regulation which decrease the ability of other systems to operate in ways that are productive

[87] 'What previously seemed normal is now impossible. The singular person can no longer belong to one and only one societal subsystem. He can engage himself professionally in the economic system, in the juridical system, in politics, in the education system and so on, and in a certain way social status follows the professionally delineated paths of success; but he cannot live in only one functional subsystem' (Verschraegen, 2002, 266, quoting and translating Luhmann).

[88] '**The inclusion of the population in society has to take a new form and this wish is framed in the form of subjective rights, because it is not realized yet**. On the level of symbolism, this figure then has a double meaning: first, that it concerns *subjective* rights (and not simply the reflexive right of an objective order), it symbolises that individuals now have to be conceived of as more personalised and more independent from social positions. Secondly, that this figure concerns subjective *rights* (and not duties), symbolises that inclusion of everyone in all function systems is not completely successful . . . corresponding to this a terminology of rights, not of duties, and a terminology of claims, not of responsibilities are created' (Verschraegen, 2002, 267, quoting and translating Luhmann, italics in original, emphasis added).

[89] Thornhill disputes this description of the Nazi state, by pointing to the historical evidence that fascist states in the first half of the 20th century were weak states, which could not perform even minimal regulatory functions. See Thornhill, 2011a, at 246.

for society (productive in the sense of allowing society to increase in its complexity).[90] As with our discussion of the rule of law the argument here is that a political system that seeks to apply political power directly to the decisions of another system risks overburdening itself by increasing the number of decisions that can only be affected through political communications, and undermining the ability of the regulated systems to develop and maintain complex programmes for the application of their own codes.[91]

Teubner and others have argued that the self-restraint provided by constitutional and human rights within the political system needs to be extended to other systems.[92] The danger of de-differentiation, which can result from the over-extension of one system to the detriment of others, is not limited to the political system, but extends to others, most notably the economy. The capacity for the economy to distort the operations of other systems, such as art,[93] sport or even politics, can be as great, if not greater, than the effects of applying political power to society's other functional systems. The economy is as capable of distorting the conditional programmes of other systems as is politics. In light of these effects, Teubner and others also argue for an express recognition that human rights operate not only to protect humans from the dangers of exclusion, but to protect communication systems, and that fundamental human rights should no longer be understood solely as self-limitations of the political system, or as individual rights, but as mechanisms[94] which protect any social system from the expansionist tendencies of another.[95] Thus, for example, we should conceive of constitutional and human rights as something which could protect the political system from the corrupting influences of the economy.[96]

In advocating these extensions of Luhmann's systems theory, Teubner and others move from a descriptive account of the conditions which have led to the evolution of human rights to a sociologically informed normative theory about the kinds of rights that are appropriate to a modern function-

[90] We discuss this further in the next Chapter.

[91] The alternative risk, and one that Thornhill claims is what has actually occurred in such situations, is that the political system loses autonomy, by distributing power through 'private' relationships, either those associated with segmentation and stratification (families, tribes, etc) or through social subsystems. Only by limiting the issues that can be recognised as political can the political system manage to resolve those issues through its own operations. See Thornhill, 2008 and 2011.

[92] See, eg, Graber and Teubner, 1998; Teubner, 2004.

[93] Graber and Teubner, *ibid*; Teubner and Fischer-Lescano, 2008.

[94] 'The horizontal effect of fundamental rights needs to be implemented through organization and procedures, rather than through subjective rights.' Teubner, 2011a, 215.

[95] On the expansionist tendencies of social subsystems, see Teubner, 1997a. Here, he considers how conflicts between systems might be dealt with by a new version of conflict of laws analysis, etc.

[96] On the need to prevent the economy's over-expansion through its own inability to control the supply of credit, and consequences in terms of a restricted political agenda for governments, see Teubner, 2011b. The author argues that an economic Constitution, in which the control of the money supply is returned to the central banks ('plain money policy') could self-limit the economy and prevent this kind of financial crisis.

ally differentiated society.[97] But in forming a view on the plausibility of these extended arguments as normative arguments, we need to consider the sociological explanation for the manner in which human rights have evolved to see if this theory not only generates arguments about the need for further extension, but also identifies the processes whereby this extension might occur. Constitutional and human rights are arguably functional for society, in the sense that they increase the ability of social systems to operate alongside each other, and continue to increase in complexity. But they did not develop simply because they are needed. Rather, the processes which led to their generation, functional differentiation, provided support for the further development of functional differentiation. Within these processes, it is apparent why human rights should have developed as self-limitations of the political system. A political system which develops autonomy from religion and custom, which increasingly seeks to regulate and control its environment, is constructing itself, and its environment, in ways that do not generate a self-observation of society as a natural order. A political system which has developed sufficiently to attempt to use legislation as a means to re-order society will have difficulty utilising communications which present societal distinctions of stratification and segmentation as 'natural' orders.[98] What replace this sense of a natural order are ideas of equality. These political ideas of equality are the political system's reconstruction of the communications of the other systems (religion, science, economy, etc) which it seeks to regulate. The recognition of equality within the political system, an equality to which politics gives expression as democracy, is the political system's own version of the system-specific basis on which other social systems allow humans to participate. The communications which lead the political system to recognise the equality of individuals – an acceptance of the legitimacy of the separate (non-segmented and non-stratified) criteria with which each subsystem constructs human participation – also generate communications which represent self-limitations of the political system.[99]

If one can accept this sociological account of the manner in which society's evolution from segmentation and stratification to functional differentiation creates the conditions in which democracy and human rights could

[97] Thornhill, 2010, claims that a normative argument is implicit in Luhmann's account of constitutional rights.

[98] A work like Thomas Paine's *Rights of Man* gains plausibility in the context of these changes within society. When the capacity of 'men' to demonstrate abilities sufficient to take them from the lowest social position to the highest is no longer rare or abnormal, but commonplace, the claim that rule should be the prerogative of a superior social class is open to ridicule, and a claim that all humans should participate in government gains plausibility.

[99] Political systems that attempted to maintain structures that were not compatible with functional differentiation, such as absolute monarchies, not only suffered from a loss in the plausibility of justifications based on natural social orders, but also failed to gain the increased political power which came from self-limitation. For example, the British state, which acknowledged subjective and constitutional rights to a much higher degree than the French, found it far easier to extract revenues and credit from the economy. See Thornhill, 2008, 179–88.

gain in plausibility within the political system, does this provide any reason to expect constitutional and human rights to develop as self-limitations within other systems? Through which social processes could we expect to see not just political Constitutions, but societal Constitutions – couplings between law and other systems which duplicate the manner in which the rule of law and human rights operate within the political system? We may be persuaded that societal Constitutions (structural couplings with law that result in self-limitations of the non-law system) are as desirable as political ones, but a normative argument does not amount to an explanation of the social processes that might be expected to generate societal Constitutions.

Teubner has acknowledged that functional differentiation has not only created the need for self-limiting mechanisms within other systems, but also generated additional barriers to any legal contribution to their creation. One may observe conflicts between social systems, and see the implications for human beings when social systems fail to restrain themselves – as when the economy puts drugs beyond the reach of those suffering from epidemics, or science treats humans as guinea pigs for experimentation.[100] But can the legal system observe these conflicts in these terms? For a start law (as with other systems) recognises only its own version of the human actor: the legal person. Law acknowledges rights granted to, and against, legal persons, and provides mechanisms for 'wrongs' (such as torts and crimes) done by one person to another. But far from bringing attention to the manner in which meaning (and with it action) is generated by social subsystems, and the risks this entails for human beings, their physical environment and the co-existence of social subsystems, the legal system sees these events (if at all) only as disputes between legal persons.

There are, however, some developments that increase the possibilities that societal Constitutions will duplicate the self-limitations that constitutional and human rights represent within the political system. The fact that legal persons include institutions increases the extent to which what law recognises as needing protection or restraint can overlap with systems. For example, a review of the right of a multi-national drugs company to set the price for anti-viral drugs in a third-world country provides something closer to a consideration of the conflict between the health system and the economy than could be the case if the legal system could only acknowledge disputes between individual human actors.[101] And in resolving disputes, the legal system will draw on its own resources, so there is reason to expect some of these disputes to be articulated in terms of fundamental rights, drawing on the legal elements of various national constitutional orders.[102]

[100] See Teubner, 2006.

[101] See Teubner's explanation of the South African case *Hazel Tau v Glaxo and Boehringer* and other examples, *ibid*, 327–30.

[102] Vesting, 2004. Vesting calls these developments 'The weak conception of social constitutionalism' (at 30).

So, for example, access to the internet has been articulated within litigation in terms of individual freedom and rights to free speech, creating the possibility that not only political restrictions on access to cyberspace, but also economic ones, will be subject to limitation.[103] But is there a sociological reason to expect societal Constitutions, as structural couplings between law and other social subsystems, to involve elements of self-limitation that are more than the occasional echo of political Constitutions?

In assessing these possibilities, one needs to remember that all structural coupling represents a relationship of co-ordination rather than external pressure, and has elements which can therefore be described as self-limitation. But this element of self-limitation does not necessarily lead to the kinds of inclusion and restraints that can be attributed to political constitutional and human rights. Take one of Teubner's own examples: patents for anti-viral drugs. This involves a structural coupling between the economy and law. As such, it is also a self-limitation, in a sense similar to the rule of law. Economic resources become attracted to activities that are stabilised and protected through legal forms, rather than those which are not. The economy only draws distinctions between a black economy and a legal one in terms of the increased costs (uncertainties and lack of enforcement) of operating in the former rather than the latter arena. Nevertheless, this distinction acts to divert economic resources to 'legal' markets rather than illegal markets, and to provide funding for a legal system that constructs and polices that market.[104] This is a self-limitation of the economy, achieved through its structural coupling with law. A market which is constituted through legal categories can rely on the legal system to establish forms of property to which the economy can then attribute value.[105] But as the example of the patenting of anti-viral drugs demonstrates, far from representing a limitation of the economy's capacity to exclude human beings from social systems (here economy and health) it can actually operate as a mechanism for their exclusion.

There is plenty of evidence that law can *constitute* social systems through structural coupling and, at the global level, by necessity, this coupling has occurred between law and other systems, particularly the economy, without

[103] Teubner, 2004, discusses the structural coupling between politics, law and the economy which results when internet providers are excluded from liability for showing prohibited material posted by their subscribers, when they 'co-operate' with the authorities. His particular example is the decision of the Paris Tribunal de Grande Instance, which in 2000 ordered Yahoo to bar French users access to auctions of Nazi objects.

[104] This is clearly not a one-way effect. The illegality of products creates barriers to entry which result in supra-profits for those prepared to expose themselves to the risks. These profits provide incentives for illegal supply, and the greater the barriers, the higher the expected supra-profits. Nevertheless, barriers to entry are self-limitations on the basis that, *ceteris paribus*, without them the economy would increase supply. The world does not stand still, so whether legality would actually result in an increased or decreased supply would depend on other factors including demand-side ones, such as the claim that legalising cannabis would reduce its attractiveness to youth.

[105] By contrast, the illegal market cannot rely on the courts for the enforcement of contracts, or for the protection of its innovations.

also involving a coupling with the political system at either the national or international level.[106] Expectations (communications which bind time and lower risk) are as necessary at the global as the national level. The need for these is met through institutions which can devise codes of conduct and procedures for adjudicating disputes. These codes of conduct and procedures for the resolution of disputes duplicate the processes associated with the rule of law at the national level. They give stability to social systems only if the code of conduct is given effect after the consensus which produced it, and the procedures for dealing with disputes are able to operate without being subjected to immediate power. With these dynamics, one can expect social systems to constitute themselves through law, and even to constitutionalise themselves through law.[107] By the latter, we mean simply that applications of the legal code can develop some conditional programmes which are identified as unalterable, thus providing immunities against change, and incentives for communications directed towards those legal provisions which are identified as open to change.[108] But these processes do not necessarily lead to a self-limitation within the system which couples with law, if that term is taken to refer to a restriction on the ability of that system to inflict damage on human beings or inhibit the operations of another system.

In recent writing, Teubner has expressed the view that social systems may develop more radical internal limitations as a result of the kinds of external and internal pressures that arise in situations of a social catastrophe: 'hitting the bottom'.[109] This approach acknowledges the resistance of systems to external or internal critique: to communications prophesying the consequences for the system or its environment if operations continue without radical alteration.[110] Systems cannot be expected to adopt self-limitations except as a response to their imminent inability to continue

[106] The examples which Fischer-Lescano and Teubner, 2004, give are the role played by the private company ICANN in regulating domain names on the internet, the development of the WTO, the internal codes of multinational corporations for their dealings with state and private actors, international trade associations, and the networks of NGOs.

[107] 'In some respects, the quasi-legal orders of world society themselves show constitutional characteristics . . . superior norms develop that define where the decision making power should be located, how violations should be handled, and how third parties should be included. By analogy to state constitutions, private regulations embody mechanisms of self-restraint to reduce intrusions on other actors and other domains' (Dilling *et al*, 2008, 8, quoted in Teubner, 2011a, 221).

[108] As Emilios Christodoulidis puts it, if societal constitutions represent self-descriptions which limit the possibilities of communication and thus allow system operations to continue without overburdening themselves with contingencies, then is 'there *any significant distinction* to be drawn here between *juridification and constitutionalisation*?' See Christodoulidis, 2011, 240.

[109] See Teubner, 2011b.

[110] Systems offer resistance to communications which cannot be incorporated into their everyday operations. The greater the loss of redundancy involved in incorporating new communications, the greater the resistance. See our Chapters on judges' communications (Chapter 2) and civil disobedience (Chapter 3).

functioning, or enormous pressure from other systems.[111] Thus whilst warnings from other systems that expansions may prove disastrous may have little influence on the systems to which those warnings are directed, it is a system's inability to continue its complex operations that provides a stimulus for quite radical change, including self-limitations. Parallels can be drawn with the political crises of France in 1789 and Eastern Europe in 1989, when political systems were able to incorporate self-limiting constitutional rights.[112] The dynamics of these political crises are described in the recent writings of Thornhill, who adopts an analysis of Constitutions which is similar to our presentation here of the rule of law. 1789 in France, and 1989 in Eastern Europe, are moments when political systems which had produced states with restricted ability to adapt to their environment were replaced by ones which had constitutional rights as self-limitations which increased their ability to respond to their environment.[113] These political systems, claiming absolute unrestricted authority to direct society, had found themselves responsible for matters which exceeded their capacity to make plausible claims to control. At the same time, the economy failed to provide these political systems with sufficient revenues to sustain their political programmes. These over-expansive political systems had bankrupted themselves by attempting political programmes which exceeded both their revenues and their ability to produce binding collective decisions. The radical changes of 1789 and 1989 represent moves from situations of relative impotence (in terms of the plausibility of claims to control their environment) to ones which represented an increase in the amount of power that could be directed through the political system. The argument is that, just as a political system gains in power by directing power with the technical precision that comes with ruling through law, so too it gains in power by withdrawing from the detailed direction of economic resources, where this results in an increase in the ability to raise taxation and influence the economy through payments.

Teubner argues that systems other than politics may over-extend themselves in similar ways, giving the example of the fiscal crisis of 2008 as an over-expansion of the fiscal sector within the economy which paralysed the financial institutions by their inability to identify which financial institutions

[111] Teubner, 2011a, admits that: 'To date, the new global constitutional orders have, for the most part, devised only *constitutive rules*, which have supported the freeing up of various systemic rationalities at the global level. Only after historical experience with their grave *effets pervers*, are counter-movements now appearing, which formulate *limitative rules*, in order to counteract self-destructive tendencies and to limit damage to social, human and natural environments' (213–14).

[112] Teubner, 2011b, in 'A Constitutional Moment?' gives three examples when the political system adopted human rights in response to internal and external pressure. He claims that France in 1789, post-war Western Europe in 1945, and Eastern Europe in 1989 were three moments when the political system incorporated human rights as self-limitations in response to catastrophe.

[113] Teubner, 2011b, cites Thornhill, 2008; see also Thornhill, 2011.

were in a position to make payments, and which were not. His hope was that such situations might lead to the fiscal sector adopting limitations which reduce its ability to bring itself to such a state of self-paralysis, and that these might take the form of constitutional limitations, self-observed within both law and the economy as unalterable.[114]

Whilst Teubner and others[115] write of external pressures as well as internal self-destruction as contributions to 'hitting the bottom' moments, consistency in the application of systems theory requires us to accept that external pressure can only be 'felt' by a system in terms of the differences which occur in its own operations. Thus, if a consequence of a system's operations is that its own reconstruction of a system in its environment alters, as with the political system's awareness that it is raising less revenue from the economy, this can be described as 'external' pressure, even though it is 'constructed' as such inside the political system.

We cannot here do full justice to the issues raised by ideas of societal constitutionalism,[116] and must content ourselves with having attempted to explain the dynamic through which such changes *may* occur. We feel the need to stress the 'may' as, whilst these changes may come to pass, the ability to describe how they have occurred in the past cannot be translated into an ability to know when, how or even if they will happen in the future (a theme which we will return to in the next Chapter).

[114] Teubner's constitutional example was a return to central bank control of the money supply (with central banks acting as a sort of 'constitutional court' for the economy), contrasted to a current situation in which 90% of the money supply is generated by commercial banks who lend by treating their debts as assets. This supply generates ever greater amounts of systemic risk, as it is based on assumptions as to the future ability of interrelated parties to make debt repayments if called upon to do so. As 2008 showed, relatively small changes in these calculations, relative to the world's total amount of finance, can precipitate a huge reduction in credit, especially if the location of expected future losses cannot be identified with any precision. Christodoulidis, 2011, questions whether this crisis, or ones like it, can be expected to result in self-limitations in the economy. He notes the political system's commitment to maintain growth and avoid recession, which has resulted in political responses to the banking crisis that has allowed the financial system to continue its operations, 'business-as-usual' (at 242).

[115] See essays in Kjaer, Teubner and Febbrajo, 2011.

[116] For example, one could discuss whether societal constitutionalism at the transnational level is only viewed as a structural coupling between two systems, law and a social system other than politics, because one's understanding of the political system is restricted to national state politics. If the political system is understood as a system that produces collectively binding decisions, then the transnational institutions that are producing structural coupling between law and other functional subsystems also involve a coupling with politics. The rule of law, at a transnational level, requires the systems of dispute resolution that spring up to determine disputes arising from the codes of guidance established by transnational institutions to be able to operate without being subjected to direct political pressure. This has to occur even when the consensus that led to the adoption of those codes no longer obtains. Only thus can the political power which circulates through these transnational institutions establish the basis of collectively binding decisions with any degree of permanence.

7

Control through Law

Towards the end of the previous Chapter we began to consider structural coupling between law and other subsystems in modern societies beyond that between the legal system and the political system. In the case of the latter coupling, we were able to demonstrate how some of the key concepts that have specific meanings within both the political and legal systems have been and continue to be stabilised by the meanings attributed by each system to the other. In other words, we can observe a certain co-evolution that despite significant differences in communicative meaning enables each system to develop its programmes and self-reflexive complexity in tandem with the other system. But we started to question whether this level of stable co-evolution between any particular system and law would necessarily be compatible with the operations of a third system. Indeed, despite developing juridification one must not exaggerate the ability of law to couple with other social systems. As each subsystem develops by generating self-reflexive communications, reliant on self-observation and self-description, the possibility of stable co-evolution between all of the various subsystems is questionable. This is not surprising, if one thinks about how subsystems become ever more complex in their attribution of meaning. In this Chapter we will explore that complexity further.

What difference does it make to understand law, and other social subsystems, as closed autopoietic systems especially with respect to developing system complexity and systems' co-evolution? One important consequence of understanding modern society as functionally differentiated through the evolution of autopoietic social subsystems, which has implications far beyond law, is the conclusion that no system can steer society.[1] This is a lesson which has enormous implications for both politics and law and any expectation that politics can use law as an instrument through which to control

[1] 'It is difficult, almost impossible, to abandon the notion of steering and to let the future come as it comes. The semantics of time of modern society, the accentuation of the differences between past and future seem to prohibit this. And on the other hand, it is not easy to see if and how at least some of the expectations related to steering could be saved' (N Luhmann, 1988a, at 41, translated and quoted in Van Assche and Verschraegen, 2008, 264, also translated at Luhmann, 1997a).

society. The limitations on steering[2] are inseparable from the theory's understanding of subsystems and the role which they play in modern society. If each system has to construct itself through linkages of its own communications, and each system can only observe the world through its own communications, then no system can see the same world. Each system can only react to its version of the world which it creates through its own communications. This is the meaning of the claim that law only reacts to the world that it builds up through its own internal monitors, a limitation which law shares with all other subsystems.[3] No system can ever experience or anticipate the full complexity of another. This is also part of what it means for something to be a system. Every system, however complex, is less complex than the environment in which it is situated. Other social subsystems form the environment of a particular subsystem (along with the physical world, psychic systems, interactions and institutions or organisations).[4] Whilst any other subsystem is only one part of the environment of another, the relationships between those subsystems are still, like that between one system and the whole of its environment, less than a replication of the complexity of one system inside another.

Beyond the limitation of one system understanding fully the complexity of another, there are other limitations on the ability of one system to control or steer another. As discussed in Chapter 5, every system takes time to complete its internal operations in response to an event in its environment. By the time that a system's operations in response to its environment have been completed, that environment has changed.[5] The ensuing problems of synchronisation disturb opportunities for steering. Further, one needs to take account of the nature of self-production. Systems reproduce themselves through their own operations. Whilst the ability of complex social subsystems to carry out their operations is dependent upon redundancies, this does not mean that the system is in a static condition, or that it returns to the same state. A social system generates a vast number of communications within a short space of time. (Imagine all the legal communications that occur even within a single national legal system if we limit ourselves to a single week.) Even if only a small percentage of those communications generate redundancies (background information), which create new variet-

[2] Schirmer and Hadamek describe the background limitation in the following paradoxical terms: 'Steering is necessary because it is impossible' (Schirmer and Hadamek, 2010, 133).

[3] 'In terms of environmental influences on law, this means that even the most powerful social and political pressures are only perceived and processed in the legal system to the extent that they appear on the inner "screens" of legal reality constructions' (Teubner, 1987a, 20).

[4] In this book, apart from some consideration given in this Chapter, we have not spent any significant time considering how systems theory can be applied to institutions and organisations. For a set of essays that does this well, see Bakken and Hernes, 2003. In particular, see Andersen, 2003, which explores structural coupling within organisations.

[5] 'Something else always happens simultaneously with the steering operations (and this means also cannot be influenced by the steering operations)' (Luhmann, 1997a, 45).

ies (new possibilities for information), this still represents a significant change in the possibilities of further communications within that system. Small changes in outputs, which re-enter the system as inputs, repeated endlessly, generate large alterations in the system's state. In the case of complex systems, these changes are unpredictable.[6]

Writing in the 1980s,[7] Gunther Teubner considered the implications for systems of attempts to steer society through politics and law and identified three kinds of regulatory failure ('regulatory trilemma'). The first of these is that laws will be produced which the intended regulated system will be unable to incorporate into their operations, and to which they will not respond. Although laws' coercive threats might well motivate actors not to make system communications, or to select communications which raise less risk of threats, in some situations other systems will be deaf to laws' demands, and those laws will be, in some fundamental ways, ineffective. Another possible 'failure' identified by Teubner is where a system responds to political or legal steering through a decrease in its ability to carry out its current level of operations: a decline in its own complexity. The regulated social system will reduce its complexity through the abandonment of redundancies which sustain a high degree of variety in favour of ones that offer lesser possibilities. An example of this might be an attempt to regulate the economy, which leads to a reduction in the economy's ability to distribute goods and services. Another example would be the claimed effect on medical practice of increasing legal liabilities: the move to 'defensive medicine'. The third form of failure identified by Teubner is that the political initiative causes law to become over-socialised. This is a result of the production of norms which are orientated to the regulated systems, but cannot be processed consistently within the legal system. This could occur, for example, when the political system uses legislation to enact norms that are specific to problems which it has recognised within the regulated system. The most obvious burden for law is an ever increasing number of specialist norms that cannot be integrated into more general legal concepts or principles.[8] We illustrated this in Chapter 5, with the example of the different

[6] If one thought of this in mathematical terms, one would take a hugely long equation and multiply it by itself a million times. Then one would change one small element of the original equation, and repeat the multiplication. A comparison of the results would demonstrate the implications of system self-production, in which the results of operations provide the starting point for the next operations. As we have described this, there is an obvious parallel with chaos theory and its analysis of the sensitivity to initial conditions. 'Chaos theory . . . reveals how many systems that are constantly changing are extremely sensitive to their initial state . . . as the system evolves in time, minute changes amplify rapidly through feedback' (Hall, 1991, 8).

[7] Teubner, 1987a.

[8] 'The disastrous state of modern positive law lies in the incoherence of large numbers of norms which are produced procedurally in response to a particular situation and are then lumped together in disordered heaps. No adequate means of coping with this material intellectually has been developed' (Luhmann, *Rechtssoziologie* (1972), 331, quoted in Teubner, 1987a, 6).

temporal dimensions of the legal and political systems. Future-oriented norms can reduce law's ability to provide consistent sets of time-binding norms.

In place of more direct forms of steering, Teubner suggested that those who wish to use law to regulate society should focus on the nature of structural coupling, and the possibilities of increased complexity which arises not through one system controlling another, but through achieving relationships of co-ordination and co-evolution: an approach which he called 'reflexive law'. We introduced the nature of structural coupling in our last Chapter on the rule of law. For politics to develop a complexity constituted by law, it has to allow law to develop its own complexity through its own operations, that is without political power being applied directly in order to steer the outcome of particular legal operations (most notably adjudication) on anything other than an exceptional basis. This example, taken as a 'lesson', invites the conclusion that steering could take the form of developments likely to encourage structural coupling between systems, rather than attempts to directly regulate one system by means of another. In this Chapter we explore the possibilities of steering society through forms of law that express or rely on structural coupling, rather than more direct forms of intervention.

Steering through Constituting Rules

Teubner himself has described the developments which occur between two systems when they form relationships of structural coupling as 'blind evolution'.[9] There is an obvious tension between describing the evolution of systems as 'blind' and any claim that insights provided by systems theory in terms of structural coupling might lead to an increase in the capacity of politics or law to steer society. Nevertheless one can make a convincing argument that the structural coupling between law and politics has led to elements of steering within the political system. As discussed in the civil disobedience and rule of law Chapters (Chapters 3 and 6), the use of law as a basis for establishing collectively binding decisions provides a technical means for the distribution of physical power (coercion), and in turn (via the distribution of the capacity to make payments generated through taxation) economic incentives. Politics uses law to steer itself – to create agencies, programmes, policies, etc. Here law has an essentially constituting role. There is no doubt that this involves elements of steering, in the sense

[9] 'Co-evolution can thus be thought of in the following way. Co-variation is triggered by the impulses to variation which stem from the various subsystems. These must pass through the needle's eye of the singular interaction, and can then exert pressure on each other for change as parts of the system which reciprocally influence each other' (Teubner, 1993, ch 4, 'Blind Legal Evolution', 62).

that operations can occur (most notably the passage of legislation) which will lead to predictable results – agencies will be formed, financial payments will be made, etc. This constituting role is basically self-enforcing. Politics exists as decisions which provide the basis for further decisions. By using legality to distribute political power, one has a situation in which the legality of one decision provides the basis for the next. Here, steering through law is the use of law, like the points used to switch traffic on a railway line, to direct political power. The steering afforded to politics through law is undeniable, compared to the less precise ways in which power can be directed through ideology, etc. So one can say that the rule of law is a condition in which politics steers itself, through law. This ability to steer itself increases the variety of responses that can be made to problems which are identified as 'political problems'. Initiatives are tried which, if they appear to produce results that are acceptable, can be retained, and if not, other initiatives can be tried (the use of modern legislation typifies this example, namely the constancy of repeated legislative change dealing with the same subject matter). This is still self-steering – the political system alters itself in response to its perception of the manner in which its environment responds to politics, or rather, to the administrative apparatus within politics.[10]

Inside the political system, developments have occurred which increase the possibilities of steering. The resonance of the first part of Teubner's regulatory trilemma within politics is an awareness of the deafness of much of the rest of society to legal norms, introduced through legislation, which take the form of obligations or duties directed to behaviour and intended to alter it. Politics registers that its environment in many instances does not alter in the manner that was expected: things don't change. Much modern legislation thereafter consists of experiments with norms, which seek to alter behaviour indirectly. Thus, for example, rather than issue detailed regulations which seek to alter the internal practices of schools or hospitals, governments have instead required institutions to provide certain kinds of information (pupil test results, hospital mortality rates, etc) with the expectation that it is the publication of this information (producing league tables of 'successful' institutions) which will produce changes in behaviour rather than substantive law imposing detailed legal duties.[11] Detailed prescriptions on how companies should conduct themselves in response to various kinds of risk which have political significance have been replaced by obligations to conduct assessments, and produce and police appropriate standards. There is awareness that the constituting role of law within politics has its parallels within other systems. HLA Hart's suggestion that law is not simply duty-imposing, but also power-conferring,[12] has been a lesson not lost

[10] See Luhmann, 1990, ch 1, sections 14, 'Bureaucracy', and 15, 'Political Rationalization in the Administration: Organization, Programs, Personnel'.

[11] See generally Power, 1997, esp ch 3, 'Auditing and the reinvention of governance'.

[12] 1961/1994.

on the political system. Politics is not the only system which responds to being offered a framework for decisions established through law. Altering frameworks by altering the law offers further opportunities for politics to produce changes in its environment (namely other subsystems), as well as itself. The claim that modern law is less substantive, and more procedural, also reflects these changes in political expectations about the kinds of legal norms that can be expected to change society.[13]

The increased elements of steering available to politics as a result of law's constitutive role points to the different ways in which law carries out its function of providing normative expectations. Normative expectations differ from cognitive ones, in that they continue in the face of counterfactual examples. So when a system recognises events in its environment that conflict with an expectation, but that recognition does not trigger communications about the need to alter that expectation, then the expectation in question is normative rather than cognitive (and contra-wise with cognitive expectations). The clearest example of law's provision of normative expectations are duty-imposing rules, such as crimes and torts, which establish acts which ought not to occur, and which are not displaced by the vast number of instances when such wrongful acts nevertheless do occur. The ability of law's normative expectations to survive counterfactual examples of this kind is an important source of structural coupling, as non-legal systems rely on the law to provide technically specific wrongs which can resolve issues and disputes within other systems. So, for example, the law, with its technical procedures and substantive offences, manages to generate narratives for the media, political scandals within politics, and ways to decide whether medical treatments should be maintained for chronically ill patients within the medical system. But the possibilities of structural coupling are increased through law's constitutive rules. Here, the differences in facts recognised by law do not trigger communications about obedience or disobedience, but only alter the legal obligations that are taken to arise. These constitutive rules operate within the political system as the means to direct political power, by providing the basis on which decisions can be taken, which in turn establish the basis for further decisions. But they also operate in other social systems. In the private sector they establish the identity and basis for decisions of corporations and firms. A corporation can break the law by committing acts of fraud, but it cannot exist as a corporation without law, and it cannot operate as a corporation within the economy without having regard to the laws which establish its identity, which include identifying the formalities through which it can own and transfer ownership of assets.

Law's constitutive rules are an important source of stability to the communications of other systems.[14] We can see this in the powerful structural

[13] See Black, 2000.

[14] Constitutional (legal) norms exist at the transnational level, within trade associations, multinational communities, etc, even in the absence of duties whose breach results in the

coupling between the economy and law represented by contract, property and the law of corporations. The economy is able to generate prices for goods and services, but it uses law to identify property and its ownership independently of the economy, which simplifies the economic communications required to make payments to the person who can provide an economic asset.[15] The economy has gained in complexity through the introduction of institutional actors[16] but the legal system, through the law relating to corporations, has given these institutions and institutional actors a stability of form and identity.[17] The economy does not give legal entitlements or legal actors the same meanings that they have in the legal system. Instead of a network of communications organised in terms of rights and obligations, the economy constructs actors as bodies likely to react to costs and benefits, and their entitlements as packages of costs and benefits. But it recognises that these actors and assets are not the creations of itself. Namely, it can recognise them as 'legal', in the same reductionist manner that the legal system recognises the processes of 'politics'[18] expressed in statutes.

This constitutive role of law provides another mechanism for politics to achieve steering through law. What has been granted can be withdrawn, or only granted pursuant to further conditions. Systems which have coupled with the legal system in this way are likely to rearrange themselves in response to legal change. So, for example, if particular types of corporation are declared invalid, this introduces uncertainty and risk into the economy. Whilst these corporations would have been interpreted within the economy in terms of their contribution to calculations of costs and benefits, they were not constituted through those calculations. These corporations would have been constituted, not through the systematic relationship of communications within the economy, but through the internal relationships between legal communications. If the legal system ceases to generate these communications, this has implications for the system that has evolved

application of nation state political force. Teubner claims that these norms have a constituting role which not only enables social subsystems to operate at a global level (without the support of nation states) but steer those systems in the direction of ever greater autonomy from nation states. See Teubner, 2011a, esp 223–25; also Teubner and Korth, 2012.

[15] See, Teubner, 1991, 131. Whilst economic analysis of law approaches the allocation of legal rights in terms of the respective ability of different actors to pay for them, it utilises a form which is resistant to this formula in order to implement it. Legal rights, especially property rights, are treated as assets which can be valued, and thereby form part of calculations about what it is rational to pay for other assets. One simply cannot do this calculation and, at the same time, deconstruct all of the legal entitlements on which it is based into provisional rights open to re-allocation to whoever is willing to pay most for them.

[16] The economic rationality of which can be explained by neo-institutional economics – see Williamson, 2000.

[17] There are obvious parallels with the manner in which law gave identity and form to political actors in the history of the political system (on which see Thornhill, 2011, 20–76).

[18] But without, of course, in the interpretation of statutes, giving those political processes the same complex meanings that they have in the political system.

through their availability. In place of communications about the corporation as a single actor, more complicated economic communications may be required. These may be wholly economic, in the sense that expectations are generated solely in terms of the inducements likely to affect the behaviour of individual actors. Or, in the alternative, the economy will reconstruct the actors and entitlements around which payment can be organised in terms of the legal categories that law offers in the new situation, for example as a series of contractual entitlements and property ownership amongst the individuals who as a corporation formerly offered a single identity and axis for transactions.[19] Withdrawing the corporate form from particular kinds of economic activity (as identified first by politics and then by law) removes or diminishes whatever benefit, within the economy, leads to business being conducted through corporations. The removal of this benefit, for a particular class of business, can be expected (*ceteris paribus*) to reduce the amount of this business which occurs.

The greater the variety of legal responses which politics is able to induce through legislation, the greater the possibilities of steering, if steering is taken to mean that the political system registers changes in its environment to which it can respond, or not, with some predictability about what will occur both within itself and in its environment. The mistake is to move from the observation that the political system's structural coupling with law creates possibilities of steering other social systems, to the conclusion that politics, or any other system, is able to control itself or any other system. Control equals the possibility of determining the outcome, and this is simply incompatible with systems theory observation. Society cannot be controlled, as there is no point outside of society where this control can be exercised. Society can only evolve. Autopoietic systems duplicate this problem. Their existence as communications which only connect to other communications from the same system means that they have no point outside themselves which can determine what they can be or do. They too can only evolve. And in their evolution, they may steer, in the sense of 'give a steer to' (have some predictable effects upon) other social systems, but there is no possibility of one system controlling itself, and even less possibility of one social system controlling another.

To have any sense of steering society, politics has to register changes in its environment. It has to learn which of its operations produce desirable changes, which produce none, and which produce undesirable changes. In this process, it is simply repeating what all systems do. Systems of communication develop programmes, which are internal responses to their own internal version of their environment. And in doing this, they register when internal operations repeatedly produce the same response. In other words, they learn. As systems can only generate meanings through their own com-

[19] For example, a return to the use of trusts as corporate actors: see Maitland, 2003, Essay 5.

munications, this process of learning does not depend on their sharing, or duplicating, the meaning of the communications of the systems they 'learn' to influence, or attempt to influence, or are influenced by. But it does depend on stability in its own communications about that environment. Where that environment is another system, it cannot recognise and respond to that environment in a stable manner without some stability in that other system's communications. This sense of stability must involve elements of structural coupling. The 'steering' system cannot identify and respond on a one-to-one basis to all the communications, or operations, of the other system. It cannot react to everything, that is, it has to construct a simplified version of the system to which it is reacting. This process will mean that many communications which have significance within the 'steered' system do not register with the system attempting to steer. Any remaining possibilities for 'steering' require that the communications which *do* register within the system seeking control must have an element of predictability, so that the steering system is not constantly 'surprised' by what happens in its environment.

With this more muted sense of what it might mean for one system to steer another, let us return to Teubner's suggestion that this might be better achieved though structural coupling rather than more direct attempts to influence another system. Systems construct themselves and their own version of their environment through their own communications. This includes their own version of other systems' communications. The fact that some communications of one system are given meaning within another allows for the possibility that changes in the communications of one system will trigger changes in another. The puzzle is not over how systems might stimulate each other – each system, along with the physical environment, provides an endless and varied supply of events which may, depending on the possibilities of communication within the observing system, generate further system communications.[20] The puzzle is how this process of constant stimulation can achieve elements of stability and co-ordination. Luhmann's answer was structural coupling – the co-evolution which occurs when two systems respond in stable ways to the communications of the other, despite the fact that they each give each others' communications different meanings. Common language, including common syntax, allows closed systems to identify the repeated communications of another system as the same 'event', to which it can have the same reaction. This process of repetition allows a system to learn, through trial and error, which of its operations are followed by which of its observable events. There will be occasions when the observable regularity of such reactions is simply a

[20] 'Luhmann describes society as being in a constant state of adjustment, with irritations or perturbations in the environment of one system setting off changes in that system which could have a ripple effect throughout all segments of the social system' (King and Schütz, 1994, 270).

matter of coincidence. The operations of the 'steering' system are actually having no effect, as they do not trigger any changes in the targeted system. Whatever induces the changes in the targeted system lies elsewhere. But the complexity of society, like the complexity of advanced organisms, is not simply a situation of coincidence, but rather it is also a situation of co-ordination. Although random stimulation appears the more probable relationship between two closed systems, the possibility also exists that one system's communications produce stabilities in the internal environment of another that are also accorded a positive value within that system, and vice versa. This leads each system to orientate more of its operations towards realising the benefits of the observable regularity, which in turn increases the possibilities of co-ordination. To refer again to our rule of law example, the political system does not have to take on board the full complexity of law when it constructs sovereignty as something to which law responds, and law does not have to take on board the full complexity of politics when it constructs sovereignty as something to which it will respond. And yet the stabilities produced (stability in the allocation of legitimacy within the political system, stability in the expectation that physical coercion will be forthcoming from the political system within the legal system) stimulate communications in both systems that allow both to evolve to higher levels of complexity.

The dynamics of structural coupling offer the possibility for systems to be both blind and able to observe translated versions of each other's communications, and translated versions of changes in each other's communications, and to interpret those changes as responses to each other's communications. This is the basis on which law might be understood (or understand itself) as capable of 'steering' another system. This is also the basis of Teubner's concept of reflexive law – law which steers social systems by inducing changes in the basis on which those systems steer themselves.

Observing Reflexive Law

John Paterson has examined the various kinds of reflexive law identified by Teubner to see if they are compatible with the premises of systems theory, in particular, the idea of social systems being closed with co-ordination being achieved via structural coupling.[21] The first is 'tangential response': 'In this case, faced with evidence that substantive regulation is unsuccessful, the response of the legal system is to abandon any attempt to "establish stable structures in the regulated area" and instead to try only "punctuated interventions" on a sort of trial-and-error basis "until the regulated area has

[21] Paterson, 2006; see also King's critical response to this essay, 2006. King, 2010, develops his arguments further against the possibilities of steering society.

moved somewhat" in the desired direction'.[22] Whilst Paterson describes this in terms of a decline in the attempts of a regulating system (here law) to establish structures in the face of disappointments, the logic of closure suggests that the situation he describes is also the beginning of all occasions of structural coupling. A system alters itself, and observes its own version of its environment to see if this changes in the manner in which its own communications predict. Where this occurs, the regulating system can be expected to repeat the communications if the effect that has occurred is given a positive value. And it may also be interpreted as an opportunity for other changes to be made that the system regards as 'similar', and therefore expected to yield similar positive effects. These responses can lead to stable structures developing within the regulating system. If the expected responses do not occur, then the process of repetition will not be stimulated, and structures will not develop. And if the response is at first predictable, but predictability declines, then structures that have developed may be abandoned.

The second kind of reflexive law discussed by Paterson is 'Reciprocal or mutual observation': 'The advance here is that instead of simply recontextualising the response of the regulated area as unpredictable, the legal system adopts a stance of second-order observation in which it "reconstructs the self-reference of the observed system" [Teubner].'[23] The problematic element of his description of Teubner's analysis is the claim that the regulating system reconstructs the 'self-reference of the observed system'. If the process of trial and error described in the last paragraph achieved predictable results, one would expect the regulating system to generate accounts of what occurs in its environment in responses to its own changes. A system will have a more systematic account of itself than it has of its environment. It understands itself as its own interlinking operations, whilst it understands its environment as not connected by those operations, and only affected (or not) by them. But in constructing its environment in terms of responses to its operations it will also generate its own accounts of what makes those responses predictable. So, to take one of Paterson's examples (though Paterson offers this as an example of 'tangential response'), if central banks were instructed by governments to intervene in the currency markets, this instruction arises in response to some account of the economy, within politics, that supports the expectation that such interventions will result in responses that have positive political values: lower unemployment, increased production, higher revenue levels, etc. Whether such accounts of its environment amount to a 'reconstruct[ion of] the self-reference of the observed system' depends on the dynamics of structural coupling. If the communications by which the regulated system accounts

[22] Paterson, *ibid*, 25.
[23] *Ibid*, 25.

for itself as a system assist the regulating system in achieving positive values through its own operations, then this process of reconstruction may indeed occur. But where they do not, the system can be expected to reject them. To develop the central bank example, the important aspect of such intervention, within politics, might be that it provides a mechanism through which politics is able to *present itself* as being able to intervene in the economy. The negative consequences which follow within politics from failing to try to control the economy (loss of office) may provide a disincentive to any account of the economy which denies the ability of government to control economies through central bank interventions.[24]

Thus where Paterson sees two levels of reflexive law, we would identify three stages in the process of structural coupling. At an initial stage structural coupling begins by a system observing predictable reactions to its environment. In response to positive changes in its environment it will repeat operations to seek similar responses. At stage two, a system will attribute relationships to its environment that account for the differences which result from its environment, and which will suggest other possibilities for operations that will/will not produce the same desired effects. At stage three, a system will utilise another system's own accounts of operations in order to anticipate predictable reactions to its operations.[25] Whilst both stages two and three involve the regulating system laying down structures to orientate itself around the production of positive effects, this is not structural coupling, as defined by Luhmann, as we have only described developments within one system. Structural coupling occurs when two systems begin to establish structures in response to each other's communications. In accordance with the strictures of closure, one could argue that structural coupling cannot move beyond the mutual experience of level two: every system's account of a system in its environment is always its own account, so all that is open to two systems in terms of co-ordination is to construct their respective accounts in forms that have this consequence, and encourage further changes (by trial and error) which increase the range and intensity of co-ordinated responses. But it seems prima facie plausible to claim that the degree of co-ordination achieved between closed systems is likely to be increased if the account of the reactions of system A con-

[24] 'All that matters for the autopoiesis of the political system is the collectively binding communication about intentions to intervene, and not the actual effects of intervention – which occur much later, or not at all' (Luhmann, 2004, 402).

[25] Some readers will find this description anthropomorphic. But it provides a means to present a more complex situation, in which humans motivated to carry out system operations will utilise the system's available redundancies. These include what, within the system, can create a meaningful (which includes plausible) claim that a particular operation will have a predictable effect on the system's environment. The changes in these redundancies cannot be reduced to what individual humans 'learn'. It is therefore more accurate to describe the evolution in terms of systems 'learning'.

structed by system B takes the form of a reconstruction of system A's account of itself.[26] Thus where the self-observations of one system can be utilised within another system as part of that system's construction of its environment, and vice versa, this might be expected to lead to closer co-ordination between the two systems.

The third kind of reflexive law discussed by Paterson is 'coupling through interference, or "bifurcation and attractors".' 'Interference is a bridging mechanism whereby social systems get beyond self-observation and link up with each other through one and the same communicative event.'[27] This offers the possibility for a regulated system 'to move from its existing attractor state into one compatible with the aims of the regulating system'.[28] Coupling through interference is a restatement of the dynamic of structural coupling: offering communications to another system which have a positive value when that system utilises them within its own operations (or at least accords them a more positive value than the alternatives). The chances of this occurring through law can be increased if the law offers more than one option, leaving the selection of the 'appropriate' law to be made within the regulated system. This applies not only to constitutive rules, but also duty-imposing ones – for example, requiring a company to carry out a risk assessment, but leaving the company to determine the procedure to be adopted or the level of risk it is prepared to accept. This additional element – the suggestion that offering a variety of legal provisions to another system increases the likelihood that structural coupling might arise – does not go beyond the premises of the theory. Neither does the suggestion that the possibilities of intervention allow the regulating system to 'probe for sensitive "intervention points"'.[29] This is what we have just described above. A system that seeks to steer its environment will focus on those of its operations which alter its internal environment in a manner that the system regards as positive. It can be expected to repeat those which are followed by positive changes in its understanding of its external environment, and avoid those which are not. Even within systems that are limited to their own internal version of their environment, and are otherwise 'blind', this can be described as 'probe[ing] for sensitive "intervention points"'.[30] And this process can be expected to be described (self-observed) within the regulating system as 'steering'.

The next form of reflexive law, 'Communicating through organisation or binding institutions',[31] is based on the observation that organisations offer increased possibilities for structural coupling to develop. To explore the

[26] We say 'prima facie' because there is a counter-dynamic, which we discuss below.
[27] Paterson, 2006, quoting Teubner, at 26.
[28] *Ibid*, 26.
[29] *Ibid*, 26.
[30] *Ibid*, 26, referring to his own earlier article with Teubner, 1998, at 474–79.
[31] *Ibid*, 28.

possibilities of structural coupling and steering represented by 'organisation or binding institutions', we have to understand the manner in which organisations operate alongside systems, and the role played by law in this. The internal communications of institutions provide opportunities for system communications to be routinely 'translated'. As with interactions, the internal communications of organisations have the possibility of a second existence within the social subsystems that form their environment. At the same time, organisations, as autopoietic systems, have to recreate their environment, and their own identity, through their own communications, and in particular their decisions. As such, organisations represent an increase in the complexity of society, as the individuals who are identified as actors making communications belonging to organisations will couple their psychic systems to the system of the organisation, as well as to the social systems that form the organisation's environment. These different aspects of organisations mean that the possibilities for structural coupling are both increased and decreased. They are increased by the greater frequency with which the communications of different subsystems will be recognised as originating from, or returning to, a common address,[32] leading to an increased intensity with which they are decoded within the organisation, and decoded by the systems in the organisation's environment. However, the unique internal selections and consequent meanings which are generated within organisations provide an additional obstacle to the co-ordination of the social subsystems which make up their environment.[33] The expectation that organisations which participate in multiple systems offer an increased possibility of structural coupling boils down to a belief that the obstacles to structural coupling represented by an organisation's own autopoiesis are less significant than the increased intensity of responses which different systems can trigger in each other through the synchronicity[34] supported by a common address. This greater intensity increases the

[32] An organisation has to be identified with sufficient stability to be recognisable across the borders of differently codified communications 'despite being ascribed different meanings in each of these communications' (Andersen, 2012, referring to Star and Greisemer, 1989, 393).

[33] Van Assche and Verschraegen, 2008, see the meta-languages that develop within organisations, with their own goals and programmes, as de-differentiation, and offer, as a normative suggestion, tighter coupling between the respective departments of organisations and the social subsystems in their environment as a way of improving the self-steering of social systems through organisations (at 279). Andersen by contrast argues that organisations replicate the closure of the systems in their environment, so that communications merely oscillate between the codes of the different systems with which they couple, maintaining differentiation (Andersen, 2012, referring to Andersen, 2003, and Andersen and Born, 2007).

[34] Synchronicity occurs when something is an event within more than one system at the same moment. Thus when a communication in one system triggers a communication in another we have synchronicity. This should be contrasted with synchronisation, which deals with the time taken to process the operations that may be triggered within different systems in response to events (an event may produce the next day's 'news' within the media, a trial after months or even years, and a government inquiry years later). See Luhmann, 2004, 383, and our fuller description in Chapter 5.

probability that productive stable reactions will be identified and focused upon within each social system.[35]

Law undoubtedly has a role to play in the creation of structural couplings through organisations. If we consider the nature of organisations, and compare these with individuals, we can see that law has provided considerable stability to other systems through legal communications which establish the identity and decision-making processes of organisations as actors. Institutions or organisations represent a form of communication which links communications in terms of some attribute of membership. It has to be established that a communication 'belongs' (can be attributed) to a particular institution or organisation.[36] Whilst each system establishes its own actors for its own purposes through its own communications – pupil, citizen, lawyer, consumer, etc – they are assisted in this process by the communications through which other systems establish an actor with the same name. In the UK there is relatively little legal formality surrounding the naming of individuals. As a result, when the economy seeks some assurance that the individual to or from whom it expects to make payments is a unique 'Mr Smith' it relies on communications from other systems as well as itself: passports, driving licences, birth certificates, educational qualifications, etc. At earlier periods, the unique identity of an individual could be produced through testimony as to a person's biography. Organisations lack a corporal body that can be tracked through the common events of a human life, which, in modern times, means that they cannot establish their identity through their role as drivers, travellers, pupils, etc. Law, through its formalities, has had, and continues to have, an important role in establishing organisations as actors within different social systems. The most important modern example is the corporation, which law constructs and recognises as a legal person. Law provides communications which establish when and how the communications of human actors can be attributed to a corporate actor. The provision of constitutive rules, particularly in the context of organisations, allows law to play an important role in facilitating structural coupling between closed social systems. State law (where law is coupled with politics via legislation) therefore provides more opportunities for politics to 'steer' other social systems than would be the case if law were limited to duty-imposing rules directed towards the behaviour of human actors.

[35] The ability of organisations to couple with separate social systems does not, in itself, produce structural coupling between those separate social systems. Organisations coupled to one system will treat its communications as events, which will trigger its own communications, which can in turn be treated as events by a different social system. But these endless reactions do not, in themselves, represent or produce structural coupling between social subsystems.

[36] Membership is not just a question of identifying who is a member. There is always the question of which communications by a 'member' can be attributed to the institution or organisation and which cannot. And indeed, it is not membership which establishes an institution or organisation for systems theory, but organisational self-description: see Seidl, 2003.

The last form of reflexive law discussed by Paterson is 'synchronising difference reduction'.[37] This focuses on the feature, common to all systems, that they develop programmes for the application of their codes, and that these programmes involve goals and purposes. Systems do not simply register their environment. They identify states of their internal environment with a view to altering that environment through their own operations. In that sense, all social systems are steering systems, and all of them steer by altering themselves in order to minimise the difference between their current environment and a more positive future environment. Synchronising difference reduction refers to the increased likelihood that the communications of one system will be taken up by another system if, when re-used in their translated form within the second system, they assist the achievement of that system's goals, purposes, etc. For example, laws which apply to the economy are more likely to meet their objectives if they reinforce and support conditions which the economy identifies with efficiency, than if they seek to impose inefficiencies. This approach is compatible with structural coupling, though it points strongly towards the limitations of using it for steering. The more synchronised the respective difference reduction of two systems, the greater their likely levels of co-ordination, and the more they support each other's continued existence as functionally differentiated social systems. But if a system adopted co-ordination as an aim (assuming for the moment that such an aim could be internalised by a system) this would imply discounting options that do not support the (internally reconstructed) aims and goals of the other system. This would represent a loss of autonomy within the 'steering' system. To maintain a residual sense of 'steering' (rather than 'supporting' or 'maintaining') the synchronisation of difference minimisation cannot be an aim in itself. This is why options are commonly given as examples of reflexive law. Here some element of difference minimisation is offered to the other system, alongside other conditions that may be neutral, or even negative. Allowing a corporation to choose which of three possible health and safety regimes it wishes to adopt allows it to identify which of the three contributes most to its aims as an organisation. In introducing such regulation, the regulating system does not need to adopt a commitment to the aims of the organisation, or to the aims of the other social systems with which that organisation is coupled (such as the economy). The regulation can be understood as something imposed on the organisation. The element of co-ordination is limited to the expectation that any selection which remains open to the organisation will be made on the basis of minimising the difference between the organisation's aims, and its current situation.

To summarise this discussion of the variants of reflexive law, Paterson is right to conclude that each of them is compatible with the blind co-evolution

[37] Paterson, 2006, 29.

that is structural coupling. 'Tangential responses' and 'interference' are restatements of the dynamics of structural coupling. 'Mutual observation' and 'synchronised difference minimisation' are based on arguments that structural coupling is more likely if systems construct internal versions of each other's cognitive and normative structures. Options are linked to variety – offering another system a variety of communications to select increases the chances that it will find at least one that is given a positive value when reconstructed within its own operations. And 'communicating through organisations and binding institutions' is based on the supposition that the intensity of communications which can be attributed to the same named actor by different systems increases where that actor is an organisation, rather than an individual, and that this in turn increases the possibilities of structural coupling between the various social systems with which the organisation is coupled. One can also accept that structural coupling can contribute to a system's ability to experience (self-observe) on its own self-steering as the steering of another system. The co-ordination of systems, through structural coupling, lessens the extent to which changes in a system's environment which result from its operations are experienced as a surprise. All of this has to be situated within the features of systems, as set out at the start of this Chapter. A system's ability to steer itself does not determine its evolution, though it will bring some stability to its operations. Steering is not controlling, even at the level of self-steering within a single system.

The ability to observe that structural coupling has occurred, *ex post*, does not enable a system, through its operations, to identify the basis on which that coupling will be further developed, or new forms of structural coupling produced.[38] Thus even if all forms of reflexive law are also examples of structural coupling, this does not mean that there can be any certainty as to which attempts to create reflexive law will result in structural coupling: it remains a hit-and-miss or 'blind' relationship. And even where structural coupling has occurred, and can be observed to be such within the regulating system, this does not provide a basis for one system to have a predictable influence on the other. The dynamics of structural coupling suggest at least two reasons why such relationships are difficult to exploit in a manner that a regulating system is likely to experience as successful steering.

[38] Luhmann is adamant that structural coupling is something that can be observed to have come into existence, *ex post*, but not something whose conditions can be identified and prescribed, *ex ante*: 'The form "structural coupling" is not a normative topic; it is not something that can be prescribed. Even if those institutions which, seen from the perspective of law, perform such a prescriptive task – and we will discuss here property, contract, and constitution – and adopt a legal form, *they cannot do this in their function of structural coupling*. This function must be presupposed as given. Its design is at right angles to the operations that the system-internal structures (norms) develop and which are guided by those structures' (Luhmann, 2004, 385, emphasis in original).

Structural Coupling Dynamics

Structural coupling is a relationship in which two systems place a positive value upon each other's communications, and are attracted to make further communications which achieve the same positive values. It is an evolution produced by attraction. Structural coupling allows for the possibilities of decoupling, where the communications which have proved attractive to another system are withdrawn (as with our example of withdrawing the corporate form from specified activities). But the options for steering through structural coupling are not symmetrical. Positive values increase the level of co-ordination, and reduce the likelihood of 'deafness' and unpredictable reactions. Negative ones decrease the level of co-ordination, and increase the likelihood of 'deafness' and unpredictable reactions. The likely consequence within a regulating system, of repeated changes to which another system gives a negative value, is a decreasing coupling of the two systems and in turn a decreasing sense of 'control' within the regulating system.

The positive value which leads to structural coupling is a result of one system producing communications which another system cannot produce for itself. Consider our various references to the law of corporations. Through this law, the legal system constitutes an actor, a legal person. The economy does not replicate the systematic relationship of duties, rights and powers that constitute this legal person. But it can utilise the stability of identity generated within the legal system to treat an organisation as a single actor for the purposes of payments and the like. Similarly, the economy, through its systematically interrelated communications, attributes value to the property and rights created by the legal system. A simplified version of these communications (valuations) is used to organise compensation, etc, when aspects of these rights are litigated. This is what Teubner has called a surplus value.[39] The relationship between systems produces potentially positive values for other systems that each system, left to itself, could not produce. The positive value which induces one system to evolve in response to the other is inescapably linked to the inability of each system to duplicate what the other is doing.[40] Each social system cannot produce, for and by itself, all the mean-

[39] Teubner uses this phrase to describe the positive effects of law translating disputes into its own issues and categories, thereby allowing decisions to be reached within law that could not be achieved within the systems that have generated the dispute. In this way law, through dispute resolution, offers other systems stability within their communications which they could not achieve for themselves, and which, if accepted within those other systems, provide new redundancy, and new possibilities of evolution. See Teubner, 2001.

[40] 'What matters – and is made visible by the concept of structural coupling – is that the reinforcement of mutual irritations depends on and remains dependent on the exclusion effect of the same mechanism. Only indifference to each other makes it possible that a specific dependence on each other is increased' (Luhmann, 2004, 411).

ings that are necessary for its current level of complexity.[41] This process places a kind of brake on the ability of one system to observe the complexity of the other. To be able to observe the complexity of a second system, the first system would have to replicate the self-observations of that system inside itself, that is, to lose the very surplus value which stimulates structural coupling in the first place. This is particularly relevant to mutual observation and synchronised difference, which are premised on the likelihood that systems will achieve greater co-ordination if they can reproduce more of each other's structures, in a translated form, inside themselves. But with these forms of reflexive law the systems involved seem likely to lose some of the surplus value produced through their coupling – the positive benefits of relying on another system to produce stable communications through operations (including self-observations) that the system cannot produce for itself. To use a term from economics, there may be a relationship of diminishing marginal returns involved in two systems incorporating more of the other's structures into each other, even in a translated form, which will produce in turn a lessening of the incentive for human actors to make the communications which perpetuate the co-evolution.[42]

These opposing dynamics make it difficult to accept that structural coupling, in the form of reflexive law, could become a programme that operated as a form of steering – altering the internal environments of law and politics without constant surprises, unexpected or unforeseen 'consequences'. Law is subjected to constant pressure to increase its approximation to other systems. In its regulation of markets, it is invited to increase its economic features. In the use of scientific evidence, it is urged to increase its scientific features. In its intervention in political affairs, it is advised to increase its sensitivity to political arguments. In its involvement in health, it is suggested that it take greater account of clinical judgements, etc. But law offers considerable resistance to these invitations, because it can only select those communications which facilitate its own operations. Whilst humans who couple their consciousnesses at the sites of structural coupling between two systems may prove adept at 'translating' the communications of each

[41] Other systems have to produce meanings that distribute other mediums: power through the political system, legality through the legal system, money through the economy, etc. This in turn means that systems have to develop ways of attracting the mediums distributed through other systems to themselves without duplicating the complex meanings of those other systems in themselves.

[42] Teubner claims that if law fulfils its integrative function by furthering reflexive processes in other social systems then its cognitive needs are less: 'the social knowledge required by the legal system is very specific and the need for model construction is much more limited than it would be in a comprehensive "planning" law' (1983, 281). This is plausible, but it does not reflect the dynamics of structural coupling – that a diminishing surplus value will result from the increased translation of another system's self-observations inside a regulating system. To reverse the loss of surplus value, the translated self-observations have to be productive for the regulating system by providing new stabilities that the regulating system cannot produce for itself, which facilitate the regulating system's operations.

into the other, the actual incorporation of one system's communications into another's remains, from the perspective of these individuals, fairly limited. Take the use of science within law as an example. Despite the presence of some (albeit comparatively rare) individuals who are familiar with both science and the legal system, the legal system continues to be unable to incorporate the complexity of scientific procedures and methods into its own procedures, preferring to rely on a simplified version of science: the expert's opinion. Increasing the number of persons who are familiar with both systems through education would reduce some of the costs of introducing more of the complexity of science into law (though it would externalise that burden into education). But the greater resistance lies in what the law seeks from its expert witnesses – an authoritative testimony on what has occurred in order to apply its substantive conditional programmes to established 'facts'. If the consequence of the greater incorporation of scientific communications into the legal system is an erosion of the certainty which law attributes to expert evidence, then the positive values which scientific communications formerly offered to law will be eroded – and the use of scientific evidence lessened. The dynamics of structural coupling offer reasons to expect resistance to any simple process of increased approximation (de-differentiation) between different social systems, as that would remove the positive values that stimulate the communications which, when selected and retained as structures, constitute co-evolution.

This is not an argument that law has a finite capacity to absorb scientific or other forms of argument. The point is rather that one cannot know in advance, at the individual or the system level, which communications from another system are capable of supporting that system's operations, and which are not, and which offer platforms of stability which the system could not generate for itself. It is a trial-and-error, evolutionary, and therefore 'blind' process.[43] Structural coupling is an observation that can only be made with any degree of stability in hindsight. It is an explanation of the dynamics which allow co-ordination between closed systems, and explains how society can continue to increase in its complexity despite the lack of any meta-language, universal values, or controlling centre. Familiarity with a system provides a considerable insight into what that system, at particular moments, *cannot* do in response to the demands of another: a sense of the

[43] In a more recent discussion of the possibilities of social constitutionalism, where the goal of steering is limited to restricting the expansionist tendencies of systems, Teubner reaffirms the elements of trial and error which accompany any attempts to induce systems to evolve in a desired manner: 'Nobody knows how such a capillary constitutionalism could be concretely achieved. *Ex-ante* prognoses are, in principle, impossible. And, for this reason, there is no alternative but to experiment with constitutionalisation. The application of external pressure means that the self-steering of politics, or law, or other sub-systems, creates such irritations of the focal system that, ultimately, the external and internal programmes play out together along the desired course. And this cannot be planned for, but only experimented with' (Teubner, 2011b, 15). Teubner has now captured the underlying thesis of his extensive writings on societal constitutionalism, pluralism and globalisation, in Teubner, 2012.

operations that could not be carried out, or only carried out with a large increase in the resources required. This is part of what it means to be familiar with the communications of a system, particularly with regard to the more systematic communications made at the centre of a system.[44] This is very different from predicting which novel forms of communication from another system will not only be incorporated (via translation) somehow or other into a system, but will contribute stability to the communications of that system and stimulate further evolution.

Systems theory does not offer any basis on which to expect differentiated social subsystems to achieve any kind of general equilibrium. Structural coupling is a relationship which is beneficial to the coupled systems, in the sense that it stabilises the communications of each, providing relatively fixed redundancies from which to generate new varieties: new ways of communicating. As such, it increases society's complexity. The alternative to structural coupling between systems is captured in Teubner's regulatory trilemma. If systems inhibit each other, along the lines of the second and third versions of the trilemma (decreasing complexity and over socialisation), then the variety of communications available will decrease, a situation that can be described as de-differentiation. Whilst increased complexity has no normative value within the theory (for example, it should not be referred to as 'progress') the possibilities of de-differentiation include the apocalyptic. For example, the totalitarian experience of the Nazi state was described by Luhmann as one of de-differentiation, with the political system extending itself in such a way as to inhibit other social systems, with terrible consequences.

The economy seems the social system which is currently most likely to over-extend itself, thereby threatening the ability of other systems to carry out their operations, which in turn may deprive the economy of the communications which stabilise its own operations. Recent, potentially catastrophic, economic events provide an example here. The development of complex financial instruments created a situation in which no financial institutions could know which of the banks held bad debts arising from the US mortgage market, so they ceased to lend, or reduced what they were willing to lend, to each other. This caused a crisis within institutions reliant on the wholesale lending market for their liquidity. This impasse was only overcome through monies provided by governments, who were able to do this on the basis that they could raise future revenues through taxation. Had the impasse continued, those financial institutions unable to borrow would have collapsed, with an expected catastrophic effect on world trade, and in turn a contraction in the complexity of political, health, economic, media, educational and scientific systems. As it is, the assumption that governments could provide an ultimate guarantee to the financial markets has

[44] Which centre we go on to explore in the next, final Chapter.

itself in turn been put into question, with the market raising the level of interest charged on some European sovereign debts to those that cannot be met through the revenues currently available to the governments in question. This in turn causes de-differentiation, with systems, and especially the political system, reducing their complexity in response to their observations of 'economic realities'.

The increasing complexity of social systems, and in particular their internal evolution as complex systems, may disrupt the structural coupling between systems, and their ability to co-evolve. In the final Chapter we go on to discuss the potential for 'crisis' to be constructed by one system (the mass media) in response to the complexities of another system (the legal system), as those complexities disrupt the structural coupling that has developed between them.

8

Appeals in Law

In this final Chapter we consider how the legal system constructs its appeals, and how what it understands as the nature of its appeals differs from external observations on these practices, most notably those of the mass media. Doctrine, the endless articulation of what, outside law, is observed as technical distinctions, is the process through which law develops especially within its centre, the courts, and the centre of that centre, the appeal courts. This is not simply a technique applied within a centre constructed through a different kind of communication. It is the manner in which that centre forms itself, and its relationships with its environment. This includes the internal relationship formed between the appeal courts and the courts and tribunals whose decisions are appealed. The premise of this Chapter is that the only resource through which law can manage its internal relationships is through the endless iteration of doctrine, which is commonly observed (when it is observed) outside of the legal system as being 'technical' and lacking substantive values, and that this has implications for law when it structurally couples with systems that have strong contrary normative expectations.

We have discussed the possibilities of law's structural coupling with politics in other Chapters, but particularly our Chapter on the rule of law. Here we introduce a new structural coupling, one between the mass media and law. Our argument, which we have articulated elsewhere,[1] but with less attention to the nature of legal doctrine, is that 'conviction' in the criminal courts provides a particularly powerful structural coupling between law and the mass media. We discuss this here, in the context of a Chapter devoted to appeals, because it is our conclusion that this particular structural coupling generates significant problems for the legal system. The form of criminal trial in the UK, with its reliance on jury trial for serious crimes, offers lesser resources through which to control the processes of appeal than is the case with criminal trials in systems that do not rely on jury trial. In addition, the structural coupling between the mass media and law, through conviction, has no parallel when it comes to appeals. The meaning which the mass media consistently, routinely and productively attributes to conviction generates an understanding of appeals which cannot couple

[1] Set out in a short form in Nobles and Schiff, 2009a.

with the legal meaning of appeals in the same routine and productive manner. Instead, the media's understanding of appeals operates as a periodic pressure on the legal system to be something which it cannot be or accomplish in the modern differentiated world: a system for the delivery of truth. This has implications for law's ability to maintain itself through the articulation of doctrine.

Appeals and Doctrine

Within law the meaning of legal appeals is relatively unproblematic. An appeal in law refers to the opportunities available to have a case or some aspect of it, whether the decision or the procedure undertaken to reach that decision, reconsidered.[2] In all developed legal systems the relevant rules determining these opportunities have evolved and become ever more complex. In other words, the opportunities to undertake appeals within law depend ever more on the complex conditions set by law for those appeals, determining who, under what circumstances, can undertake an appeal as a legal appellant.[3] The particular example of appeals which we consider here lie at the centre of the legal system: appeals to the Court of Appeal (Criminal Division). This court shares with other appeal courts a responsibility for ensuring the finality of the legal system's decisions.[4] The premise of all courts' operations is that every issue which they are called upon to decide is capable of a legal answer – the courts have a duty to decide even when there are no good reasons for deciding one way rather than another. And even where courts decide that they have no jurisdiction, they have to give legal reasons, constructed from available and recognisable legal communications, why they have no jurisdiction to decide the matter in question. This is a dynamic process, as those who stress the indeterminacy of

[2] The range of matters that can now be considered on appeal is wide and can only be summarised in these general terms unless a full list of examples is given. Here is one example in relation to cases that may be referred to the Court of Appeal (Criminal Division) by the Criminal Cases Review Commission, as set out in the Criminal Appeal Act 1995. Matters that can be considered in an appeal include 'a condition, verdict, finding or sentence'. But, for example, verdict includes 'a verdict of not guilty by reason of insanity', and sentence includes 'any other sentence (not being a sentence fixed by law) imposed on, or in subsequent proceedings relating to, the conviction', etc.

[3] This is the relevant general term in relation to a person whose appeal reaches the courts, but other terms may refer to someone who is attempting to have a legal decision reopened prior to court proceedings, such as an application by an applicant (see Criminal Appeal Act 1995, Part II). In addition, opportunities for prosecution appeals in different forms now also exist: see, Ormerod, Waterman and Forston, 2010.

[4] This is not because the Court of Appeal (Criminal Division) is the only court dealing with criminal appeals, or the final court, but it is the main appeal court from the decisions of the Crown Court which deals with serious crimes, and an appeal to the Supreme Court is rare and normally requires leave from the Court of Appeal. On the range of appeal bodies dealing with criminal appeals, and their arguably inconsistent state, see Spencer, 2006.

legal decisions would agree. In constructing their answers to legal questions, courts are engaged in what is called, within systems theory, re-entry. The application of a system's code, here legal/illegal, is a distinction that is constantly reapplied, in that the results of one application of the distinction, including self-observations on the reasons for that application, are the object of the next application of the distinction. This can be a reversal of the previous application, but also, and more importantly as a contribution to the increased complexity of a system, it can be a reapplication of the distinction to one side of the previous application. So, having described what, in a previous situation, made something illegal, there can be a qualification, or exception, which identifies something within that previous situation that can result in the conclusion that it is legal. One can observe the 're-entrance of the distinction into what the distinction has distinguished and the virtual space of possibilities which the system opens up through this operation'.[5] This process of re-entry involves ever increasing system complexity: 'Such a re-entry into complexity of the unity of what is complex is a more or less evident characteristic of all processes. Otherwise it would not bring about an intensification of their selectivity.'[6] As described in Chapter 4, this leads to the technicalisation of the application of the code, with the identification of differences within situations that make a difference within the system, but that difference is often not recognised as making a difference outside the system.

This process of re-entry is common to all systems, and is what generates their increasing complexity, and is particularly intense within the centre of a system. This process, as applied within the courts, generates what lawyers familiarly describe as doctrine, and involves techniques which are also familiarly known as distinguishing, not following, overruling, etc. The benefits of applying this more general term are that it draws attention to the features that the legal system shares with other systems – in particular, that the process has no foundation outside itself. The communications that are available to a system to achieve re-entry are a system's available store of communications. These can be re-worked, with the application of new distinctions. In re-working these materials, to provide legal answers, there is always the danger of undoing previous answers, and thereby inhibiting the operations that were facilitated by the redundancy represented by those previous answers. The costs of re-entry are experienced from within a system in terms of meaning. What does it mean for the environment of the system, and the system itself, if a new reason for the application of the code is provided? How will the operations of law alter, and what is the likely effect of these alterations on law's environments? As stated in the last Chapter, it is always easier for a system (and for those articulating within a system) to

[5] Luhmann, 2004, 107–08.
[6] Luhmann, 1995, 451.

identify the consequences for the system than for the environment, as the system is understood to be connected by its operations, whereas the environment is only taken to be *affected* by the system's operations.

The legal system is identified with legal norms, and these are integrated with each other on the basis that they establish the legality of events in law's environment. The communications that recognise law's environment are brought into an ordered relationship with each other, within law, through the relationship between its norms. Other possibilities of connection are only recognised within the legal system to the extent that law, through its norms, integrates those communications into its own operations. One has an internal selection of externally created combinations. In this combination of communications, those constructing the legal system as norms, and those constructing its environment through the selections indicated by those norms, one has conflicting elements which have to be reconciled. There are parallels here with Dworkin's description of legal reasoning. But in keeping with the wider sense of what constitutes a system (outside observation of a system can observe that the system creates both itself and its environment) the competing pressures are both more than and different from normative consistency and substantive moral justification. Re-entry within the legal system requires a consideration of the implications of any change for the system's operations. But it also involves consideration of the plausibility of communications which the legal system has opened itself to through its norms. So, for example, law cannot incorporate scientific evidence into its procedures for deciding upon facts without opening itself to pressure to reconsider 'events' that scientific communications which construct facts may 'change'. Having accorded plausibility to science, and incorporated that plausibility into the decisions through which it carries out its operations (such as finding persons guilty of particular crimes) it has to respond to that plausibility, either by accepting that its norms have a different application, or by identifying a normative reason why there should be no response. What brings diverse events within the environment into an ordered relationship with each other are law's norms. But this is an ongoing and temporary arrangement, in the sense that the challenge to legal answers is never ending.[7] In building up ever more complex relationships between legal norms, the legal system creates conditions in which norms conflict, generating the need for further re-entry (qualifications, exceptions, or re-statements which dissolve its contradictions).

The production of doctrine through the articulation of distinctions not only generates the norms which have to be applied by the appeal courts, and the courts which they supervise, but also, as just said, constructs the appeal courts themselves, in terms of the conditions under which cases can be appealed, and the consequences of different outcomes on appeal. The

[7] Hart referred to this in terms of the relative indeterminacy of aims and ignorance of fact.

premise which underlies all this is that like cases should be treated alike. This formula is not, as we discussed in Chapter 1, empty of content. Doctrine cannot develop in complexity if anything can, at any point, be taken to be 'like' anything else. It is only by constructing redundancies, and their repeated use within self-observation (generating eigen values), that the courts and particularly the appeal courts are able to develop complex legal programmes to direct the application of the legal code.

Within these processes, certain kinds of communications are not available to the legal system. One is the idea that legal rights, including rights of appeal, should be sold to the party who values them the most in terms of their ability to pay. Whilst this is a perfectly normal economic communication about rights established within the legal system, it is not a communication available within the legal system to self-observe on the establishment of legal rights (except as a wrongful application of rights, that is, corruption). This provides a problem for the legal system. Economic resources (the ability to make payments) have to be attracted to the legal system, without de-differentiating the legal system. The legal system cannot apply a different code than legal/illegal. And its conditional programmes, what makes something legal rather than illegal, are not the same conditional programmes which the economy has constructed in order to determine what has, and can be, paid for.

So, whilst there is no doubt that the process of appeals favours those with access to economic resources, the communications through which appeals are constructed cannot acknowledge ability and willingness to pay as grounds for appeal. Whilst greater willingness to pay is exactly what disturbs any existing allocation of assets within the economy, it cannot be the basis for self-observation on an earlier legal decision. An appeal, as the correction of an earlier application of the legal code, has to engage with the reasons why that code can be taken to have been applied. Just as the ability to purchase that earlier legal decision is not an appropriate ground for the decision, the ability to purchase its reversal is not an appropriate ground for its re-examination. The parties who wish to appeal have to find whatever resources (counsel, fees, etc) this involves, and the opportunity which this represents within the economy for increasing wealth will provide economic meanings (incentives) for appealing. But the processes of appeal cannot themselves be constructed by reference to these economic meanings. Access to appeals has to be constructed through a legal version of a meritocracy: are there good legal arguments for overturning this decision? Which is also the question: were there good legal reasons for reaching this decision?[8]

[8] This is a development of the 'tragic choice' analysis we applied in *Understanding Miscarriages of Justice* (2000). That analysis is set out in Calabresi and Bobbitt, 1978, which focuses on the distortions which occur when decisions which allocate resources cannot refer to this fact when making those allocations. For an alternative understanding of the implications of economic analysis of legal appeal systems, see Schapiro, 1980.

The idea that there have to be grounds for appeal, and that these grounds have to replicate elements of the original decision, is a trite observation. Its importance for understanding the nature of law's appeals lies in the fact that the creation of doctrine (observation on what can be distinguished from what – treating like cases alike) is not simply what is available for the construction of substantive rules, it is also the basis for the construction of procedural rules, including rules on the basis for appeals. Doctrine which treats like cases alike is not simply the means by which the courts generate substantive law, it is also the basis on which they control the tap through which cases can proceed to an appeal.

The ability of the law to control its own operations through its own communications has implications for all the relationships between law and other subsystems. For example, can the legislature use law to exclude any possibility of an appeal to the courts? Attempts to establish such rules produce iconic cases endlessly discussed by academic lawyers.[9] For systems theory the discussion takes the following form: if the use of law necessitates the integration of statutory provisions within the rest of law, and this can only be achieved through secondary observation within the legal system, how does one exclude the possibilities of observation upon that observation, that is, appeal? A fixed limit to the number of appeals that could be entertained within any period, with the right of appeal ceasing once that number were reached, would provide a mechanism to couple the appeal courts with the economic resources needed to administer them. But this would generate endless observations that like cases were not being treated alike, since it would be difficult to observe on the basis for selection for appeal in any manner that connected with communications about the reasons for having appeals: correcting legal mistakes. The introduction of time limits for allowing appeals and for bringing cases at first instance operates to provide some relief from the pressure to offer appeals – as does the build-up of backlogs, which provide disincentives to appeal, or to continue with appeals, but this latter development will also inevitably generate an internal critique from within the legal system, which cannot reverse any earlier decision on appeal without also recognising the period during which a mistake of law, an 'injustice', has continued.[10] A requirement of leave for appealing reduces the burden on the appeal courts, and eliminates the idea of an absolute right to appeal, but only by introducing a further procedure, and reinforcing the idea of appeal as a meritocratic right: that those who can show

[9] For example, the House of Lords case *Anisminic Ltd v Foreign Compensation Commission* [1969] 2 AC 147. For the endless discussion, see any UK administrative law academic text.

[10] Law creates its own internal pressure to manage its procedures. Whilst it resists any attempt to pre-empt its own decisions as a denial of justice (see our analysis in Chapter 5 on the presumption of innocence) it cannot reach its own decisions without acknowledging how long its subjects have remained in their former legal category. This is also part of its inability to acknowledge that its adjudicative decisions create law, rather than reflect law – any legal wrong acknowledged by a court always acknowledges a period of injustice.

grounds for appeal should have access to this procedure. (So, for example, introducing a quota on appeals that had already received leave would be subject to a particularly strong internal critique in terms of injustice).

We have written elsewhere about the need for workable systems of appeal, and the role played by deference within them.[11] Only by generally respecting the procedures through which legal decisions are reached at first instance can appeal courts hope to keep the number of appealed decisions within a level compatible with their resources. In keeping with Chapter 2 on judges' speech, we can acknowledge here that this respect need not be a conscious internal commitment. It is a commitment exhibited by the communications through which appeal courts articulate what constitute grounds for appeal. In order to identify what was 'wrong' with a decision at first instance, the appeal court cannot help but re-affirm what was 'right'. They cannot declare the whole first instance procedure to be a mistake, without abandoning considerable redundancy. For example, what legal resources would enable the Court of Appeal to construct a judgment in which the whole practice of trial by jury was declared inappropriate, that is, to find that the continued detention of every prisoner who had been convicted following a jury trial is an error? A judge's own knowledge or experience of the jury might lead her/him to have a deep scepticism as to the jury's fact-finding abilities, and these views might be expressed in academic lectures or even through the mass media. But in constructing an appeal which claims that there has been an error in the course of a jury trial, the judge cannot begin to identify the error without using communications which contain the implicit meaning that a jury trial, properly conducted, would reach a verdict that is correct. To approach the issue on the basis that jury trial itself was an inappropriate basis for deciding someone's guilt would clash with the normative commitment to jury trial implicit in so much statute law and precedent which, within the UK, constructs the procedures for criminal appeals. This normative commitment would also involve an awareness of the difficulties which such findings would create for law's internal version of its environment. Introducing communications which exhibit a general scepticism toward the accuracy of jury trials into the communications which establish the basis for deciding whether jury verdicts could be upheld would remove the current basis for deciding who has committed what serious offences, without offering a replacement. These environmental considerations and normative commitments also link to more general legal communications about the nature of judicial authority: on what basis is the judge (rather than Parliament) authorised to create such change (and hiatus) within the legal system?

Not all appeal processes need to be conducted through communications which exhibit deference. Appeals by way of a re-hearing, such as appeals

[11] Nobles and Schiff, 2002.

from convictions for lesser crimes by magistrates, may involve a re-trial.[12] Quashing a conviction is then not dependent on the identification of error, except in the sense that the appeal court takes a different view as to whether the offence has been committed by the particular defendant. The small percentage of persons convicted in the Magistrates' Court who seek these re-hearings, and the smaller number who thereby obtain a quashing of their convictions, does not seem to have caused particular problems. By contrast, appeals from jury trials have always involved deference. Before 1907 criminal appeals were limited to questions of law (narrowly drawn compared to what is possible today). There was no provision for an appeal which simply questioned whether the jury had, after a trial conducted without any mistake of law, reached the wrong decision: 'appeal on questions of fact'. The introduction of a system for appeal against jury verdicts on questions of fact was strongly resisted by the judiciary throughout the nineteenth century. This resistance, expressed within the political system and the media, invites the conclusion that the nineteenth-century judiciary were hypocritical, or complacent, or both. No system could be expected always to produce correct results, however perfect, let alone one which involved unrepresented and illiterate defendants. But another way of viewing this resistance is that these judges, familiar with the complex communications which operate at the centre of the legal system, were aware how limited were the communicative resources available to them to dispose of these kinds of appeal. Without a re-hearing of all the evidence presented at the trial, on what basis were they to form a view that the conclusion by the jury as to the defendant's guilt or innocence was inappropriate?

In civil proceedings, the appeal court is presented with an account of the facts found and manner in which those factual conclusions were determined. This provides communicative resources for an appeal court not only to decide that the law has been improperly applied, but also that they would not have made the same connections between one conclusion and another (whether to believe particular witnesses, what to conclude from disbelieving them, etc). Even this involves elements of deference. It is not a process whereby an appeal court simply reads the transcript of evidence and substitutes its own assessment for that of the trial judge. It is the trial judge, through her/his reasoned judgment, which provides the materials through which an appeal court can construct a different conclusion regarding the relevant facts. A civil trial judge's statement of reasons not only provides a basis for agreeing or disagreeing with her/his overall conclusions, it also provides a basis on which access to appeals can be controlled through doctrine. The distinction between law and fact is important in circumstances where the right to appeal is excluded, or more restricted, for appeals on questions of fact than law. This is a distinction which illustrates

[12] See Keogh, 1999.

the systems theory claim that the environment of a system is constructed internally, within the system. It is a boundary that is constructed as a question of law, that is, where and how to draw the distinction is subject to endless re-articulation. These different articulations offer different possibilities of appeal, so that the possibilities of appeal can differ both between tribunals, and can vary at different times in respect of a particular tribunal. This opportunity to re-articulate the boundary, especially in response to perceptions that large numbers of cases are otherwise likely to be the subject of appeals, operates to stimulate or dampen the possibilities of appeal. Through this use of doctrine, and others like it, appeal courts insulate themselves from appeals.[13]

The Structural Coupling between Law and the Media through Conviction

Law, and particularly trials, is a source of 'news' or, to refer to the positive side of the code of the media as a whole, 'information'.[14] Despite the enormous range of media outlets, there is a remarkable degree of consistency in what the media will identify as 'news' on any particular date. This is not surprising, as one of the conditional programmes which operate in deciding what can be selected as 'news' on a day is the selection of other media on the same day. Differences can be justified by reference to an outlet's construction of its intended readership/audience, or a judgment that the rest of the media have mistakenly selected something as 'news' which is not. But the selection of output from another media outlet or programme is both a cheap source of 'news', a prima facie confirmation that the selection is indeed 'news' and also the hypothetical object of selections: if a media outlet correctly diagnoses what is 'news', their selections can expect to be followed by others.[15]

[13] These techniques operate alongside articulations of substantive law. They also operate to reduce or increase the incentive to litigate and appeal. Articulations of doctrine that provide incentives to litigate and appeal also offer repeated opportunities to reduce those incentives. There is an asymmetry here – articulations that reduce the incentive to litigate or appeal do not offer the same opportunities for reconsideration as those that open up legal questions. Delay caused by the inability to process appeals generates an internal critique in terms of the period of 'injustice', the period between the original decision and its reversal on appeal.

[14] The code of the mass media is information/not information, that of the news media within the media generally 'news/not news' – see Luhmann, 2000, ch 5.

[15] This is most obviously a feature of television and radio, where the news broadcast by one station or programme is updated by another. When the 'latest news' is broadcast, it is an update of what has already been established as news, earlier. Where newspapers have different 'editions', one observes the same process. A paper, or programme whose 'news' is not picked up by the other channels, is being presented with evidence that its coverage has not managed to identify 'news'. It is hard to sustain the claim that a media outlet is delivering 'news', rather than information only of interest to its own readers/audience, if no other news outlet picks up the story, and thus vindicates the original selection.

Within these media processes, convictions represent a stable source of news. Civil trials or appeals can generate news, but the factors involved are more varied. The involvement of celebrities will make civil actions newsworthy, and some actions can be re-interpreted within the media as 'political' issues, and presented in terms of their consequences for government. But there is little stability in the verdicts in civil trials, let alone civil appeals, as news. Indeed, it usually takes a 'legal' correspondent familiar with legal and media communications to extract a 'story' from a civil trial or appeal.[16] By contrast, criminal trials, particularly those involving serious offences, are a stable diet for media reporting. Persons who lack celebrity status in the rest of their lives can expect to be the subject of media reportage once they have been convicted of a serious crime. The convictions most likely to be reported are those which the media can most easily present in terms of moral failings: rape, theft, assault, and murder.

So much of law's communications are inaccessible to the media, in the sense that they cannot be presented as 'news'. This applies to both substantive and procedural law, and the processes through which each is generated. There is generally no correspondence between what is significant within law, and what can be reported as significant within the media. *Donoghue v Stevenson* is on every common lawyer's list of significant cases, but a dispute over an illness resulting from the ingesting of a decomposed snail is not high on the media's list of newsworthy items, and even then its reportage as a novel event would only be possible if it were presented as having actually occurred, and not as a hypothetical incident, which was its actual status in the case. Although crime is a constant source of media news, the exploration of doctrine that establishes what, within law, actually constitutes the crimes of rape, theft, assault and murder is similarly inaccessible. So too are the decisions which establish the evidence that can be admitted to prove a case, or the exact wording of the instructions which need to be given to a jury. The complexity of these decisions excludes the possibility of their reportage as news, not only because legal communications involve linkages and language that may be unfamiliar, but because they involve decisions to apply distinctions that cannot, or can only with great difficulty involving significant explanations, be understood as differences outside the legal system. However important changes in doctrine may be for the ongoing generation of legal communications, so much of law's decisions, especially at the level of its appeals, can only be described as 'technical', and coded as 'not news', by the media.

With conviction for serious crimes, the media can couple with a legal operation to which they can give a stable meaning: 'x happened'. The sig-

[16] Though there is evidence that law firms are taking over this translating role, by offering press releases in civil actions that present the legal issues involved in forms that can be used by journalists to create stories. This usually requires law staff to undertake training on how to communicate to (that is, within) the media.

nificance of crime is not an internal construction of the legal system, signified by the severity of the sentence. Indeed, the perceived inadequacy of the sentence will often be part of the media's story. What the media determines to be significant crime is determined internally, by reference to its own programmes. But the media have no routine way of establishing either the definition of a crime, or the fact that particular persons have committed that crime. The ability of investigative journalism to generate a story that a crime has been committed, in the absence of a police investigation and prosecution, is rare. Rare, that is, compared to the number of occasions when law, through convictions, establishes for the media the 'truth' that a particular person, or persons, has committed a particular crime. A conviction moves the story beyond a presentation of evidence, and the allegation of 'possible' guilt, to a freedom to report what has occurred. Legal processes, such as contempt of court, are part of this freedom. But the most important aspect of conviction, as shown by reportage in countries which do not operate contempt of court laws which prevent 'prejudicial' comment, is that the legal system provides something which the media can treat as an authoritative fact: 'x happened'. This is an example of structural coupling.[17] When reporting the 'fact' that a person has committed a crime, little of the trial will be reported.[18] The prosecution case is likely to be summarised on the basis that this represents an accepted truth of why and how the crime occurred. But the endless back and forth of questioning – examination, cross-examination, and re-examination – the legal arguments, and the exploration of alternative possibilities within the judge's summing-up, are likely to be omitted once the conviction has been achieved. Indeed, like the difficulties of deconstructing what one wishes to say at the same time as one says it, these other aspects of trial have the capacity to undermine the newsworthiness of the conviction if they are introduced into the story at the same time that the newsworthiness of the 'event' demonstrated by the conviction is being presented. The drama of what happened, and why it happened, cannot be combined with statements which point to the contingency of the processes by which the conclusion has been reached without reducing the drama of the event. Without compensating factors (often present in reportage on overseas convictions, where the suspect nature of 'their' procedures can form part of the story), introducing the procedures of the criminal trial and pointing to the possibility that they might not have established the 'truth' of

[17] Structural coupling occurs when a system 'presupposes certain features of its environment on an ongoing basis and relies on them structurally . . . the forms of a structural coupling *reduce* and so *facilitate* influences of the [system's] environment on the system' (Luhmann, 2004, 382).

[18] It is even rarer for the elements of an offence to feature in reporting, so, for example, someone is reported to have committed theft, or murder, without reference to the complexities of intention, including recklessness, property, permanently depriving, dishonesty, common purpose, or multiple causes of death. Some of these matters might have been reported during the course of the trial, but rarely at the time of conviction.

the conviction not only complicates the story, it removes the certainties which are pivotal to the conviction being 'news'.

The media are not the only system to couple with law at the moment of conviction, or to give convictions meaning in terms of information about the truth of what has occurred, removed from the legal communications that have generated that truth. As well as the story of what an individual has done, we also have an operation that can generate the routine production of statistics about crime 'solved' (a coupling with the political system)[19] and provide a record relevant to a person's 'character', for the purposes of employment, immigration, political office, rehabilitation,[20] etc. Nor, within the legal system, at the moment of conviction, is this sense of convictions as statements of truth absent. Counsel who have spent days arguing for their client's innocence will, following conviction, in nearly all instances switch to a form of speech that acknowledges their guilt: mitigation. Similarly judges who have constructed a summing-up which sets out the possibilities that the defendant could be innocent as well as guilty, will deliver a speech which justifies the selected sentence, not in terms of the possibilities of the defendant being guilty, but on the basis that the jury's verdict *has established* that they did in fact commit the crime. The interior beliefs of judge or counsel regarding the accuracy of the jury's verdict cannot form part of these communications. Thus there is nothing in the moment of conviction, within the legal system, that can disturb the media's re-use of conviction as a statement of the truth of a unique event – but a truth that would not be recognised as such by the system which has primary responsibility for establishing truths within our functionally differentiated society – the science system.[21]

[19] Conviction, misread as a statement of the truth that a particular person has committed a particular crime, is a 'performance' of law that is productive for other systems. For example, the political system utilises the legal system to identify criminals, a necessary step to discussions about what should, or should not, be 'done' to them. This dependence is part of what attracts the political system to make collective decisions that the economic resources at its disposal should be used to fund the criminal courts.

[20] For example, the prison service treats continued denial of guilt as evidence that a prisoner is not eligible for admission to the programmes that prepare them for release.

[21] The ability of law, through its norms, to establish its environment (its facts) is both extraordinary and problematic. On the one hand, the legal system, through its procedures of trial, including witnesses, examination and cross-examination, etc routinely establishes the guilt of accused persons. In the UK, thousands of people each year are found to have committed particular crimes. The legal system, through its procedures, establishes what has happened. In these procedures, the legal system makes claims to have established the truth of events 'beyond reasonable doubt' in circumstances where science, even when it may offer some contribution to the process, could not plausibly claim to know the truth of this unique event. Whilst scientific evidence has relevance in many trials, there are few trials where the contention that a person had committed the facts of a particular crime could be established in a manner that would be accepted as 'fact' within the science system. Indeed, the legal system insists that the guilt of a person cannot be decided by scientists, however relevant their expertise, and whatever degree of consensus exists within the scientific 'community' (system) as to the meaning of the scientific evidence. The decision, for serious crimes, in nearly all situations, is assigned by law to the jury.

Implications of Criminal Appeals for the Structural Coupling between Law and the Media

While the legal system speaks in terms of the truth of a conviction at the end of a trial, appeals take a different form. An appeal to the Court of Appeal (Criminal Division) is not a re-hearing of the evidence with a view to establishing the truth that the defendant did or did not actually carry out the actions which constitute her/his crime. Instead, it is primarily a review of the processes and procedures which constructed the original conviction, undertaken with a presumption that the original trial, properly conducted, would produce an accurate verdict. The focus of this procedure is not on truth, but rights, and not on rights that would necessarily be recognised as such within moral or political philosophy, but rights which are simply the correlatives of the procedures which, properly conducted, are assumed to produce accurate, or at least appropriate, results. Was the procedure properly conducted? Were there significant deviations from these expected procedures? These processes translate into the parochial rights of a particular legal system. For an appeal court the question is: did defendants receive the rights that the legal system has constructed for them?[22]

This is not a claim that the legal system has no interest in truth as part of the process of appeal. In identifying a failure of procedure, an appeal court has to form some idea of its significance. And whilst there are rankings in the importance of procedures in terms of the rights which they are taken to represent, and even some breaches of procedure that are self-observed within the legal system as being so important that they justify quashing a conviction even in the absence of any plausible connection between the breach and an accurate verdict,[23] it is more usual for the appeal courts to justify quashing a conviction on the basis that the breach of the procedure could have some plausible connection with a factually inaccurate verdict. The Court of Appeal (Criminal Division) identifies breaches of procedure that 'may' have led to an erroneous verdict of guilt.[24] This is a review of the effect of a breach of rights on the correctness of the conclusions presumed to have been reached by the original trial (the jury having provided no reasons for their decision). The appeal does not involve the hearing of any evidence relating to 'facts', unless that evidence is considered 'new'.

[22] Legal rights are articulated within the legal system in terms of values that resonate within political and moral philosophy – rights to fairness and truth as preconditions to punishment. But the system generated distinctions which are orientated by, and provide the substance of, these more general concepts are not easily integrated into these moral and political communications. See Nobles and Schiff, 2006a.

[23] For example, see *R (Mullen) v Secretary of State for the Home Department* [2005] AC 1 (HL); [2003] QB 993 (CA), and for commentary, Nobles and Schiff, 2006b.

[24] But oscillates (for reasons we will come to) between an assessment that the original jury might have been led to a different verdict, and the conclusion that the members of the Court of Appeal are persuaded to have doubts, regardless of the likely effect on the original jury.

New evidence stimulates communications on the need to revisit a conviction both inside and outside the legal system. Within the media, the relevance of new evidence is linked to the meaning of conviction: new evidence raises the possibility that the defendant was factually innocent. And just as the media's understanding of conviction is separated from the processes that produced it within the legal system, so too is their understanding of evidence able to reverse that understanding. New evidence, for the media, is anything that they can present as not having been considered at the original trial which suggests that the 'criminal' may actually be innocent. Within the legal system, the situation is different.

It is difficult for a legal system to deny the possible relevance and importance of new evidence, as it challenges the communications by which a legal system typically seeks to articulate the relationship between the original tribunal and the appeal body. As said before, to construct an appeal from a court or tribunal which is anything less than a complete re-hearing, the appeal body has to develop communications which exhibit deference towards that first instance body and its proceedings. But new evidence, in the sense of evidence that was not available to the original hearing, cannot usually be accounted for by these communications. The original court or tribunal may be more democratic, practical, imbued with more common sense, or have the advantage of seeing witnesses and judging their demeanour. But once somebody, whether within the legal system or outside, has identified evidence which the original court or tribunal ought to have considered, and which it was unable to do without any fault on the part of the appellant, it is difficult to resist the conclusion that the appellant has suffered from injustice. Thus, both within the legal system and outside, there is acknowledgement that new evidence provides a reason to revisit a conviction. But thereafter understandings diverge.

Within the legal system, new evidence has to be 'admissible' – not simply in the sense that it has to meet the rules which exclude certain kinds of evidence from trial, but admissible in the sense that it has to be capable of being inserted into the legal system through legal procedures. In the case of the English legal system, this means that it has to be introduced and probed through the legal procedures of examination and cross-examination. Interviews that represent powerful testimony within radio and television programmes or newspaper articles will be transformed through this process. Similarly, scientific knowledge, which is generated within the science system via refereed journals, has to be introduced as the opinion of expert witnesses, and similarly subjected to questioning by legal counsel. There is no reason to suppose that what appears credible when communicated within one system will retain this quality within another.

What is 'new' will also differ. The evidence has generally to have been unavailable at trial, not to have been available but unused. This additional consideration generates considerations as to what kinds of failures to find or adduce evidence at the original trial will be excused, and which will not. Aside from the formal rules of admissibility, some elements of what is available to the media to construct a news story regarding a claim of miscarriage of justice are simply unrecognised as 'evidence'. So, for example, if investigative journalism produces ever more biographical information about the character of a prisoner, which challenges their characterisation generated in their trial, this is unlikely to be recognised by the legal system as evidence.

The same communications within the legal system that open it to appeals based on new evidence also serve to construct its closure towards what the media can utilise. Whatever processes the legal system constructs to reach its verdicts have to be treated with deference within the legal system. This is most obvious in the situations when an appeal takes the form of a review. If a decision is to be reviewed, rather than retaken after a complete rehearing, then the appeal court has to construct that decision in a form that is capable of being reviewed. Some part of the processes and procedures of the original body must be taken to be capable of producing something which is *not* a mistake, so that the relevant mistake can be identified. This is a relationship of deference (in that the appeal court has to find aspects of the original hearing that are both correct and to be respected) and hierarchy (in that it is the appeal court who can identify a mistake, and require its rectification). Thus, whatever the appeal court identifies as a mistake is something which cannot continue to form part of the original court's procedures without generating grounds for appeal.[25]

To allow new evidence to enter into an appeal without conducting a full re-hearing requires the appeal court to consider what difference the new evidence might have made to the original verdict. In the case of a civil trial, this would be assisted by the judge's statement as to what evidence she/he had accepted as true, and what reliance she/he placed upon that evidence in reaching further conclusions. In the case of jury trials, these reasons are absent. Instead they have to be reconstructed on the basis of what the jury must be treated as having accepted and what conclusions they drew from it in order to reach the guilty verdict. There is a heavy reliance on the judge's summing-up, which presents the evidence as a series of either/or options, indicating what choices need to be made in order to justify a conclusion of 'guilty'. At the level of appeal, deference towards the trial involves starting from the conclusion that options necessary to reach a verdict of guilty were accepted, and have to be regarded, for the purposes of the appeal, as

[25] A full re-hearing does not generate the same communications about mistake. Whilst a different verdict is a communication that the verdict was a mistake, a re-hearing that adopts the same procedures and limits on evidence as the original hearing is also an affirmation of the ability of those procedures to achieve a correct result. Whatever self-observation justifies the ability to reach a different conclusion on appeal does not necessitate changes to the original tribunal.

correct. The new evidence has to be inserted into this background matrix, with a view to assessing whether it could have made a difference to the verdict reached.

This process is again different from that likely to be undertaken by the media, which does not start with this background assumption, which is both more conservative and more liberal than that adopted by the media. It is more liberal, in that the Court of Appeal (Criminal Division) does not have to be certain that the new evidence would have produced a different verdict, only that it 'may' have done so. On the other hand, the interpretation of the jury's verdict as something which establishes the truth of the prosecution's case, as outlined by the judge in summing-up, weakens the impact of new evidence to the point where it is sometimes claimed that the Court of Appeal operates a reverse burden of proof in appeals based solely on new evidence.

With these differences between the two systems, the legal system's communications on appeal do not reverse the understandings generated within the media at the moment of conviction. The breaches of procedure are difficult to communicate in the media as something fundamental or even important. Self-observations on rights as important contributions to the fairness of verdicts are important within the legal system, as they help to orientate the endless iteration of distinctions which give substance to those rights. But this process of iteration is not communicated about within the media as the drawing of distinctions which make a difference. The story generated by conviction pivots on what the defendant is taken to have done. The conclusion that the defendant had not done it is, in itself, no more newsworthy than most acquittals. 'Man did not bite dog' is not a story. Acquittals which do not involve celebrities are rarely reported. What makes a quashed conviction more newsworthy than an acquittal is the assumption that someone has been punished for something that they did not do – that they were, after all, factually innocent. But the legal system is rarely able to offer the media communications which support this interpretation of an appeal. The co-ordination of meaning that occurs on conviction – with both systems articulating the conviction as a factual truth – is not repeated at the level of appeal. The most common basis for a successful appeal is that there has been a breach of the defendant's legal rights. And whilst this may be delivered along with a general conclusion that the trial was 'unfair', neither that general conclusion, nor the specific communications that led to it, generate news. 'Man receives unfair trial' in a legal system that overturns approximately one quarter of jury convictions appealed to the Court of Appeal each year is about as newsworthy as 'dog bites man'. The particular features of what constitutes an unacceptable breach of procedure, set alongside all the variations that would not amount to the same, can only undermine any sense, in the media, that something important has occurred. The distinctions that establish the importance of the breach within the legal system generate the sense that these breaches are 'technical', within the media, and therefore not 'news'. To be able to use the general label of 'unfairness', and distinguish it from run-of-the-mill successful appeals based on breach of rights, the media need to combine it with an understanding that a person who is innocent has been wrongly punished. Most appeals based on breaches of rights will also involve a consideration of the likely effect of that breach on the sustainability of the conclusion that the defendant did in fact commit the crime, and this will always be the case with appeals based on new evidence. But the conclusion that this breach or new evidence 'may' have made a difference to the original trial is not the firm statement of innocence that the media needs for its story of miscarriage of justice as the wrongful punishment of the factually innocent.[26]

The Pressures Generated by the Differences between the Media and the Legal System's Understanding of Appeal

If the media report on criminal appeals at all, they invariably do so in terms of a reversal of the meaning generated at conviction. A person considered factually guilty through conviction is reported as 'innocent', their 'name cleared' through appeal. These cases allow the legal system to be presented within the media as a system that can correct what the media understands as its mistakes. But there are circumstances when the media misreading of both convictions and appeals generates significant pressure on the legal system. This occurs when the media begin to report particular convictions as miscarriages of justice, in the sense of the wrongful conviction of the factually innocent, and the legal system fails to respond. Such responses date back to before the creation of the first Court of Criminal Appeal, and created the political conditions which led to its introduction.[27]

The most recent period in the UK for sustained media reportage of this kind was in the period 1989–1992.[28] This was a period in which the press became increasingly convinced of the factual innocence of a number of high-profile prisoners convicted in the 1970s of murders arising out of an

[26] For a case study that systematically demonstrates these differences, see Nobles and Schiff, 2004.

[27] The demand for a legal procedure to reconsider jury verdicts was a political reaction to press campaigns to secure redress for prisoners reported in the press as being innocent and the perceived inadequacy of the only then-available remedy: the pardon. Whilst the pardon operated on a rational basis within a structurally differentiated society (see Hay, 1976, Rolph, 1978), the political system offered few communicative resources for its routine operation in a functionally differentiated society. It was perceived by the Home Office as a legal matter. The judiciary had no wish to take up this function, repeatedly speaking out against the 31 Bills proposed between 1844 and 1906 for the introduction of a right to appeal jury verdicts other than for a mistake of law. See Pattenden, 1996, ch 1; Nobles and Schiff, 2000, 39–55.

[28] See Nobles and Schiff, 2000, ch 4, esp 117–49.

IRA bombing campaign in England. Press reportage included 'evidence' which was not treated by the legal system as such: the belief of important political and religious persons in the innocence of these prisoners; the changing understanding of the organisation and discipline of the IRA, combined with knowledge of these prisoners' biographies and attributes, which made them unlikely candidates for an IRA active service unit; the confession of the actual active service units to the crimes for which some of these prisoners had been convicted (including a TV interview with the IRA's then current high command); and various books which conducted complete reassessments of the evidence against the prisoners and found it wanting. Reporting on this 'evidence' generated a media expectation that the status of the prisoners should be changed to recognise their factual innocence, and an increasing frustration with a legal system that failed to respond. These led to stories which no longer saw these unremedied miscarriages as insulated instances, but as indicating a systemic failure, reported as a 'crisis of confidence' in the criminal justice system. What followed included the resignation of the then Lord Chief Justice, further appeals which resulted in quashed convictions in cases that had been identified within the press as long-outstanding miscarriages, a statutory change to the grounds for appeal, and the introduction of a new body to investigate claims of wrongful conviction and refer appropriate cases back to the Court of Appeal. These events and reforms removed the pressure being placed upon the legal system by the media.[29] But what they did not alter was the basis on which the legal system conducted its appeals, that is, the conditions which can be expected to generate similar pressures in future. Both systems remain closed to each other. Neither could take the meanings generated by the other's communications into their own operations. In the case of the media, the dominant and routine reporting of convictions remains, and even did so during their period of reporting 'crisis', one that treated convictions as proof of the truth of the offenders' guilt without reference to the legal rights which orientate and construct the legal processes that produce those convictions.

Educating journalists about appeal rights in law is the apparent solution to what appears to be a lack of understanding. But, from a systems theory perspective, there is no form of uniform education that could enable such legal operations (decisions about whether a conviction is 'unsafe') and stories about miscarriages of justice in the mass media to represent the same

[29] The crisis of confidence theme was a media construct, the confidence of any individual, let alone whatever individuals are believed to make up 'the public', not being directly accessible to journalists, and certainly not on the daily basis on which they construct their stories. Reportage that the legal system could not identify and remedy 'known' miscarriages, and that these were the 'tip of an iceberg', invited the conclusion that a rational 'public' would have no confidence in the legal system's convictions. The changes removed the consensus that had generated this story of 'systemic' failure.

meanings, because the links made by each subsystem of communication will not mirror each other; each subsystem will operate through its different memories associated with its programmes and code. Attempts to 'educate' the media during this period were noticeably unsuccessful. Lord Donaldson, then a former Master of the Rolls, wrote an article in 1994 expressing his frustration at the ignorance of journalists and the general public of the nature of trial processes. He stressed the importance of procedures as matters of fairness, rather than a single-minded pursuit of the truth. He wanted both journalists and the public to understand: 'The question of whether someone is innocent or not is not one that is addressed in a criminal trial in our legal system.'[30] We can see a similar approach in a book written by Louis Blom-Cooper QC in 1997, *The Birmingham Six and other Cases*. The thesis which informs his book is that if the public understood the constitutional importance of trial by jury, the implications of deferring to the jury on appeal, the role played by circumstantial evidence, and considerations of fairness rather than truth, then the public would not lose faith in the criminal justice system when faced with cases where innocent persons might have been convicted.

Neither of these actors[31] explored the implications, for both the legal system and the media, of successfully transmitting these messages. How are the media expected to publish stories about convicted criminals alongside a genuine understanding that their trial has not established that they have in fact committed the crimes in question? How could the media continue to tap into public desires for vengeance against individuals who have committed shocking crimes while simultaneously presenting the criminal justice system as an unjust set of procedures which routinely punishes the innocent? How are statistics on matters such as the clear-up rate to continue to be produced? And what value does the legal system offer to the rest of society if its verdicts are no longer read (or misread) as a successful resolution to the investigation of crime? The costs of this 'education', in terms of the things that could no longer be routinely communicated within the media, public administration and politics indicate why it will not in fact occur. One must also add the inability of actors within the legal system to avoid using communications, at the moment of conviction, which reinforces this 'misreading' of the legal system by the media.

The closure of the legal system brings us back to where this Chapter began – the process of re-entry, whereby the legal system constructs itself though the generation of endless distinctions, that is, doctrine. The changes

[30] *The Mirror on Sunday*, 28 August 1994, quoting Professor Michael Zander (a member of the Runciman Royal Commission on Criminal Justice).

[31] And there are many more recent examples of such sentiments being expressed by prominent members of the legal profession. See, for example, the speech by the current Lord Chief Justice, Lord Judge, 'The Judiciary and the Media' (www.judiciary.gov.uk/media/speeches/2011/lcj-speech-judiciary-and-the-media).

which followed the above 'crisis' included the replacement of Lord Chief Justice Lane with the more 'liberal' Lord Taylor. Lord Lane had been found too unwilling to accept that there were systemic failings in the criminal justice system, including the system of appeals. This change of personnel was expected to result in a greater willingness to accept that trials may result in factual errors (and a corresponding lessening of the deference shown to juries). But how is this 'greater willingness' to form part of legal operations? Through what communications is it to be communicated? How can the legal system construct a form of appeal which is 'more open' to the possibility that trial procedures generate mistakes?

For the legal system, an appeal operates at its centre and involves so many of its programmes that despite possible adverse publicity it has little room to manoeuvre and respond to 'bad press' reporting. If the appeal court identifies mistakes in the procedures of investigation or trial, these are interpreted as grounds for appeal, and within the trial court, as instructions as to what should not occur. Through these kinds of communications an appeal court can change the basis of trial, but this is not what is meant by a greater willingness to accept that the trial system, in whatever form it takes, makes more mistakes than has hereto been recognised.[32] Indeed, these kinds of decision, which alter the trial process, are self-observed as the reduction of the potential for mistakes. They construct the trial system as superior to what went before. The ability to recognise these kinds of mistake is restricted by the inability to remove what cannot be replaced through judicial communications – as per our earlier example of a general scepticism towards jury verdicts.[33] In addition, whatever is found to have been a mistake is, in keeping with the legal system's construction of time, typically found to have been a mistake from an earlier period (the passing of a statute, or for a past without limits in the case of common law aspects of procedure). These mistakes have to be managed through restrictions on the right to appeal (which again will not be 'understood' within the media).[34]

The media call for a greater willingness to admit errors set the Court of Appeal the task of articulating a basis for appeal that can identify mistakes in a jury's verdict without identifying errors in the procedures of the trial

[32] What Naughton, 2007, 189 describes as a 'move from exceptionalist understandings of miscarriages of justice towards a more inclusive depiction of the miscarriage of justice terrain'.

[33] Another example would be general scepticism towards police evidence.

[34] One characteristic of the Criminal Cases Review Commission, which has stimulated considerable judicial communication, is its ability to refer cases to the Court of Appeal without any time limits (Nobles and Schiff, 2005, 179–81). This has the potential to burden the court with huge numbers of appeals based on new interpretations of law made by the court itself (Elks, 2008, ch 7). The spectre with which the judges frightened themselves was the prospect of an appeal by Guy Fawkes. This possibility was partly due to an unintended consequences of doctrinal development – responding to the 'injustice' of Giuseppe Conlon, one of the Maguire 7, losing his right to 'clear his name' through his death in prison, the Court of Appeal had removed the rule that only living parties could bring an appeal.

court. Two doctrinal routes open to it are 'new evidence' and 'lurking doubt'.[35] Both of these routes are inadequate for this task. 'Lurking doubt' is an acceptance that, despite no error at the trial, and in the absence of any new evidence, the Court of Appeal takes a different view of the evidence at trial to that taken by the jury. It is a doctrine that comes closest to what the media expect from appeals, but it provides no basis on which to indicate which cases should be appealed and which not. It is not a ground of appeal which identifies what cases should not expect to be taken to appeal, so much as an abandonment of grounds of appeal. Reaching judgments of irrefutability itself involves an investigation not only of the new evidence but all the evidence into which it is to be integrated which moves the process closer to a full re-hearing. And even this approach can only defer and not exclude the necessity for deference – otherwise how is an appeal turned down for lack of doubt to be insulated from a further appeal on the same basis?[36]

New evidence allows some deference towards the trial court procedures to remain part of the appeal court's communications, but how much? Following the crisis reportage there was a call for 'less deference' to jury verdicts.[37] There is some confirmation that this occurred immediately after the 'crisis' in that the Court of Appeal quashed the convictions of a number of cases which had been the subject of repeated appeals to the Court of Appeal. But this 'attitude' was never included within the court's judgments. Deference to the jury continued to be central to the construction of the process of review – the assumption that the jury are able to reach an accurate verdict on factual guilt within a properly conducted trial. One can hypothesise that the more liberal attitude remained permanent, or that it faded away when the pressure from media reporting evaporated. But in the absence of any way of registering attitude which is not communicated, and in the presence of ongoing communications which construct appeals in terms of deference to the jury, there are few resources available for the legal system to refute or resist media stories about the legal system's reluctance

[35] A third is the discretion to admit evidence that was available at trial, but not used. This relaxes deference, as it allows the appeal to consider something not before the jury. But, as the Court of Appeal has regularly articulated, it creates the danger that the appeal has to examine all the lines of argument and evidence discarded by the defendant's legal team – turning the appeal into a re-hearing. Attempts to articulate reasons for exercising this discretion threaten to create a doctrinal right to a re-hearing of unused evidence. The Court of Appeal recently announced that their decisions on the exercise of this discretion should not be read as precedents, and only the leading cases which articulate general principles should be cited to them (see *R v Erskine and Williams* [2009] EWCA Crim 1425, and commentary by Ormerod, 2010).

[36] See Leigh, 2006; his legal analysis suggests that the doctrine of 'lurking doubt' has no current legal credibility. For the original formulation of 'lurking doubt' within legal doctrine, see Lord Widgery's judgment in *R v Cooper* (1968) 53 Cr App R 82.

[37] Especially as urged in the Report of the Royal Commission on Criminal Justice (the Runciman Report), Cm 2263, 1993, ch 10.

to remedy miscarriage, if the conditions which generate those stories should reoccur.[38]

Postscript: A Comment on Human Involvement

The focus of this postscript is the individual, the human being who, according to some of the critics of systems theory, is excluded from its consideration, or at least offered a less prominent position from which this theory organises its observations. As with all potential structural coupling between systems, there is human involvement in that individuals as human actors have to be motivated to make the operations (communications) within each system that are facilitated by the coupling.[39] Individuals who regularly participate in more than one system may find themselves familiar with the communications available on each side of a particular coupling, and what it means to make different communicative selections from each system as a result. Everyday examples of this are commercial lawyers, who package business deals into legal contracts, or parliamentary draftsmen, who turn political programmes into legal ones, or legal correspondents and court press officers who turn court judgments into newsworthy stories. This kind of familiarity is an extension of the experience which makes complex systems possible in the first place. If the operations of social systems, and the communications necessary to achieve those operations, were not something with which human actors could gain familiarity, then they would not be able to participate in social systems. And the heightened familiarity of some actors with systems' communications (tighter structural coupling between individual psychic systems and social systems) is in turn a precondition for the increased complexity of social systems. Thus, for example, without the development of a separate legal profession, with its specialist training, it

[38] Meanwhile the legal system continues to fine-tune its appeals with doctrinal changes that have little resonance outside itself. The internal adjustment in attitude to jury verdicts is reflected in an oscillation between the approach in the House of Lords decisions in *Stafford* [1974] AC 878 and *Pendleton* [2001] UKHL 66 (although the different judgments in each case offer various possibilities). The majority judgment in the latter case looks to the likely effect of an error of procedure or new evidence on the assumed characteristics of a jury. The former invites the members of the court to decide how it would have affected them if they had been called upon to decide the case. Both operate alongside an assumption that the jury has accepted the other uncontested aspects of the trial. Neither has a clearly liberal or conservative effect. The assumption that there is any difference between these two approaches implies that some evidence, and some mistakes, would have a greater effect on one body than the other, with the implication that the Court of Appeal would be more forensic than the jury. But greater forensic skills can rebuild prosecution cases as well as deconstruct them.

[39] We refer to the issue of human involvement in social systems without making any claim that Luhmann's systems theory has an answer to the ontological question of the way that individuals are so engaged, particularly as observers. We recognise that such a claim would open up a range of questions that we do not consider here. As an example of one analysis that tries to offer some plausible answers to such questions, see Brier, 2007.

would not have been possible for the legal system to have, at its centre, a court system which processes system communications that have a complexity beyond what would be possible with only lay involvement.

Moving to the possibilities of participation in more than one system, the first point to note is that this is an everyday experience for individuals within a functionally differentiated society. Individuals have to make medical, scientific, educational, political, legal and economic communications. They must also couple their consciousnesses with systems in which they may not be called upon actively to participate, such as the mass media (assuming that they are not journalists or television or radio presenters, but only newspaper readers, or television viewers or radio listeners, although active involvement is now more readily experienced through forms of social networking). And, as we pointed out in our Chapter on legal pluralism, the possibilities of making complex communications at levels below social subsystems, such as those made during interactions, are increased by individuals' experiences of operating within social subsystems. But the ability of human beings to engage, through their consciousnesses, with more than one social system should not be confused with the ability of individuals to take control of social systems in themselves,[40] including relationships of structural coupling between systems.

The difficulties of achieving this are formidable. Controlling a social system means determining the possibilities of its evolution: selecting from the available variety of communications, new communications, which are then retained by the system as structures which offer new redundancies which in future offer the variety of communications allowed to the system by the 'controlling' system. The ability of individuals to participate within systems that have achieved structural coupling by anticipating the operations which will commence within more than one system as a result of communications within another is a far cry from having the ability to anticipate the ongoing future of those communications within each system, let alone their capacity to contribute to each system's evolution. And whilst a familiarity with systems theory[41] may give an individual a different understanding of the nature of their participation in multiple systems, again, this should not be confused with a claim that through this understanding, individuals could gain control over the systems in which they participate.

This is not to deny that law (as other systems) will offer individuals particular possibilities, and of course have particular impacts on and implications

[40] This is an experience with which academics should be quite familiar. One participates in academic issues (the education system) through publication and public speaking, and one hopes that one's contributions alter the basis (redundancies) of further communications in one's subject area. However, it would be impossible to claim with any degree of credibility, no matter how skilled one is at selecting communications, that one's participation within that system could be described as 'control'.

[41] A familiarity that requires coupling of consciousness with systems theory within a system, such as the education system or the science system.

for particular individuals. Indeed, without these effects on individual human actors, those actors would not be encouraged to participate in systems, such as the legal system. This participation is motivated by the expectations which law generates in human actors as to what may be achieved or avoided by the operations which legal communications affect. To the extent that these expectations exist as thoughts and emotions within the individual (namely that individual's psychic system) they are unknowable. But the expectations of human actors have a social existence through participation in systems of communication.

As we have tried to demonstrate throughout this book, individuals are constrained by the systems within which they operate and their need to adopt systems' communications. Each system co-opts individuals by constructing their statuses, whether as legal subject, citizen, economic actor, etc. Individuals are not unimportant, but like the modern societies which they inhabit, they are fractured not psychically but socially. When they wish to participate in society they need to adopt the communications that are available. Those communications are not static. They continue to evolve, and individuals can participate in that evolution by using their creative abilities and aptitudes. When they do so they may perturb the systems within which they are constructed and encourage those systems towards new redundancies, stimulating them through the expectations created by those systems' own communications. In colloquial terms, systems may become hoisted on their own petards.[42] However, in the case of the legal system, and especially at its centre, and the centre of that centre in its appeal courts, the opportunities for participation in its evolution are rigorously constrained.

Lay individuals (even with legal advice from legal professionals) who seek to extend the reviewing operations of legal decisions can perturb the legal system by creating arguments that the legal system will recognise as potential reconstructions of its own appeal practices. They are not pushing at a closed door, but they are pushing at a system's doors and, in relation to appeals and the legal system, they are pushing towards the centre of that system. This is demanding for any lay individual (or their professional lawyers) as an individual, because that individual will need to reconstruct their expectation about their 'rights' in relation to appeals to meet the challenge of the legal system's re-entry and potential reconstruction.[43] An individual needs not only a precise understanding of the legal system's communications to enable them to succeed in this task, but they may well need more in order to engage

[42] A systems theory version of Shakespeare's 'hoist with his own petard' (Hamlet).

[43] For those interested in exploring further how demanding this is, consider the recent case of *R v Dunn* [2010] EWCA Crim 1823 in which the appellant unsuccessfully appealed against the refusal of the Court of Appeal to certify that his case involved a 'point of law of general public importance', which would enable it to be considered by the Supreme Court (Criminal Appeal Act 1968, section 33.2). It appears that the UK Supreme Court is only able to decide up to 70 cases per year.

the appeal courts' attention, and for it to be willing to reconstruct its re-entry operations at the level of the distinctions that construct its appeals.

In this book we have been observing the observations of systems, and in particular the self-observations of the legal system. We have been exploring the differences between those self-observations concerning some of the legal system's most common or significant operations, and contrasting them with external observations relating to the same subject matter. We have tried to show how systems theory offers an observational standpoint from which one can observe these differences and thus make some sense of the modern differentiated social world as it is constructed through differentiated communications. And we have addressed the question whether systems theory makes a difference. At this point we want to make one further suggestion about how it may do so for individuals.

Individual human beings are outside of social systems and may fail to respond to them. Social systems form part of their environment. But in order to respond, human beings, as psychic systems, have to couple with social systems, which they do through making system communications. In undertaking this, they are offered roles within systems which circumscribe (that is, provide context) for the communications available to them. Like any other actor (which includes institutional and non-human actors)[44] individuals are constituted by the systems in which they participate – legal subjects within the law, economic actors within the economy, pupils within education, patients within the health system, etc. Particular human beings participate as actors in multiple systems, often at the same moment, making selections from the redundancies, which include roles that the particular system affords to them, at that point in the system.

When we explore how individuals exist from this understanding of the modern social world we can observe the way in which they are fractured socially, but not psychically, by the subsystems that name them and construct them. That fracturing might lead to a certain disassociation from the modern social world (including a sense of frustration as to the inability to control the operations of systems within which they are organised). Apart from the perceptions available to systems theorists to understand the modern differentiated world, systems theory enables individuals to make sense of the social world in which, as individuals, they might feel disassociated. Without being systems theorists, people recognise that systems are complex, difficult to understand and be part of, without considerable loss of control. Systems theory gives people the opportunity to explain this disassociation and lack of control to themselves. It is not our suggestion that systems theory understanding may then enable individuals to respond to their sense of disassociation more positively, that they might somehow gain control, but merely that they might better understand from where their disassociation derives.

[44] Consider Teubner, 2006a.

Bibliography

Abbott, A, *Time Matters: On Theory and Method* (Chicago, University of Chicago Press, 2001)

Ackerman, B, *We The People, Volume 1: Foundations* (London, Belknap Press, 1991)

Adam, B, *Time* (Cambridge, Polity Press, 2004)

Agamben, G, *State of Exception*, trans K Attell (Chicago, University of Chicago Press, 2005)

Andersen, NA, 'Polyphonic organisations' in Bakken, T and Hernes, T (eds), 2003, ch 8

——,'The Semantic Analytical Strategy and Diagnostics of Present' in John, R, Henkel, A and Ruckert-John, J (eds), *Die Methodologien des Systems* (VS Verlag, Wiesbaden, 2010) 161–80

——,'Luhmann as Analytical Strategist' in John, R, Henkel, A and Ruckert-John, J (eds), *Die Methodologien des Systems* (VS Verlag, Wiesbaden, 2010a) 97–117

——,'Contract as a form of intersystemic-communication', to be published in Febbrajo, A and Hartse, G (eds), *Law and Intersystemic Communication* (Aldershot, Ashgate, 2013 forthcoming)

—— and Born, A, 'Heterophony and the postponed organisation – organizing autopoietic systems' (2007) 6 *Tamara Journal for Critical Organizational Inquiry*, 176–86

Appelbaum, A, *Gulag: A History of the Soviet Camps* (London, Allen Lane, 2003)

Arnaud, A-J, 'We Are All E.T.'s' (1998) 41 *Journal of Legal Pluralism and Unofficial Law* 1–14

Ashworth, A, 'Ignorance of the Criminal Law, and Duties to Avoid it' (2011) 74 *The Modern Law Review* 1–26

Baghai, K, *Three Systems Theoretic Essays in the Sociology of Law* (Aldershot, Ashgate, 2013 forthcoming)

Bakker, T and Hernes, T (eds), *Autopoietic Organization Theory: Drawing on Niklas Luhmann's Social Systems Perspective* (Oslo, Abstrakt, 2003)

Bankowski, Z, 'How does it Feel to be on Your Own? The Person in the Sight of Autopoiesis' in Nelken, D (ed), *Law as Communication* (Aldershot, Dartmouth, 1996) ch 4

Barden, G and Murphy, T, *Law and Justice in the Community* (Oxford, Oxford University Press, 2010)

Bausch, K, *The Emerging Consensus in Social Systems Theory* (New York, Kluwer, 2001)

Beck, A, 'Is Law an Autopoietic System' (1994) 14 *Oxford Journal of Legal Studies* 401–18

Bedau, HA (ed), *Civil Disobedience in Focus* (London, Routledge, 1991)

von Benda-Beckmann, F, 'Who's Afraid of Legal Pluralism?' (2002) *Journal of Legal Pluralism and Unofficial Law* 37–82 von Benda-Beckmann, F, and von Benda-Beckmann K, 'Changing One Is Changing All: Dynamics In The Adat-Islam-State Triangle' (2006) *Journal of Legal Pluralism and Unofficial Law* 239–70

Benewick, R and Smith, T (eds), *Direct Action and Democratic Politics* (London, George Allen & Unwin, 1972)

von Bertalanffy, L, *General System Theory: Foundations, Development, Applications*, revised edn (New York, George Braziller, 1976)

Black, J, 'Proceduralizing Regulation: Part I' (2000) 20 *Oxford Journal of Legal Studies* 597–614

Blom-Cooper, L, *The Birmingham Six and Other Cases: Victims of Circumstance* (London, Duckworth, 1997)

Bredemeier, HC, 'Law as an Integrative Mechanism' in Evan, WM (ed), *Law and Sociology* (New York, Free Press, 1962) 73–90

Brier, S, 'Applying Luhmann's System Theory as Part of a Transdisciplinary Frame for Communication Science' (2007) 14, 2/3 *Cybernetics and Human Knowing* 29–65

Brunsson, N, *The Organization of Hypocrisy* 2nd edn (Oslo, Abstrakt forlag AS, 2002).

Burke, E, *Reflections on the Revolution in France*, O'Brien, C (ed) (London, Penguin, 1986)

Calabresi, G and Bobbitt, P, *Tragic Choices* (New York, WW Norton, 1978)

Cane, P (ed), *The Hart-Fuller Debate in the Twenty-First Century* (Oxford, Hart Publishing, 2010)

Castellani, B, *Sociology and Complexity Science* (Berlin, Springer, 2009)

Charlesworth, H, 'Human Rights and the Rule of Law after Conflict' in Cane, P (ed), 2010, ch 2

Checkland, P, 'Soft Systems Methodology' in Rosenhead, J and Mingers, J (eds), *Rational Analysis for a Problematic World Revisited: Problem Structuring Methods for Complexity, Uncertainty and Conflict*, 2nd edn (Chichester, Wiley, 2001)

Chiba, M, 'Legal Pluralism in Sri Lankan Society: Toward a general theory of non-western law' (1993) 33 *Journal of Pluralism and Unofficial Law* 197–212

——,'The Intermediate Variable of Legal Concepts' (1998) 41 *Journal of Legal Pluralism and Unofficial Law* 131–43

Christodoulidis, E, *Law and Reflexive Politics* (Dordrecht, Kluwer, 1998)

——,'Of Boundaries and 'Tipping Points': A Response to Gunther Teubner' (2011) *Social & Legal Studies* 238–43

Coleman, J (ed), *Hart's Postscript. Essays on the Postscript to the Concept of Law* (Oxford, Oxford University Press, 2001)

Cotterrell, R, *Law, Culture and Society: Legal Ideas in the Mirror of Social Theory* (Dartmouth, Ashgate, 2006)

Cover, R, 'Nomos and Narrative' (1983) 97 *Harvard Law Review* 4–68

——,'Violence and the Word' (1986) 95 *Yale Law Journal* 1601–29

——,*Narrative, Violence and the Law: The Essays of Robert Cover* (Ann Arbor, University of Michigan Press, 1993)

Davies, M, 'The Ethos of Pluralism' (2005) 27 *Sydney Law Review* 87–112

Dewey, W, 'System' in Baldwin, J (ed), *Dictionary of Philosophy and Psychology* (New York, Macmillan, 1901)

Dilling, O, Herberg, M and Winter, G (eds), *Responsible Business: Self-Governance and Law in Transnational Economic Transcations* (Oxford, Hart Publishing, 2008)

Dworkin, R, *Taking Rights Seriously* (London, Duckworth, 1977)
——, 'Is Wealth a Value' (1980) 9 *Journal of Legal Studies* 191–226
——, *A Matter of Principle* (Cambridge, Mass, Harvard University Press, 1985)
——, *Law's Empire* (London, Fontana, 1986)
——, *Justice in Robes* (Cambridge, Mass, Harvard University Press, 2006)
Edmundson, WA (ed), *The Duty to Obey the Law: Selected Philosophical Readings* (Lanham, Md, Rowman & Littlefield, 1991)
Elias, N, *Time: An Essay* (Oxford, Blackwell, 1992)
Elks, L, *Righting Miscarriages of Justice? Ten years of the Criminal Cases Review Commission* (London, Justice, 2008)
Febbrajo, A and Teubner, G (eds), *State, Law, Economy as Autopoietic Systems* (Milan, Giuffre, 1992)
Finnis, J, 'The Fairy Tale's Moral' (1999) 115 *Law Quarterly Review* 170–5
——, *Natural Law and Natural Rights* (Oxford, Clarendon Press, 1980)
Fischer-Lescano, A and Teubner, G, 'Regime Collisions: The Vain Search for Legal Unity in the Fragmentation of Global Law' (2004) 25 *Michigan Journal of International Law* 999–1045
Fisher, L, *Constitutional Dialogues: Interpretation as Political Process* (New Jersey, Princeton University Press, 1988)
Fitzpatrick, P, 'Law and Societies' (1984) 22 *Osgoode Hall Law Journal* 115–38
Friedman, L, *The Legal System: A Social Science Perspective* (New York, Russell Sage, 1975)
Fuller, L, 'Positivism and Fidelity to Law – A Reply to Professor Hart' (1958) *Harvard Law Review* 630–72
——, *The Morality of Law* (New Haven, Yale University Press, 1964, revised edn, 1969)
Galanter, M, 'Justice in Many Rooms: Courts, Private Ordering and Indigenous Law' (1981) 19 *Journal of Legal Pluralism and Unofficial Law* 1–47
Galligan, D, *Law in Modern Society* (Oxford, Oxford University Press, 2007)
Gardbaum, S, 'How Successful and Distinctive is the Human Rights Act? An Expatriate Comparatist's Assessment' (2011) 71 *Modern Law Review* 195–215
Gies, L, 'The Empire Strikes Back: Press Judges and Communicative Advisers in Dutch Courts' (2005) 32 *Journal of Law and Society* 450–72
Goodale, M, 'Locating rights, envisioning law between the global and the local' in Goodale, M and Merry, SE (eds), *The Practice of Human Rights: Tracking Law Between the Global and the Local* (New York, Cambridge University Press, 2007), Introduction
Graber, C and Teubner, G, 'Art and Money: Constitutional Rights in the Private Sphere' (1998) 18 *Oxford Journal of Legal Studies* 61–73
Greenawalt, K, 'Discretion and Judicial Decision: the elusive quest for the fetters that bind judges' (1975) 75 *Columbia Law Review* 359–99
——, *Conflicts of Law and Morality* (Oxford, Oxford University Press, 1989)
Grey, T, 'Origins of the Unwritten Constitution: Fundamental Law in American Revolutionary Thought' (1977–78) 30 *Stanford Law Review* 843–93
Griffin, S, 'Constituent Power and Constitutional Change in American Constitutionalism' in Loughlin, M and Walker, N (eds), 2007, ch 3
Griffith, J, 'The Political Constitution' (1979) 42 *Modern Law Review* 1–21

Griffiths, A, 'Legal Pluralism' in Banakar, R and Travers, M (eds), *An Introduction to Law and Social Theory* (Oxford, Hart Publishing, 2002) ch 15

Griffiths, J, 'The Division of Labor in Social Control' in Black, D (ed), *Towards a General Theory of Social Control: Vol 1 Fundamentals* (London, Academic Press, 1984) 37–70

——,'What is Legal Pluralism?' (1986) 24 *Journal of Legal Pluralism and Unofficial Law* 1–55

——,'Legal Pluralism and the Theory of Legislation' in Petersen, H and Zahle, H (eds), *Legal Polycentricity: Consequences of Pluralism in Law* (Aldershot, Dartmouth, 1995) 208–16

Hall, N, 'Introduction' in *The New Scientist guide to Chaos* (ed N Hall) (London, Penguin, 1991)

Hart, HLA, 'Positivism and the Separation of Law and Morals' (1958) *Harvard Law Review* 593–629

——,'Legal and Moral Obligation' in Melden, AI (ed), *Essays in Moral Philosophy* (Seattle, University of Washington Press, 1958a) 82–107

——, *The Concept of Law* (Oxford, Clarendon Press, 1961; 2nd edn 1994)

Hassard, J (ed), *The Sociology of Time* (Basingstoke, Macmillan, 1990)

Hay, D, 'Property, Authority and the Criminal Law' in Hay, D *et al*, *Albion's Fatal tree: Crime and Society in Eighteenth-Century England* (London, Allen Lane, 1976) 17–63

Himma, K, 'Law's Claim of Legitimate Authority' in Coleman, J (ed), 2001, ch 8

Holmes, S, 'Lineages of the Rule of Law' in Maravall, JM and Przeworski, A (ed), *Democracy and the Rule of Law* (Cambridge, Cambridge University Press, 2003) 19–61

Husserl, G, *Recht und Zeit: Fünf Rechtsphilosophische Essays* (Frankfurt am Main, Vittorio Klostermann, 1955)

Hutchinson, A, *Evolution and the Common Law* (Cambridge, Cambridge University Press, 2005)

—— and Monahan, P (eds), *The Rule of Law: Ideal or Ideology?* (Toronto, Carswell, 1987)

Huxtable, R, *Euthanasia, Ethics and the Law: From Conflict to Compromise* (Abingdon, Routledge/Cavendish, 2007)

Jakobson, R and Halle, M, *Fundamentals of Language*, 2nd revised edn (Berlin, Mouton de Gruyter, 1971)

Jacques, E, 'The Enigma of Time' in Hassard, J (ed), *The Sociology of Time* (Basingstoke, Macmillan, 1990) ch 1

Jones, J, 'Cultural Differences in Temporal Perspectives: Instrumental and Expressive Behaviors in Time' in McGrath, J (ed), *The Social Psychology of Time: New Perspectives* (California, Sage, 1988) ch 2

Kelsen, H, *General Theory of Law and State*, trans Wedberg, A (Cambridge, Mass, Harvard University Press, 1945)

——, *Pure Theory of Law*, trans Knight, M, 2nd edn (California, University of California Press, 1967)

Keogh, A, *Criminal Appeals and Review Remedies for Magistrates' Court Decisions* (London, Blackstone Press, 1999)

Kersch, K, *Constructing Civil Liberties: Discontinuities in the Development of American Constitutional Law* (New York, Cambridge University Press, 2004)

King, M, 'The Muslim Identity in a Secular World' in King, M (ed), *God's Law versus State Law* (London, Grey Seal, 1995) ch 11

——, 'Comparing Legal Cultures in the Quest for Law's Identity' in Nelken, D, (ed), *Comparing Legal Cultures* (Aldershot, Dartmouth, 1997), ch 7

——, 'What's the Use of Luhmann's Theory?' in King, M and Thornhill, C (eds), 2006, ch 2

——, *Systems, Not People, Make Society Happen* (Holcombe, [E]Publishing, 2010)

—— and Schütz, A, 'The Ambitious Modesty of Niklas Luhmann' (1994) 21 *Journal of Law and Society* 261–87

—— and Thornhill, C, *Niklas Luhmann's Theory of Politics and Law* (Basingstoke, Palgrave/Macmillan, 2003)

—— and Thornhill, C, ' "Will the real Niklas Luhmann stand up?" A reply to John Mingers' (2003a) 51 *The Sociological Review* 276–85

—— and Thornhill, C (eds), *Luhmann on Law and Politics. Critical Appraisals and Applications* (Oxford, Hart Publishing, 2006)

Kjaer, P, Teubner, G and Febbrajo, A (eds), *The Financial Crisis in Constitutional Perspective: The Dark Side of Functional Differentiation* (Oxford, Hart Publishing, 2011)

Klir, G, *Facets of Systems Science* (2nd edn, New York, Plenum Press, 2001)

Koselleck, R, *Futures Past* trans Tribe, K (New York, Columbia University Press, 2004)

Kramer, L, *The People Themselves: Popular Constitutionalism and Judicial Review* (Oxford, Oxford University Press, 2004)

Kramer, M, *In Defense of Legal Positivism. Law without Trimmings* (Oxford, Oxford University Press, 1999)

—— *et al* (eds), *The Legacy of HLA Hart: Legal, Political and Moral Philosophy* (Oxford, Oxford University Press, 2008)

Ladeur, K-H, 'Globalization and the conversion of democracy to polycentric networks: can democracy survive the end of the Nation State?' in Ladeur, K-H (ed), *Public Governance in the Age of Globalization* (Aldershot, Ashgate, 2004) ch 5

Laermans, R and Verschraegen, G, 'Modernity and Individuality: a Sociological Analysis from the Point of View of Systems Theory' in Van Harskamp, A and Musschenga, A (eds), *The Many Faces of Individualism* (Leuven, Peeters, 2001) 111–27

Leigh, L, 'Lurking Doubt and the Safety of Convictions' [2006] *Criminal Law Review* 809–16

Lempert, R, 'The Autonomy of Law: Two Visions Compared' in Teubner, G (ed), 1987, 152–90

Levine, R, 'The Pace of Life Across Cultures' in McGrath, J (ed), *The Social Psychology of Time: New Perspectives* (California, Sage, 1988) ch 3

Lewis, D, *Convention: A Philosophical Study* (Oxford, Blackwell, 2002)

Loughlin, M, *Foundations of Public Law* (Oxford, Oxford University Press, 2010)

—— and Walker, N (eds), *The Paradox of Constitutionalism: constituent power and constitutional form* (Oxford, Oxford University Press, 2007)

Luhmann, N, *Grundrechte als Institution* (Fundamental Rights as an Institution) (Berlin, Duncker & Humbolt, 1965)

——, 'Sociologische Aufklarung' (1967) 18 *Soziale Welt* 97–123

——, 'Differentiation of Society' (1977) 2/1 *Canadian Journal of Sociology* 29–53
——, 'The Improbability of Communication' (1981) 23 *International Social Science Journal* 122–32
——, *The Differentiation of Society*, trans Holmes, S and Larmore, C (New York, Columbia University Press, 1982)
——, *Protest: Systemtheorie und Soziale Bewegungen* (Frankfurt am Main, Suhrkamp, 1982a)
——, 'The World Society as a Social System' (1982b) 8 *International Journal of General Systems*, 131–8
——, 'The Self-Description of Society: Crisis Fashion and Sociological Theory' (1984) XXV, 1–2 *International Journal of Comparative Sociology* 59–72
——, *Religious Dogmatics and the Evolution of Societies* trans Beyer, P (New York, Mellen, 1984a)
——, *A Sociological Theory of Law*, trans King-Utz, E and Albrow, M (London, Routledge & Kegan Paul, 1985)
——, 'The Representation of Society within Society' (1987) 35 *Current Sociology* 101–8
——, 'Closure and Openness: On Reality in the World of Law' in Teubner, G (ed), 1987, 335–48
——, 'The Third Question: The Creative Use of Paradoxes in Law and Legal History' (1988) 15 *Journal of Law and Society* 153–65
——, *Die Wirtschaft der Gesellschaft* (Frankfurt, Suhrkamp, 1988a)
——, 'Law as a Social System' (1989) 83 *Northwestern University Law Review* 136–50
——, *Ecological Communication*, trans Bednarz, J (Chicago, University of Chicago Press, 1989a)
——, *Essays on Self-reference* (New York, Columbia University Press, 1990)
——, *Political Theory in the Welfare State*, trans Bednarz, J (Berlin, de Gruyter, 1990a)
——, 'The Coding of the Legal System' in Febbrajo, A and Teubner, G (eds), 1992, 145–86
——, 'Operational Closure and Structural Coupling: The Differentiation of the Legal System' (1992a) 13 *Cardozo Law Review* 1419–41
——, 'The Code of the Moral' (1992–93) 14 *Cardozo Law Review* 995–1009
——, *Risk: A Sociological Theory*, trans Barrett, R (New York, de Gruyter, 1993)
——, 'Speaking and Silence' (1994) 61 *New German Critique* 25–37
——, *Social Systems*, trans Bednarz, J (Stanford, Stanford University Press, 1995)
——, 'The Paradoxy of Observing Systems' (1995a) 31 *Cultural Critique*, Part II 'The Politics of Systems and Environments' 37–55
——, 'Legal Argumentation: An Analysis of its Form' (1995b) 58 *The Modern Law Review* 285–98
——, 'On the scientific context of the concept of communication' (1996) 35 *Social Science Information*, 257–67
——, *Die Gesellschaft der Gesellschaft* (Frankfurt am Main, SuhrkampVerlag, 1997)
——, 'The Limits of Steering: chapter 10 of Wirtschaft der Gesellschaft' (1997a) 14 *Theory, Culture and Society*, 41–57
——, *Observations on Modernity*, trans Whobrey, W (Stanford, Stanford University Press, 1998)

——, *The Reality of the Mass Media*, trans Cross, K (Oxford, Polity Press, 2000)
——, *Art as a Social System*, trans Knodt, E (Stanford, Stanford University Press, 2000a)
——, 'Answering the Question: What is Modernity?' (An Interview) in Rasch, W, *Niklas Luhmann's Modernity: The Paradoxes of Differentiation* (Stanford, Stanford University Press, 2000b) 195–221
——, *Theories of Distinction: Redescribing the Descriptions of Modernity*, trans O'Neil, J *et al* (Stanford, Stanford University Press, 2002)
——, *Risk: A Sociological Theory*, trans Barrett, R (New Brunswick, Transaction Publishers, 2002a)
——, 'Deconstruction as Second-Order Observing' in Luhmann, 2002, ch 4
——, *Law as a Social System*, trans Ziegert, K (Oxford, Oxford University Press, 2004)
MacCormick, N, *Legal Reasoning and Legal Theory* (Oxford, Clarendon Press, 1978)
——, *HLA Hart*, 2nd edn (Stanford, Stanford University Press, 2008)
Maitland, F, *State, Trust and Corporation*, ed Runciman, D and Ryan, M (Cambridge, Cambridge University Press, 2003)
Marmoor, A, 'Legal Conventionalism' in Coleman, J (ed), 2001, ch 6
Meadows, DH, *Thinking in Systems* (London, Earthscan, 2009)
Melissaris, E, 'The More the Merrier? A New Take on Legal Pluralism' (2004) 13 *Social & Legal Studies* 57–79
——, 'The Chronology of the Legal' (2005) 50 *McGill Law Journal* 839–68
Merry, SE, 'Legal Pluralism' (1988) 22 *Law & Society Review* 869–96
——, Levitt, P, Rosen, M and Yoon, D, 'Law From Below: Women's Human Rights and Social Movements in New York City' (2010) 44 *Law & Society Review* 101–28
Midgley, G, *Systemic Intervention: Philosophy, Methodology, and Practice* (New York, Kluwer, 2000)
Mingers, J, 'Observing organizations: An evaluation of Luhmann's organization theory' in Bakken T and Hernes, T (eds), 2003, ch 6
Moeller, H-G, *Luhmann Explained: From Souls to Systems* (Chicago, Open Court, 2006)
Morin, E, *La Méthode: la Nature de la Nature* (Paris, Seuil, 1977)
Moore, SF, 'Law and social change: the semi-autonomous social field as an appropriate subject of study' (1973) 7 *Law & Society Review* 719–46
Moore, SF, *Law as Process* (London, Routledge & Kegan Paul, 1978)
Muller, H, 'Luhmann's Systems Theory as a Theory of Modernity' (1994) 61 *New German Critique*, 39–54
Naughton, M, *Rethinking Miscarriages of Justice* (Basingstoke, Palgrave Macmillan, 2007)
—— (ed), *The Criminal Cases Review Commission: Hope for the Innocent?* (Basingstoke, Palgrave Macmillan, 2010)
Nelken, D (ed), *Law as Communication* (Aldershot, Dartmouth, 1996)
Nobles, R, review of Chris Thornhill, *A Sociology of Constitutions: Constitutions and State Legitimacy in Historical-Sociological Perspective* (2012) 75 *The Modern Law Review* 290–95
—— and Schiff, D, 'Optimism Writ Large: A Critique of the Runciman Commission on Criminal Justice' in McConville, M and Bridges, L (ed), *Criminal Justice in Crisis* (Aldershot, Edward Elgar, 1994) ch 4

—— and Schiff, D, 'Criminal Appeal Act 1995: The Semantics of Jurisdiction' (1996) 59 *Modern Law Review* 573–81
—— and Schiff, D, *Understanding Miscarriages of Justice* (Oxford, Oxford University Press, 2000)
—— and Schiff, D, 'The Criminal Cases Review Commission: Reporting Success?' (2001) 64 *Modern Law Review* 280–99
—— and Schiff, D, 'The Right to Appeal and Workable Systems of Justice' (2002) 65 *Modern Law Review* 676–701
—— and Schiff, D, 'A Story of Miscarriage: Law in the Media' (2004) 31 *Journal of Law and Society* 221–44
—— and Schiff, D, 'The Criminal Cases Review Commission: Establishing a Workable Relationship with the Court of Appeal' [2005] *Criminal Law Review* 173–89
—— and Schiff, D, *A Sociology of Jurisprudence* (Oxford, Hart Publishing, 2006)
—— and Schiff, D, 'Theorising the Criminal Trial and Criminal Appeal: Finality, Truth and Rights' in Duff, A, Farmer, L, Marshall, S and Tadros, V (eds), *The Trial on Trial, Volume 2* (Oxford, Hart Publishing, 2006a), ch 14
—— and Schiff, D, 'Guilt and Innocence in the Criminal Justice System: A Comment on *R (Mullen) v Secretary of State for the Home Department*' (2006b) 69 *Modern Law Review* 80–91
—— and Schiff, D, 'Review of Paradoxes and Inconsistencies in the Law' (2007) 70 *Modern Law Review* 505–16
—— and Schiff, D, 'Jurisprudence as Self-Description: Natural Law and Positivism within the English Legal System' in G-P Calliess, A Fischer-Lescano, D Wielsch and P Zumbansen (eds), *Soziologische Jurisprudenz: Festschrift fur Gunther Teubner* (Berlin, de Gruyter Recht, 2009), 359–74
—— and Schiff, D, 'Public confidence in criminal justice: the lessons from miscarriages of justice' (2009a) 48 *Howard Journal of Criminal Justice* 461–71
—— and Schiff, D, 'Why do judges talk the way they do?' (2009b) 5 *International Journal of Law in Context* 25–49
—— and Schiff, D, 'Disobedience to Law – Debbie Purdy's case' (2010) 73 *Modern Law Review* 295–304
Oakshott, M, 'The Rule of Law' in *On History and Other Essays* (Oxford, Blackwell, 1983) 119–64
Ormerod, D, 'Commentary on *R v Erskine and Williams*' [2010] *Criminal Law Review* 52–4
——, Waterman, A and Forston, R, 'Prosecution Appeals – Too Much of a Good Thing?' [2010] *Criminal Law Review* 169–94
Orren, K and Skowronek, S, *The Search for American Political Development* (Cambridge, Cambridge University Press, 2004)
Parsons, T, *The Social System* (London, Routledge, 1951)
—— and Smelser, NJ, *Economy and Society* (London, Routledge, 1956)
Paterson, J, 'Who is Zenon Bankowski Talking to? The Person in the Sight of Autopoiesis' in Nelken, D (ed), 1996, ch 5
——, 'Reflecting on Reflexive Law' in King, M and Thornhill, C (eds), 2006, ch 1
—— and Teubner, G, 'Changing Maps: Empirical Legal Autopoiesis' (1998) 7 *Social and Legal Studies* 451–68
Pattenden, R, *English Criminal Appeals 1844–1994* (Oxford, Oxford University Press, 1996)

Penner, J, 'The Current Debate: The Semantic Sting, 'Soft Positivism', and the Authority of Law according to Raz' in Penner, J, Schiff, D and Nobles, R (eds), *Jurisprudence and Legal Theory* (London, Butterworths/LexisNexis, 2002) ch 10

Pennock, JR and Chapman, JW (eds), *Political and Legal Obligation* (Nomos XII, New York, Atherton Press, 1970)

Perez O and Teubner, G (eds), *Paradoxes and Inconsistencies in the Law* (Oxford, Hart Publishing, 2006)

Perry, S, 'Hart's Methodological Positivism' in Coleman, J (ed), 2001, ch 9

Philippopoulos-Mihalopoulos, A, 'Dealing (with) Paradoxes: On Law, Justice and Cheating' in King and Thornhill (eds), 2006, ch 10

——, *Niklas Luhmann: Law, Justice, Society* (Abingdon, Routledge, 2010)

Poole, T, 'Tilting at windmills? Truth and illusion in "The Political Constitution"' (2007) 70 *Modern Law Review* 250–77

Postema, GJ, 'Melody and Law's Mindfulness of Time' (2004) 17 *Ratio Juris* 203–26

——, 'Conformity, Custom, and Congruence: Rethinking the Efficacy of Law' in Kramer, M *et al* (eds), 2008, ch 3

Power, M, *The Audit Society: Rituals of Verification* (Oxford, Oxford University Press, 1997)

Priban, J '(Review of) Niklas Luhmann: Law, Justice, Society by Andreas Philippopoulos-Mihalopoulos' (2010) 73 *Modern Law Review* 893–7

—— and Nelken, D (eds), *Law's New Boundaries: the Consequences of Legal Autopoiesis* (Aldershot, Ashgate, 2001)

Quint, PE, *Civil Disobedience and the German Courts* (London, Routledge, 2008)

Rasch, W and Knodt, E, 'Systems Theory and the System of Theory' (1994) 61 *New German Critique*, 3–7

——, *Niklas Luhmann's Modernity: The Paradoxes of Differentiation* (Stanford, Stanford University Press, 2000)

Rawls, J, *A Theory of Justice* (Oxford, Oxford University Press, 1971)

Raz, J, *Ethics in the Public Domain* (Oxford, Clarendon Press, 1994)

——, *Practical Reasons and Norms* (Oxford, Oxford University Press, 1999)

Raz, J, *The Authority of Law* 2nd edn (Oxford, Oxford University Press, 2009)

——, *Between Authority and Interpretation* (Oxford, Oxford University Press, 2009a)

Reid (Lord), 'The Judge as Law Maker' (1972) 12 *Journal of the Society of Public Teachers of Law* 22–9

Roberts, A and Garton Ash, T (eds), *Civil Resistance and Power Politics: The Experience of Non-Violent Action from Gandhi to the Present* (Oxford, Oxford University Press, 2009)

Roberts, S, 'Against Legal Pluralism' (1998) 42 *Journal of Legal Pluralism and Unofficial Law*, 95–106

——, 'After Government – On Representing Law Without the State' (2005) 68 *Modern Law Review* 1–24

Rodger, A, 'A time for everything under the law: some reflections on retrospectivity' (2005) 121 *Law Quarterly Review* 57–79

Rolph, C, *The Queen's Pardon* (London, Cassell, 1978)

Rousseau, J-J, *The Social Contract and other later political writings*, trans Gourevitch, V (Cambridge, Cambridge University Press, 1977)

Sampford, C, *The Disorder of Law: A Critique of Legal Theory* (Oxford, Basil Blackwell, 1989)
——, *Retrospectivity and the Rule of Law* (Oxford, Oxford University Press, 2006)
Santos, B de Sousa, *Toward a New Legal Common Sense: Law, Globalisation and Emancipation* 2nd edn (London, Butterworths, 2002)
——, 'The Heterogeneous State and Legal Pluralism in Mozambique' (2006) 40 *Law & Society Review* 39–75
Schapiro, M, 'Appeal' (1980) 14 *Law & Society Review* 629–61
Schirmer, W and Hadamek, C, 'Steering as Paradox: The Ambiguous Role of the Political System in Modern Society' (2007) 2/3 *Cybernetics and Human Knowing* 133–50
Schmitt, C, *Political Theory: Four Chapters on the Concept of Sovereignty*, trans Schwab, G (Chicago, University of Chicago Press, 1922/2005)
Searle, J, *Speech Acts: An Essay in the Philosophy of Language* (Cambridge, Cambridge University Press, 1969)
Seidl, D, 'Organisational identity in Luhmann's theory of social systems' in Bakken, T and Hernes, T (eds), 2003, ch 7
Seung, T and Bonevac, D, 'Plural Values and Indeterminate Rankings' (1992) 102 *Ethics* 799–813
Shannon, B, 'The retroactive and prospective application of judicial decisions' (2003) 26 *Harvard Journal of Law & Public Policy* 811–76
Shklar, J, 'Political Theory and the Rule of Law' in Hutchinson, A and Monahan, P (eds), 1987, 1–16; reprinted in Hoffman, S (ed), *Judith N Shklar – Political Thought and Political Thinkers* (Chicago, Chicago University Press, 1998) ch 2
Simmonds, N, 'Why conventionalism does not collapse into pragmatism' (1990) 49 *Cambridge Law Journal* 63–79
——, *Law as a Moral Idea* (Oxford, Oxford University Press, 2007)
——, 'Reflexivity and the Idea of Law' (2010) 1 *Jurisprudence* 1–23
Simpson, Brian, 'The Common Law and Legal Theory' in Twining, W (ed), (Oxford, Blackwell, 1986), ch 2
——, *Leading Cases in the Common Law* (Oxford, Oxford University Press, 1995)
Snyder, F, 'Law and Anthropology' in Thomas, P (ed), 1996, ch 5
Spencer, J, 'Does our present criminal appeal system make sense?' [2006] *Criminal Law Review* 677–94
Spencer-Brown, G, *Laws of Form* (London, Allen & Unwin, 1969)
Star, S and Greisemer, J, 'Institutional ecology, "translations" and boundary objects: amateurs and professionals in Berley's museum of vertebrate zoology, 1907–39' (1989) 19 *Social Studies of Science* 387–420
Summers, R, *Lon L Fuller* (London, Edward Arnold, 1984)
Strawson, PF, 'Intention and Convention in Speech Acts' in *Logico-Linguistic Papers*, ch 8 (London, Methuen, 1971)
Sunstein, C, *Why Societies Need Dissent* (Cambridge, Mass, Harvard University Press, 2003)
Tamanaha, B, 'The Folly of the "Social Scientific Concept" of Legal Pluralism' (1993) 20 *Journal of Law and Society* 192–217
——, 'A Non-essentialist Version of Legal Pluralism' (2000) 27 *Journal of Law and Society* 296–321

——, *A General Jurisprudence of Law and Society* (Oxford, Oxford University Press, 2001)
——, 'Enhancing Prospects for General Jurisprudence' (2007–08) 15 *University of Miami International and Comparative Law Review* 69–84
——, 'Understanding Legal Pluralism: Past to Present, Local to Global' (2008) 30 *Sydney Law Review* 375–411
——, 'Rescuing Ehrlich from "Living Law" (2011) 36 *Law & Social Inquiry* 297–318
Teubner, G, 'Substantive and Reflexive Elements in Modern Law' (1983) 17 *Law & Society Review* 239–85
——, 'After Legal Instrumentalism? Strategic models of post-regulatory law' in Teubner, G (ed), *Dilemmas of Law in the Welfare State* (Berlin, de Gruyter, 1986) 299–35
—— (ed), *Autopoietic Law: A New Approach to Law and Society* (Berlin, de Gruyter, 1987)
——, 'Juridification: Concepts, Aspects, Limits, Solutions' in Teubner, G (ed) *Juridification of the Social Spheres: A Comparative Analysis in the Areas of Labor, Corporate, Antitrust and Social Welfare Law* (Berlin, de Gruyter, 1987a) 3–48
——, 'How the law thinks: toward a constructivist epistemology of law' (1989) 23 *Law & Society Review* 727–57
——, 'Autopoiesis and Steering: how politics profit from the normative surplus of capital' in In 't Veld, R *et al* (eds), *Autopoiesis and Configuration Theory: New Approaches to Societal Steering* (Dordrecht, Kluwer, 1991), ch 11
——, 'The Two Faces of Janus: Rethinking Legal Pluralism' (1992) 13 *Cardozo Law Review* 1443–62
——, 'Regulatory Law: Chronicle of a Death Foretold' (1992a) 1 *Social & Legal Studies* 451–75
——, *Law as an Autopoietic System*, trans Bankowska, A and Adler, R (Oxford, Blackwell, 1993)
——, '"Global Bukowina": Legal Pluralism in the World Society' in Teubner, G (ed), *Global Law Without a State* (Aldershot, Dartmouth, 1997) 3–28
——, 'Altera pars Audiatur: Law in the Collision of Discourses' in Rawlings, R (ed), *Law, Society and Economy: Centenary Essays for the London School of Economics 1895–1995* (Oxford, Oxford University Press, 1997a) ch 7
Teubner, G, 'Alienating Justice: On the Surplus Value of the Twelfth Camel' in Priban, J and Nelken, D (eds), *Law's New Boundaries: the Consequences of Legal Autopoiesis* (Aldershot, Ashgate, 2001), ch 2
——, 'Economics of Gift – Positivity of Justice: The Mutual Paranoia of Jacques Derrida and Niklas Luhmann' (2001) 18 *Theory, Culture & Society* 29–47
——, 'Breaking Frames: Economic Globalisation and the Emergence of *lex mercatoria*' (2002) 5 *European Journal of Social Theory* 199–217
——, 'Societal Constitutionalism: Alternatives to State-Centered Constitutional Theory?' in Joerges, C, Sand, I-J and Teubner, G (eds), *Transnational Governance and Constitutionalism* (Oxford, Hart Publishing, 2004) 3–28
——, 'Global Private Regimes: Neo-Spontaneous Law and Dual Constitution of Autonomous Systems' in Ladeur, K-H (ed), *Public Governance in the Age of Globalization* (Aldershot, Ashgate, 2004a) 71–87
——, 'The Anonymous Matrix: Human Rights Violations by "Private" Transnational Actors' (2006) 69 *Modern Law Review* 327–46

——, 'Rights of Non-humans? Electronic Agents and Animals as New Actors in Politics and Law' (2006a) 33 *Journal of Law and Society* 497–521

——, 'Fragmented Foundations: Societal Constitutionalism Beyond the Nation State' in Dobner, P and Loughlin, M (eds), *The Twilight of Constitutionalism?* (Oxford, Oxford University Press, 2010) 327–41

——, 'Social Constitutionalism Without Politics? A Rejoinder' (2011) 20 *Social & Legal Studies* 248–52

——, 'Constitutionalizing Polycontexturality' (2011a) 20 *Social & Legal Studies* 210–29

——, 'A Constitutional Moment? The Logics of "Hitting the Bottom"' in Kjaer, P, Teubner, G and Febbrajo, A (eds), 2011b, ch 1

——, 'Self-Constitutionalizing TNCs? On the Linkage of "Private" and "Public" Corporate Codes of Conduct' in Calliess, G-P (ed), *Governing Transnational Corporations: Public and Private Perspectives* (2011c) 18 *Indiana Journal of Global Legal Studies* 617–38

——, *Constitutional Fragments: Societal Constitutionalism and Globalization*, trans Norbury, G (Oxford, Oxford University Press, 2012)

—— and Fischer-Lescano, A, 'Cannibalizing Epistemes: Will Modern Law Protect Traditional Cultural Expressions?' in Graber, C and Burri-Nenova, M (eds), *Traditional Cultural Expressions in a Digital Environment* (Cheltenham, Edward Elgar, 2008) ch 2

—— and Korth, P, 'Two Kinds of Legal Pluralism: Collision of Transnational Regimes in the Double Fragmentation of World Society' in Young, M (ed), *Regime Interaction in International Law: Facing Fragmentation* (New York, Cambridge University Press, 2012) ch 1

——, Lindahl, H, Christodoulidis, E and Thornhill, C, 'Debate and dialogue: constitutionlizing polycontexturality' (2011) 20 *Social and Legal Studies* 209–52

——, Nobles, R and Schiff, D, 'The Autonomy of Law: An Introduction to Legal Autopoiesis' in Penner, J, Schiff, D and Nobles, R (eds), *Jurisprudence and Legal Theory* (London, Butterworths/LexisNexis, 2002) ch 18

Thomas, P (ed), *Legal Frontiers* (Aldershot, Dartmouth, 1996)

Thornhill, C, 'Luhmann's Political Theory: Politics After Metaphysics?' in King, M and Thornhill, C (eds), 2006, ch 4

——, 'Niklas Luhmann, Carl Schmitt and the Modern Form of the Political' (2007) 10 *European Journal of Social Theory* 499–522

——, 'Towards a historical sociology of constitutional legitimacy' (2008) 37 Theory and Society 161–97

——, 'Niklas Luhmann and the Sociology of Constitutions' (2010) 10 *Journal of Classical Sociology* 315–37

——, *A Sociology of Constitutions: Constitutions and State Legitimacy in Historical-Sociological Perspective* (Cambridge, Cambridge University Press, 2011)

——, 'Constitutional Law from the Perspective of Power: A Response to Gunther Teubner' (2011a) 20 *Social & Legal Studies* 244–47

Traynor, RJ, 'Quo Vadis, Prospective Overruling: A Question of Judicial Responsibility' (1999) 50 *Hastings Law Journal* 771–804

Tur, R, 'Time and Law' (2002) 22 *Oxford Journal of Legal Studies* 463–88

Twining, W (ed), *Legal Theory and Common Law* (Oxford, Blackwell, 1986)

——, *Globalization and Legal Theory* (London, Butterworths, 2000)

——, 'A Post-Westphalian Conception of Law' (2003) 37 *Law and Society Review* 199–257

—— and Miers, D, *How to do things with rules* 4th edn (London, Butterworths, 1999)

Urry, J, 'The Complexity Turn' (2005) 22 *Theory, Culture & Society* 1–14

Van Alstyne, W, 'A Critical Guide to *Marbury v Madison*' (1969) 18 *Duke Law Journal* 1–47

Van Assche, K and Verschraegen, G, 'The Limits of Planning: Niklas Luhmann's Systems Theory and the Analysis of Planning and Planning Ambitions' (2008) 7 *Planning Theory* 263–83

Van de Kerchove, M and Ost, F, *Legal System Between Order and Disorder*, trans Stewart, I (Oxford, Oxford University Press, 1994)

Verschraegen, G, 'Human Rights and Modern Society, A Sociological Analysis from the Perspective of Systems Theory' (2002) 29 *Journal of Law and Society* 258–81

——, 'Systems Theory and the Paradox of Human Rights' in King, M and Thornhill, C (eds), 2006, ch 5

Vesting, T, 'Constitutionalism or Legal Theory: Comments on Gunther Teubner' in Joerges, C, Sand, I-J and Teubner, G (eds), *Transnational Governance and Constitutionalism* (Oxford, Hart Publishing, 2004) ch 2

——, 'Politische Verfassung? Der moderne (liberale) Verfassungsbegriff und siene systemtheoretische Rekonstrucktion' in Cailliess, G-F, Fischer-Lescano, A, Wielsch, D and Zumbansen, P (eds), *Sociologische Jurisprudenz* (Berlin, de Gruyter, 2009) 609–26

Vinx, L, *Hans Kelsen's Pure Theory of Law: Legality and Legitimacy* (Oxford, Oxford University Press, 2007)

Waldron, J, *The Law* (Routledge, London, 1990)

——, *Law and Disagreement* (Oxford, Oxford University Press, 1999)

——, 'Legal Pluralism and the Contrast between Hart's Jurisprudence and Fuller's' in Cane, P (ed), *The Hart-Fuller Debate in the Twenty-First Century* (Oxford, Hart Publishing, 2010), ch 7

Walzer, M, *Obligations: Essays on Disobedience, War and Citizenship* (Cambridge, Mass, Harvard University Press, 1970)

Whitrow, G, *The Nature of Time* (New York, Wiley, 1975)

Whittington, K, *Constitutional Construction: Divided Powers and Constitutional Meaning* (Cambridge, Mass, Harvard University Press, 1999)

Williamson, O, 'The New Institutional Economics: Taking Stock, Looking Ahead' (2000) 38 *Journal of Economic Literature* 595–613

Zinn, H, *Disobedience and Democracy: Nine Fallacies on Law and Order* (New York, Random House, 1968)

Zwiebach, B, *Civility and Disobedience* (Cambridge, Cambridge University Press, 1975)

Index

Index

Index

Printed by Libri Plureos GmbH in Hamburg,
Germany

9 781849 462181